EAST ANGLIAN ARCHAEOLOGY

This volume is dedicated to the memory of John Hurst, 1927–2003, who did so much to further the study of medieval rural settlement archaeology in Britain.

Without the inspiration provided by his example, the excavation of the medieval villages at Thuxton, Grenstein and North Elmham in Norfolk would not have taken place, nor would the many earthwork surveys embodied in this report.

(PW-M)

Earthworks of Norfolk

by Brian Cushion and Alan Davison

EAST ANGLIAN ARCHAEOLOGY
REPORT NO.104

Published by
Archaeology and Environment Division
Norfolk Museums and Archaeology Service
Union House
Gressenhall
Dereham
Norfolk NR20 4DR

in conjunction with
ALGAO EAST

Editor: Peter Wade-Martins
Managing Editor: Jenny Glazebrook

Editorial Sub-committee:
Brian Ayers, Archaeology and Environment Officer, Norfolk Museums and Archaeology Service
David Buckley, County Archaeologist, Essex Planning Department
Keith Wade, Archaeological Service Manager, Suffolk County Council
Peter Wade-Martins
Stanley West

Set in Times Roman by Jenny Glazebrook using Corel Ventura™
Printed by Witley Press Ltd., Hunstanton, Norfolk

ISBN 0 905594 38 X   1003520526

For details of *East Anglian Archaeology*, see last page

This volume is published with the aid of a grant from English Heritage

Cover photograph:
Horsford Castle, a small motte and bailey.
Photo by Derek A. Edwards (ref: TG 2015/ACT)

Contents

List of Plates

List of Figures

Manorial sites and isolated settlements

List of Contributors

Brian Cushion
Archaeological Surveyor

Alan Davison, MA, FSA Scot
Landscape Archaeologist

Acknowledgements

The authors wish to thank all those landowners who allowed their property to be surveyed and Helen Paterson for facilitating access to many of the sites. The advice and comment on the earthwork surveys and descriptions by Dr Andrew Rogerson was much appreciated. The staff of the Norfolk Record Office are thanked for producing the many documents and maps examined during the course of the survey, so also is Mrs Christine Hiskey, Archivist at the Holkham Estate, for her help.

All of the line drawings are by Brian Cushion, except Figs 32, 33, 80 and 126 (T. Williamson); Fig. 35 (A. Rogerson and S. Ashley) and Figs 98; 105 (Royal Commission). The photographs were provided by the Norfolk Air Photographs Library and were taken by Derek Edwards, except Pl. XXXVII (Eileen Horne); and Pls XI, XII, XXIII, XLIX and LV which are 1946 RAF photographs, reproduced with the permission of the Controller of Her Majesty's Stationary Office. Pls I, VIII–X, XV, XXVI, XXX, L and LI are provided by the Cambridge University Collection of Air Photographs (CUCAP), and reproduced by kind permission.

Summary

This volume represents a corpus of most of the best preserved earthworks known to exist in Norfolk grassland. With each site plan there is a descriptive text and a summary of the available documentary evidence.

The settlement earthworks are almost entirely medieval and include deserted villages and the more numerous shrunken settlements as well as manorial sites where more than a single moated platform survives. Monastic sites and castles where, in some instances, additional earthworks have been found, form two important sections. Water features include some fishponds together with plans of Norfolk's few water meadows. Ridge and furrow, another rarity in the county, also appears and the survey ends with a selection of parkland earthworks.

Résumé

Ce volume représente un corpus formé par la plupart des ouvrages en terre les mieux préservées de la région des prairies du Norfolk. Chaque plan du site est accompagné d'un texte descriptif et d'un résumé des preuves documentaires disponibles.

Les ouvrages en terre du site sont presque tous de l'époque médiévale. Ils comprennent des villages abandonnés et un nombre plus important d'implantations réduites ainsi que des sites seigneuriaux où subsistent quelques plates-formes fossoyées. Deux ensembles importants sont formés par des sites monastiques et des châteaux où plusieurs ouvrages en terre ont été découvertes. On trouve également quelques étangs ainsi que les plans de plusieurs prairies humides du Norfolk. La présence de sommets et d'étendues basses, que l'on rencontre rarement dans le comté est également mentionnée. Enfin, l'étude se termine par un choix d'ouvrages en terre intégrées à des espaces verts.

(Traduction: Didier Don)

Zusammenfassung

In diesem Band sind die meisten der besterhaltenen Erdwerke zusammengestellt, deren Existenz im Grasland Norfolks bekannt ist. Zu jedem Lageplan findet sich ein beschreibender Text und eine Zusammenfassung der vorhandenen dokumentarischen Belege.

Die auf Siedlungen zurückgehenden Erdwerke stammen fast gänzlich aus dem Mittelalter. Zu ihnen zählen Ortswüstungen und, in größerer Zahl, abgegangene Siedlungen und größere Anwesen, von denen mehr übrig ist als nur eine von Gräben umgebene Plattform. Zwei wichtige Abschnitte formen Klosteranlagen und Burgen, bei denen in einigen Fällen zusätzliche Erdwerke gefunden wurden. Unter den Wasser aufweisenden Strukturen sind einige Fischteiche und Grundrisse der wenigen Wasserwiesen Norfolks zu finden. Ebenso aufgeführt sind Wölbäcker, eine weitere Seltenheit in der Grafschaft. Abgeschlossen wird die Übersicht mit einer Auswahl an Erdwerken, die aus Parklandschaften hervorgingen.

(Übersetzung: Gerlinde Krug)

Editorial

by Peter Wade-Martins

This volume represents the results of a six-year study of the earthworks of Norfolk. The project started in 1994 as part of a wider monument conservation initiative which was designed to identify and safeguard all of the county's most significant surviving earthwork archaeology. The results published here demonstrate for the first time an extraordinary richness of earthwork monuments even in a county where there has been such intensive cultivation. Even quite well known sites like Castle Acre Priory (pp136–7) and Langley Abbey (pp143–5), as well as lesser known ones like Anmer deserted village (pp10–11), have been found to be more intact and more extensive than was previously realised.

Norfolk has been greatly affected by agricultural change and land improvements since the late 18th century. Then, the enclosure of the commons was often accompanied by widespread reorganisation of the field systems. In some parishes this led to major landscape changes, with marginal land being brought into cultivation. After this great period of improvement, change in the countryside was more gradual until the drive for increased food production in and after the Second World War. Of the hedgerows in Norfolk in 1945, only 55% remained by 1970. The ploughing up of grassland, assisted by government subsidies to increase the acreage in cereals, brought about unprecedented change. Most of the earthworks lost then went without record unless they happened to show well on the RAF 1946 air photographs or were seen and photographed by that remarkable Cambridge air photographer, J.K. St Joseph. By the time Derek Edwards started the Norfolk Archaeological Unit's air photography programme in 1973, destruction had slowed, although it continued well into the 1980s.

With the change in farming subsidies and the move towards conservation in the countryside, it is now time to take stock, identify what remains and develop policies and programmes which will ensure the conservation and better appreciation of this most important part of the county's heritage.

Norfolk's own earthwork conservation programme began in August 1990 with the establishment of the Norfolk Monument Management Project (NMMP). The aim of the project has been to visit and assess every significant earthwork in the county, whether or not it is already legally protected by scheduling. From 1990 up until March 2000 some 450 sites were visited by the project officer, Helen Paterson, and it is hoped that the whole county will have been covered by the end of 2002. The range of monuments visited includes deserted villages, fishponds, moated sites, burial mounds, castles and monasteries.

By February 2002 forty-seven legally binding grant-aided Section 17 Agreements had been signed with landowners or tenants. Dossiers containing earthwork plans, air photographs and site descriptions are assembled and presented to the farmers as part of the ongoing management discussions. While the academic value of the data assembled on these sites is important, it is also recognised that the earthwork plans provide a yardstick against which the success of monument conservation can be measured for years to come.

Under the NMMP, funding for up to 100% of the capital costs of stock fencing, scrub clearance, tree felling and initial rabbit control can be followed by annual payments calculated by the hectare to maintain the benefits of the initial works. Tax-free lump sum payments are made at the commencement. The Agreements usually last for five years, and they can be renewed thereafter.

In many instances sites are being well managed already, and owners are willing to undertake improvements without grant aid. In these cases a non-legal management statement is frequently signed. This provides a record of the understanding about site management reached during the project officer's visit. To date 185 owners have willingly signed these statements. Over 70 owners have preferred not to sign but have given instead a verbal undertaking to provide beneficial management. A more detailed summary of the progress of this project can be found in Paterson and Wade-Martins (1999), and a more up-to-date account is due to be published (Paterson and Wade-Martins forthcoming).

The initial selection of sites to be surveyed for the Norfolk Earthworks Survey was made by Helen Paterson after trawling through the county Sites and Monuments Record and the Norfolk Air Photographs Library. Once identified, the earthworks were then assessed on the ground by Brian Cushion and the better preserved and more complete examples were recorded — usually at a scale of 1:1,000.

The detailed analysis of the air photographs and all the survey work was carried out with great dedication and with very limited resources by Brian Cushion, a former Ordnance Survey surveyor, who single-handedly recorded most of the sites illustrated in this volume. Alan Davison, a landscape and documentary historian who had already published notable fieldwalking and documentary research in the county (Davison *et al.* 1988; Davison 1990; Davison 1994; Davison *et al.* 1993; Rogerson *et al.* 1997), joined the project in its later stages. The surveys were compared with early Ordnance Survey maps, Bryant's and Faden's printed maps of Norfolk (Bryant 1826; Faden 1797), all the relevant manuscript maps, particularly the Tithe and Enclosure Maps, and the other local documentary sources.

By incorporating into this volume some previously published plans (Cushion 1994, 29; 1995, 35; 1996, 40; 1997, 32-33; 1998, 44; 1999, 347; Cushion and Davison 1997, 494-7; Cushion *et al.* 1982; Davison *et al.* 1988, 8, 61; Davison with Cushion 1999, 208; Rogerson *et al.* 1997, 28; Wade-Martins P. 1980a, 25; Wade-Martins, S. and Williamson 1994, 28), the authors have assembled a virtually complete corpus of the county's most significant earthwork archaeology. Not included here are prehistoric burial mounds (already studied in Lawson *et al.* 1981 and Lawson 1986), Iron Age forts (described and discussed by Davies *et al.* 1992), linear earthworks (discussed in Wade-Martins 1974) and moats (in many cases adequately recorded on Ordnance Survey maps and also recorded and discussed in Dollin 1986).

This volume does not contain plans of all the sites surveyed under the Norfolk Earthwork Survey. A further sixty-three sites were recorded, but the sites were not sufficiently significant to justify publication. Brian Cushion's reports and plans of all the sites surveyed are available for study in the County Sites and Monuments Record.

One justifiable criticism of this volume might be that these surveys are presented largely out of context; they often appear removed from the known archaeology and the landscapes around them. Further plans and maps could have been produced showing recorded surface finds, cropmarks and other landscape features, particularly greens and commons. However, this option had to be rejected at an early stage on grounds of cost because the project was funded with very limited resources. Readers are therefore advised to study these plans alongside the relevant large-scale Ordnance Survey maps and the printed versions of Faden's and Bryant's maps of Norfolk (Faden 1797; Bryant 1826).

Most of the earthworks located in this survey were in grassland. It may well be that there are significant earthworks still to be discovered in the county, particularly in woodland, and it is hoped that the project can be followed by another which ensures that there is a thorough search for earthworks in Norfolk woodlands. Sample searches of areas of the conifer forests in Breckland have already revealed several well-preserved round barrows and many boundary banks not previously recognised. More extensive searches of both these comparatively recent plantations and the older deciduous woodlands are likely to produce worthwhile results. Not until all the woodland in the county has been fully examined can we say that our record of the county's earthworks is complete.

The information in this volume is particularly relevant to the publication of the *Monuments at Risk Survey of England* (Darvill and Fulton 1995). In the strategy document published with this report English Heritage made a number of commitments, including the following:

> to maintain support for the Monument Protection Programme (for site scheduling), and

> to target the work of the Monument Protection Programme to take account of the regions with the highest levels of monument loss (South East), regions with highest levels of reported risk (West Midlands and North West), and monument forms hitherto subject to the heaviest casualty rates (large single monuments and field systems).

Sites in this volume clearly qualify for extra English Heritage effort, being in the South East.

It can be said that Norfolk has led the way in developing an integrated approach to earthwork conservation, involving a very detailed assessment of all the surviving evidence and then linking that to conservation measures. It is to be hoped that English Heritage will follow the conservation process to its logical conclusion and consider scheduling most of the monuments illustrated here, although at the moment only some 40% have legal protection.

Despite the considerable loss during the post-war years, the amount of information which has survived has surprised all those who have been involved in the project. Now that the countryside has entered a period of more stable and sustainable management, let us hope that most, if not all, of the earthworks of Norfolk can endure for future generations to enjoy.

Introduction

(Fig. 1)
Norfolk is, and has been, an essentially arable county. The only general exceptions have been the floors of river valleys and the marshes around the coast and the lower Bure, Yare and Waveney valleys. Areas safe from the plough for many years ultimately went under cultivation particularly during the Napoleonic Wars and the emergencies of 1914–18 and 1939–45. They included commons still shown intact on Faden's map of Norfolk (1797), areas of heathland and even parts of the Acle marshlands taken into cultivation since the Second World War.

Norfolk is also a county of villages. From the high point of the 13th and 14th centuries rural population has declined and many villages listed in the Domesday Survey of 1086 have either shrunk or, in some cases, disappeared. Many of the vacant sites have been ploughed as few of the dwellings consisted of materials which would offer prolonged resistance to the cultivator. It has been suggested that the additional fertility of house sites with their gardens and crofts may have provided an additional incentive to plough.

In the 1970s, the Norfolk Archaeological Rescue Group and the Norfolk Archaeological Unit initiated a project to investigate and record sites of some of the known deserted villages which then remained at least partially intact. The results of these surveys were published in *East Anglian Archaeology* (Cushion *et al.* 1982; Davison *et al.* 1988). It is significant that while this work was being undertaken one site was destroyed, another was found to have been destroyed earlier and one has subsequently been partially ploughed despite its status as a scheduled monument.

Later investigation using aerial photography followed by ground inspection revealed that, despite the centuries of destruction, many more areas of earthworks remained. In the light of this, a new recording programme of mapping and describing these sites was organised by the Field Archaeology Division of Norfolk Museums Service from 1994 to 2000. As a part of this project all pieces of related work were reviewed. Many of these consisted of surveys of moated sites carried out by the late Bert Dollin and published in the reports of the Moated Sites Research Group in the 1970s. Other surveys included, most notably, the work of Dr Tom Williamson of the University of East Anglia. The total number of sites examined up to the year 2000 was over 300 and included castles, monastic sites, manorial sites, deserted villages, shrunken villages, parkland features, ridge and furrow, fishponds and water meadows, as well as other smaller features.

With such a surprisingly wide range of subjects it seemed appropriate to make a selection of the more notable sites and to publish each of them with a brief account and its documentary background.

It was decided to exclude sites which were prehistoric and to dispense with moats unless they had additional features associated with them. It has to be remembered that many isolated moats not considered here probably had associated features, now long gone, and are not really a separate group. Hilgay and Hockwold have medieval earthworks but are thought to include Romano-British features. Apart from these exceptions the remainder of the sites are mostly medieval. There are some post-medieval examples, mainly in parkland which, nevertheless, include features of a fossilised medieval landscape. A number of post-medieval water meadows have also been surveyed.

Deserted villages with good earthworks which have already appeared in *East Anglian Archaeology* (Cushion *et al.* 1982; Davison *et al.* 1988) are republished here in summary, as is the survey of Hautbois Castle by Dollin (1986) and the surveys of Baconsthorpe Castle and St Benet's Abbey by the Royal Commission of Historical Monuments (Everson and Wilson-North 2002). Two sites, Bixley and Godwick, are represented by fresh surveys containing additional information. The great majority of the sites presented here are published for the first time.

Most sites have been surveyed at a scale of 1:1,000 and reduced for publication to 1:2,500 and this publication is an attempt to bring together in one volume detailed surveys of all significant earthwork monuments in the county, with the exceptions already stated. The purpose is to provide a source of information for further research as well as a record of the present condition of the earthworks, thus giving a yardstick against which their future conservation may be measured.

The accompanying accounts have been divided equally as far as possible between an abbreviated description of the earthworks and a brief summary of the documentary evidence. The latter has proved more difficult since it has depended on the nature of the documents accessible and has to respect the limitations of space in the volume. More detailed descriptions of the earthworks can be found in the County Sites and Monuments Record (henceforth SMR).

The following general practice has been adhered to. Where previous full treatment exists in *East Anglian Archaeology*, the *Victoria County History*, or *Norfolk Archaeology*, there is just a reference to the work at the end of the account. Where additional information has been acquired, or where a particular emphasis has been deemed necessary, a more specific reference is given at the appropriate point.

Where an entirely new site has a key source such as a field book or an early map allowing a relatively easy reconstruction of the past landscape, the documentary account will be based primarily on that and all necessary references given. However, this rarely happens and conclusions of a more general nature may be inferred from a variety of sources. Changes in the status of a settlement from 1086 (Domesday Book) to 1676 (The Compton Census) can be portrayed but the flesh is absent from the bones.

Domesday Book, for example, is an enigmatic document with many obscurities and needs to be used with discretion. Ellingham, in 1086, was awarded one line about five sokemen, with 15 acres, half a plough team and a church supported by 24 acres, the whole being treated under Stockton. There must have been much more; the

Location of sites

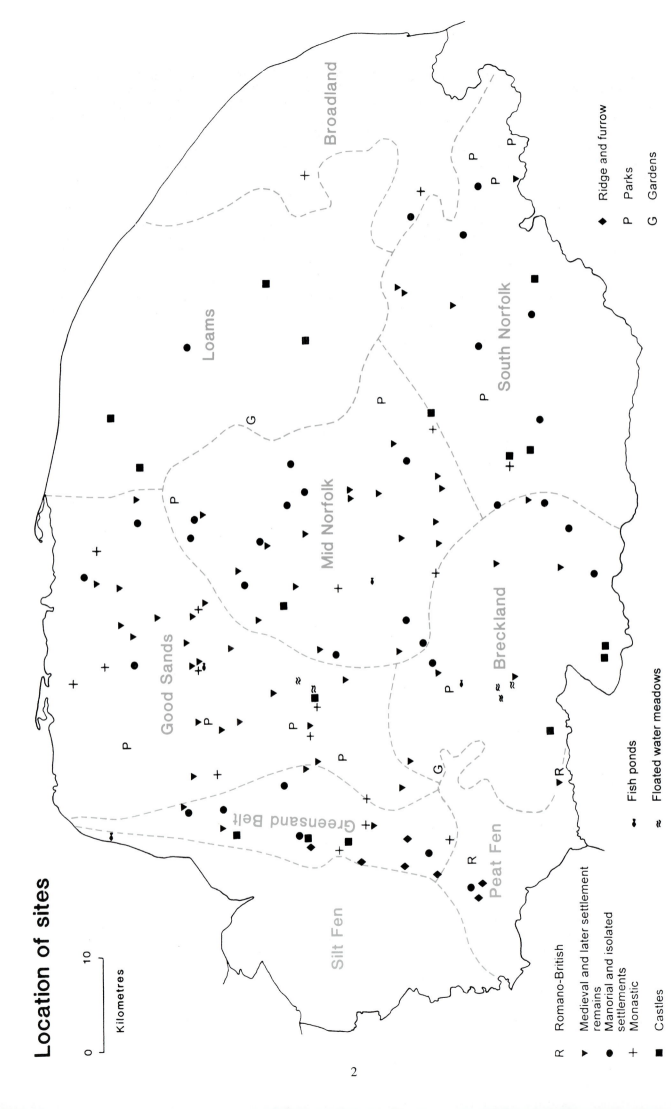

Figure 1 Location of earthwork surveys included in this volume, with sub-regional divisions after Darby (1952) and Williamson (1993). Scale 1:400,000

R Romano-British

▶ Medieval and later settlement remains

● Manorial and isolated settlements

+ Monastic

■ Castles

◆ Ridge and furrow

⌇ Fish ponds

≈ Floated water meadows

P Parks

G Gardens

0   10

Kilometres

Broadland

Loams

South Norfolk

Mid Norfolk

Breckland

Good Sands

Greensand Belt

Peat Fen

Silt Fen

church is the only feature of archaeological significance mentioned. In other cases, the Domesday account is very full. Taxation figures levied at differing rates also present hidden pitfalls. A recent publication by the Public Record Office *Lay Taxes in England and Wales 1188–1688* (Jurkowski *et al.* 1998) gives some welcome insight into the complexities of such returns. They, however, deal solely with lay persons. Throughout the medieval period exemptions to these taxes were granted to ecclesiastical persons and the lands and chattels in their charge. The use of such sources, though necessary, gives only the barest outline and may conceal much of great interest. It should be noted that more satisfactory documentary evidence, in the shape mainly of field books or dragges, is absent for many parishes in the eastern half of the county. Though there are exceptions, this may be because estates there seem to have been smaller than those in many parts of the west.

The sites have been subdivided into groups according to their nature: Romano-British Sites, Medieval and Later Settlement Remains, Manorial and Isolated Sites, Monastic Sites, Castles, Ridge and Furrow, Fishponds and Water Meadows, Parks and Gardens. Each group is preceded by a separate introduction discussing them in detail and placing them in relationship to the county as a whole. A glance at Figure 1 shows the distribution of sites within the county and reveals sub-regional inequalities. There is a belt of sites bordering Fenland but that area itself has few significant earthworks. The major concentration lies in a north-to-south band across the county coinciding roughly with the soils developed on the chalky boulder clay and chalky glacial deposits of the Good Sands and Mid Norfolk areas, noticeably thinning out on the sandy Breckland soils and in the extreme north-west. Eastern and north-eastern Norfolk are poorly represented. This does not appear to be a reflection of soil types necessarily so much as of some other factor, possibly past agricultural practice.

HILGAY

SMR 4455

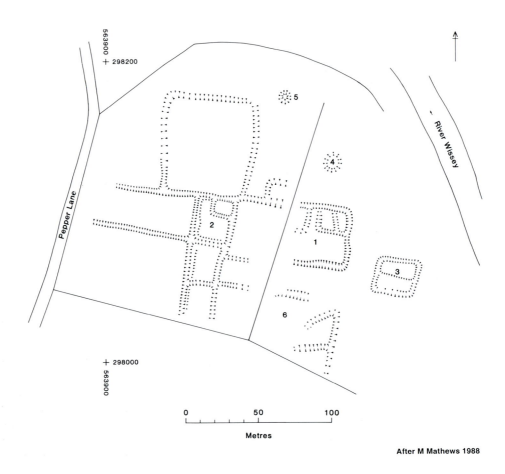

Figure 2 Hilgay, probable Romano-British enclosures. Scale 1:2,500

Romano-British Sites

Few examples of Romano-British earthworks remain, as might be expected, given the lapse of time since the ending of the Roman occupation and the arable nature of the county. However, before the Fens suffered intensive post-war ploughing, earthworks of Romano-British settlements were a feature of the landscape (Phillips (ed) 1970, IV; Silvester 1988a, 195). Particularly notable were those at Flaggrass and Grandford House near March, at Hacconby Drove near Bourne, at Weston Fen south-east of Spalding and at Cottenham and at Willingham Middle Fen to the north of Cambridge (Phillips (ed) 1970, 221, pl. IV; 197, pl. V; 263, pl. XI; 282, pl. X; 206, pl. XXI). These were all ploughed in the post-war period and only a few isolated fragments survive in any of the Fenland counties.

One possible site is the small area of earthworks at Hilgay interpreted by Silvester (Silvester 1988b, 195) as the remains of a farmstead with attached fields of pasture and with small circular features which are probably Romano-British but which some believe to be medieval. Finds of late 3rd- or 4th-century pottery from the site appear to confirm the general Romano-British origin.

The second area is at Hockwold on the margins of Fenland on a tongue of the fen extending eastwards towards Brandon. This is known to be a rich area of Romano-British activity, with important finds made in the locality, including a villa at Feltwell, temple sites in Hockwold and buildings in Weeting (Gurney 1986, 2; Gregory 1982, 370). The earthworks here are composite, those near the road are medieval in origin and surface finds of pottery support this. On the lower ground further south, approaching the modern Cut Off Channel which has truncated them, are earthworks of Romano-British origin; here pottery finds include both Iron Age and Romano-British material. These two sites are rare and important survivals which warrant particular care and protection.

Hilgay SMR 4455, TL 640 981
(Fig. 2)

The remains are of a small Romano-British farmstead consisting of enclosures with small raised platforms suggesting buildings. Small ditched circular features of uncertain purpose are also present.

Hilgay lies about 5km south of Downham Market on a former island in the Fenland which it shares with the village of Southery. The earthworks are on the eastern side of the island on sloping ground close to the River Wissey. They are bisected by a relatively modern hedge and ditch.

The earthworks consist of several small near-rectangular shallow ditched enclosures. The focus of the site is in two enclosures, one to the east, large and rectangular (1), the other further to the west and much smaller (2). Each has a small raised platform in its north-east corner. Further to the east of these is a third (3) which appears subdivided, the northern portion raised above the southern one. There are also two small ditched circles to

the north (4 and 5); the more northerly one has a slightly raised interior.

One large enclosure lies to the north of the smaller western one (2) and there are others, more or less intact, attached to the south of the main group. It appears that the construction of the modern hedge and ditch has probably destroyed some linkage between the surviving features.

Finds made from molehills, particularly from a mounded area (6) some 30m south of the main enclosure, suggest Romano-British occupation in the area.

It seems likely that this is the remnant of a small Romano-British farmstead, and the raised platforms within the three central enclosures probably represent the sites of buildings placed above ground that was seasonally damp. The other enclosures are likely to be surrounding paddocks.

The two small ditched circles are of particular interest. A number of features of this kind have been noted previously at various sites in Fenland and their dating has been disputed, some have dated them as medieval (Hall 1978, 27; Wilson 1978, 45; Lawson *et al.* 1981, 30). These ones appear Romano-British. They may may have served as stack stands for grain or hay, the shallow circular ditches serving as drainage channels. An alternative use may have been to store peat (Christie and Rose 1987, 184).

It is, of course, possible that the origin of these earthworks, as a whole, may be medieval. However, the form and location strongly support the earlier date.

Hockwold SMR 5357 and 5461, TL 728 877
(Pl. I, Fig. 3)

The remains of rectangular ditched enclosures are of Romano-British date and are overshadowed by extensive medieval earthworks to the north.

Hockwold-cum-Wilton lies about 6km west of Brandon on the north bank of the Little Ouse and on the edge of Fenland. The present village forms a continuous east-to-west street with two churches, one at the Wilton (eastern) end and one, Hockwold, at the western end. The two parishes have been linked since the time of Domesday (Brown (ed) 1984, 8,34;35) and were taxed as one under Wilton in 1334 (Glasscock 1975, 204).

The earthworks lie south of Hockwold and north of the Cut Off Channel. Those in the northern area, Site 5357, show considerable variation in form, indicating differing origins, but are essentially of former medieval settlement. In the north-eastern portion, a curving length of probable hollow way (1) divides as it heads south and has an indeterminate northern end, possibly partly infilled. A north-to-south ditched trackway (2) has a separate section to the south, probably originally associated with it. Both have some links to (1) forming incomplete enclosures. Further incomplete sub-rectangles exist to the east. South-east of (1) is a large rhomboidal enclosure (3) containing three depressions, almost certainly fishponds. 'The Lilacs'

Plate I Hockwold: primarily medieval earthworks with Romano-British features in the foreground. CUCAP AEX 10
(Photography by Cambridge University Collection of Air Photographs)

has remains of a moat (4) possibly extending round the outbuildings, while a depression (5) to the south has three deeper pits within it. To the west, a north-to-south linear feature (6) of varied form was probably an access trackway to the south and also formed part of an outer enclosure to 'The Lilacs' along with (1) and (2).

The north-westerly portion has an extensive system of ramifying ditches, a former roadside ditch (7) and many small pits. The whole of this northern area appears to have been bounded to the south by a long curving ditch (8) from which roughly parallel ditches extend southwards. 'The Lilacs' is the successor of a former significant farmstead, possibly manorial. The incomplete enclosures east and west probably represent tofts facing two roads. The southern area, truncated by the Cut Off Channel, is more regular in character. The western portion has vestiges of small rectangular ditched enclosures at its southern end. The eastern section, Site 5461, has a reversed L-shaped raised area (9) and two truncated rectangular enclosures. To the north are less clearly-defined features (Wade-Martins (ed) 1987, 42).

Scattered finds suggest that the southern area is Romano-British, with Iron Age and even Beaker material.

Finds from the northern part have been medieval. When similar earthworks west of Station Road were ploughed in the 1970s large quantities of Romano-British material were recovered. This suggests that the surviving earthworks are part of a larger Romano-British fen-edge settlement.

Although this medieval fen-edge village was prosperous it was allowed a 20.8% reduction on its Lay Subsidy payment in 1449 (Hudson 1895, 274). A 16th-century survey (NRO Rudling and Co 18/11/1971) gives further evidence of decline particularly in Hockwold. In Church Street, seven out of fifteen messuages were described as 'void'; elsewhere there was other evidence of change or decline with ways stopped up. The decline of the Hockwold portion of the settlement seems to have continued; there were 173 communicants in 1603 and 154 in 1676, whereas Wilton showed a slight increase (Whiteman 1986, 209–10). There appears little doubt that the earthworks in the north represent part of this deterioration. The Romano-British earthworks are part of a more extensive spread of fen-edge settlement in neighbouring Feltwell and Wilton (Gurney 1986).

6

Medieval and Later Settlement Remains

It is now over 40 years since Keith Allison published a list of Norfolk Deserted ('Lost') Villages (Allison 1955, 116–162) drawing attention for the first time to what has since become recognised as commonplace. Since then there has been further research and his list has received additions and deletions. The most notable additions are Bixley, Anmer, Dunton and Tattersett, while those omitted include Petygards (now shown to have been a common-edge hamlet of Sporle), Keburn (entirely fictitious, Keburna is Ickburgh, the site mentioned in Bromehill is Otringhithe) and Norton (actually Wretton, not recorded in Domesday), (Davison 1982, 102–07; 1985, 33,10; 1990, 5,27; Dymond 1998, 161–168).

As work has progressed it has become increasingly difficult to continue to maintain this list. Much of the pioneer work done by Canon Foster in Lincolnshire, W.G.Hoskins in Leicestershire and Maurice Beresford in the Midlands and Yorkshire was carried out in areas where nucleated settlements are numerous.

In Norfolk such settlements certainly existed but methods have to be modified to allow for the peculiarities of the overall pattern in which migratory dispersal of medieval settlement around greens and commons is frequent, especially in eastern and southern Norfolk. This movement began early in the 12th century and sometimes resulted in the abandonment of an original site near the church which remained in isolation. Subsequent decline in population brought variations on the theme of desertion; sometimes the relatively new satellite disappeared, sometimes the original was depopulated. Large villages lost limbs and developed gaps in surviving streets. Work carried out in the Launditch hundred (Wade-Martins 1980b), in various parts of Norfolk (Davison 1990; 1994, 57–59; 1995, 160–184; Davison with Cushion 1999, 257–274) and in the parishes of Barton Bendish and Fransham (Rogerson 1995; Rogerson et al. 1997) has revealed something of the complexity of rural settlement in the county.

All this contrasts markedly with the classic desertions portrayed by Beresford and others in nucleated settlements such as Wharram Percy (E.Riding; Beresford 1954, pl.1), Whatborough (Leics.; Beresford 1954, pl.5), East Lilling (W.Riding; Beresford 1954, 32–33) or South Middleton (Northumberland; Beresford and Hurst 1971, pl.15). These are not common in Norfolk, Pudding Norton being one of the few examples which can be confidently cited.

The more usual Norfolk settlement type is comparatively small and variable in shape and in the more easterly parts of the county it becomes even more varied in form with straggling limbs and isolated clusters. They have some superficial similarities with the dispersed settlements found at Hanbury (Worcs; Dyer 1991) or on the higher grounds of the Chilterns (Lewis et al. 1997, 127), but have, not surprisingly more in common with the dispersed pattern of Felsham in Suffolk (Taylor 1983, 180). The subsequent modifications brought about by a variety of causes pose even greater variations. Coupled with this are instances where the rise of commercial activity, mainly in

the form of markets, has caused the migration of a settlement to a site around the centre of the new activity. It was not possible to sustain the division between 'deserted' and 'shrunken' settlements simply because it was impracticable, in such a varied and complex situation, to draw a clear distinction between them and it was necessary to take into account the various shifts in settlement which have occurred.

One of Allison's major contributions was to isolate two chief causes of desertion in Norfolk; the late medieval/early post-medieval activities of sheep-rearing landlords and the later enthusiasm for landscaped parks. Since then it has become apparent that desertions of the first kind began earlier and extended later than was immediately obvious and were quite often more complex than previously thought. Emparking often happened on sites already substantially deserted.

Of the fifty or so cases selected here, Waterden, Godwick, Egmere and Pudding Norton seem to be, in general, good examples of late medieval/early post-medieval landlord action, while Rougham, a remnant of a vanished limb of an existing village, is a case of desertion resulting from a series of events. Bixley is an interesting case; details of the cause of desertion are lacking but the plan suggests a dispersed form prior to the event. Whether this was the original shape or whether it represents a later degeneration from an earlier concentration is unknown. Thuxton is an amalgamation of two separately named Domesday vills and is the only site selected here, apart from North Elmham, which has been partly excavated. Little Bittering, never large, declined rapidly in the medieval period from unknown causes while Great Palgrave may have been an example of medieval decline because of the earlier actions of a sheep-rearing lord. West Raynham is an example of post-medieval shrinkage while Anmer, which probably experienced some medieval decline was displaced by early 19th-century emparking. Houghton is a well-known example of displacement by emparking in the 18th century, though some of the earthworks may have already been abandoned.

Beachamwell All Saints and Tattersett are deserted parts of what had been multi-parish or multi-focal settlements. Shotesham St Mary, formerly considered a deserted village, is a particularly complicated case. It once contained three parish churches of which only one remains and the most obvious site contains little that is medieval having been occupied by an early park. Recent work has shown that the now-vanished village survived as common-edge settlement in 1650 only to disappear later. Shouldham is an example of a shift away from the original site to a new one around a market place. Whether this occurred at once, or whether it was the result of gradual drift over one or two generations remains to be discovered.

Houghton-on-the-Hill suffered considerable decline in the 15th century and did not recover. Roudham, though declining in the medieval period survived in restricted form until the mid 18th century when it appears to have succumbed to purchasing-in by the landlord, the ultimate event in a long process of decay, often inexplicable, since the Middle Ages. Dunton, recently considered, is apparently an instance of the slow decline of a settlement over a lengthy period for no identifiable cause. West Tofts is a special case, a place which had remained quite stable throughout the medieval and early post-medieval period but was partially emparked in the 18th century and finally, when the hall had gone, largely depopulated by the creation, in 1942, of the Stanford Training Area.

Many of the remaining sites are examples of parts of surviving villages which have gone or are cases of outlying satellites which have disappeared. It is by no means easy to venture upon a date or cause of the abandonment, though general inferences may be drawn from the economic fluctuations of the parent settlement. In some cases, these earthwork areas are quite extensive; Wilby appears as a northern portion of the main village while the case of East Walton involves an extension and a common-edge development.

It should be remembered that earthwork remains represent only the visible proportion of the abandoned settlements in the county. Norfolk is arable and in the eastern parts in particular sites are often completely obliterated as surface features, leaving concentrations of pottery as almost the only evidence of their existence. Examples of such deserted sites can be seen at Mannington and Wolterton in South Erpingham, Ashby, Oby and Herringby in Flegg, and Holverston south-east of Norwich. Wickmere has a centre abandoned in favour of a common-edge site, as has Heckingham which has become scattered, while the deserted sites around Hales Green are former common-edge settlements (Allison 1957, 142–154; Davison 1990, 21–22; 1995, 160–184; 1991, 30).

The selected distribution of earthworks is interesting. The majority, save Bixley, Shotesham St Mary, Ellingham and Arminghall are in the western half of the county, though some, like Thuxton, are more centrally placed. Of these, Arminghall is strangely enigmatic, consisting more of marked roadways than of noticeable settlement. Ellingham has part of a vanished medieval settlement located alongside riverine pastures.

The reason for the greater western survival of earthworks is unclear though there are a few factors which may go some way towards explaining it. The first is the greater frequency of settlements which approach the nuclear form as opposed to dispersed settlement. The second is that the western sites lie within the sheep-corn area of husbandry as recorded by a 17th-century writer (Allison 1957, 13).

In the east, in the wood pasture area, convertible husbandry (the ploughing of grassland for short periods of cultivation before restoring it to sown grass) and the more dispersed form of settlement may account in part for the difference. Dispersed settlements may have found it easier to adapt to changing circumstances than the more concentrated village forms. Nevertheless, shrinkage of settlement, from whatever cause, is something found throughout the county.

Anmer SMR 3514, 30492 (part); TF 738 293
(Fig.4)

The former village, with tofts and a manorial site, was emparked in the early 19th century. Old roads and field boundaries lie to the south.

Anmer lies about 17km north-east of King's Lynn where the Good Sands border on soils of the chalk escarpment. The parish takes Peddars' Way as its eastern boundary. From map evidence (Faden 1797; OS 1st Edition c.1824 with later additions) it is clear that changes to Anmer are relatively recent. The earthworks in the northern part of the park, especially north of the Hall, represent the remains of the 18th-century village street (1) partly obscured by the driveway and, to the north of it, vestiges of tofts, building platforms, boundary banks and ditches, apparently eroded by ploughing. North-west of the church similar features (2), approached from the west by another hollow way (3), appear more likely to represent a large property.

West of the church, the street (1) becomes a substantial hollow way c. 2m deep where it turns to the south before merging with the present road. South of the Hall is a series of subdued banks marking probable pre-park field boundaries, with two possible roadways, one hollow (4), the other a shallow-ditched causeway-bank (5). A third, very short linear ridge (6) east of the Hall may be the remains of another way (Cushion 1994, 27–29). A substantial ditch (7) denotes the park boundary in the south.

Anmer (OE Aened + mere — 'duckpool'; Mills 1991, 10; Gelling 1984, 26) had a recorded Domesday population of twenty-one; sheep figured prominently in the economy and salt pans implied some coastal right (Brown (ed) 1984, 5,2. 8,31). Evidence from Subsidy returns (Hudson 1895, 271–2) shows that by 1334 Anmer was relatively small and, in 1449, had received a larger-than-average reduction of tax. In 1517 it was reported that 100 acres had been laid down as pasture for sheep (Leadam 1893, 194–5). In 1603 there were fifty-four communicants; in 1676 there were sixty-three (Whiteman 1986, 228). In the 1664 Hearth Tax there were thirty-two hearths in thirteen charged households (Frankel and Seaman 1983, 30). Fortunately surveys made in 1600 (NRO MC 40/7 484 x 7; ANW/S/2/16) and 1679 (NRO MC 40/52 485 x 7) describe the village at this period. In 1600 Anmer was a village of about seventeen houses, one of them a shepherd's together with the rectory and the 'sites' of two manor houses. In 1679 it was, perhaps, a little larger.

According to the surveys the houses were disposed on either side of the street with the rectory south of the church and with the site of Castle Hall manor to the east of it. The other manorial site, Anmer Hall, was north-west of the church and the earthworks (2) west of the pond probably mark its position. The building of the Georgian Hall may have obliterated sites south of the street including Castle Hall. In 1679 one of the houses recorded was that of James Couldham who had been charged for eight hearths in 1664.

A series of Road Orders, particularly in 1782 (NRO RO Book 1) and 1793 (NRO RO Bk 3) shows how a later Couldham obtained the diversions of roads entering the street from north and south. In 1803 (NRO RO Bk 9) the enlargement of the park northwards was accomplished enclosing the church within it. The plan accompanying this order shows that the churchyard had been bounded by roads on all sides in the old village. The Road Orders confirm the identification of features in the park as roads.

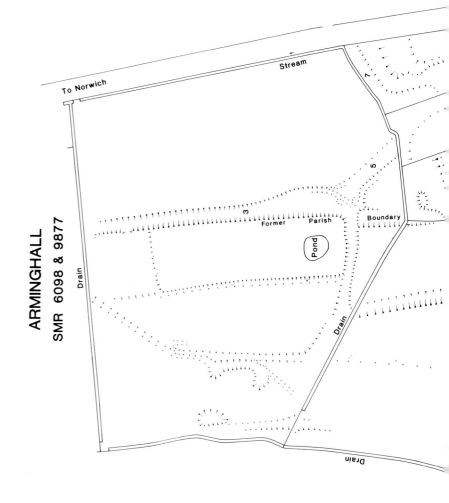

ARMINGHALL
SMR 6098 & 9877

Figure 5 Arminghall, shrinkage of medieval village and later roadways and enclosures. Scale 1:2,500

12

Plate II Arminghall: shrunken village features looking north. TG 2504/J/AHB 16

Arminghall SMR 6098, 9877; TG 254 045
(Pl. II, Fig.5)

Marked hollow ways and enclosures, including possible tofts, lie near the boundary of two villages, one of them, Bixley, deserted.

Arminghall is a small village immediately south-east of Norwich, formerly separate but now within the modern parish of Bixley. The earthworks lie between the inhabited area and B1332 Norwich-to-Bungay road and are divided north-to-south by the former parish boundary between Arminghall and Bixley. The western, Arminghall, part is characterised by a distinct curving hollow way (1), extending north-eastwards from the part-moated Hall site (SMR 6098). Small enclosures to its east (2) may have originally been tofts and closes. A sharp eastward turn in the roadway links it to another north-to-south hollow way (3) which the old parish boundary follows; the boundary is marked by a hedge and ditch further south. In the extreme south, a ditch (4) represents the rear boundary of former tofts.

The eastern Bixley section is linked to (3) by a shallower hollow way (5), broken by the gardens of Meadow Cottages and seen to the south as a very sharp hollow way (6). East of the cottages, a fragment of roadway (7) links with the former village of Bixley (pp19–21). Fragments of toft or close boundaries straddle the drive to them. Further subdivision to the south of the cottages represents probable post-medieval field boundaries.

Arminghall, in the hands of Norwich Cathedral Priory in 1334, made the smallest payment, apart from neighbouring Bixley, to the Lay Subsidy but was allowed no reduction in 1449. However, only a limited amount of church property was liable for taxation so the village was not necessarily as small as figures suggest (Hudson 1895, 271; Glasscock 1975, XVII–XX). By the 17th century much shrinkage had certainly occurred; the 1664 Hearth Tax was exacted on only eleven households (Frankel and Seaman 1983,45) while in 1676 there were forty-two communicants (Whiteman 1986, 217).

A map of 1779 (NRO DCN 127/6) shows a landscape much enclosed and the hall as a three-gabled building facing south onto a common but with no moat. The curving roadway (1) leading northwards is shown as a road turning sharply to join a road called Dead Man's Lane following the parish boundary. The field within the curve of the road was Home Close, the smaller features facing it were a hempyard and three pightles.

Earlier documentary evidence suggests a landscape of contraction, early enclosure and many roads. An undated terrier (NRO NRS 13169 37 F12) refers to Beckles Way. A court book (NRO MS 12819 31 F1) mentions at least eight roads of which the common way from Arminghall to Bixley (1572), Saffron Lane (1573) (*c.f.* Lower Saffron Pightle, 1779) and Bungay Way (1606), deleted in favour of Newgate Way with Dead Man's Grave nearby, appear relevant to the earthworks. Some of the enclosures mapped in 1779 appear to have been in existence for some time.

Arminghall presents a picture of a small contracting settlement with relatively early enclosure and with a changing road system. Dead Man's Lane, not shown on a map of 1813 (NRO DCN 127/22), was probably a procession way. The western roadway with its sharp bend survived until 1813 at least. The eastern one looks suspiciously like an earlier alignment of the Norwich-to-Bungay road.

BABINGLEY

SMR 3257

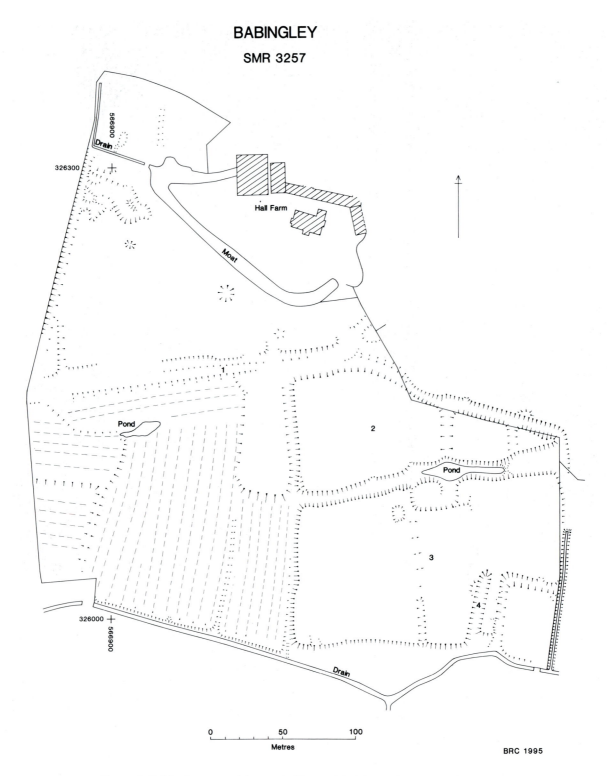

Figure 6 Babingley, part of deserted village with ridge and furrow. Scale 1:2,500

Babingley SMR 3257, TF 670 261
(Pl. III, Fig.6)

A surviving fragment of a deserted medieval village includes a hollow way, a moated site, enclosures and ridge and furrow.

Babingley is a deserted medieval village about 8.5km north-east of King's Lynn. Because of coastal accretion it is now about 6km inland but it may have seen the maritime activity suggested by Havengate Lane in Castle Rising further up the Babingley River.

The earthworks lie to the south and west of the moated Hall Farm and extend southwards to the edge of the former estuary. A prominent feature is the ditched causeway (1) of a former road. To the south-east of it are two substantial ditched enclosures (2,3); a long narrow incision (4) in the south of (3) may have been a dock. The remaining features are ridge and furrow on three distinct alignments. The moat is considered to be much altered.

14

Plate III Babingley deserted medieval village: hollow way, enclosures and ridge and furrow. TF 6726/P/ARO 18

Babingley may have been an early Christian site; its ruined church of St Felix, 200m west of the earthworks, is the only one so dedicated in Norfolk and there is a suggestion that Felix founded a church there (Williamson 1993, 144). Fieldwalking in the early 1980s revealed a strong concentration of Middle Saxon pottery around the churchyard (Moralee 1982–3, 7–12), while Late Saxon and medieval pottery has been found at various times over a broader area, including medieval sherds on the earthworks. Domesday Babingley was substantial with a recorded population of about seventy and there was a flourishing salt production (Brown (ed) 1984, 29,3. 34,1.). In 1334 only nine places in all Freebridge Hundred paid more to the Lay Subsidy; only one of those (other than the Lynns) was outside Fenland (Hudson 1895, 271–2). No relief was given after the Black Death but by 1449 Babingley had suffered decline; the reduction of 21.4% allowed on the Subsidy payment was the seventh largest in Freebridge (Hudson 1895, 271–2).

The 1517 Inquiry reported 86 acres converted to pasture and one house decayed (Allison 1955. 143). In 1602 the church was greatly decayed, the inhabitants few and the chief landowner, Cobbe, was said to be responsible (Allison 1955, 142). In 1603 there were only eight communicants, with eleven in 1676 (Whiteman 1986, 144).

A survey of 1610–11 based on one of 1593 (BM Stowe 765; trans. NRO MC 1086/1 MS 34045) conflicts with this, describing a landscape with six or seven named streets. References are made to land of 'diverse men' north of the church and to messuages east of Paternoster Lane, location unknown. However, Woodethorpes, a messuage and croft was decayed. Of three manors named the sites of only two are mentioned; all three were held by the Cobbe family. West Hall, the moated site on the plan, was said to be west of Butler's Cross, a junction 500m to the east of the earthworks, while Butlers is the isolated moated site 300m to the east of the surveyed area. The causewayed road on the plan is named as Bradgate Way and led westwards to the church. The map of Rising Chace (1588) shows only the church and Butler's Cross (Allison 1955, 143); however, this may have illustrated features solely relevant to the Chace.

Evidence gathered in 1956–8 led to the conclusion that a deserted village had been, perhaps, re-settled in the 17th century with some survival into the 19th (Hurst 1961, 332–42) and this is reflected in the reduced structure of the church (Batcock 1991, 83–88).

Plate IV Barton Bendish: Blind Lane and enclosures from the west. TF 7106/F/ATZ 13

Barton Bendish SMR 18851, TF 718 061
(Pl. IV, Fig.7)

A remnant of a hollow way with tofts and enclosures provides evidence of post-medieval shrinkage.

Barton Bendish lies about 10km east-north-east of Downham Market just beyond the north-western margin of Breckland. Much of the parish is well-drained upland but at the southern end there are peat-filled valleys draining to the Wissey. Until 1929 the Devil's Dyke (Bichamditch) served as the eastern parish boundary. The main village is close to the north-western corner of the parish, and, in medieval times, contained three parish churches, St Mary's, All Saints' and St Andrew's and a chapel of St John. A separate common-edge settlement, Eastmoor, grew up in medieval times in the south-east of the parish. Barton Bendish has been the subject of a recently-published parish study (Rogerson *et al.* 1997).

The earthworks lie at the north-eastern end of the main village to the west of Abbey Farm. A hollow way (1), partly cut by a pit, runs from south-west to north-east and is flanked by three ditched enclosures to the north. These are probably toft sites and there are more rectangular ditched closes to the north (2). The earthworks south of the way are much less evident because of ploughing.

Documentary evidence allows identification of the hollow way as Blind Lane, a name still in use in the early 17th century. It originally formed part of an elongated settlement about 1.5km long with only one side street. Fieldwalking evidence suggests a Middle Saxon core of the village near St Mary's at the western end of the settlement with a second site developing in Late Saxon times near St Andrew's. In medieval times the inhabited area grew eastwards and Barton Bendish became one of the more prosperous places in its hundred. It maintained its standing through the troubled 14th and 15th centuries though some decline occurred. A 17th-century survey mentions gaps in the village street which may once have supported buildings and there are definite references to decayed tenements and evidence of losses west of St Mary's.

Fieldwalking finds support the picture of shrinkage from and abandonment within the area established in the medieval period. All Saints' church, close to St Andrew's, was demolished in the 18th century and a comparison of the survey with the modern map reveals other subsequent losses.

The earthworks, medieval in origin, are visible evidence of settlement contraction (Rogerson *et al.* 1987, 1–66; 1997, 1–76).

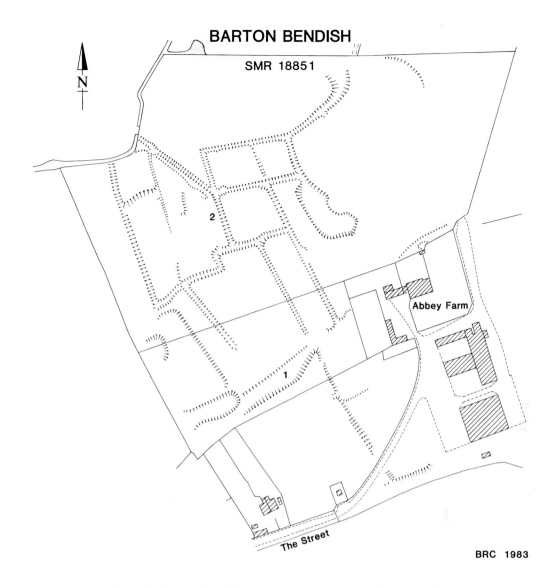

BARTON BENDISH

SMR 18851

N

2

1

Abbey Farm

The Street

BRC 1983

Figure 7 Barton Bendish, roadway and enclosures. Scale 1:2,500

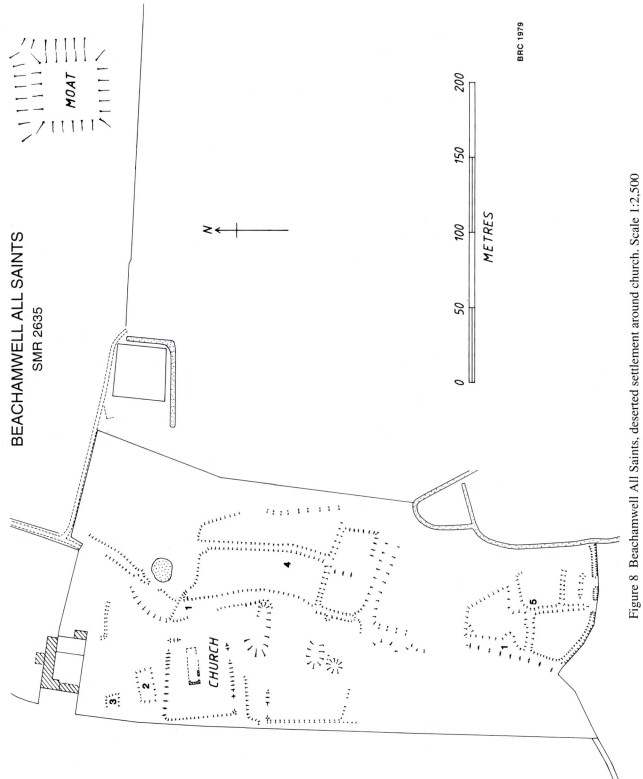

BEACHAMWELL ALL SAINTS
SMR 2635

MOAT

N

CHURCH

METRES

0   50   100   150   200

BRC 1979

Figure 8 Beachamwell All Saints, deserted settlement around church. Scale 1:2,500

Beachamwell All Saints' SMR 2635, TF 750 046
(Fig.8)

A sinuous hollow way is flanked by a ruined church and probable tofts.

Beachamwell is about 8km south-west of Swaffham and lies on the north-western margin of Breckland. The village was formerly very much larger and was divided into three parishes, of which only one church, St Mary's, remains intact. The earthworks are to the south of the present village around the ruined All Saints' church. The site straddles a sinuous linear depression (1) indicating a roadway which led southwards to the deserted village of Caldecote. To the west of this hollow way the church stands within a discernible churchyard. Two possible building platforms (2 and 3) lie north of it. Two groups of tofts (4 and 5) survive to the east of the hollow way.

From the earthworks and surrounding grassland many medieval sherds have been recovered together with some Late Saxon and Romano-British wares. Some 350m east-north-east of the church is a large ploughed-over moated platform. Finds from land north, west and north-east of the earthworks show that the site was much larger with evidence of Middle and Late Saxon activity.

The portion of Beachamwell around All Saints' church seems to have been called 'Well' in early medieval times. Later, the three parishes appear to have been sometimes named distinctly. That of the surviving church was known as 'Bicham St Mary', All Saints' parish as 'Bichamwell' and the third parish, St John's, was 'Little Bicham'. All Saints' was near the southern end of a crescent-shaped inhabited area proved by fieldwalking.

By 1334 the Lay Subsidy list shows that the settlement was treated as one unit called 'Bychamwell' and was one of only sixty places in Norfolk charged £10 or more. Figures for 1449 show only slight decline (Hudson 1895, 286). Of the several medieval manors, the ploughed-over moat can be plausibly identified as Well Hall. Will requests in the 16th century suggest that burials at All Saints' were few and that scarcely any occurred at St John's. St Mary's had become the centre of the surviving village. The reasons for the contraction remain unknown.

A Faculty of 1721 (NRO FCB/1 559(b)) recorded the ruinous state of All Saints' and stated that there were only seven families left in the parish. These attended St Mary's church which was near and convenient. It also said that All Saints' had been dilapidated for 33 years. It is interesting that the Tithe Map of All Saints' (1845, NRO E1) showed that some houses around St Mary's were actually in All Saints' parish so the Faculty did not exaggerate. Before All Saints' became dilapidated it may have served as little more than a private chapel for the Athow family who repaired it in 1612 and whose arms were on the western gable. Parts of the walls of the church were 12th-century and when they collapsed in 1989, part of a Late Saxon cross was found in the rubble (Gurney 1990, 108).

Beachamwell had 224 communicants in 1603 but only 123 in 1676 (Whiteman 1986, 210). A map of 1766 shows only a few buildings near All Saints' with the village grouped around St Mary's in a vaguely planned form; the landscape was largely enclosed apart from a large warren to the north (Davison *et al.* 1988, 3–17).

Bixley SMR 9660, TG 260 049
(Pl. V, Fig.9)

The earthworks of a scattered deserted medieval settlement.

Bixley lies 3km south-east of Norwich on a fertile, well-drained boulder clay plateau between the Tas and Yare valleys. The surviving earthworks lie in four pastures close to and mainly east of the church of St Wandregeselius, a dedication said to be unique in England.

A former course of the Norwich-to-Bungay road (1) runs past the western side of the churchyard. To the east of this is another north-to-south road in part infilled (2) the remainder still marked by a hollow way (3). A short partially infilled way (4) south of the church links the two. Another road (5) extends south-westwards from the church. A further north-to-south roadway (6) can be seen in the eastern field where features are particularly well-preserved and an obvious group of tofts lies on either side of this. Other tofts lay south-east and north-east of the church with a remnant of another near Park Cottages. Ploughing and infilling have reduced some features in the north field since 1966 when they were first surveyed (Cushion *et al.* 1982, 91–2); on the new plan these are shown by pecked lines. Dredging from the ponds has caused other minor changes (Wade-Martins (ed) 1999, 58).

The documentary evidence for this, the most extensive deserted village site in eastern Norfolk, is sparse. Bixley (Biskele 1086, from OE Byxe 'box'; Schram 1961, 146) may mean a clearing or pasture associated with box trees and thus indicate a relatively late settlement. Domesday, in five entries, records a total population of twenty-seven and a half including four and a half freemen and thirteen sokemen. There was a church. Slight increase in plough teams since 1066 suggests that it was flourishing, and freemen from Bramerton were added to make up the manor (Brown (ed) 1984, 9,32;42;45;114; 66,81)

In 1334 Bixley contributed the lowest total of its hundred, its payment being well below the average. However, it was allowed no reduction in 1449 nor was it exempt from the parish tax in 1428. Only very small numbers of people paid the Lay Subsidies in 1524 and 1581. Few Bixley wills were recorded after 1400. There were twenty-five communicants in 1603 and thirty-five and a Non-conformist in 1676 (Whiteman 1986, 201). The Hearth Tax of 1664 was charged on twenty-nine hearths; fifteen of these belonged to Sir Edward Ward, two others paid for five and four respectively and there were four other houses charged (Frankel and Seaman 1983, 42).

The Wards lived in the Hall built about 1565–70. It stood well to the south of the village site. Faden (1797) showed the Bungay road close to the church and the Hall standing within a park.

Limited fieldwalking in 1997 on the north field yielded finds of Late Saxon and medieval dates on the areas of the tofts and the road line, but pottery was markedly absent near the church. Apart from the 15th-century tower little early fabric of the church remains. The scattered settlement pattern may represent some degree of late dispersal or may show a series of scattered farmsteads reflecting the rather large proportion of freemen and sokemen in the earliest record. The reasons for decay on such an apparently favourable site remain obscure (Cushion *et al.* 1982, 93–4).

Plate V Bixley deserted medieval village: earthworks seen from the west. TG 2504/R/ATT 28

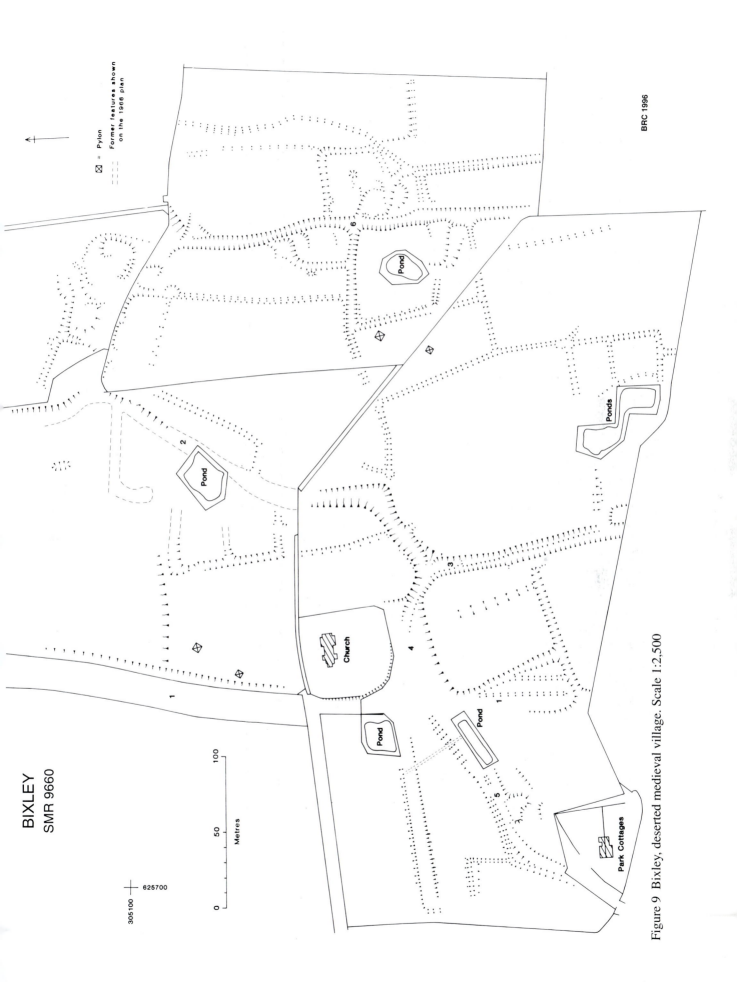

BIXLEY
SMR 9660

⊠ = Pylon

┄┄┄ Former features shown
on the 1966 plan

BRC 1996

305100
625700

Metres
0   50   100

Figure 9 Bixley, deserted medieval village. Scale 1:2,500

21

Brinton SMR 29585, TG 035 352
(Fig.10)

Complex earthworks include tofts, a roadway and a possible moated platform.

Brinton is a small village about 5km south-west of Holt. The site continues south-westwards from the existing curving linear settlement to the south and west of a small valley. It is within the angle formed by the roads to Gunthorpe and Briningham and close to the parish boundary.

The site is a fairly confused area, now cut by the modern course of a stream with linking drains. There is a hollow way (1) crossing the valley; to the south of it are two enclosures (2,3) close to the Gunthorpe road and a straight ditch (4) with a pronounced eastern edge.

To the north of the hollow way is a complicated pattern of features dominated by a small moated platform (5) (17m x 16m) now cut in two by the stream. The moat is linked to a gently curving ditch (6), possibly marking an outer enclosure, and is joined by a ditch from the road. A possible outflow channel (7), very degraded, leaves the north-east corner of the curving ditch. Finally, in the extreme north of the site, a small brick and flint building stands within a terraced enclosure subdivided by two depressions.

From Domesday onwards (Brown (ed) 1984, 10,8) where it appears briefly as an outlier of Thornage, Brinton has a somewhat obscure history, appearing to be a small village with no apparent period of decline (Hudson 1895, 280; Sheail 1968), with an increasing number of people in the 17th century (Whiteman 1986, 226–7) and without a notably large house (Frankel and Seaman 1983, 45).

A field book of 1618 (NRO MS 18623/155 726 x 3) unfortunately covers parts of Brinton within the manor of Thornage and deals with areas in the north of the parish, referring to lands west of Gunthorpe Way and south-east by Briningham Way. The same is true of a map of 1780 (NRO MC 37/149 482 x 5). Nothing can be safely identified with the earthworks. Faden (1797) shows a road crossing the site, apparently the hollow way, and this appears as a field boundary in 1818 (NRO Hayes and Storr 18).

The Enclosure Map of 1807 (NRO C/Sca 2/53) shows the enclosure to the north with two buildings described as a messuage and buildings, still shown as existing on Bryant's map (1826) and on the 1st Edition of the OS One-Inch map. Finds made on site indicate a medieval origin but the site remains largely a mystery.

Carleton Forehoe SMR 29608, TG 095 058
(Fig.11)

Earthworks of an apparent common-edge extension of the surviving settlement.

Carleton Forehoe is a small rectangular former parish 4.5km north-west of Wymondham. It faced south-eastwards onto the River Tiffey and is now part of Kimberley. 'Forehoe' refers to tumuli; one of them, Forehoe Hill, which lay, according to Blomefield (1739, I, 652), in a field on the south side of the road from Norwich to Hingham, was the place where the Hundred met.

The earthworks are to the north-west of Low Road which was the boundary of Low Common on the 1766 Enclosure Award (NRO C/Sca 2/65). They lie in three areas, interspersed with marshy natural spring-fed depressions. The most easterly one (1) consists of rather subdued enclosure boundaries and depressions. The central area contains firmer evidence of medieval settlement. There is a boundary ditch (2) which may mark the edge of the former common and, facing it, three abutting ditched enclosures. The eastern enclosure has some building evidence (3). The western field has few easily identifiable features, although one may be a possible sinuous continuation of the common edge (4).

Fieldwalking has produced a thin spread of medieval pottery over the surveyed areas, particularly the central toft and also on an unsurveyed ploughed area still further to the west, not shown on the plan.

Carleton Forehoe appears not to have undergone any major setbacks. Of modest size, it seems to have persisted quite successfully showing only slow decline over the centuries. In 1676, for example, it had sixty-four communicants as against the figure of seventy-six in 1603 (Whiteman 1986, 206). The 1st Edition One-Inch OS map of 1838 shows two buildings on the site which are no longer there.

A deed of 1490 (NRO Phi/80 577 x 1) records a messuage with another to the west, land to the east and north, and common to the south which probably refers to this area. A later document, probably of the 17th century (NRO Woodhouse 2P/34), is a schedule of abuttals of a messuage and 56 acres of land in forty-three pieces. From this it appears that there were two areas of common in Carleton Forehoe, one of them being on higher ground near the boundary of Barnham Broom to the north-west. The abuttals of the messuage, however, suggest that it faced south onto the Low Common and had other messuages to the east and west. These cannot be identified with certainty as they may refer to areas still under occupation. It would appear that this particular area developed, perhaps, as a part of a common-edge extension to the original body of the village which lay to the west near the church.

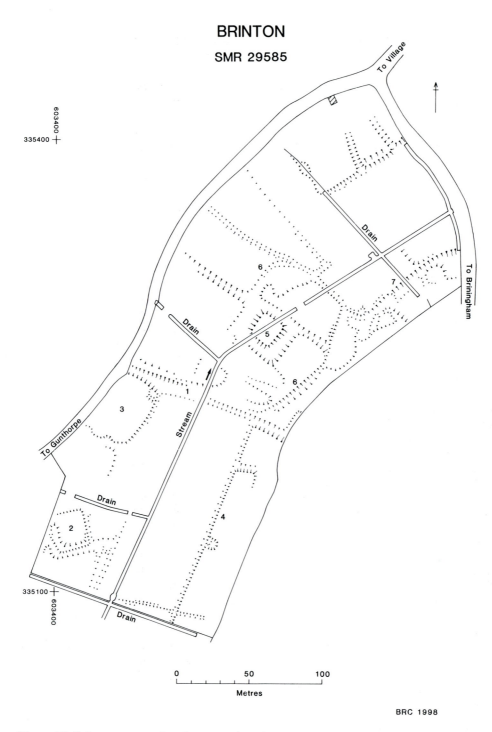

BRINTON

SMR 29585

To Village

To Briningham

To Gunthorpe

Drain

Drain

Drain

Drain

Stream

603400

335400 +

335100 +

603400

1

2

3

4

5

6

6

7

0   50   100

Metres

BRC 1998

Figure 10 Brinton, scattered settlement and enclosures south-west of village. Scale 1:2,500

23

CARLETON FOREHOE
SMR 29608

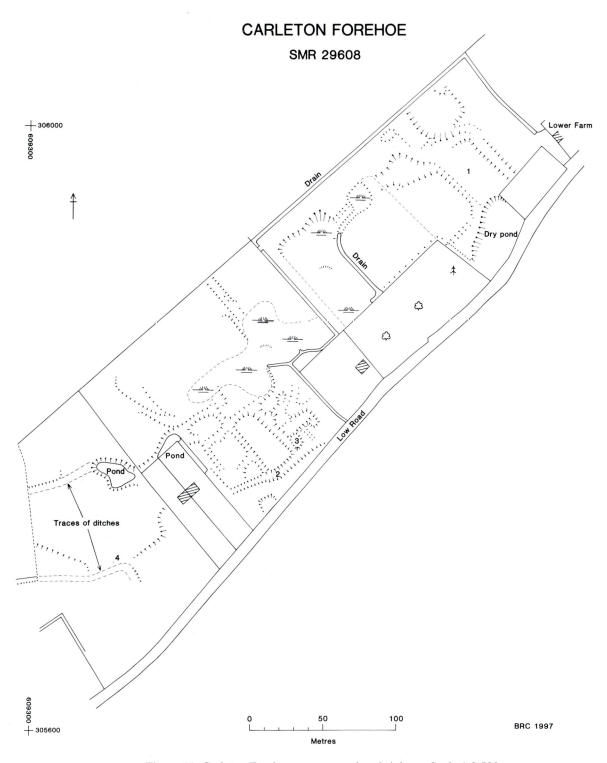

Lower Farm

Drain

Drain

1

Dry pond

Low Road

Pond

Pond

Traces of ditches

2

3

4

306000

609300

609300

305600

| 0 | 50 | 100 |
Metres

BRC 1997

Figure 11 Carleton Forehoe, common-edge shrinkage. Scale 1:2,500

CRANWORTH
SMR 25910

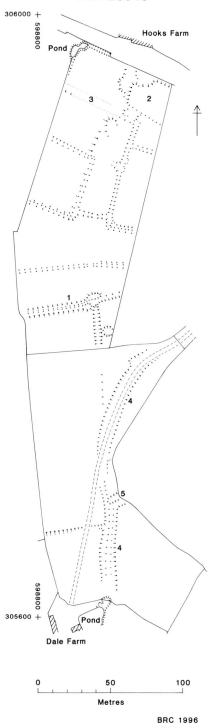

306000 +
598800
Hooks Farm
Pond
3
2
1
4
5
4
598800
305600 +
Pond
Dale Farm

0   50   100
Metres

BRC 1996

Figure 12 Cranworth, possible common-edge
settlement. Scale 1:2,500

Cranworth SMR 25910, TF 988 058
(Fig.12)

An intriguing survival of apparent medieval date, which is possibly part of Letton deserted medieval village or a relic of the vanished Swathing.

Cranworth is a scattered village about 13km west-north-west of Wymondham; it is now united with the former parishes of Wood Rising, Southburgh and Letton, the last being deserted. The earthworks are 1km north-north-east of the church and lie across the former boundary with Letton which appears as an east-to-west linear bank (1). To the north of it is a meadow with a series of rectangular enclosures, partly truncated by a relatively modern hedge to the east. A raised area in the north-east corner (2) may be the site of a building but there is no surface evidence for this. The enclosures are bounded by ditches, some of them with banks. There is some evidence of infilling of a former depression (3).

The field to the south of the parish boundary has a hollow way (4) about 11m wide and 0.6m deep partially followed by the modern drive which diverges from it to reach the farmhouse. South of the divergence the way is partly blocked by a gateway access ramp (5) before continuing as a hollow way with flanking ditches.

The identity of these earthworks is obscure; pottery found to the east of the northern field suggests a medieval origin. The Domesday entries for this hundred show a very complicated pattern of settlement with a number of places which have since disappeared. One, Swathing (Suatinga), was associated with Cranworth and Letton; William de Swathing was a lord in Letton and Rising with Cranworth in 1316 (Blake 1952, 285). In 1086 Cranworth and Swathing were of about equal size; by 1334 Swathing was unmentioned and its location has been a matter for speculation since. Its association with Cranworth and Letton has been supported by Blomefield (1775, V, 1176): 'a town many centuries passed, destroyed and depopulated and the lands belonging to it now included in the townships of Cranworth and Letton'. The arms of the Swathings were in Cranworth church and they presented to the living there (Blomefield 1775, V, 1179–80).

As the earthworks straddle the old parish boundary it is tempting to suggest a connection with Swathing. A stronger possibility is that the northern part represents a remnant of a medieval common-edge settlement on High Common. The earthworks lay in the deserted parish of Letton and a building was shown here in 1783 (Davison *et al.* 1988, 44). The hollow way in the southern part was an access way to Dale Farm or a predecessor.

DEOPHAM

SMR 21116

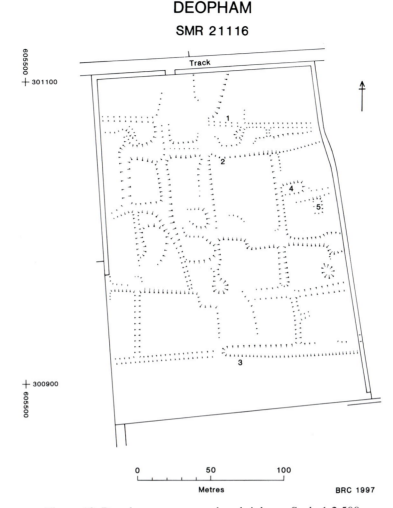

605500
+ 301100

Track

+ 300900
605500

0   50   100

Metres   BRC 1997

Figure 13 Deopham, common-edge shrinkage. Scale 1:2,500

Deopham SMR 21116, 2960; TG 056 010, 041 006
(Figs 13,14)

Two groups of medieval earthworks which were on the margins of the former Low Common.

Deopham is a large straggling village about 7km south-west of Wymondham: at present it extends almost 3km from north to south. The earthworks are in two groups, widely separated, at the northern end of the village.

The first (SMR 21116) is quite small and lies to the north-east of the village. It consists of a number of earthworks lying between two east-to-west features. These features represent former field boundaries shown on relatively recent maps and may not be older than the late 18th century. The northern one (1) has a less clear scarp (2) to the south of it, probably representing an older boundary. Between this and the southernmost boundary (3) are at least six irregularly subdivided enclosures separated by ditches with two probable building platforms (4,5) in the eastern one. Less convincing features in the western enclosures may represent other buildings. Medieval and Late Medieval Transitional pottery has been found.

The second site (SMR 2960) is much more extensive and lies to the south-west of Crown Farm. It is a series of ditched enclosures on a gently north-facing slope to the south-east of Sea Mere. The site has been subjected to some

ploughing and reseeding which has led to subduing and truncation of some features. It is divided by six main enclosure boundaries (1–6) still seen on early 19th-century maps. Subdividing features suggest the whole layout may be a good deal earlier. The most significant are in the extreme western enclosure where medieval pottery occurs on an incomplete ditched platform (7). Medieval pottery has also been found in the next two more easterly enclosures where there are also probable earlier features. North-west of Crown Farm next to a track is a small raised area (8) on which early post-medieval pottery occurs (Cushion 1997, 32).

Field evidence suggests that these sites date originally from the medieval period but there is unfortunately no real documentary evidence from that time. A relatively high contribution to the 1334 Lay Subsidy was reduced in 1449 by 28.6% (Hudson 1895, 278–9). Some further decline may have happened by 1524/5 (Sheail 1968): on the other hand 1676 communicant figures suggest recovery (Whiteman 1986, 206–08).

Faden's Map (1797) shows a number of commons still in existence in the parish; Deopham Stolland to the south-west, Hookwood Common to the south and the large Low Common to the north. Both sites appear to have been close to the edge of Low Common, but with Crown Farm shown in isolation. The Enclosure Map of 1814 (NRO C/Sca2/86) shows the northern and southern field

DEOPHAM
SMR 2960

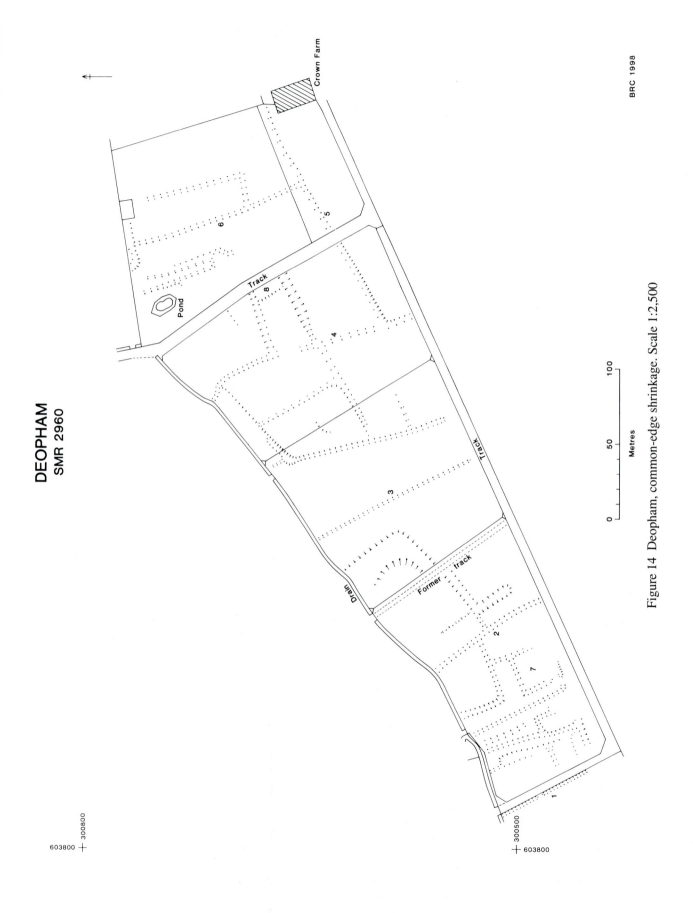

Figure 14 Deopham, common-edge shrinkage. Scale 1:2,500

BRC 1998

27

DERSINGHAM
SMR 17436

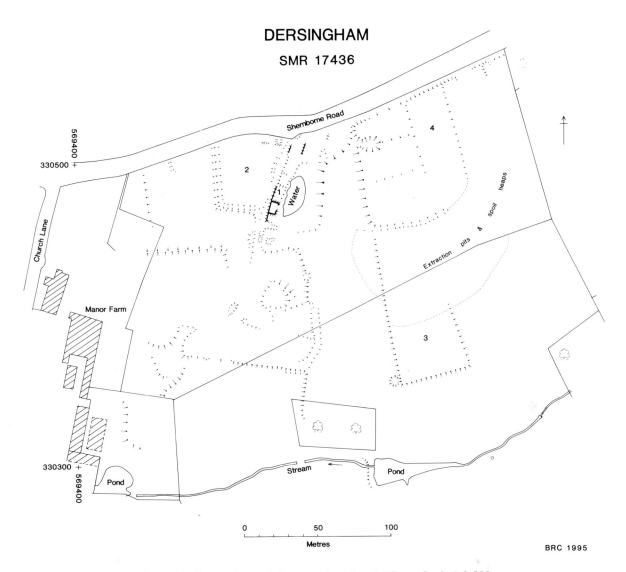

Figure 15 Dersingham, shrinkage of medieval village. Scale 1:2,500

boundaries on SMR 21116 and the remnant of a moat to the north-east of Crown Farm beyond the surveyed area on SMR 2960. Here irregular linear water features are shown instead of the modern drain: some field boundaries shown now appear as earthworks.

The Tithe Map of 1843 (NRO DN/TA 743) shows the southern boundary on SMR 21116 quite clearly with an arable Long Pightle to the south of it, the remainder being pasture. On the other site Crown Farm is shown, but the moat, also mapped by Bryant (1826), is not depicted. The linear ditches are all shown as field boundaries but the modern drain is not visible. One enclosure was said to be arable, the two most westerly and the easternmost enclosures were woodland; the one crossed by the modern track was pasture.

These relatively modern maps explain the more recent earthworks quite well. The northern field boundary on SMR 21116 appears to have replaced an earlier irregular common-edge boundary close to the south. The approximate boundary of the common on SMR 2960 is shown by the modern drain.

It appears likely that the abandonment of these sites was the result of adjustment within the parish as, in addition to Crown Farm near SMR 2960, modern settlement survives near SMR 21116.

Dersingham SMR 17436, TF 695 304
(Fig.15)

A deserted eastward extension of the village was probably associated with a former manor.

Dersingham is a large village about 13km north-east of King's Lynn. It seems likely from the evidence of the Tithe Map (NRO DN/TA 274) that by the early 19th century, at least, the village had partly drifted away from a possible early nucleus around the church and to the west of it, to develop a common-edge fringing settlement to the north-west. It is clear from the earthworks described here that medieval settlement also extended well to the east of the church.

The earthworks lie east of Manor Farm and the church in grassland between the Shernborne Road and a steeply incised stream. The major feature is a building range with subdivisions (1); it is about 33m north-to-south and about 5m wide and there are signs of possible other buildings nearby. The visible remains of walls include fragments of carstone, limestone and medieval bricks. To the west of it is a complete enclosure (2) with banks and ditches, while to the east is an obvious boundary which appears linked to

Plate VI Dunton deserted medieval village, seen from the south-west. TF 8830/D/ALY 1

the western limit of an incomplete enclosure (3). The south-east of the area has been disfigured by the remains of more recent carstone pits, truncating enclosures (4) facing onto Shernborne Road. War-time ploughing has degraded many features including incomplete enclosures to the south of the building outlines.

From surface evidence it is clear that the features are in part, at least, medieval as a substantial quantity of pottery of that period was collected. The Tithe Map shows Snoring Hall Close on the north side of the Shernborne Road and this coincides closely with the site of the medieval manor of Snoring Hall still indicated on modern maps by scanty remains of a moat. A field book of 1692 (NRO MC 40/54 485 x 7) mentions Snoring Hall, Snoring Hall Close and Snoring Hall Dike in describing this area, confirming the later maps. The earthworks lie on the opposite side of the road and may have been associated with the manor, possibly the forerunner of Manor Farm.

Dunton SMR 17329, TF 880 302
(Pl. VI, Fig.16)

The earthworks are of a deserted medieval village diminished by slow wastage.

Dunton lies about 4km west of Fakenham; it has a roughly rectangular parish based on the River Wensum and includes Doughton, a lost hamlet nearer the river.

The earthworks are in south-sloping meadows around the church and Dunton Farm on either side of the street. To the north-west of the church are flint masonry outlines of buildings (1) which appear intact on pre-1939 OS maps, while neighbouring features appear as field boundaries. A small east-to-west depression (2) north of the church may be an earlier churchyard boundary. South of the church are earthworks including old field boundaries, possible remnants of tofts, and pits indicating multi-period activity.

To the east of the street two salient features are a well-defined ditch (3) separating a featureless area to the north from earthworks to the south; it corresponds with a boundary shown on older OS maps. The other is a marked

29

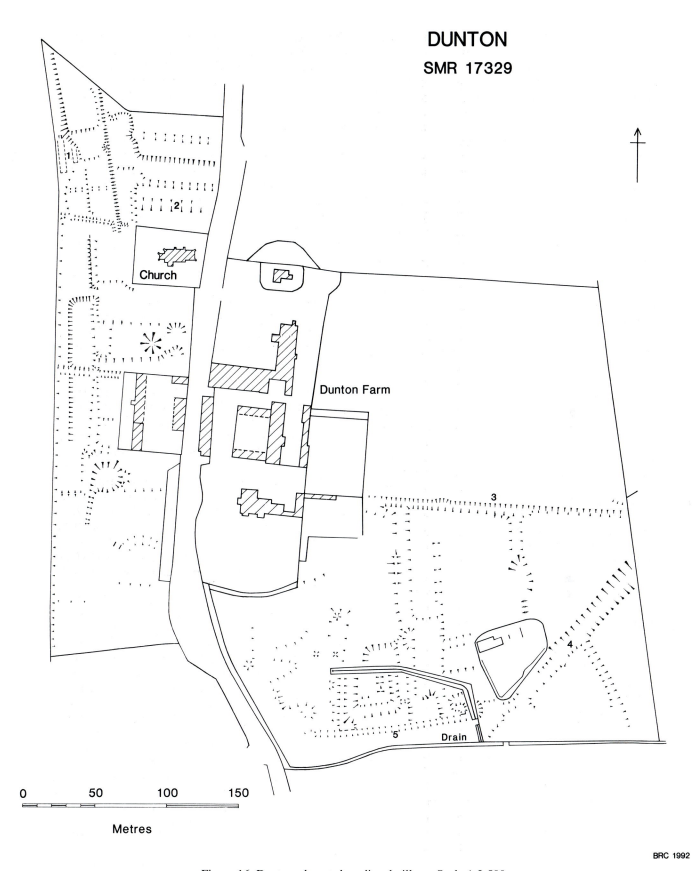

DUNTON
SMR 17329

Church

Dunton Farm

3

4

5   Drain

0   50   100   150

Metres

BRC 1992

Figure 16 Dunton, deserted medieval village. Scale 1:2,500

hollow way (4) extending north-eastwards and passing a fenced enclosure containing remains of post-medieval cottages which may lie on the southern remnant of a toft. Other linear features to the west suggest possible tofts, although the southern portions, cut by a modern drain, appear more complicated. Building remains exist on the north side of a ditch (5) which was probably the northern edge of a continuation of the hollow way.

Dunton with Doughton, in medieval times appears to have been quite stable judging by its Lay Subsidy payment in 1334. It was allowed a reduction of 14.6% to the 1449 payment, quite modest compared with reductions allowed neighbouring settlements (Hudson 1895, 273). Some loss may be attributable to the Black Death as three clergy were installed between 8th April and 10th July in 1349 to the church of Dunton with the chapel of Doughton (Pobst 1996, 85, 89, 114).

A field book, dated on internal evidence to the early 16th century (Holkham MS, Vol 3, Bundle 5, 65), lists thirty-one messuages and six cottages, all apparently occupied, and sixteen messuages described as unoccupied. There was also a grange and a barn. There is no direct reference to the church or to the chapel. The latter disappeared probably in the 14th century (Batcock 1991, 54). The unoccupied buildings suggest contracting settlement and the overall description indicates a northern cluster of nine messuages with two empty ones; a main group of eleven messuages, including the parsonage, one cottage, a barn and six empty ones; and a southern group near a riverine Dunton Common of eleven messuages, five cottages and eight empty messuages, probably in the vicinity of Doughton.

It appears that the parsonage was immediately north of the Dunton church path and there were four messuages nearby together with an empty one and a number of minor enclosures including an orchard. This seems to describe some of the earthworks near the church. Other entries in this group record messuages associated with Dunton Common which may refer to earthworks on the eastern side of the road where Faden (1797) shows a small embayment of the common approaching the street.

Slow decline continued; there were seventy communicants in 1603 and sixty-two in 1676 (Whiteman 1986, 212) while the Hearth Tax of 1666 recorded sixteen taxable households with thirty-seven hearths. A rate list of 1643 names seventeen people (NRO HMN 6/380 772 x 6). A map by Biedermann dated 1781 shows a very small settlement much diminished with earthwork areas depicted as pasture; the hollow way to the east of the street was shown petering out eastwards (Holkham MS). Faden shows the common surviving, the Hall where Dunton Farm now stands, a few other buildings near the church, and the hollow way continuing as a road towards Sculthorpe. This is repeated by Bryant (1826) who does not show any common land, and on the OS One-Inch 1st Edition.

East Walton SMR 30996, 31091; TF 740 167, 749 153
(Figs 17,18)

The earthworks are of a northern expansion of the village along a drove road with a second group of common-edge features to the south.

East Walton is a shrunken village about 14.5km east-south-east of King's Lynn and about 8km west-north-west of Castle Acre. It is situated between the chalk escarpment to the east and an important area of periglacial features on Walton Common to the west. Decline of the settlement is shown by the ruins of St Andrew's church abandoned in the 15th or 16th century (Batcock 1991, 52).

Earthworks immediately south of St Mary's church may include a manorial site while to the north a series of rectilinear field boundaries extend from the present road westwards towards the common. A slight element of settlement in this area is not convincing.

Site 30996 consists of a series of sub-rectangular and rectilinear enclosures, themselves subdivided, which extend from a northern boundary of banks and ditches (1) to front south onto Common Lane. Existing buildings may be the remains of a linear settlement. The central portion has the best surviving enclosures, with a raised area (2) close to the road possibly including building foundations. Features (3), (4) and (5) may be further building sites. While the remains of a series of tofts may be the original earthworks, it is possible that later superimpositions of farmsteads may best explain the complex features surrounding the sites of buildings. The western parts extend into the area of periglacial features which must have presented difficulties for settlement and suggest that pressure on land must have been quite marked.

Site 31091 lies at Summer End along the northern edge of a common and consists of up to five tofts facing south. An internal boundary ditch (1) is shown on the Tithe Map (1840) as dividing the area into two unequal portions. To the west of this, two ditches (2,3) run from north to south and there are short ditches linking them with the divide. To the east, two more complex earthworks appear to contain building platforms; the more westerly has three (4,5,6) and the easternmost has one (7) with signs of foundations. Pottery finds support a medieval origin for these earthworks.

East Walton in 1086 was in an area of moderate population density where sheep were numerous (Darby 1952). By 1334 the region was assessed at £20–29 per sq. mile (Glasscock 1975, XXVII) but East Walton was granted a 21% reduction on Lay Subsidy payment in 1449. The earlier medieval prosperity probably explains the development of the Common Lane area and possibly the move to Summer Common.

Two surveys of East Walton (NRO BIR/26 and BIR/27 396 x 7) include references to commons or pastures such as Walton Common next to Bilney Fen; those near to Walton Slack; 'over the Welles' against the common spring; others next to Thorpe Brook, one called Reed Acre and yet another 'next the common called the Wroe', a clear reference to the angular projection of Walton Common towards Bilney. The Drove mentioned with these commons may well be Common Lane along which part of the village grew.

The surveys, one dated 1593, the other probably 16th century, record a field called Emenhow or Southmore in which there was a Southmore Crofts furlong next to the common of South More. 'Summer' is an obvious modern corruption. Southmore Street is also mentioned together with messuages and probably relates to these earthworks. One survey (BIR/26) refers to a manorial site here, the other describes it without comment and it cannot be clearly identified.

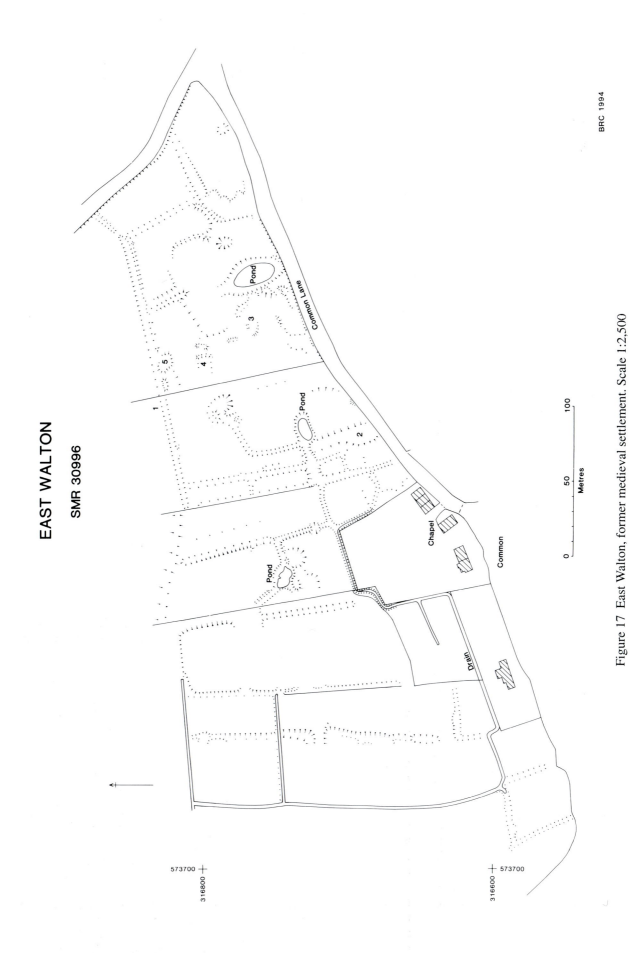

EAST WALTON

SMR 30996

BRC 1994

Figure 17 East Walton, former medieval settlement. Scale 1:2,500

EAST WALTON

SMR 31091

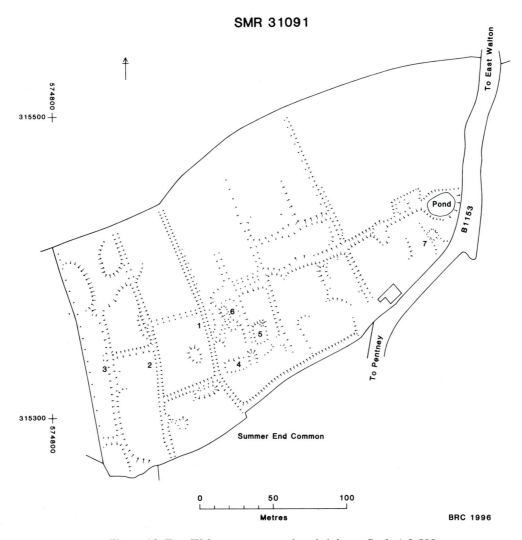

Figure 18 East Walton, common-edge shrinkage. Scale 1:2,500

Egmere SMR 1955, TF 895 375
(Fig.19)

The earthworks lie in three fields linked by hollow ways and dominated by the ruins of a church.

Egmere lies about 8km north-north-west of Fakenham near the head of a seasonally dry valley draining southwards towards Waterden. The surviving earthworks are in three fields but the site is dominated by the ruined St Edmund's church standing on a knoll with street lines flanking its north-western and eastern sides (Batcock 1991, 134–136). The first of these (1) continues as a linear depression on arable land and crosses the valley, being traceable afterwards as a soil mark in arable land to the west. On the valley-floor is a short length of hollow way (2) leading south with the remains of tofts at the intersection. The pond here is probably a later feature and the southerly road now holds a watercourse. The road linking church and valley floor followed the boundary with Waterden; fieldwalking revealed medieval occupation on its northern side only. Medieval pottery also occurs, with some evidence of Middle and Late Saxon activity, on the arable to the west

of the valley. To the south of the church features appear to be associated with a roadway (3) and a manor farm shown on maps of 1797 and 1807 respectively. Pit digging has added confusion here.

The area north of the modern road is enigmatic, a well-defined hollow way (4) with flanking ditches being the only obvious feature. To the west is what appears to be a series of enclosures, possibly medieval, without evidence of settlement. Again, gravel or marl pits have introduced complications (Cushion *et al.* 1982, 84–7).

Egmere (Ecga's Pond — Gelling 1984, 26, 278) is reliably recorded twice before 1086. The Bishop of Elmham bequeathed land there between 1035 and 1040 while a list of holdings of Bury Abbey (1044–1065) included stock at 'Eggemere' (Hart 1966, 82, 91; Sawyer 1968, 417). In 1086 the greatest part of Egmere was held by the Bishop of Thetford and seemed to have suffered some decline, as had a smaller holding of the King (Brown (ed) 1984, 1,36; 8,117; 10,11).

In paying the Lay Subsidy of 1332 Egmere was linked with Quarles now also deserted; between them they mustered thirty-one named contributors. In 1334 the two paid a sum ninth in order of size in a hundred of fifteen places. There was no reduction in payment after the Black

33

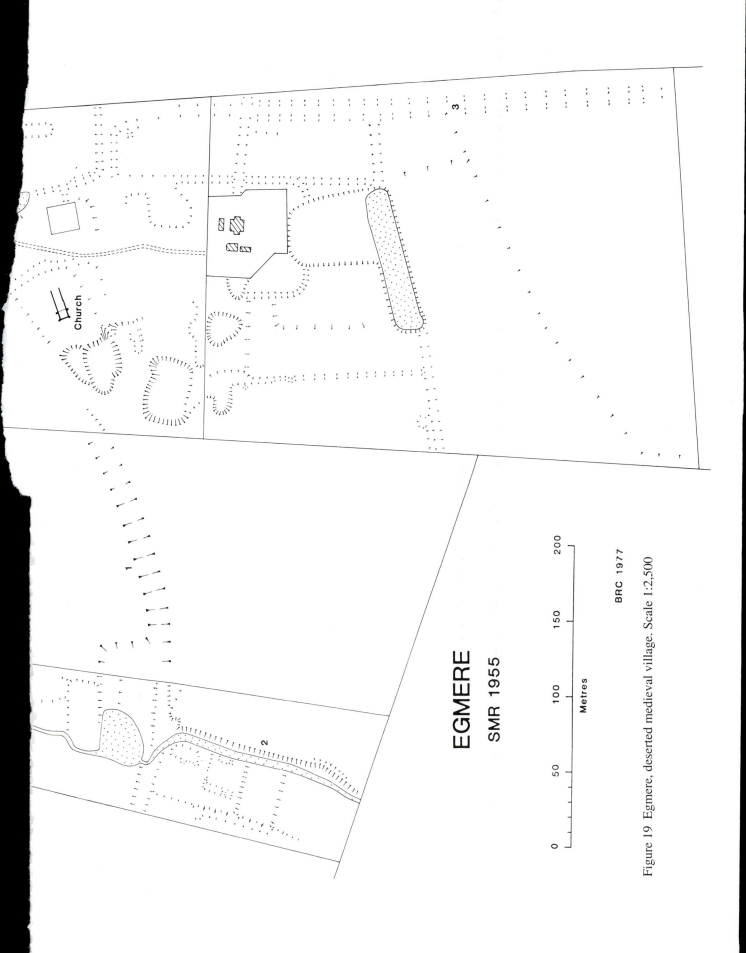

EGMERE
SMR 1955

Church

0   50   100   150   200

Metres

BRC 1977

Figure 19 Egmere, deserted medieval village. Scale 1:2,500

To Walsingham

To the Creakes

4

Death, seemingly the village was in reasonably good heart. However, in 1428 Egmere had less than ten households and, with Quarles, was allowed a 40% reduction in the Lay Subsidy payment of 1449. It is thus interesting that the fine church tower is of the 14th century. The decline seems to have begun in the 15th century.

By the 1550s the church had been partly demolished, the lead looted and the largest bell sent to the coast for export. The parson was one of the culprits. In 1602 decay and profanation of the church was blamed on Sir Nicholas Bacon, the lord, and Thomas Bostock, the incumbent (Allison 1955, 147; Cushion *et al.* 1982, 84–7). Bostock was also rector of Blofield, 30 miles away, in 1592/3 (Smith and Baker 1990, Vol 2, 234).

Ellingham SMR 30620, TM 379 914
(Fig.20)

The earthworks are of a medieval riverine extension of the village.

Ellingham is in the Waveney valley about 3.5km north-east of Bungay. Broadly-based on the valley floor, it has a narrow and curiously attenuated extension north-westwards as far as the boundary of Loddon. The present settlement straggles over a considerable area north of the isolated church and includes some development astride the Kirby Cane boundary, 1km north-west of the site.

The earthworks are in the extreme south-eastern corner of the parish, close to the parish boundary, and consist of a series of sub-rectangular ditched enclosures and tofts on the edge of the flood plain, spread over three fields. A meandering scarp (1) 1m in height corresponds with the edge of the common on the Enclosure Map of 1806 (NRO C/Sca 2/102). An old ditched causeway (2) runs south to the common edge in the central field. In the western field there are five enclosures, one cut in two by a more modern ditch (3). One of these (4) still existed in 1806, approached from the present causeway, and may represent the last phase of pre-grassland use. The central field is subdivided by ditches into enclosures two of which have possible building sites (5 and 6). The eastern field includes an area (7) shown as common in 1806 together with an enclosure of rhombic form (8) in the south-west, also shown then. The boundary of this last feature cuts into a platform yielding medieval pottery and late medieval tiles. Ploughing in the western and eastern fields has subdued some features (Cushion 1997, 32).

There is no sign of any marked decay in the standing of the parish. The Domesday record (Brown (ed) 1984, 1.239) mentions a church and it may be assumed that the original settlement was near the present building which is close to a crossing place of the river. 14th- and 15th-century taxation lists suggest a village of moderate prosperity

(Hudson 1895, 269) with no great evidence of decline, as do the communicant figures for 1603 (106) and 1676 (108) (Whiteman 1986, 201).

There is no indication as to the form of the settlement in medieval times but it might reasonably be assumed that early medieval population increases may have resulted in a spread along the edges of the riverside common pasture in keeping with known river valley sites at Scole in the Waveney valley and West Harling in the Thet. This is borne out by the discovery of medieval pottery at a number of points on the site. At some subsequent period these sites were abandoned to farmland and the population became centred at various points to the north along the main Bungay-to-Beccles road (A 143) with a mill and a farm near the isolated church.

Gateley SMR 12160, TF 958 240
(Fig.21)

An enigmatic cluster of earthworks near the 17th/18th-century hall which is detached from the village; some may be parkland relics.

Gateley is a small village in central Norfolk about 11.5km north-north-west of East Dereham and about 4km north-west of North Elmham. The earthworks are in grassland north of Gateley Hall and consist of a linear depression (1) aligned from north-north-east to south-south-west with enclosures (2,3) on its south-eastern side. Faint north-to-south ridging on the other side of the depression was once more extensive and may represent ridge and furrow, probably post-medieval as it is too straight to be convincingly medieval. Shallow quarrying may be responsible for surface irregularities within the enclosures. West of the Hall a causeway marks a former track or road while a curious near-rectangular platform (4) may be a forgotten parkland feature. The linear depression (1) has narrow stretches with limited flat surfaces and is reminiscent of a drain although it is probably a partially infilled hollow way.

Gateley seems to have had a normal existence from Domesday onwards and it is almost impossible to say, from the lack of documentary evidence, what these features may be. The Hearth Tax returns for 1660 and 1666 show fourteen or fifteen households charged in Gateley, the largest having eight hearths (Frankel and Seaman 1983, 57; Seaman (ed) 1988, 26). It is tempting to see this eight-hearth house of Mr Henry Lancaster 'and j for old Couldhams' of 1666 as a forerunner of the present hall but proof is absent. The hall itself, somewhat detached from the village, has an 18th-century facade but includes a 17th-century part and some of the earthworks may be relics of associated landscaping or gardens (Cozens-Hardy 1961, 179–180; Pevsner and Wilson 1999, 352).

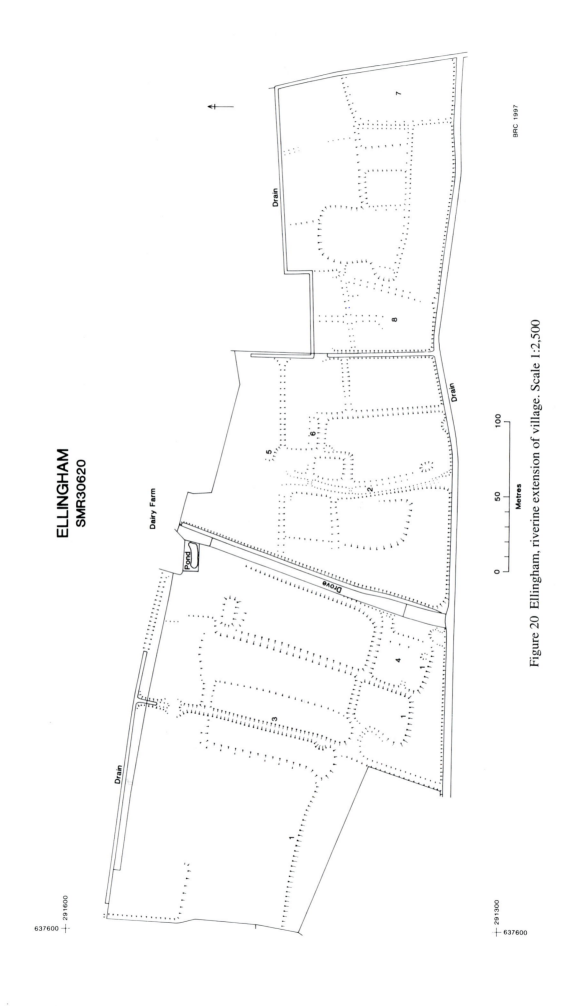

ELLINGHAM
SMR30620

Dairy Farm

Pond

Drove

Drain

Drain

Drain

BRC 1997

Metres

0   50   100

Figure 20 Ellingham, riverine extension of village. Scale 1:2,500

637600
291600

291300
637600

36

GATELEY

SMR 11929

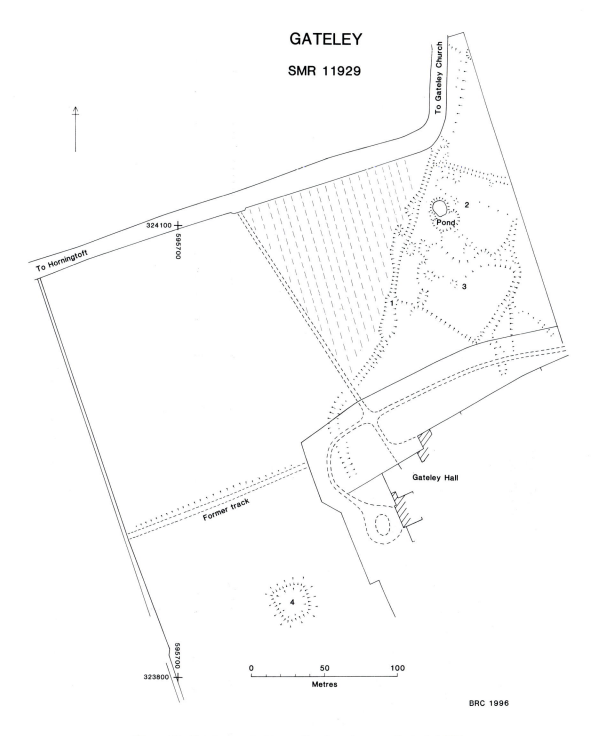

Figure 21 Gateley, probable medieval enclosures. Scale 1:2,500

Plate VII Godwick deserted medieval village: church tower, hollow ways and enclosures. TF/9022/S/ALX 17

Godwick, Tittleshall SMR 1104, TF 904 220
(Pl. VII, Fig.22)

Extensive earthworks are of the deserted medieval village with later changes imposed by the post-medieval building of a hall and barn and more recent farm buildings.

The site lies within Tittleshall parish, about 5km north-east of Litcham, on heavy wet land on the flat boulder clay plateau. The surviving earthworks, among the most impressive in the county, include a hollow way (1) which represents the main street, once part of a way linking Tittleshall and Whissonsett. Two others ran south from the main street and the church tower stands within the angle made by one of them. Only faint outlines of the rest of the church remain but the boundaries of the churchyard are distinct.

Set back from the main street on either side were near parallel ditches (2,3). These were the rear toft boundaries, and the often fragmentary banks and ditches joining them to the street represent property divisions. Seven tofts survive north of the street as earthworks and about four to the south, one of the latter still with platforms and depressions (4) which almost certainly represent buildings marked on a map of 1596. Others have been obliterated by later developments. These include the changes made by the building of a 16th-century hall and, still later, a 17th-century barn and the digging of various clay pits, as well as more modern farm buildings.

The near-rectangular pattern of earthworks around the hall in the eastern part of the village were, on the evidence of late 16th- and early 17th-century maps, laid out in the 17th century and may represent formal gardens and orchards. Depressions (5) and a mound south-east of the Hall may represent the position of buildings shown on 18th- and early 19th-century maps. The barn was built across the line of the street (Cushion *et al*. 1982, 59–63), a slight hollow way still seen to the east, while a former drive (6) to the hall also crossed the hollow way. Earthworks to the north of the barn include some field boundaries recorded in 1596, while south-east of the farm very enigmatic earthworks include incomplete enclosures and the channel of a former natural watercourse (7) leading to a possible degraded fishpond complex (8). A semi-natural scarp (9) may have been in part the eastern edge of a millpond shown on the 1596 map in the extreme north-east corner of the site (Wade-Martins (ed) 1987, 41). The remains of the mill dam, since destroyed, are recorded on an earlier survey. The mill is depicted on the map of 1596 (Wade-Martins 1982, 60,61).

The 'wick' element in the name suggests a farm concerned mainly with grazing; in this case one on damp clay land (Williamson 1993, 89). Godwick in 1086 had a small recorded population compared with Tittleshall. Numbers of taxpayers in 1327, 1332 and 1377 only just reach double figures. The Lay Subsidy contribution in 1334 was 24s compared with the average payment of 61s 11d made by six neighbours (Allison 1955, 128). The reduction to the Lay Subsidy payment allowed in 1449 was almost 28%, one of the highest in the Launditch hundred. Godwick had less than ten households in 1428. A survey of 1508 lists eleven out of eighteen messuages north of the street as being 'void'. A survey of 1588 mentions further empty messuages. The map of 1596 shows the 16th-century hall and three remaining dwellings besides the church. Documentary evidence shows that enclosure and consolidation of holdings had been practised by certain tenants as well as the Lord of the Manor. It seems likely that Godwick was included in the communicant returns for Tittleshall in 1603 and 1676; the benefices were united in 1630 (Whiteman 1986, 225).

The hall was demolished in about 1962; the present farm buildings are of the 19th century. In 1981 part of the church tower collapsed. The surviving portion suggests a Norman origin for the church with some 13th- and 14th-century alterations. It seems that a 17th-century rebuilding of the tower was intended to preserve it as a folly (Cushion *et al.* 1982, 63–67; Batcock 1991, 136–138).

Great Breckles SMR 11929, TL 960 945
(Fig.23)

Surviving features between the church and the hall were abandoned in favour of common-edge sites.

Breckles Magna is about 8km west of Attleborough and 7.5km south-east of Watton and is now within Stow Bedon on the eastern margin of Breckland. Breckles Parva is a neighbouring deserted site near Shropham Hall in Shropham.

The earthworks lie between St Margaret's church and the grounds of Breckles Hall, a 16th-century house built for the Woodhouse family (Pevsner 1962, 96). A hollow way (1) *c.* 1m deep runs from the direction of the Hall towards the north end of the churchyard and there are ditched enclosures on either side. Those to the south are connected to irregular enclosures (2,3) and depressions fronting the B1111 to the west which are likely settlement sites. Medieval pottery has been found, mainly to the south of the hollow way, but the enclosures either side of it appear to be fields rather than tofts.

The earliest reference to Breckles is in Domesday which has seven entries for 'Breccles', the total recorded population was twenty-seven (Brown (ed) 1984, 1, 5; 7; 9; 10; 137. 9, 123. 22, 22). The church has a round tower in which Pevsner (1962, 95) saw possible 11th-century work. The village gave its name to the Deanery of Breccles, perhaps an indication of early status.

By 1334 Breckles was one of the smallest contributors to the Lay Subsidy in Wayland Hundred. All the settlements in the hundred were allowed reductions in 1449; Breckles with a 14.2% reduction had the fifth largest (Hudson 1895, 287). Thereafter, though small, it appears to have held its own. In 1603 it had fifty-two communicants

and three recusants; the number of communicants was forty-three in 1676 (Whiteman 1986, 227) suggesting totals of about ninety and seventy. The Hearth Tax list for 1664 appears incomplete; the Hall appears to have escaped and the seven named householders mustered only eight hearths among them (Frankel and Seaman 1983, 120).

A map of 1757 (NRO BAR 32 Harvey) shows some twenty buildings, the majority spaced in an arc along the edge of Breckles Common to the south-west which fringed the southern boundary of the parish. This common lay along the course of a stream carrying the outflow from Hockham Mere. Besides the Hall, a building stood opposite the church and another lay to the south of that. Hall Farm bordered the common further south again. Only one surveyed feature (4) corresponds to close boundaries of 1757. The three buildings nearest the church and west of what is now the B1111 and part of the earthwork sites could be a lingering survival of an original village site abandoned in favour of a common-edge location to the south-west.

Great Cressingham SMR 31839, TF 844 016
(Fig.24)

Earthworks lying to the west of the village are probably associated with the medieval Strawhall manor.

Great Cressingham lies about 7km west of Watton. The earthworks lie to the west of the present village on the western bank of the Wissey. A series of at least six medieval tofts extends from a well-defined hollow way (1) south-eastwards to the edge of the flood plain of the River Wissey. There is some subdivision within the ditched enclosures with at least two building platforms, including one (2) bounded by a shallow spring-fed ditch which could be a later insertion into the tofts. Over forty sherds of mainly medieval pottery have been found on the surface.

Medieval Great Cressingham was a large village with several manors, a church and a chapel of St George (formerly a church). Part of the village was in the hands of the Cathedral Priory of Norwich (Priory Manor, later Collins). The rest had a rather complicated pattern of manorial holdings which, after various changes, became known as Hockham's, Rysley's and Glosbridge. A further manor was known as Streethall, Streathall or Strawhall; this was added to the preceding three by purchases in 1540.

Glosbridge manor has been identified in a detached position to the south-west of the village (Davison 1994, 67,73). It seems likely that Streethall was closer to the village but lay some distance from the present southern end, since, in 1647 (NRO PD 131/83), a description of a piece of land south of Cley Way or Water End Street ended 'in this lies the site of the manor of Strawhall'. Earlier in 1563, a court roll presentation for not scouring a ditch at Strawhall Close and Waterend Field was recorded. Similarly, in 1566, the common drain at the east side of Strawhall Close was not scoured. It seems from these that the earthworks are most likely to have been associated with this manor.

590100

322200 +

2

Track

Ba

6

Pond

Street

1

Church

3

3

4

Drain

Road

Road

0   50

Metres

321700 +

590100

Figure 22 Godwick, deserted medieval vi

39

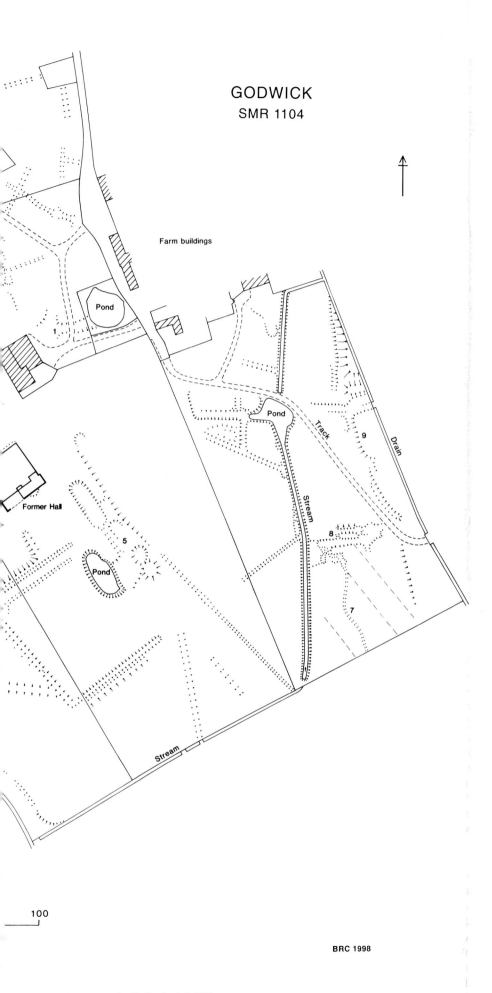

GODWICK
SMR 1104

Farm buildings

Pond

1

Pond

Track

9

Drain

Former Hall

5

Pond

Stream

8

7

Stream

100

BRC 1998

age with 17th-century hall. Scale 1:2,500

GREAT BRECKLES
SMR 11929

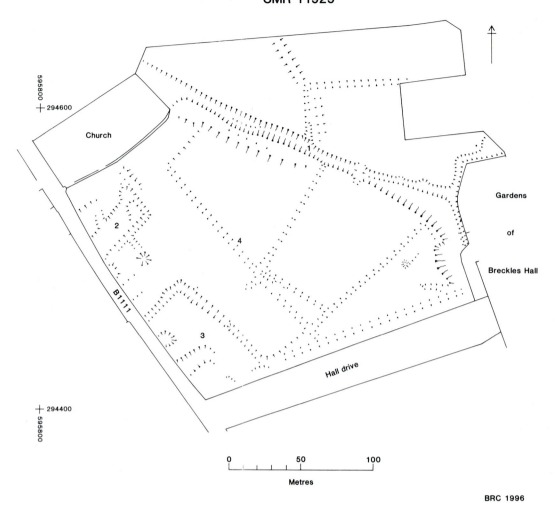

Figure 23 Great Breckles, settlement near the church.
Scale 1:2,500

BRC 1996

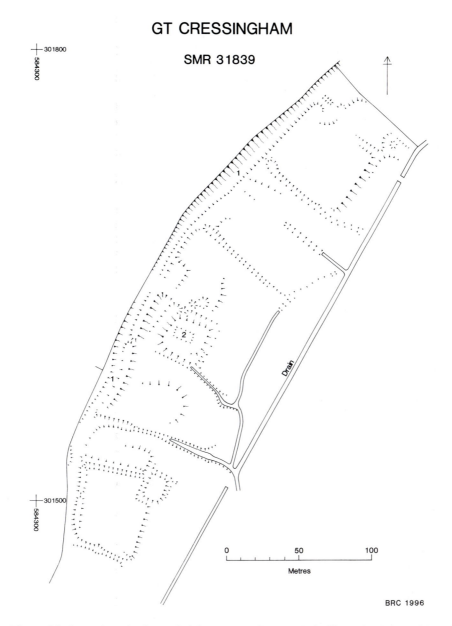

Figure 24 Great Cressingham, shrinkage at southern end of village. Scale 1:2,500

Great Dunham SMR 4194, TF 872 148
(Fig.25)

Confusing earthworks are probably part of a common-edge development with some possible garden features to the south.

Great Dunham is a village 8km north-east of Swaffham. The earthworks lie to the west of Church Farm and extend northwards from the gardens of the Old Rectory where the church of St Mary stood until the mid 16th century (Batcock 1991, 54). They present a confusing picture and it seems that much modification has occurred. In the north is a fragment of a curving hollow way or substantial former roadside ditch (1) which disappears southwards; it has a rectangular enclosure (2), slightly subdivided, to the south-west. To the south the scene is complicated. There are vestiges of brick walls, indicating buildings and/or yards, with the central of three ponds part-revetted with

similar bricks. Further west is an area (3) where infilling occurred after 1965, which explains many irregular features.

To the south-west a ridge (4) now cut by a ditch at its eastern end may have been the remains of a road leading to fields. Incomplete enclosure boundaries and amorphous irregularities exist to the south, possibly remnants of tofts and closes or gardens associated with the Old Rectory. The only remaining thing of note is the 'moated platform' (5) opposite Church Farm which, because of its size, is unlikely to have been occupied.

Great and Little Dunham were not separated in 1086. Of the three entries, two can be allocated to Great Dunham; the larger was an outlier of Mileham with half a market, the smaller one was reckoned with Necton. It was scarcely larger than Little Dunham. By 1334 its status had altered with the place occupying sixth position in the hundred and from then on it appears to have maintained its standing, despite a 12.7% decline in 1449 (Hudson 1895, 276–7) and the loss of its second church. Unfortunately there seems to

41

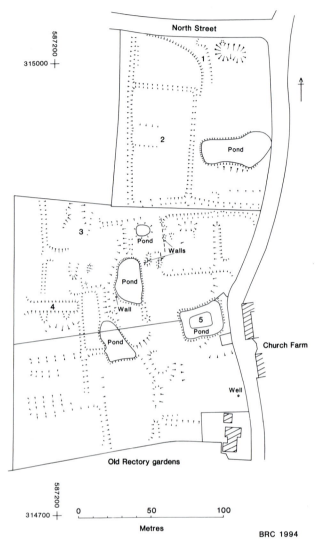

GT DUNHAM
SMR 4194

587200

315000 +

North Street

2

Pond

3

Pond

Walls

Pond

4

Wall

Pond

5

Pond

Church Farm

Well

Old Rectory gardens

587200

314700 +

0   50   100

Metres

BRC 1994

Figure 25 Great Dunham, shrinkage of village north of church. Scale 1:2,500

be little documentary evidence of individual plots. There is (NRO MS 12831 31 E5) a reference to a piece divided by a ditch which abutted on Northyard Grene at a place called Botilde Croft but this and another piece abutting north-east on the common pasture, is too vague for certainty.

Faden's map (1797) shows a large sweep of Dunham Common extending from the site on the plan around to the east, south-east and south of the village. From this it is clear that the area is to some extent a common-edge feature with the northern hollow way representing the rounded edge of the common shown by Faden. It is possible that this area was abandoned at the same time as St Mary's church, undergoing substantial alterations over the years.

Great Palgrave (Pagrave), Sporle SMR 1058, TF 834 122
(Pl. VIII, Fig.26)

The remains of a deserted settlement include a hollow way and tofts and a moat with associated features.

Great Palgrave lies about 3km north-east of Swaffham on a small spur separating two valleys leading towards the Nar. With Little Palgrave to the north, also deserted, it is within Sporle-with-Palgrave parish.

Two areas of earthworks survive. A small group of tofts (1) lies north of the road and west of the farm. A large area to the south consists of a hollow way (2) with flanking ditches and five tofts on its western side. The western flanking ditch has been truncated by extraction and the modern track. Of two moated sites one, north-west of the farm, has associated outer earthworks. The other, to the north of the present house, has no trace of a southern arm and has lost a western one. Aerial photographs (1946) show that earthworks east, west and south-west of the farm have since been removed (Cushion *et al.* 1982, 78–80).

Palgrave ('Pagrava') was first recorded in Domesday; of three entries the most significant described it as an outlier of the King's land in Sporle, as were parts of the Acres and Pickenhams. Distinguishing the Palgraves from each other and from Sporle in documents is difficult. Little Palgrave had a church by 1157 but none is recorded for Great Palgrave. There were two manors in Great Palgrave, East Hall and Wood Hall. A late 13th- or early 14th-century cartulary of Sporle (NRO MS 18199) records a grant by William de Wudehall to William de Larling, who held East Hall, of, among other property, two 'vivaria' with fishponds. The Woodhalls also granted their messuage, buildings and outbuildings to de Larling. Another charter records the lord of Sporle as granting William de Larling another messuage in Palgrave with two fishponds next to it as well as land. These charters probably relate to the moated sites. The Tithe Map of Sporle-with-Palgrave shows Dam Close north-east of the present farm, a probable reference to fisheries (NRO 378).

When Palgrave was deserted is unclear. The 14th-century Register of Coxford Priory records a free tenant in 'Pagrave' between two other messuages (NRO Bradfer-Lawrence 1b/1). In 1339 William de Esthalle was taxed as a producer of wool suggesting that he had large flocks. In 1381 insurgent peasants looted 400 sheep from John de Pagrave as well as stealing property and causing damage valued at £100 (Reid in Cornford *et al.* 1984, 20–21). This may indicate some motive such as response to landlord oppression rather than mere theft. By 1517 a manor in Palgrave, in decay, had been completely laid to pasture (Leadam 1892–3, 205).

A survey of Sporle dated 1598 contains little to suggest that Great Palgrave still existed and mid 17th-century documents describe only a landscape of farms and farm buildings there. With so little evidence it is only possible to suppose that Great Palgrave declined after the 14th century, in part, at least, because of large-scale sheep farming (Cushion *et al.* 1982, 80–83).

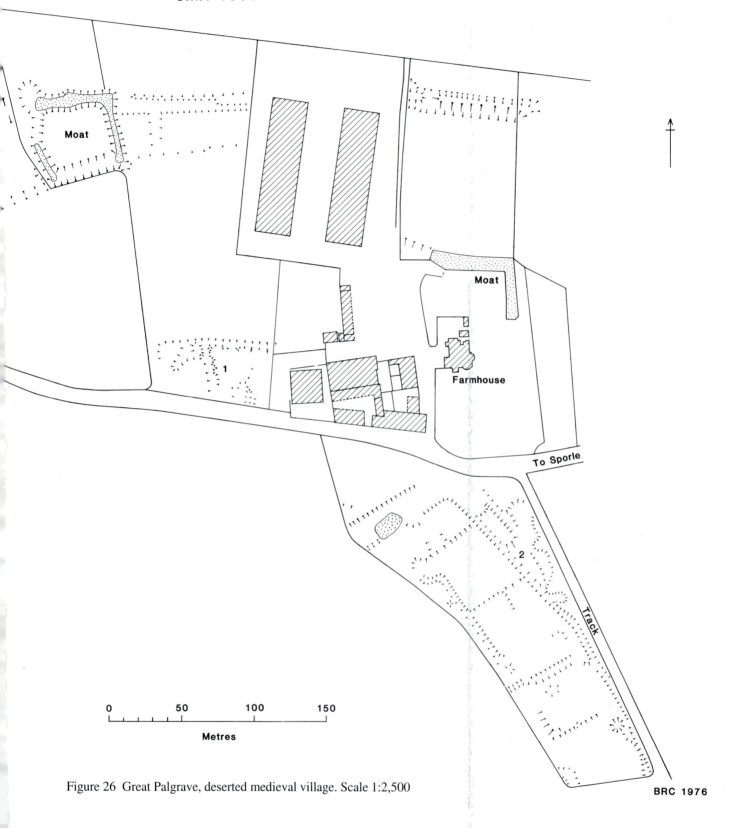

GREAT PALGRAVE

SMR 1058

Moat

Moat

Farmhouse

1

To Sporle

2

Track

0   50   100   150

Metres

Figure 26 Great Palgrave, deserted medieval village. Scale 1:2,500

BRC 1976

To South Acre

Plate VIII Great Palgrave, hollow way and enclosures from the south.
CUCAP AAQ 68
(Photography by Cambridge University Collection of Air Photographs)

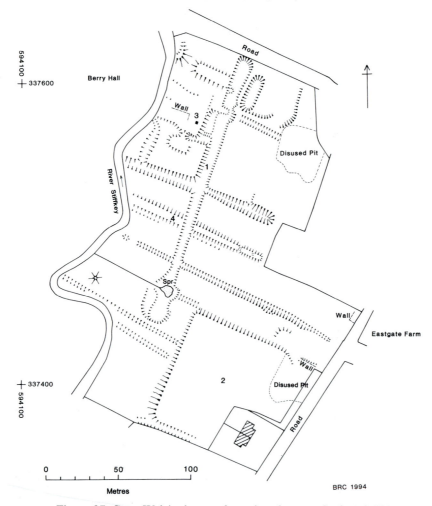

Figure 27 Great Walsingham, tofts and enclosures. Scale 1:2,500

Great Walsingham SMR 30697, 11951,
TF 942 375
(Fig.27)

Rather confusing earthworks are partly explained but were much altered by later activity.

Great Walsingham is about 8km north-north-east of Fakenham. The 'Great' is now a thing of past time. Little Walsingham has been the larger settlement for many centuries, beginning to grow at the middle of the 12th century when the Priory of Austin Canons was founded and the cult of the Virgin Mary became established there.

The earthworks lie in grassland between the River Stiffkey and Eastgate Farm. The major features are a series of rectilinear enclosures on either side of a linear depression (1) which has a spring at its southern end. There is a square enclosure (2) to the south-east bounded on the north and west by terraced banks, on the east by the road and by a fragment of hollow way and a ditch on the south. Two cottages have been built here and a length of flint walling was exposed during work on a driveway.

In the north, on the far side of the linear depression, is another platform (3), rather uneven, on which there is a flint masonry pillar with knapped surfaces, and an L-shaped flint wall evident at ground level. There is the remnant of a culvert

across the depression with a slight hollow way extending eastwards to a small disused pit. Other features in the area include a number of ditched enclosures and a substantial bank (4) which has been cut by the linear depression.

The Enclosure Map of 1808 (NRO C/Sca 2/312) shows a building standing where the flint walling was revealed during driveway construction; the building now standing to the south was not there then. Also shown on the site of Berry Hall on the far side of the river was a moat and associated water features; these are opposite the features on the northern platform (3) which may have been the site of an entrance gate although there is no visible evidence for a bridge.

An 18th-century field book (NRO MS 18623/156 726 x 3) gives a detailed account of Great Walsingham although hardly any of the names of roads and fields appear to have survived. However, part of the description of the North Field does seem to describe the area of the earthworks. This records a cottage abutting north on Briggate and another two cottages and a messuage apparently abutting east on Southgate. These two 'gates' or roads appear to be the two roads shown on the plan. Possibly the messuage was on the site of the revealed wall facing the eastern road. The others are probably masked by present-day buildings.

Apart from this little else seems to relate to the various ditches or enclosures. It appears that by the 18th century many features had already disappeared.

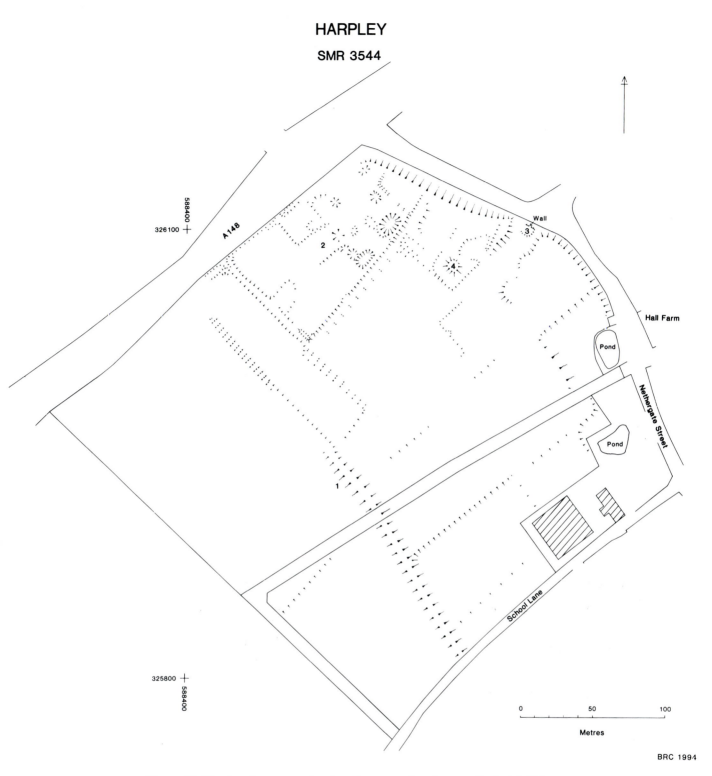

HARPLEY
SMR 3544

A148

588400
326100 +

2

Wall
3.

4

Hall Farm

Pond

Netheгgate Street

Pond

1

School Lane

325800 +
588400

0   50   100

Metres

BRC 1994

Figure 28 Harpley, former medieval settlement and enclosures. Scale 1:2,500

Harpley SMR 3544, TF 786 260
(Fig.28)

Enclosures west of the surviving village were abandoned at some time and no documentary evidence for them appears to exist.

Harpley is a village about 17.5km north-east of King's Lynn. The earthworks lie on the western side of the village in former parkland belonging to Harpley Hall. The site has been, in its western and southern parts, ploughed and reseeded since 1946 subduing features there.

The most prominent feature is a still pronounced bank (1) which narrows considerably in its northern extent where it is flanked by a western shallow ditch. In the northern part of the site much more survives. A well-marked enclosure (2) possibly representing a small farmstead faces onto two existing roads and is bounded by a double bank to the south-west and a terraced bank to the

HEMPTON

SMR 7120

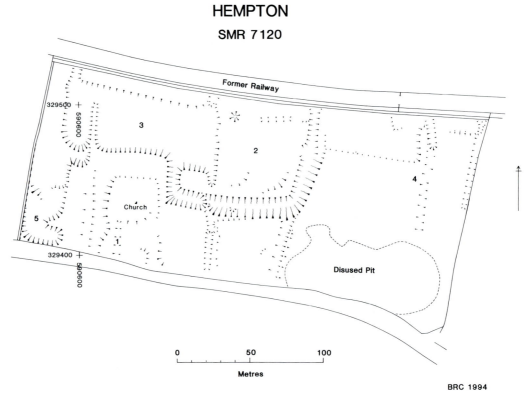

Figure 29 Hempton, former church and surrounding earthworks. Scale 1:2,500

south-east; within it are two small enclosures which display no evidence of buildings. To the east a short length of possible hollow way divides the remaining features. At its entrance is a small platform (3) with about 6m of flint and stone masonry. To the north of the hollow way is another platform (4) (*c.*5m x 7m). These two comparatively small items may have been parkland features probably inserted into an area of former tofts.

Harpley seems to have been of moderate size throughout its career. The population in medieval times appears to have altered little with only a 9.6% decline shown in 1449 (Hudson 1895, 271–2) and about thirty-five contributors in 1524/5 (Sheail 1968). However, an unusually large acreage was reported as being converted to grass in 1517 (Leadam 1893, II, 188, 190). A map of the Estate of John Raven, Esq., dated 1839, shows the area of the earthworks as being occupied by two pieces of land. Most of the features lay in a small enclosure called 'The Old Wood'; the other remains were in a large featureless piece called 'The Meadow' but no other information was given. The only details shown were the pond opposite Hall Farm and the house (NRO BRA 705/1 716 x 2).

It looks as though the earthworks were probably remains of part of the village abandoned at some unknown date.

Hempton SMR 7120, TF 907 294
(Fig.29)

Earthworks include a vanished church and an incomplete moated enclosure, possibly abandoned at the Dissolution.

Hempton is a village immediately to the south-west of Fakenham and separated from it by the River Wensum. In

modern times it has had something of the character of a suburb of its larger neighbour.

The earthworks lie on the north side of the road to Shereford at a little distance to the west of the present settlement. The site slopes gently towards the floodplain of the river and has been truncated by the construction of a railway, now abandoned. A fragment of flint masonry marks the position of St Andrew's church but no convincing building outline remains. A shallow depression on the western side may indicate a churchyard boundary, and a small hollow way (1) might represent an entrance path. The major feature is an incompletely moated enclosure (2); the L-shaped moat appears to be linked to a large subdivided pond (3). Further enclosures lie to the east (4). Quarrying in the extreme south-west (5) as well as the larger marked pit has disfigured the remains.

The manor of Hempton was held, with the Rectory with other rights, by Hempton Priory. When Dissolution came in 1534 the Priory manor and Rectory were acquired by Sir William Fermour, a notable flockmaster (Doubleday and Page 1906, II, 381). The church was still standing in 1552 (Walters 1945, 171).

Batcock's suggestion (1991, 12,53) that Hempton was deserted possibly because of the proximity of Fakenham is mistaken. In 1666 nineteen persons were charged for a total of fifty hearths; there were several substantial houses, including that 'at ye Abby' (Seaman (ed) 1988, 39) and there were seventy-nine communicants in 1676 (Whiteman 1986, 224). It seems likely that the church and probable manorial site were abandoned, post-Dissolution, when they passed into lay hands and that activity in Hempton drifted eastwards to the road leading to Fakenham market.

HINGHAM

SMR 33856

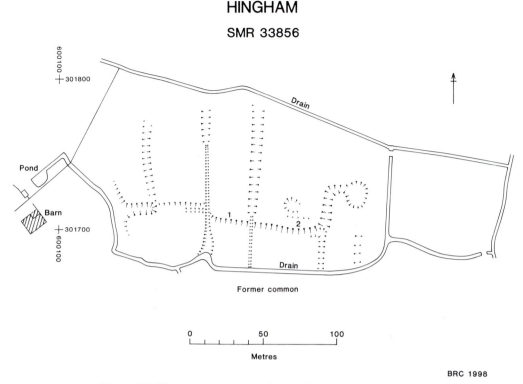

Figure 30 Hingham, common-edge enclosures. Scale 1:2,500

Hingham SMR 33856, TG 002 017
(Fig.30)

A very small detached group of earthworks facing south onto former High Moor Common.

Hingham is a large village or small town about 8km west of Wymondham. It functioned as a market centre until quite recently and has two large central open spaces, the eastern one a market place, the other a Fairstead. The earthworks are far from the centre of the village, close to the parish boundary with Scoulton.

The earthworks lie close to a barn near the B1108 leading to Scoulton and are contained within one field. The southern edge of the field is marked by a rather irregular drain leading from a pond close to the barn. A south-facing scarp to the north (1) marks the edge of higher, drier land. Two well-maintained ditches or drains link the northern and southern boundaries of the field: to the west is another shallow ditch which may once have extended north. There are two other features, a broad shallow ditch and what may have been a pond. Only one possible building platform (2) is visible.

The commercial prosperity of Hingham seems assured throughout the Middle Ages as no decline in Lay Subsidy payment from the high level of 1334 was recorded in 1449 (Hudson 1895, 278–9). In the 16th century it was second only to Wymondham in its hundred (Sheail 1968) while in the 17th century onwards to 1811 it was inferior only to East Dereham and Wymondham (Whiteman 1986, 206–08; CXX). However, much of this importance must have been linked to its market and its annual fairs, masking any fluctuations in agricultural prosperity.

A map of 1776 (NRO C/Ca 2/4) shows that there were quite extensive commons not shown by Faden (1797). One

called High Moor Common, extending into Frost Row Common and by a narrow entrant into Hall Moor, stretched to the Scoulton parish boundary where it joined Scoulton Common shown by Faden. The 1776 map shows two buildings and the earthwork field facing onto High Moor Common, the southern drain marking the common boundary. The Tithe Map (NRO DN/TA 539) of 1841 shows a differently arranged group of buildings with the earthwork field as part of an unnamed arable area, the western portion not appearing on the plan. The common was then divided for cultivation but names such as Furze Meadow and Common Pightle remain suggestive. A Tollgate was shown by the road as it crossed the parish boundary.

It seems most likely that the modern barn is the survivor of a farmstead of 1776 which may in turn have superseded a small medieval common-edge settlement formed at the height of medieval population density; the finding of sherds of medieval pottery immediately to the west adds weight to the supposition that this is an area of medieval common-edge settlement.

Hoe SMR 2810, TF 998 166
(Fig.31)

A large group of earthworks — part of a shrunken village — consisting of a moated enclosure, tofts backed by a ditch, hollow ways and former field boundaries.

Hoe lies immediately north of East Dereham, of which its living has long been a chapelry. The extensive earthworks, mainly in three fields, lie to the north and east of the church and Hall. In the most westerly field a rectangular moated enclosure (1) is dominant, while other features there may

47

be remains of tofts backed by a boundary ditch (2). This ditch extends southwards to form a boundary, first to a wood, and then to further toft-like features (3) in the central field. To the east of the ditch the remainder of the field is marked by a banked part-enclosure (4) extending to the easternmost field. In the eastern field there are two apparent hollow ways. The southernmost (5) is aligned to pass between church and Hall; the other (6) leads away from it in a northerly direction. The remainder of the field is marked by banks and ditches of probable old field boundaries.

Described by Blomefield (1795, V, 1062) as only a hamlet of East Dereham, Hoe seems to have been a settlement of substance, despite its status as a chapelry. In 1334 it contributed the eighth largest payment in Launditch Hundred to the Lay Subsidy and was allowed no reduction in 1449 (Hudson 1895, 276–77). Its subsequent fortunes are not easy to ascertain as it was considered with Dereham or with neighbouring Dillington, but there were eighty-five communicants there in 1676 (Whiteman 1986, 225). There is no obvious sign which could account for the apparent contraction suggested by the earthworks.

There were references (Blomefield 1775, V, 1062; NRO MC 254/7/22 682 x 7) in 1609 and 1615 to the watermill and house with adjoining osier ground and a fishery from the mill to the Chapel Mill which may refer to this area. A map of 1773 (NRO MS 4532) shows that the tofts of the central field lay in Home Meadow while the area beyond the boundary ditch formed part of Deadmans Close. A building within an oddly-shaped enclosure stood in Home Meadow facing onto the road and can be associated partially with some features on the plan.

The north-western field was shown as property of John Lambe; a member of this family was lord of the manor in 1845 (White 1845, 335) and it is thus possible that the moat may mark a manorial site. However, the Grounds family were also important landowners then and in 1773, and a three-limbed moat, no longer visible, was shown on the enclosure map of 1811 north of the hall (NRO C/CA1/32). The southern hollow way in the eastern field was shown as a former road running between the church and the Hall on Faden's map (1797) and in 1811, but had been realigned to its present course by the 1830s. The linked road had become a field boundary by 1811 and appears to have been replaced by the present road to the east.

Houghton SMR 28476 and 3543, TF 794 290
(Figs 32,33)

A well-known emparked village: the surviving northern portion consists of a hollow way with tofts and enclosures, the southern part, which still existed near the church in the 18th century, has been largely obliterated. Other features include a probable park boundary and farmstead and various parkland developments.

Houghton is an emparked and relocated village about 12km west of Fakenham. The earthworks of the medieval village (SMR 28476) lie within the park, north-east of the hall, and consist of a sinuous hollow way (1) flanked on both sides by enclosures, some undoubtedly representing tofts and cut by the north drive. On the western side two parallel banks reach almost to the remains of another bank (2) extending north-north-west. The hollow way extends northwards to interrupt a partly banked scarp (3) which, together with other earthworks (4) to the south of it, probably represent an early park boundary and associated features, possibly a farmstead. There are also vague vestiges of earthworks near the church (SMR 3543).

Other earthworks shown include four parallel banks (5), obvious parkland boundary features including a roadway, a great cutting (SMR 3542) extending south-south-eastwards from a position in front of the Hall, and a huge mound covering an ice-house (SMR 3523); this and other mounds for tree clumps were composed of spoil from the cutting. A barrow (SMR 3522) is also located here.

Houghton was an outlier of Rudham in 1086 with a recorded population of at least fourteen (Brown (ed) 1984, 8,108). By 1316 the Walpole family and Castle Acre priory held it (Blake 1952, 273). In 1334 the village contributed £6 to the Lay Subsidy, the second largest total out of twenty-two from the hundred. In 1449 it was allowed a reduction of 11.1%, the average for the hundred being about 17% (Hudson 1895, 273). A tithe list for 1578–9 (Yaxley 1988b, 84) lists eighty-two persons, a minimum level of population, probably excluding young children, indicating modest prosperity. In 1666 Sir Edward Walpole was charged for eighteen hearths 'and for his new building 3' with two added in the margin; seventeen others were charged for thirty-one hearths between them (Seaman (ed) 1988, 39). In 1676 there were eighty communicants (Whiteman 1986, 212). This gives some indication of the standing of the old village.

A park was probably created in the late 17th century (Williamson 1998, 40) and is shown on a map of 1719 and, with some extension, on one of 1720 (Houghton Hall Archive Maps 2,1; Yaxley 1988b, 86,87). The village was shown south of the park, ranged along an east-to-west street near the church. There was no indication of anything on the site of the hollow way to the north. Sir Robert Walpole began building a new hall to the east of the old one in 1721 and work continued until the mid-1730s (Yaxley 1988b, 84). The park was expanded to the south and east and a new settlement, New Houghton, replaced it outside the park. In 1731 a visitor described how 'Sir Robert has removed about 20 houses of the Village to a considerable distance and he proposes to remove the rest. The new Building they call *New Town*' (Markham 1984, 88).

The church was left standing isolated in the middle of open parkland and 'landscaped' in fashionable gothick mode (Yaxley 1994, 46–50).

The park contains numerous relict field boundaries, headlands and hollow ways, together with others of more modern and Second World War date. The great cutting was opened in the 1740s to improve the vista from the hall but was, it seems, abandoned incomplete in 1743 when Sir Robert died (Williamson pers. comm.).

The hollow way and its associated features must represent part of the old village which, if not already abandoned, must have been removed when the first park was made.

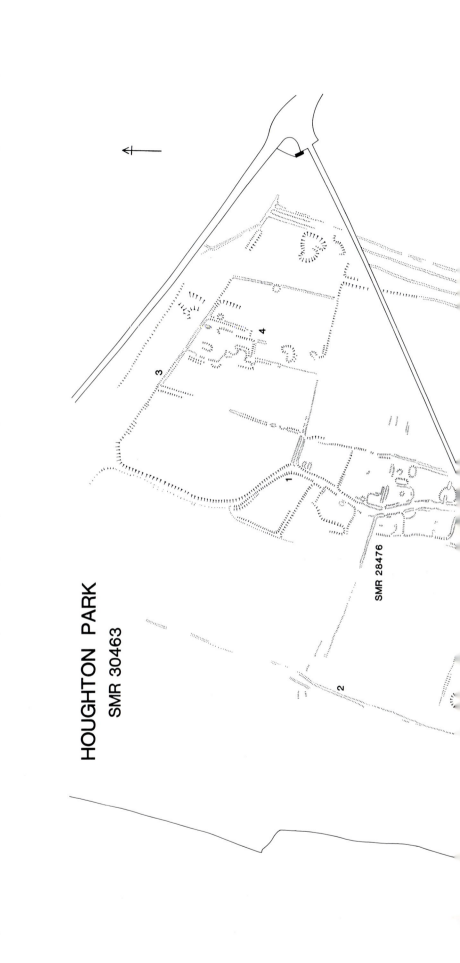

HOUGHTON PARK
SMR 30463

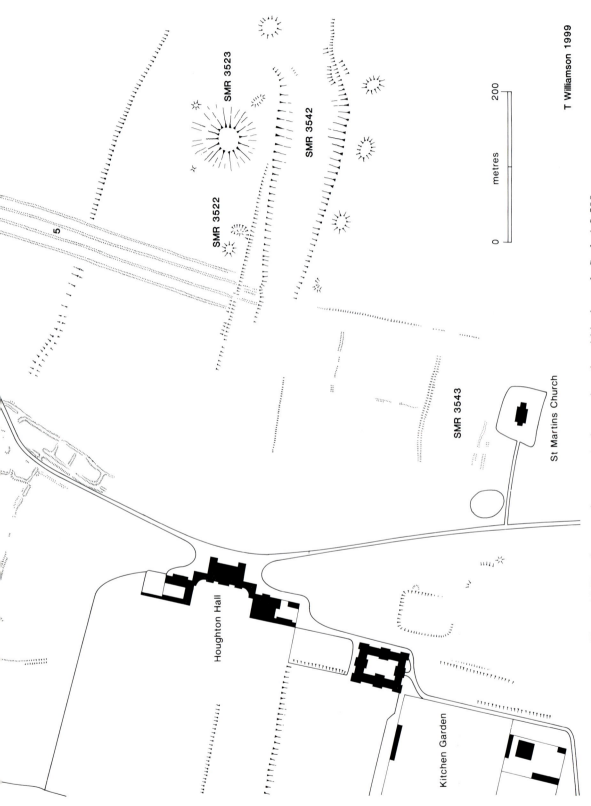

Figure 32 Houghton, settlement and other earthworks within the park. Scale 1:2,500

SMR 3523

SMR 3542

SMR 3522

SMR 3543

5

St Martins Church

Houghton Hall

Kitchen Garden

0   metres   200

T Williamson 1999

50

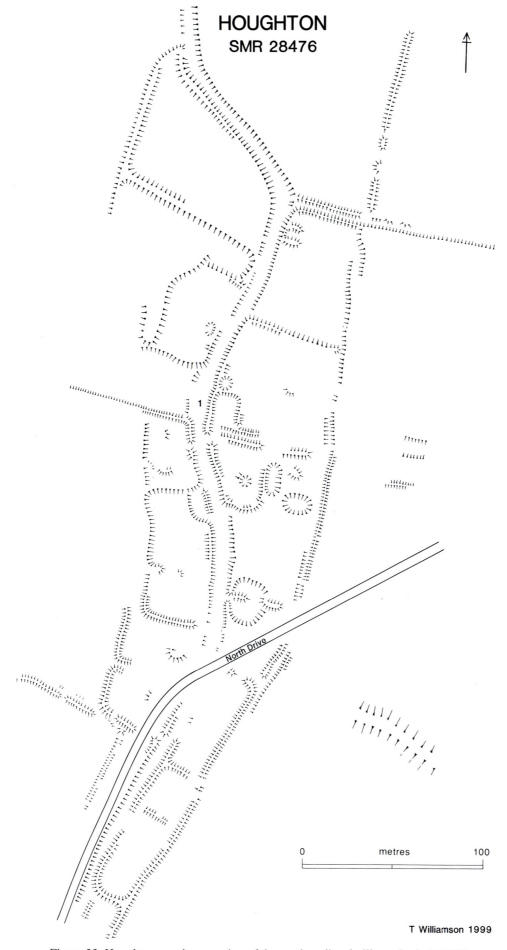

HOUGHTON
SMR 28476

North Drive

0   metres   100

T Williamson 1999

Figure 33 Houghton, northern section of deserted medieval village. Scale 1:5,000

Houghton-on-the-Hill, North Pickenham
SMR 4630, TF 869 055
(Fig.34)

A tiny survival of a deserted medieval village consists of a branched hollow way and former tofts or enclosures.

Houghton-on-the-Hill is within the parish of North Pickenham about 6km south-east of Swaffham. The site lies in pasture north of the church and slopes gently north-westwards. The earthworks consist of a hollow way (1) up to 1.5m deep which extends northwards and is overdeepened by a pit at one point (2) where a branch heads eastwards towards arable land. To the west of the way are ditched or scarped enclosures probably representing former tofts or closes. The one on the eastern side opposite the church is said to have been the site of the rectory. The full extent of the settled area remains unknown as no systematic fieldwalking has yet been undertaken.

Houghton (OE hoh + tun; Gelling 1984, 167) appears to mean 'settlement or farm on a spur', an appropriate description in this instance. Unfortunately, the earliest documentary reference, in Domesday, merely records a freeman with 16 acres valued at 16d (Brown (ed) 1984, 21,15). To the Lay Subsidies of 1327 and 1332 respectively, eighteen and seventeen inhabitants of Houghton contributed (Allison 1955, 150). In 1334 Houghton's contribution was one of the lowest in the hundred, although it paid slightly more than South Pickenham and only a little less than North Pickenham. It received no relief after the Black Death but was allowed a reduction of 26% in 1449 suggesting a major loss over the intervening century. Contributions to the 1524/25 Subsidy imply that there was no significant recovery (Sheail 1968). There were fifteen communicants in 1603 and eighteen in 1676 (Whiteman 1986, 209). The 1664 Hearth Tax recorded seven individuals charged for fourteen hearths, seven of them in one household (Frankel and Seaman 1983, 87).

Some details of this tenuous survival of a community appear in manor court entries made between 1625 and 1696 (NRO NNAS 5784, 5785 18D1). Courts were held at infrequent intervals with the homage numbering only three or four jurors and with repetitive transactions concerning only the same small number of properties. Roads mentioned were Drove Way, Foxhole Way, Watton Way, Swynesgate and Spring Way. There was a feature called 'fyshpitt', a Guildhall Croft mentioned in 1630, and a watermill in 1684. The fields appear to have remained at least partially open. Blomefield mentions St Mary's Gild as existing in 1497. He also recorded that, in his day, Houghton comprised 'only a farm or two and a cottage or two' (Blomefield 1769, III, 450–51).

The living was united with North Pickenham in 1715 but the church remained in use until *c.* 1945. The nave is of the 11th century, the tower of the 15th and the chancel of the 18th (Batcock 1991, 51). Recent discoveries of very important wall-paintings in the church dated to about 1090 may point to an earlier phase of some significance for Houghton. It was a victim of later medieval decline but specific details remain unknown.

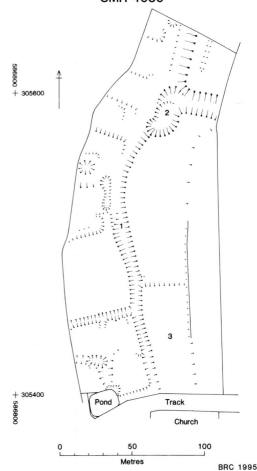

HOUGHTON ON THE HILL
SMR 4630

Figure 34 Houghton-on-the-Hill, remnant of deserted medieval village. Scale 1:2,500

Little Bittering, Beeston with Bittering
SMR 7266, TF 937 176
(Pl. IX, Fig.35)

A moat and outer enclosure, a row of tofts with another moated platform and a third moat are the remains of one of the least documented deserted medieval settlements in Norfolk.

Little Bittering is a very small deserted village located on gravel soils 2.5km south-east of Mileham and to the north of the line of a major east-to-west Roman road.

The present east-to-west road through the site seems to follow the line of a medieval road which Faden (1797) showed entering a V-shaped piece of common land to the west. The small church of Sts Peter and Paul mainly dates to the 12th and 13th centuries and lies to the south of the road. To the north, abutting the road is a moat linked with the remains of a now destroyed large outer enclosure (1) to the east, which appears to have linked with the churchyard. Both moated platform and enclosure were entered from the east. Traces of the road through the enclosure are visible in the ploughsoil.

Plate IX Little Bittering: the church with an associated moat, a possible moated platform and tofts. CUCAP BLP 12
(Photography by Cambridge University Collection of Air Photographs)

Up to eight tofts, somewhat damaged by later drainage ditches, lie to the north of the street; one of the tofts contains what appears to be a small moated platform (2). The mounds and hollows in the extreme east of the site (3) are considered natural undulations. There are the remains of another moat (SMR 1055) near Manor Farm house with cropmark evidence for an outer enclosure with a building.

Documentary evidence for Little Bittering is slight; Domesday entries for 'Britringa' may include Great Bittering, now absorbed within Gressenhall, and they are indistinguishable in some other records. By the 14th century Little Bittering was lumped together with nearby Beeston and again its individual status is concealed. However, in 1428 it was exempt from the parish tax as it

had fewer than ten households. A list of contributors to the 1543 Subsidy revealed only two names. In 1603 there were nine communicants in the parish; the total had risen to fourteen by 1676 (Whiteman 1986, 224). The Hearth Tax of 1664 was levied on just four households for fourteen hearths (Frankel and Seaman 1983, 62).

It seems obvious that this settlement, with its obscure history, was never more than a tiny place (Cushion *et al.* 1982, 94–99), yet the earthworks are still largely intact.

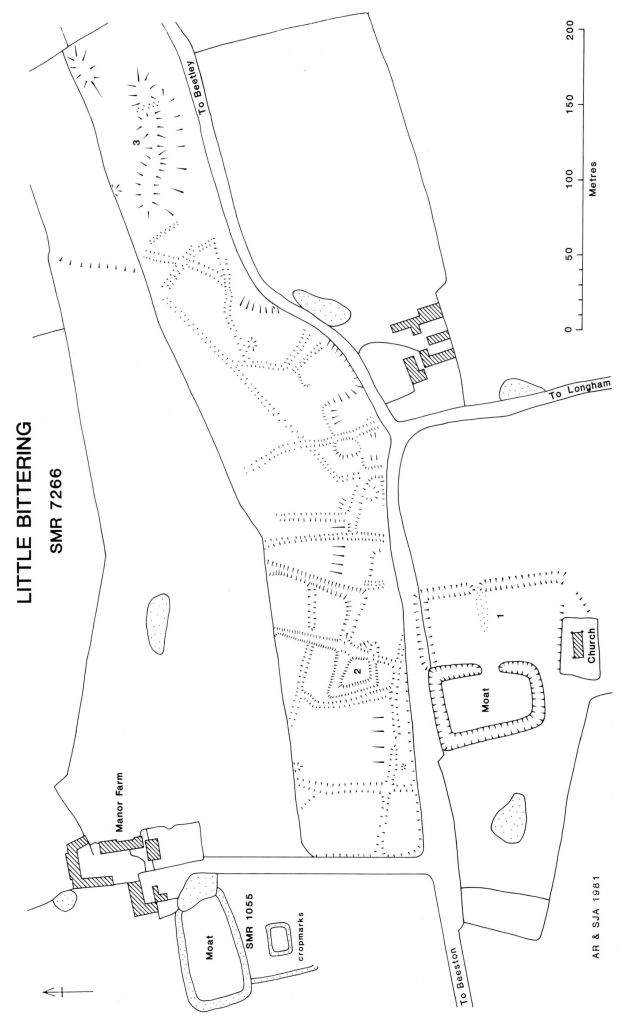

Figure 35 Little Bittering, deserted medieval village. Scale 1:2,500

LITTLE BITTERING

SMR 7266

To Beetley

3

To Longham

To Beeston

Manor Farm

Moat

SMR 1055

cropmarks

Moat

1

Church

2

Metres

0   50   100   150   200

AR & SJA 1981

54

LITTLE MASSINGHAM

SMR 25139

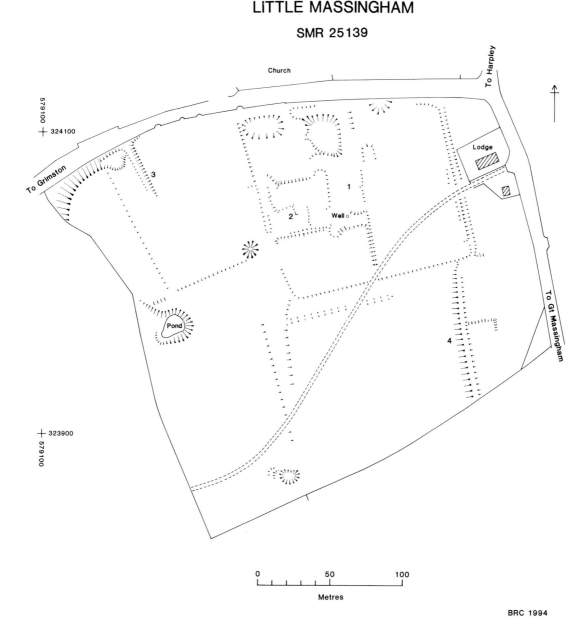

Figure 36 Little Massingham, settlement site near the church. Scale 1:2,500

BRC 1994

Little Massingham SMR 25139, TF 793 240 (Fig.36)

Undocumented earthworks near the church are probably medieval in origin, but with later modifications including conversion to parkland.

Little Massingham is a small village roughly equidistant between King's Lynn and Fakenham and about 1.5km north of Great Massingham. The earthworks lie in parkland opposite the church on the southern side of the village street.

The major feature is a large rectangular enclosure (1) directly opposite the church and extending eastwards, ditched on its eastern and partly on its western sides and embanked to the south. It is subdivided by a north-to-south bank with the western half containing irregular banks, platforms and depressions. An L-shaped section of flint masonry (2) is probably the south-western corner of a

building and there is a scattering of brick fragments nearby. A section of a flint-lined well is also present. To the west is another enclosure with a short length of hollow way (3) leading to it, while to the south is a well-defined bank (4) extending southwards.

It seems quite likely that the earthworks are medieval. This is supported by the presence of medieval brick fragments and a few sherds of pottery. They probably date from a period of 14th to 15th-century decline. The house within the major enclosure appears to have been of some substance and being opposite the church may have been manorial. As the site lies within parkland this seems likely.

Little Massingham is not easily separated from its larger neighbour Great Massingham as they were simply called 'Massingham' in Domesday Book. The implication here is that the Domesday surveyors may have seen it as part of a large extended settlement only separated subsequently. By the medieval period the settlements were considered separate. In 1334 it contributed one of the smaller totals to the Lay Subsidy, the sum being twenty-seventh in order of diminishing size out of thirty-four places. In 1449 it was allowed a large reduction of 25% in its payment (Hudson 1895, 871–2); this was the third highest percentage for the hundred and implies a quite severe reduction in prosperity. The position seems not to have improved to any marked extent. In 1603 there were seventy-six communicants dwindling to fifty-nine with a Dissenter and a Papist in 1676 (Whiteman 1986, 229). The picture thus obtained is of a settlement which persisted but at no great level of prosperity.

The sole available map is the Tithe Map of 1838 (NRO DN/TA 29) which is singularly uninformative; however a later Altered Apportionment map shows a featureless area with a small enclosure immediately south-west of the church.

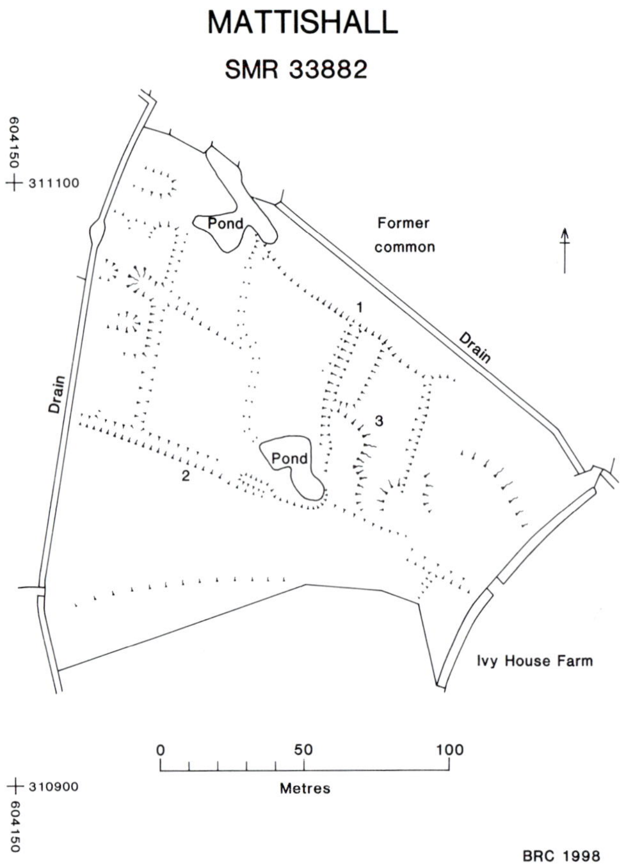

Mattishall SMR 33882, 29473, TG 042 110, 034 110

(Figs 37,38)

Two areas of earthworks, the second of them distant from the village and near Old Hall Farm, probably associated with the edges of common land. Some features may be comparatively recent.

Mattishall is a substantial village about 11km north-west of Wymondham and 6.5 km south-east of Dereham. It is a compact settlement with some rather straggling westward development and it now includes the formerly separate parish of Mattishall Burgh to the north.

The earthworks are in two areas. The first (SMR 33882: Fig.37) is to the west of the village centre and just to the north-west of Ivy House Farm. It consists of a group of ditched enclosures which has suffered some degradation through infilling. There is a north-facing scarp (1) which marks the edge of a former common. There are two ponds which appear to be linked by a sinuous drain. To the west of this is a cruciform pattern of ditched enclosures, bounded by a ditch (2) to the south. To the east is another ditched enclosure (3).

The second group (SMR 29473: Fig.38) lies further to the west near Old Hall Farm and consists of incomplete ditched enclosures to the north-west of the farm buildings. Some earthworks(1) near the Barn may be the sites of former buildings, while the ditch (2) to the east is a probable former common boundary. Further to the north-west is a somewhat confusing group of features, including redundant ditches (3) probably contemporary with the present field boundaries. To the west is a ditch (4) which has a sinuous western arm and has been partly obliterated; within it are what seem to be two small enclosures (5,6). Beyond that, to the west again and linked to it by a ditch, is a well-defined bank and ditch (7) with a spread bank further north.

In 1334 Mattishall was paying the third highest contribution to the Lay Subsidy in Midford Hundred after East Dereham and Shipdham but was allowed a reduction of 20.7% on its 1449 payment (Hudson 1895, 274). This may be taken as a sign of some medieval decline. After this the village appears to have retained its status with substantial numbers of communicants in 1603 and 1676 (Whiteman 1986, 207). On neither of the sites has any medieval pottery been found but it is quite probable that

MATTISHALL

SMR 33882

Figure 37 Mattishall, common-edge enclosures.
Scale 1:2,500

they date from a 14th-century high-water mark of population.

The first area was close to the southern edge of West Green, a common shown on a map of 1783 (NRO FX 263/1) and an Enclosure Map of 1803 (NRO C/Sca 2/194). Its boundary seems to have been the north-facing scarp. The Enclosure Map does show a pond in the centre of the area, though shaped differently. The Tithe Map shows no ponds but reveals that the vague earthworks at the southern edges mark the boundaries of two small woods (NRO DN/TA 195). It also shows that the piece was called Lower Harlestones. A family of that name lived in Mattishall in the 1550s and 1560s; one gave two houses and other property to the poor (NRO NCC Ingold 219).

The second area (SMR 29473) was also marginal to common land; the probable common boundary on the plan relates quite closely to the actual feature shown in 1783 and 1803. Two of the small probable enclosures to the north-west are shown in 1783 and 1803 while the remains of two others still exist. The central earthworks near the pond pre-date the two maps cited; the large ditch with the sinuous western arm may be a survival of features related to the Old Hall. The most westerly features are shown on the two early maps. The Tithe Map shows field boundaries which are close to the modern ones. A vertical RAF air photograph (3G/TUD/UK 52 Part II 13 January 1946 5009) shows that many features have been degraded by infilling.

56

MATTISHALL

SMR 29473

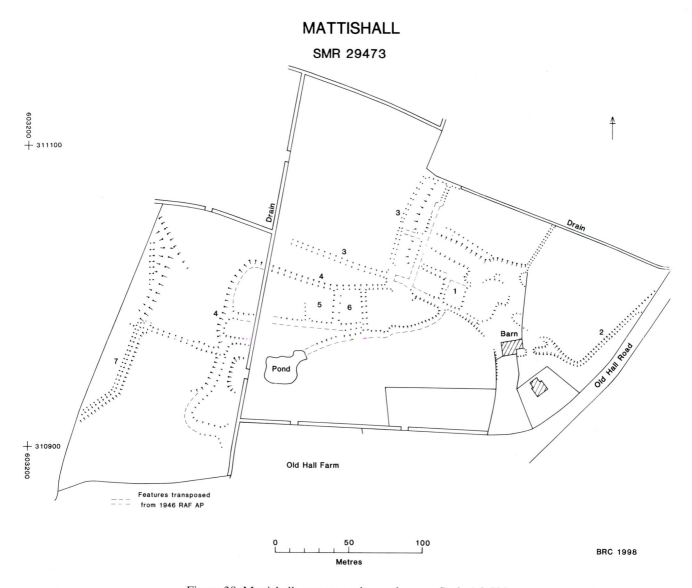

Figure 38 Mattishall, common-edge enclosures. Scale 1:2,500

North Elmham SMR 1013, TF 987 215
(Fig.39)

The remains of an entire street, partly excavated in 1967–72. It was probably abandoned by the 17th century and was later emparked.

North Elmham lies about 8km north of Dereham. A large village even today, it served in the 11th century as the seat of the diocese. The earthworks of a complete street lay in the park to the west of the present main street; the northern part was removed by archaeological excavation in 1967–72 (Wade-Martins 1980a).

The main feature of the site is a hollow way (1) which leaves the existing street just north of the Town Beck and rejoins the line of the main street to the west of the earthworks of the cathedral or chapel. It has been interrupted by a causeway crossing it and carrying the drive to the hall.

On either side of the hollow way are the sites of buildings; the building platforms on the eastern side, some situated within toft boundaries, though quite impressive, are less regular and rather heavily pitted. A short length of track connecting the hollow way with the existing street occupied roughly the position of the modern drive and has been obscured by it. To the west of the hollow way the earthworks are less obvious; they are marked by a featureless raised platform (2), virtually continuous, and bounded to the west by the remains of a bank or scarp. To the south-west are further scarps of uncertain origin.

The site is unusual in being partly excavated with a thorough investigation of its documentary background (Yaxley 1980, 517–625). Thus more than is customary is known about it.

Excavation has shown that the earliest levels were of Middle Saxon date and at the northern end of the site. Late Saxon occupation grew until the Domesday survey revealed that North Elmham was a very large village though its loss of cathedral status shows that it was essentially rural (Yaxley 1980, 317). The earthworks on the plan are those of the late medieval village.

The hollow way was known as Walsingham Way and continued northwards past the cathedral site. In 1454 it was one of three streets, the others being the surviving road and the vanished Rectory Road lying to the east of the church (Wade-Martins 1980a, 231). The short length of connecting road actually crossed Walsingham Way and, as Lawndgate, now visible only on aerial photographs, continued westwards towards the Old Park (Wade- Martins 1980a, 17). North of this road, on the western side, there were three messuages and four cottages and to the south four messuages and one cottage. North of it on the eastern side were two messuages and seven cottages; to the south were four messuages and two cottages. At the northern end of Walsingham Way and between it and the Bishop's manor or cathedral was a market place which overlay portions of the earlier settlement and a cemetery (Wade-Martins 1980a, 23; Yaxley 1980, 534–536).

It seems likely that the majority of the sites on Walsingham Way were abandoned by the 17th century, By the time of enclosure in 1831 the road remained without a sign of settlement (Wade-Martins 1980a, 21,22) and Lawndgate had vanished, probably when the present park was first constructed. Walsingham Way (and Rectory

Road) were closed by a Road Order in 1829 and the present street remained to carry traffic northward (Wade-Martins 1980a, 21).

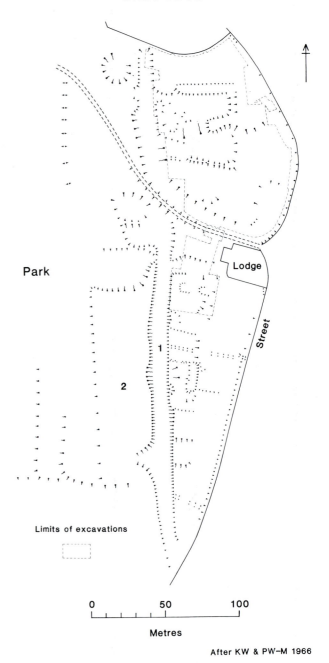

NORTH ELMHAM
SMR 1013

Figure 39 North Elmham, former village street.
Scale 1:2,500

Plate X Pudding Norton deserted village, from the north-west. CUCAP AQS 45
(Photography by Cambridge University Collection of Air Photographs)

Pudding Norton SMR 7111, TF 924 277
(Pls X, XI, Fig.40)

Probably the best example of a 'nucleated' deserted medieval village to be seen in Norfolk with a classic association with a well-known family of flockmasters.

Pudding Norton survives still as a parish south of Fakenham, one of a cluster of deserted or shrunken places another of which, Testerton, is now part of the parish. The site is on a gentle east-facing slope inclining towards a north-flowing stream. The ruin of St Margaret's church dominates the earthworks (Batcock 1991, 142–144). These consist of a street line, now largely followed by a farm track, which divides in two at the south end of the field. There are two side lanes. One lies south of the churchyard (1), the other (2), further north, opens out eastwards.

Long straight banks, former toft boundaries, run back from the street; thirteen to the east and nine to the west. Six appear to have signs of buildings and in some there are access gaps from the street. The central group east of the street is irregular, those further away are more uniform in

shape suggesting a planned layout of unknown date. Two possible small moated platforms existed until recently. Aerial photographs suggest that the earthworks formerly extended north of the farm. Pudding Norton Hall is of 18th-century date with a modern facade (Cushion *et al.* 1982, 42–5; Wade-Martins (ed) 1987, 40).

Pudding Norton, on Domesday evidence, was part of an estate dominated by Fakenham. It was small but a church was recorded. Thereafter little firm evidence appears available. Its Subsidy payment in 1334 was the lowest in its hundred but no reduction in tax was allowed thereafter and it was not exempt from the parish tax of 1428 suggesting that, though small, it had a stable existence. Wills show that there were gilds of St Margaret and St Katherine pointing to an active community.

A Lay Subsidy of 1543 (PRO E 179 150/310) shows that Sir William Fermour was the major landholder and contributed most of the sum collected. Living at East Barsham, he was the son of Sir Henry who was one of the greatest flockmasters in the county (Allison 1958, 97–100). He presented clergy to the living in 1532 and 1549 and, by acquiring Hempton Priory Manor in 1545,

PUDDING NORTON

SMR 7111

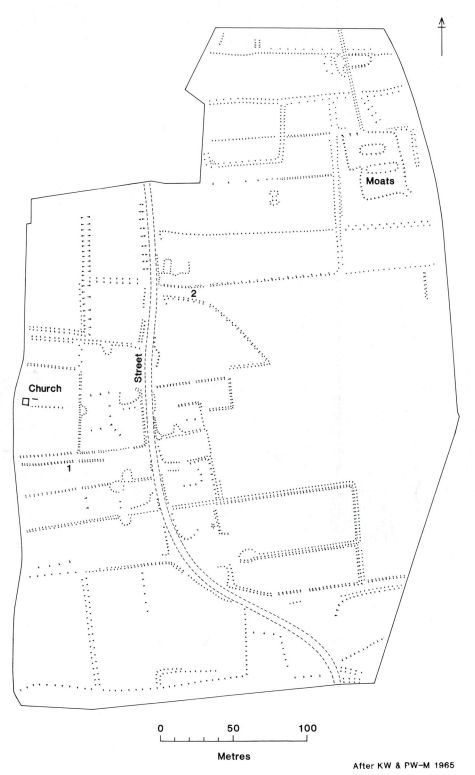

Church

Street

Moats

1

2

0   50   100

Metres

After KW & PW-M 1965

Figure 40 Pudding Norton, deserted medieval village. Scale 1:2,500

60

Plate XI Pudding Norton, 1946 RAF vertical, looking south, showing earthworks north of the farm buildings, since destroyed.
RAF 6139 3E/TUD/UK50 (Part)

seems to have had extensive control of the village. After his death, his improvident nephew sold off many manors (Smith 1974, 199) and Pudding Norton came into other hands.

By 1602 the church was decayed and those responsible were unknown. The new lords were recusants and this offers a partial explanation of the decay (Cushion *et al.* 1982, 47–48; Davison *et al.* 1988, 100; Davison 1996, 51–3). Although there is no absolute evidence, it seems likely, given the known activities of Sir Henry Fermour at nearby Thorpland (Allison 1955, 159) that he or his son had some responsibility for the demise of this village.

Roudham SMR 1057, TL 959 872
(Pl. XII, Fig.41)

The most extensive area of earthworks to be found in a Breckland deserted village; one which finally declined in the 18th century.

Roudham lies about 9.5km north-east of Thetford on the eastern edge of Breckland. The village earthworks extend for almost 1km on the southern and western flanks of an ill-drained basin, containing deep fen peat, which could well have been a mere.

The western portion near the church consists of a series of enclosures, often subdivided. Those north of the church have a north- to-south alignment with an L-shaped building outline (1) being notable. These may have cut through part of a series of tofts still seen to the north-west. They extend south-westwards from the fen edge, marked by a curving ditch (2), to the former medieval road to Illington. The central area includes a moat to the north of the hall, with some flint revetting on its internal bank and with its south-west corner obliterated by a farm road. Another moated enclosure (3) to the north-west has an outer enclosure extending northwards onto the lower ground, and a possible causeway approaching it from the south. Linear forms to the west may represent further boundary features of the manorial complex.

The lawns to the south-west of the hall have enclosure boundaries which could be those of tofts, while to the south-east there are two hollow ways (4 and 5) with remnants of associated enclosures linking and flanking them and extending into what is now arable land. Considerable quantities of medieval pottery have been found on the earthworks, particularly in the western portion, as well as on adjacent arable land. Fieldwalking suggests that areas to the east and west of the earthworks were once occupied as was that immediately south of the church (Cushion *et al.* 1982, 48–59; Wade-Martins (ed) 1987, 8).

Roudham in medieval times was divided between two manors: Westacre (held by the Priory) and New Hall. After the Dissolution they were united in 1584 when the owner of Westacre manor purchased New Hall. Lay Subsidy figures for 1334 show a settlement more prosperous than places in central Breckland but poorer than its neighbours on richer soils to the east. Figures for 1449 show a serious decline (Cushion *et al.* 1982, 54–59). Afterwards some stability was maintained. In the early 16th century Westacre manor had nineteen tenants (Cul Dd 8.42) while, in about 1580, other sources suggest at least thirty heads of families in the village. In 1603 there were eighty-six communicants declining to sixty-three in 1676 (Whiteman 1986, 206).

The Hearth Tax of 1672 recorded fourteen taxable households (one empty) and eleven discharged (PRO E179/154/697; 26708). By 1750 purchasing-in had taken place and by the 1770s all that remained was the ruined church, Hall Farm, one other farm, an inn and some newly built cottages. Ogilby's road map (1675) shows Roudham Church 'ye Hall' and a 'row of houses', the latter placed in a position roughly matching concentrations of late pottery discovered by fieldwalking.

The church was destroyed by fire in 1734. The original building probably dated before 1200, but a small early 13th-century church was lengthened and widened and a tower porch built on the southern side in the 14th century. In the 15th century the chancel was rebuilt to the same width as the nave.

Rougham SMR 3673, TF 825 207
(Fig.42)

A deserted area of an existing village consists of the remains of two streets and associated tofts and enclosures, modified by later activity to the east.

Rougham is about 13km north of Swaffham and 16km south-west of Fakenham. It lies on the southern margin of the Good Sands region of the county. The existing village lies on either side of the main street with the church and hall near its northern end. The remains of a small park lie on its north-western flank and in pasture beyond that again are the surviving earthworks.

The earthworks are most distinct at the western end where there are two well-marked broad hollow ways (1,2) which appear to converge eastwards. The more southerly one can be traced westwards into a plantation and has five truncated toft boundary banks on its southern side. The area between the two hollow ways is divided into four by three boundary banks; two of the divisions have what appear to be smaller enclosures at their northern ends.

The eastern section of the earthworks begins where a complex deeply-cut channel (3) breaks across the ends of the hollow ways. Beyond that is a possible combination of the two ways into one less convincing linear hollow (4). The area is much disturbed by quarry pits, one water-filled, and by channels for brick works in the wood to the north which itself may have been imposed on possible 18th-century fishponds constructed by Roger North. Foundations of buildings can be detected, notably beside what may be a road (5) coming from the south. Many features here are probably post-medieval.

Further east, to the west of the present hall, is the site of an earlier house. The hollow (6) may represent part of garden landscaping associated with this house as has been discussed in some detail by Tom Williamson (1996, 275–290; 1998, 28–30, 271–273; Wade-Martins (ed) 1999, 59).

Documentary evidence shows that the present street was the core of the medieval village. Archaeological evidence suggests that the area of the earthworks was first occupied *c.* 1100 and also shows that they are only a small part of a large western extension of Rougham. The southern hollow way, Hildemere Gate, led to further settlement areas in the two arable fields to the west. The northern one, Massingham Gate or Overgate, had a green called Bradmere Green to the north of it. The green had settlement on both sides with a manorial site, Green Hall, at the south-east corner near the pond (Broadmere).

Rougham underwent economic decline in the period between 1334 and 1449, being allowed a 27.3% reduction in Subsidy payment. In 1349 there was a flurry of land transactions, many of them concerning the lord, John Reed, who had a reputation as a grasping man of wealth and who was targeted by rebellious peasants in 1381. He seems to have been keeping large flocks of sheep. Soon after the events of 1381 Reed continued the enlargement of his demesne and this may coincide with the abandonment of western parts of the village. In 1517 (Leadam 1893, 176)

To East Harling

A.D., G.F. & B.C. 1977

Plate XII Roudham deserted medieval village, 1946 RAF vertical showing earthworks.
RAF 3G/TUD/UK 59 5132 and 5133 composite

William Yelverton, a later lord, converted 200 acres of arable in Rougham to sheep pasture; a document of 1511 describes pastures which appear to cover the area of the earthworks. The absence of any significant quantity of pottery later than 1400 from that area seems to support this view.

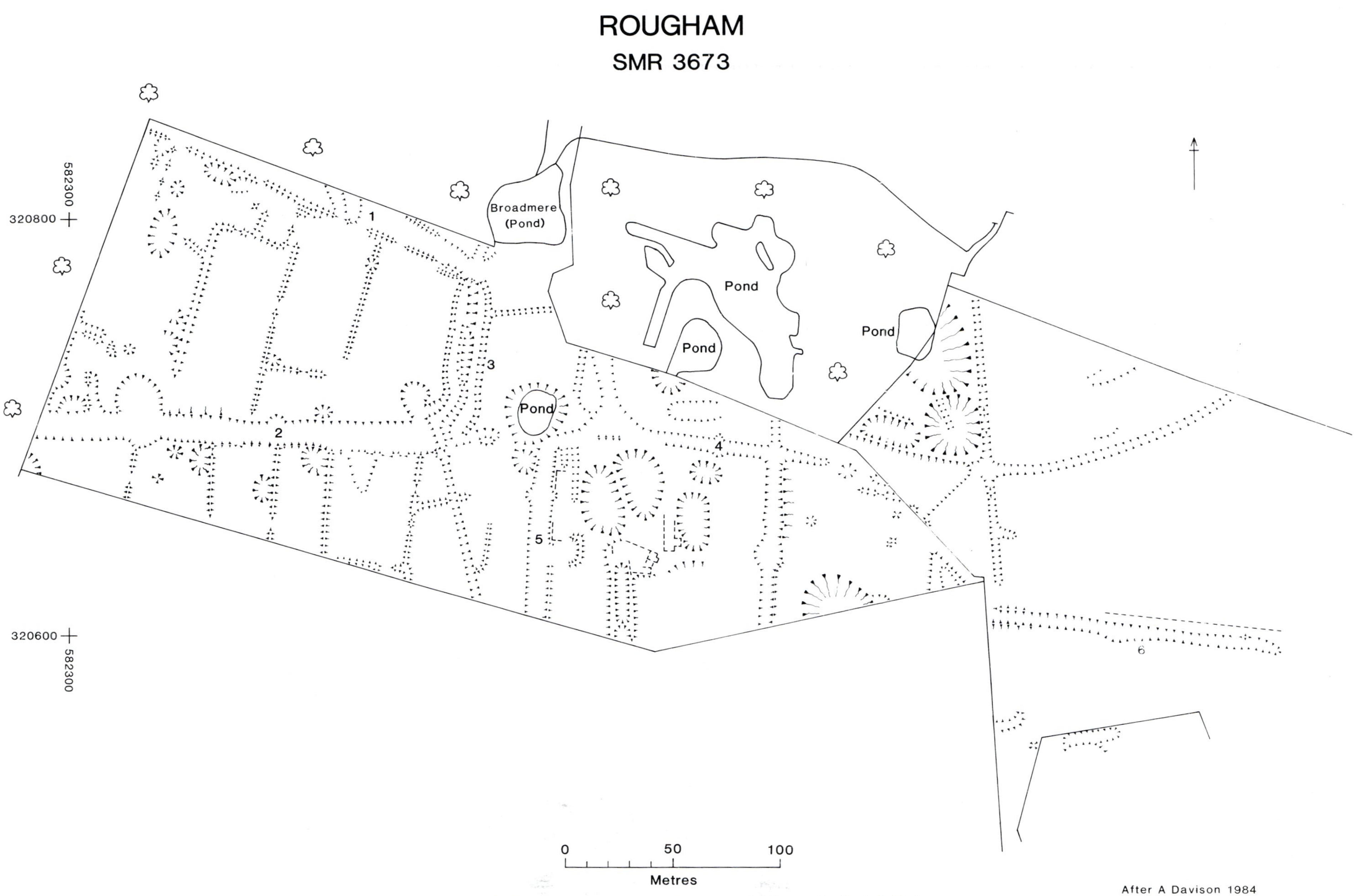

ROUGHAM
SMR 3673

Pond

Pond

Pond

Broadmere
(Pond)

Pond

1

3

2

4

5

6

582300

320800

582300

320600

After A Davison 1984

Figure 42 Rougham, western extension of village. Scale 1:2,500

Metres

0   50   100

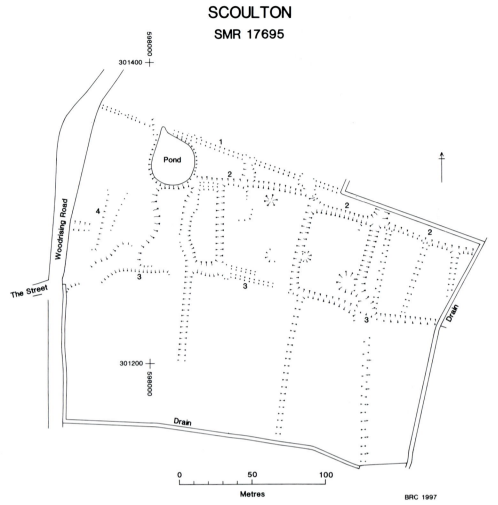

Figure 43 Scoulton, common-edge settlement. Scale 1:2,500

Scoulton SMR 17695, TF 981 012
(Fig.43)

A deserted common-edge settlement, probably medieval in origin, lies within a scattered parish.

Scoulton is a scattered settlement about 13km west of Wymondham with an isolated church and widely distributed groups of buildings; within it is a large mere containing a substantial island.

The earthworks are in grassland to the east of The Street and to the west of the mere. They are bounded on the north by a drain (1) which marked the approximate limit of a former common. The most westerly section of the earthworks is rather confused but to the east, the form is much more obvious. Three tofts abut an east-to-west ditch (2) to the north and this appears to have been a common-edge ditch linked to the later one to the north (1). Subdivisions of the tofts make it uncertain as to their actual number but their relationship with the croft boundaries immediately to the south suggests three. A modern drain truncates the easternmost toft and croft. The tofts and crofts are separated by an irregular feature which is, in part, a narrow hollow way, part causeway, part ditch (3), and seems to form some kind of continuation of The Street.

Faden's map of 1797 shows that a large proportion of Scoulton parish was common; this extended from the parish boundary with Hingham and included Scoulton Mere within it. It stretched north of the mere to join Woodrising Common while part of its southern boundary was what is now called Back Lane. Faden may not be entirely accurate but he does show a group of buildings in the position of the earthworks with the edge of the common to the north.

The Enclosure Award Map of 1807 (NRO Smith 29/9/73) shows the pasture with buildings on the area nearest the road as does the Tithe Map of 1838 (NRO 78). Both show the grouping in roughly identical fashion: a long building, described as a messuage in 1807 and as a cottage and garden in 1838 when it was shown in a small enclosure, and behind it three buildings, one of them said to be a barn. Bryant (1826) calls it 'Mason's Farm'. The pasture as a whole was called 'Mason's House Pasture' in 1838. Neither the Enclosure Map nor the Tithe Map shows the large pond, suggesting that it may be a relatively modern feature.

The property nearest the road was demolished in the 1950s. A small terrace (4) may indicate the position of this building with the three others standing to the east on the area south of the pond. It may be assumed that the remaining tofts are medieval though the only supporting evidence is provided by two sherds of medieval pottery found to the south of the westernmost toft.

66

Plate XIII Shotesham St Mary viewed from the west: moated platform surrounded by trees, a hollow way and early parkland features. TM 2398/Y/DXP 10

Shotesham St Mary SMR 5391, TM 236 988
(Pl. XIII, Fig.44)

A probable medieval site with a surviving moat; most other features have been obliterated by a late medieval/early post-medieval park with later subdivisions.

Shotesham lies about 9.5km south-south-east of Norwich on either side of a small valley draining into the Tas. The present village, dominated by All Saints'church, is on the eastern side of the valley. The deserted area is on higher ground to the west of the valley and includes three parish churches, St Martin's (ruined), St Botolph's (foundations only) and St Mary's (still in use).

The earthworks are in the vicinity of St Mary's surrounding a circular moat, within which is the Old Hall, probably the remnant of a larger building of 16th-century date with much later modification, (Pevsner 1962, 314; Pevsner and Wilson 1999, 650). Between the moat and St Mary's church and to the north-west of it are features which may be equated with the sites of vanished buildings. To the north of the church is a possible hollow way (1). To the west of it is a well-defined ditch (2) with a bank on its eastern side and to the west of that two enclosures, just possibly tofts, and former field boundaries. To the west of the moat is a ridge (3), possibly a terrace walk into gardens, extending to the sinuous former field boundary (4). To the

south-west and south is a marked hollow way (5), part of a road which linked Shotesham Mill and St Martin's church which, in ruins, is a striking feature (Wade-Martins (ed) 1987, 48). Some earthworks, now vanished, were noted and Late Saxon pottery found near St Botolph's church (Smith D. 1969, 173, 175–6).

'Shotesham' has a complex history beginning with Domesday which refers to 'the other Shotesham' indicating some duality. Of the three churches on the west side of the valley, St Botolph (probably pre-Conquest; Hart 1966, 93) was united with St Mary in 1311 and in 1428 St Mary and St Martin (pre-Conquest; Hart 1966, 93) each had less than ten households. Decline recorded for Shotesham as a whole in 1449 (22%) may have been on the western side. In 1517 Shotesham St Mary had 60 acres of land enclosed, the tenants being deprived of shack (grazing after harvest; Allison 1955, 135, 156–7; Smith D. 1969, 170–185).

Although pottery finds near St Mary's suggest early settlement, a map of 1650 (NRO FEL 1077) shows the manor house within a circular moat and St Mary's church with three buildings enclosing a courtyard between them. A small building still surviving by the church was possibly a dovehouse (NRO DN/TA 588). All, save St Martin's, lay within a circular park divided into enclosures also shown, with further subdivisions, on a map of 1721 (NRO FEL 1079). Earthworks east of the hall are related to the buildings which had vanished by 1721; most other features are associated with the park.

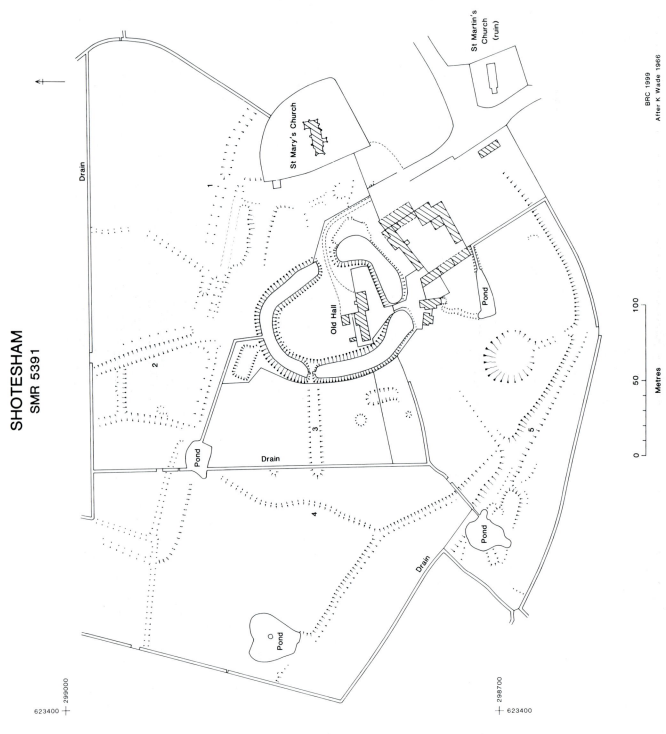

SHOTESHAM
SMR 5391

St Mary's Church

St Martin's
Church
(ruin)

Old Hall

Drain

Drain

Drain

Pond

Pond

Pond

Pond

1

2

3

4

5

BRC 1999
After K Wade 1966

0   50   100
Metres

Figure 44 Shotesham St Mary, remnant of deserted medieval village with early parkland enclosures. Scale 1:2,500

Plate XIV Shouldham, various earthworks east of the present village. TF 6708/L/EU1

The map of 1650 shows that the site is that of an early park which appears to have obliterated most signs of medieval activity. It also reveals that Shotesham St Mary, a shifted village, was not deserted; twenty-one buildings faced Reddmarsh Common by the Tas, two more, one of them a mill, lay within the common and there were eight facing Bates Greene south-east of the hall. In 1731 Shotesham was acquired by the Fellowes family. The first owner's son, Robert, employed Sir John Soane to relocate the hall in 1784. The Reddmarsh site seems to have been within a new park created soon after and must have been removed then, a case of very late desertion.

Shouldham SMR 4283, TF 680 089
(Pl. XIV, Fig.45)

Tofts facing Eastgate Street, hollow ways, enclosures and possible ridge and furrow result from a shift westwards to a market place.

Shouldham lies about 12km south-south-east of King's Lynn and 14km west of Swaffham. The present settlement forms an irregular loop based on Eastgate and Westgate Streets surrounding an open area. There is a small former market place on the south-eastern side; the surviving parish

church (All Saints') is isolated to the east while the site of the Gilbertine Priory lies to the north-east of the village.

The earthworks lie between Eastgate Street and the church. Those in the north-western part of the plan (1) appear to have been associated with four properties facing onto Eastgate Street. To the east of them, beyond a low bank, is a featureless area. This northern section is flanked to the south by a shallow hollow way (2), still shown as a road on the 1st Edition One-Inch map. To the south of this is a rather enigmatic ditched causeway (3) leading east from Colt's Hall, and an area of banked and ditched enclosures (4) partly terraced, with drainage ditches to the west. There is a small area of subdued ridge and furrow (5) in the south-east corner of the site.

Domesday entries for Shouldham (Brown (ed) 1984 21,7. 31,22.) as distinct from Carbois (Shouldham) Thorpe (Brown (ed) 1984, 21,8. 31,23. 66,14.) suggest a settlement pattern already somewhat complicated. One holding, that of Reynold, formerly Thorkell's, had a recorded population of twenty-seven. The others, formerly Aethelgyth's but, in 1086, Ralph Baynard's, were described as 'Shouldham', with two churches and a population of thirty-one, and 'the other Shouldham', also with thirty-one.

Fieldwalking in 1976/77 around the sites of the two churches (Smallwood 1977, 23–25) revealed Middle Saxon, Late Saxon and medieval pottery, suggesting an

SHOULDHAM
SMR 4283

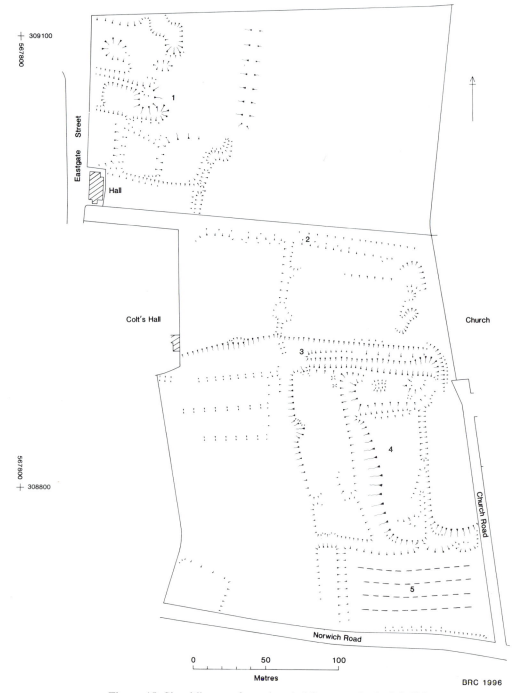

Figure 45 Shouldham, tofts and varied features. Scale 1:2,500

abandoned focus of settlement. The establishment of a market (Dymond 1993, 77) appears to have resulted in a westward movement of settlement and it seems likely that the earthworks may represent part of the abandoned area.

The area is described in a field book of 1633 by William Hayward (NRO 2495 232 x). The shallow hollow way is identifiable as 'the church lane called the Beerway'. To the north of it the features fronting Eastgate are shown to have been two pightles and an orchard. To the east of them was

a close of pasture with some wood called Olkyard and the remainder of the featureless area was then a close called Batchelors. Colt's ('capital messuage') and four tenements and yards are recorded facing onto the street and market place as now. Colt's seems to have extended eastwards to the south of the Beerway. The remaining earthworks are described as Alder Carr (western part, 6.75 acres) and a close of wood called Appletons (5.5 acres).

70

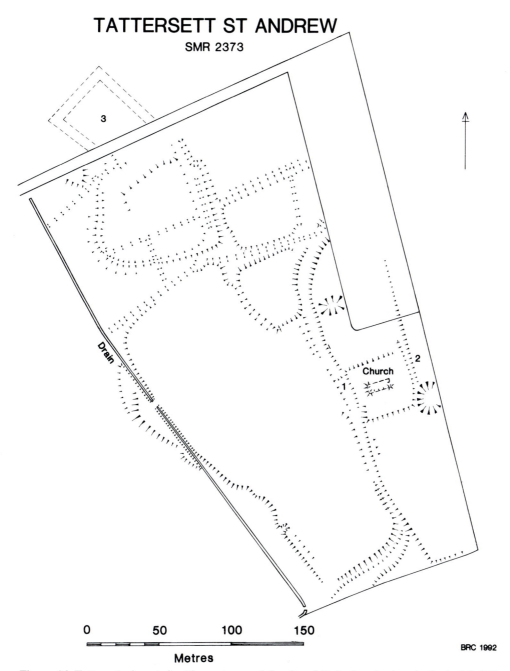

TATTERSETT ST ANDREW
SMR 2373

3

Drain

2
Church
1

0   50   100   150

BRC 1992

Metres

Figure 46 Tattersett, deserted settlement around the site of St Andrew's church. Scale 1:2,500

A 16th-century survey, made for the Mildmays who gained the Priory estate after the Dissolution, mentions Bachelers as being formerly the site of tenement Bachelers but with only a barn by then. Appletons Close was described as having a 'regia via' to the north as well as the south and west, and demesne land to the east. This and other descriptions of land in this area south of the former Priory suggest that some changes took place after the 16th century. St Margaret's church, to the south of All Saints', was abandoned in the 16th century (Batcock 1991, 54).

The 13.5% reduction to the Lay Subsidy payment allowed in 1449 suggests that some contraction as well as movement may have been involved (Hudson 1895, 285–6).

Tattersett SMR 2373, 22443; TF 853 287, 850 292
(Figs 46,47)

Two areas of earthworks in an abandoned part of the village which survives, in name at least, to the north. The southern one is associated with the foundations of a church and a ploughed-out moat; the northern one with a surviving isolated church and another moated platform.

Tattersett is on a terrace on the eastern side of the Tat valley, about 9.5km west of Fakenham. The present village lies almost entirely north of the old course of the A148. The earthworks lie to the south of the road and are overlooked by the isolated All Saints' church. There are two groups of features separated by an arable field within which medieval pottery has been found (Cushion and Davison 1997, 492).

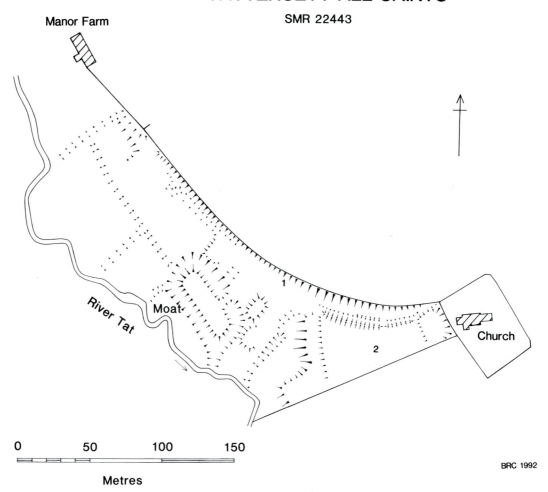

Figure 47 Tattersett, settlement north-west of All Saint's church. Scale 1:2,500

The southern group (SMR 2373) has a well-defined road-line (1), partly hollow, partly terraced. To the east of it are the foundations of St Andrew's church within a banked enclosure, on the eastern side of which is a short hollow way (2). To the west are banks and ditches with some possible toft sites. In the north-western corner of the group is a fragment of a moated platform (3) largely destroyed by ploughing.

All Saints' dominates the northern group (SMR 22443). A hollow way (1) links it with the vicinity of Manor Farm and is continued north-westwards as the modern village street; one possible toft (2) lies on its southern flank. To the south of the hollow way is a well-defined moated enclosure linked by leats to the river channel.

There were two churches recorded in 1086 (Brown (ed) 1984, 8,110) thus suggesting the dual nature of the place. By the late 12th century the Pinkenys were lords but they appear to have divided their holdings at various times and it is thus easy to visualise more than one site of manorial status. Coxford charters mention land in Tattersett and Sengham, said to be next to Tattersett village, and refer to features near All Saints' and the bridge. Other documents mention Sengham Street.

Ecclesiastical tax lists of 1254 and 1291 record the two churches as being in Tattersett and of no great difference in valuation. However, St Andrew's parish was exempt from tax in 1428 as it had less than ten households; the village as a whole was allowed a reduction of over 15% in payment to the 1449 Lay Subsidy. Decline at the southern end of the settlement could account for this, at least in part. St Andrew's church had been given to Castle Acre Priory by one of the Pinkenys and it is likely that the church finally became disused at the Reformation.

Documents referring to the 'field of Sengham' show that it lay at the northern end of the village and it is possible that the surviving part of Tattersett is in reality the street or hamlet of Sengham (Cushion and Davison 1997, 492–505).

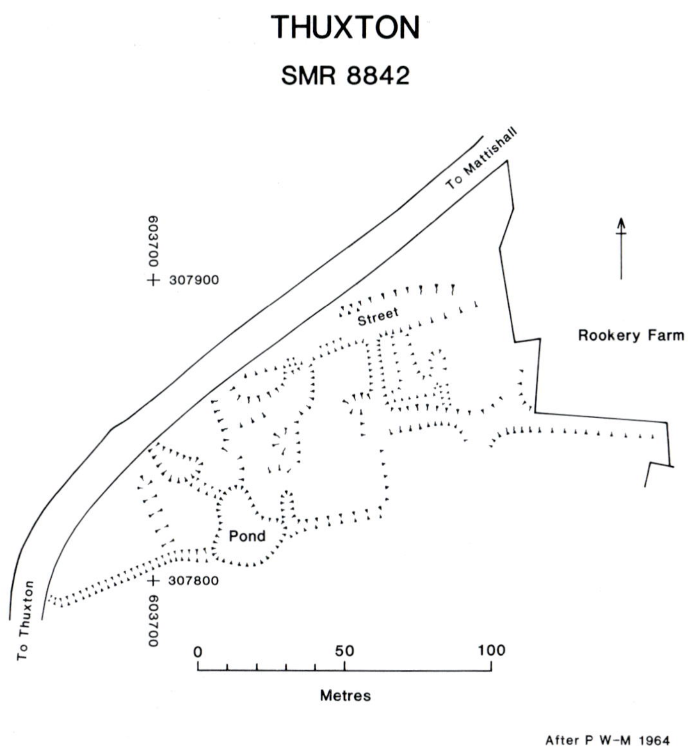

THUXTON

SMR 8842

Figure 48 Thuxton, remnant of deserted medieval village. Scale 1:2,500

Thuxton, Garvestone SMR 8842, TG 038 078
(Fig.48)

One of the few excavated sites in Norfolk; the plan shows a street and adjoining tofts, all that remains of this village which almost certainly resulted from the amalgamation of two settlements in early medieval times.

Thuxton is midway between Wymondham and East Dereham on a plateau drained by the Yare and is now within Garvestone. The earthworks, largely removed by ploughing and levelling in 1962–63, lay on higher ground north-east of the church. The complete outline of the medieval village has been recovered using aerial photographs (Butler and Wade-Martins 1989, figs 4,5; pl. 1). The plans in that report should be used to put Fig.20 in context.

A wide street with flanking ditches ran roughly east-to-west through the village; a short straight road similarly ditched led northwards to the outer enclosure of a moated site at the east end of the village. To the west, a group of thirteen tofts lay on either side of the street. Earlier ploughing had, at some time, obliterated features in the neighbouring area to the west, but beyond it, a second cluster of earthworks survived until they were largely destroyed in the 1960s. Twelve tofts on either side of the street had gone, but up to four remain to the south of the street west of Rookery Farm. Another moated site to the north of this survived complete in 1845. A third moat, long

ploughed over, lay near the church on the edge of marshy riverine meadows 500m to the south. Thuxton is one of only two deserted villages in Norfolk which have been partly excavated, the other being Grenstein (Wade-Martins 1980b, 93–161; (ed) 1987, 43).

Thuxton was originally two places, THUR(E)STUNA or TORUESTUNA and TURSTANESTUNA (Brown (ed) 1984, 1,86. 8,81. 9,134. 15,21. 66,26.), with the church in Thurestuna. It was not until *c.* 1300 that they were called Thuxton. In 1316 there were three principal landholders, possibly matching the three moats. Small in 1334, it received quite a high relief after the Black Death, the Rector dying in 1349. By 1379 it had declined further and it was allowed a high percentage reduction to the Lay Subsidy payment in 1449. Communicant numbers in the 17th century point to a total population of about sixty-five (Whiteman 1986, 207) and Hearth Tax returns suggest that they were of yeoman status (Frankel and Seaman 1983, 66).

Faden (1797) shows a small cluster of houses near the church with two farms further from the river. Various suggestions can be made about the disposition of the original settlements and these are outlined by Butler and Wade-Martins (1989). The changing structure of the church echoes the fortunes of the village. The earliest fabric is *c.* 1100 with considerable enlargement early in the 13th century with a south aisle and threefold enlargement of the whole building. After some additional work in the 15th century the south aisle later decayed and was demolished in 1757.

Plate XV Waterden deserted medieval village seen from the west: the earthworks in the foreground have since been levelled. CUCAP AMU 77 *(Photography by Cambridge University Collection of Air Photographs)*

Waterden SMR 1071, TF 887 362
(Pl. XV, Fig.49)

Neighbouring the deserted village of Egmere, these earthworks are centred on a former green with later modifications due to a post-medieval hall and pond-digging.

Waterden was the southernmost of a group of three abandoned settlements, the others being Quarles and Egmere. It lay in a valley to the north-west of Waterden Farm, east of South Creake and about 7km north-west of Fakenham. Only a part of the earthworks remain as, in about 1966, the western portion was levelled. However, recording was carried out so enabling a complete plan of the site to be made.

The main street can be seen as a hollow way (1) to the east of three ponds. It led north-eastwards to a green where three other roads converged (2,3 and 4); pond-digging has destroyed most of the green but it is shown on a map of 1713/14 by Halsey. The main street (4) continued north-east from the green, along the line of the existing farm road, with six tofts facing it on the eastern side with a boundary ditch at their rear. Further to the south, to the east of the ponds, there were probably three more tofts. To the west of the green there are earthworks of about three tofts while further north are some which mark the site of the later Hall (5). The Hall, apparently of about 1600, is shown as a sketch on Halsey's map. A barn of this date survives among the buildings of Waterden Farm; these were completed by 1784 (Wade-Martins, S. 1980, 143–4) and the ponds are probably contemporary. To the north of the Hall, incomplete enclosures west of the street are probably tofts (Wade-Martins (ed) 1999, 61).

In 1086 Waterden was in the hands of one lord; after a succession of medieval lords it was sold in 1483 to the Sefoules who held much property in north-west Norfolk. At the close of the 16th century it was bought by Sir Edward Coke and it has remained with the family ever since. In 1334 Waterden paid a very small contribution to the Lay Subsidy and, although it received no reduction after the Black Death, it was allowed a drastic reduction of over 31% on its payment in 1449 when the average for its six neighbours was only 19%. However, unlike Egmere and Quarles, it had more than ten households in 1428. It must have suffered some severe setback in prosperity in the late 14th or early 15th centuries so that by 1603 there were about twenty communicants and sixteen in 1676, among whom a solitary household from Egmere was numbered (Whiteman 1986, 212,225n).

It seems likely that the last houses may have disappeared finally in the 17th century during the times of the later Sefoules or Sir Edward Coke.

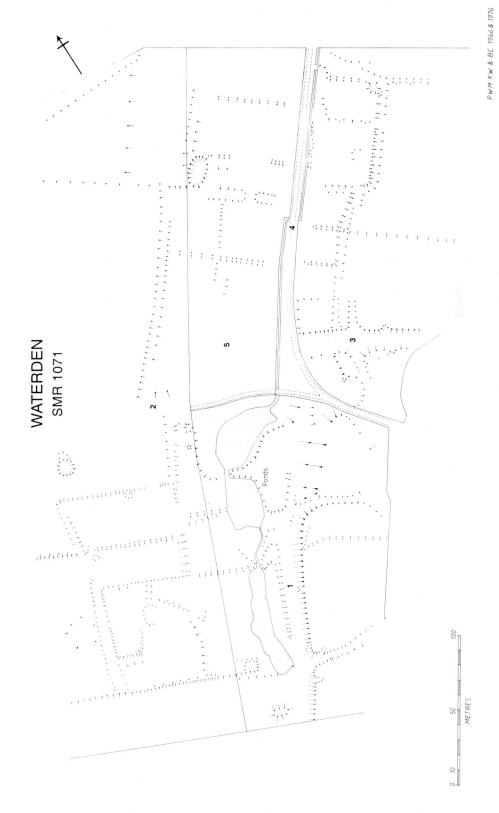

WATERDEN
SMR 1071

Ponds

PWM KW & BC. 1966 & 1976

Figure 49 Waterden, remnant of deserted medieval village. Scale 1:2,500

Plate XVI West Acre earthworks, seen from the south-east. TF 7815/AT/CV 10

West Acre SMR 29470, TF 785 155
(Pl. XVI, Fig.50)

Eastern tofts of the village, probably abandoned by the end of the 16th century at the latest.

West Acre is a small village in the Nar valley about 2.5km west of Castle Acre. The earthworks lie between Warren Farm and the existing village in 4.5ha of south-sloping grassland on the north bank of the Nar.

The most striking features are at the western end between two abandoned chalk pits. They consist of a well-marked probable building platform (1) abutting an enclosure with a frontage of 40m on the road. To the south, in the same enclosure, is a second ramp-like platform (2) raised above the valley floor where there is a substantial ditch (3) draining into the river. The boundaries of the eastern chalk pit appear to respect property divisions; this could indicate near-contemporary quarrying. The easternmost earthworks include several small building outlines, some of them (4,5) carrying footings of brick, flint and ashlar. Further features here include the remains of an old river channel and what may be part of a former garden of Warren Farm.

Medieval West Acre declined comparatively little between 1334 and 1449; in the latter year it was allowed a reduction of payment to the Lay Subsidy of only 7.7%.

Only five places in Freebridge Hundred were allowed lesser reductions: Tilney, Terrington and Walsoken, all wealthy Fenland settlements; Grimston, which had a flourishing pottery industry, and Castle Rising (Hudson 1895, 271–72). The presence of the Priory probably helped to boost the village economy. It seems likely from this that abandonment of this site has a later origin.

A survey dated 1432 (NRO BIR/1 396 x 2) mentions several properties which fronted on a '*regia via*' (king's highway) to the north and which had the river or land close by to the south. Property descriptions which seem to fit the easternmost group fairly closely are those of Robert Randes who had Calkpityard with the river to the south, a messuage to the east, the '*regia via*' to the north, an empty messuage to the west (also abutting south on the river) with a messuage held by Robert Hoo to the north of it (also abutting on the road). Also in this general area was the property of a fuller (Robert Nabbes) with a fulling mill and dam nearby; this may have been further east. The fulling mill was still recorded in a survey of 1598 (NRO BIR/4 396 x 2). Also recorded in this survey were twelve empty messuages on Estgate, probably including these earthworks.

Finds of pottery confirm medieval activity in this area while the occurrence of Thetford-type ware on the westernmost features suggest earlier occupation there.

WEST ACRE
SMR 29470

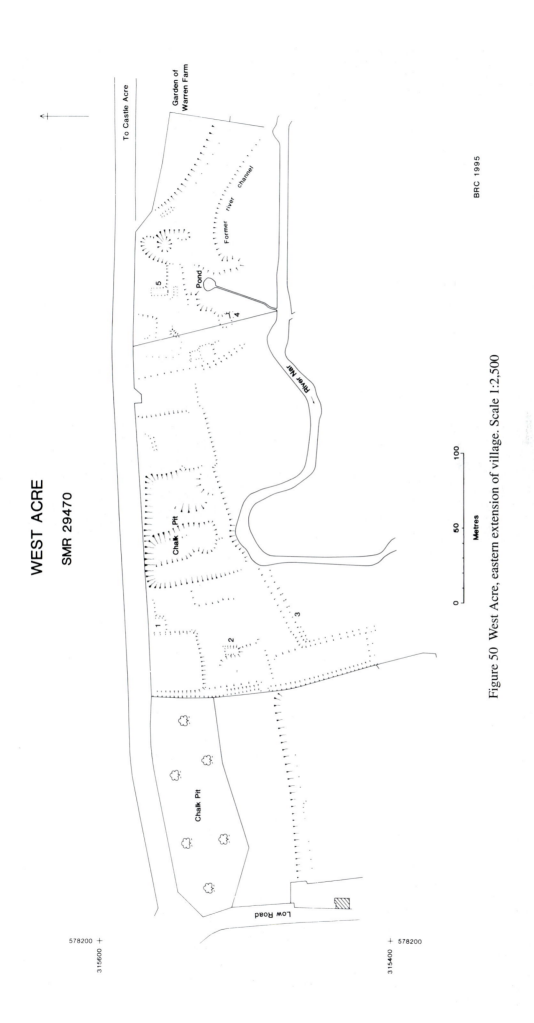

Figure 50 West Acre, eastern extension of village. Scale 1:2,500

BRC 1995

Plate XVII West Barsham, enigmatic earthworks seen from the south-west. TF 9033/K/AEA 28

West Barsham SMR 2115, TF 905 335
(Pl. XVII, Fig.51)

A puzzling and extensive site comprising roadways and enclosures for which there is virtually no documentary evidence, though a medieval presence is clear.

The Barshams are three small settlements about 4km north of Fakenham; this is the most westerly. The earthworks are almost 1km in length and lie east and south of West Barsham Hall, straddling a tributary, culverted in part, of the Stiffkey River.

The easternmost feature is a hollow way (1) extending south from a surviving track and ending south-east of Meadow House. Two ways are linked to this; one (2) led towards the church, the other (3), more northerly and interrupted by the lake, extends across the valley south of the hall. The former course of the culverted stream (4) is to the east of Meadow House where there is also a terraced enclosure (5) with a western entrance, possibly a garden when Meadow House was the manorial site.

A marked linear depression (6) to the west of the stream is possibly a hollow way; it is crossed by a depression (7) which extends across the valley to reach the southern end of the first hollow way. The linear depression (6) continues south to link with another (8) running east to west and has a boundary bank and ditch lying *c.* 40m to the west (9); between the depression and the bank are two small possible tofts (10).

There is a possible enclosure (11), much degraded, west of the pond and another to the north-east while to the south-west is a curious banked enclosure (12) which has been interpreted by Edwin Rose as a knot garden (Wade-Martins (ed) 1987, 64). To the south of this is a fragmentary ditch (13) which crosses the area and breaks the line of a terraced scarp (14). Other features in the extreme south include an east-facing scarp overlooking the remnant of the early watercourse and a flat-topped mound (15).

This is a very problematic site. Domesday does not distinguish between the three Barshams. One of the three churches mentioned had a large acreage and may have been a minster. West Barsham, with surviving early features, may have been the church in question (Pevsner and Wilson

78

WEST RAYNHAM
SMR 17449

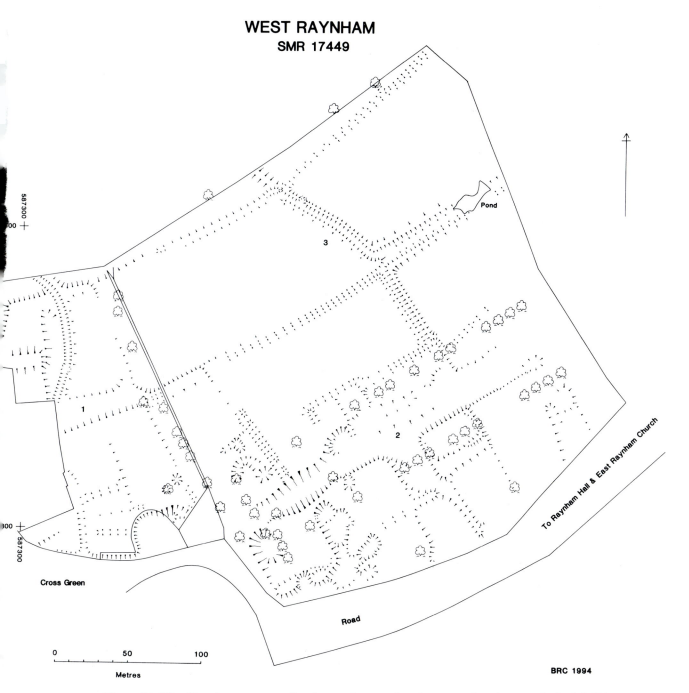

Figure 52 West Raynham, post-medieval emparkment of settlement and enclosures. Scale 1:2,500

1999, 761–62). West Barsham seems to have survived the medieval period but underwent some decline thereafter (Sheail 1968; Whiteman 1986, 212).

The earliest evidence, other than the church, is Meadow House, a fragment of an early 17th-century building. Map evidence is provided by Faden (1797) and the Tithe Map (1844; NRO DN/TA 913). They show the north-eastern track extending further south, so explaining the hollow way. The road leading towards the church appears on Faden and the 1st Edition OS One-Inch map. The Meadow House was 'The Hall' in 1844, the present hall being completed in 1921 (Pevsner and Wilson 1999, 762). The Tithe Map shows the stream already regulated and culverted, though the lake and central pond appear later. The apparent absence of early documents makes further certainty impossible. Medieval pottery found on both sides of the stream indicates a presence though features of that date are limited to a few possible tofts while some broader depressions suggest roadways.

Much of the southern part of the site could be manorial while it is clear from the numerous features and from possible cropmarks not shown on the plan, that much unrecorded activity has occurred.

WEST BARSHAM

SMR 2115

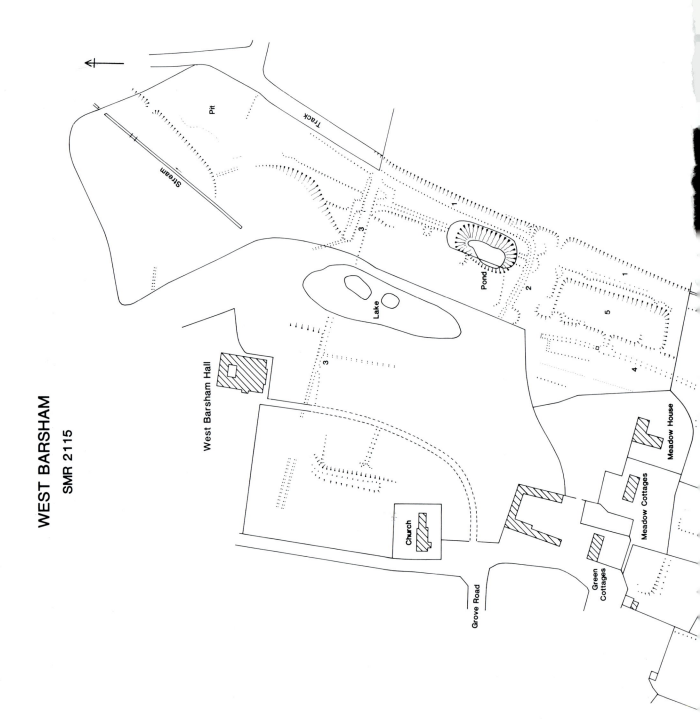

West Barsham Hall

Stream

Pit

Track

Pond

Lake

Church

Grove Road

Green Cottages

Meadow Cottages

Meadow House

590300
333900

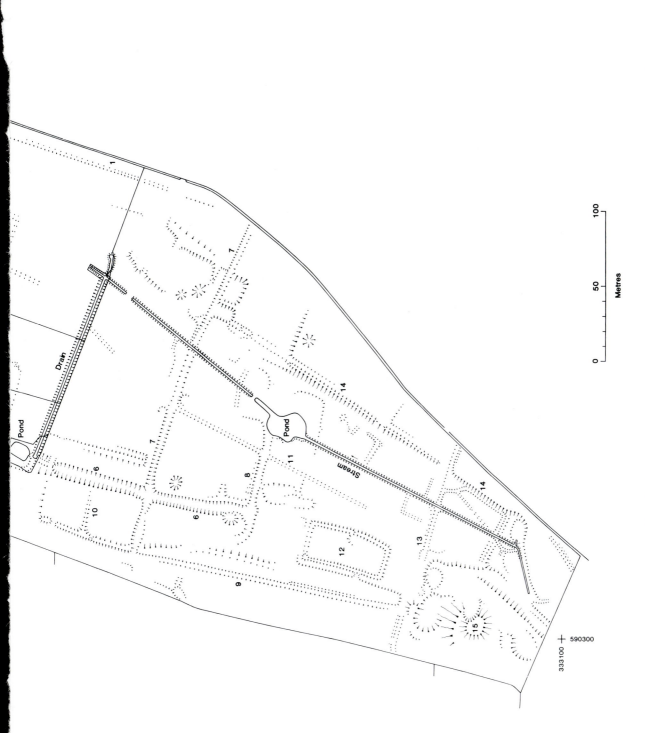

Figure 51 West Barsham, a puzzling site including village and manorial features. Scale 1:2,500

BRC 2000

3255

St Margarets Church
(ruin)

West Raynham

325

Plate XVIII West Raynham, hollow way with associated features and field boundaries, looking south.
TF 8725/ABH/DPS 2

West Raynham SMR 17449, TF 875 254
(Pl. XVIII, Fig.52)

The earthworks represent desertion near the church and a former eastward extension of the village abandoned in post-medieval times when, together with enclosures to the north, it became part of East Raynham's parkland.

The Raynhams, South, East and West, are a group of villages about 7.5km south-west of Fakenham. The earthworks lie within 9.5ha of parkland between the village of West Raynham and a lake near St Mary's church, East Raynham. They are in three fairly distinct groups. Those in the west (1) appear to be related to the ruined St Margaret's church and the surviving inhabited areas of West Raynham. The second consists of sub-rectangular features on either side of a linear depression or hollow way (2) lying within an avenue of trees which runs up to Raynham Hall. The third is a series of banked and ditched linear features (3), possibly field boundaries and tracks.

Domesday entries for the three Raynhams are often indistinguishable and reflect considerable manorial complexity. By the 16th century, however, the lands were all in the hands of the Townshends. It is clear from the reduction in payment to the Lay Subsidy allowed in 1449 that West Raynham had declined, as its reduction of just over 36% was the second largest among the seventeen

places asked to pay less (Hudson 1895, 273). By the 16th century it seems to have been less prosperous than East Raynham (Sheail 1968).

It has been shown that in the 16th century there was a considerable reduction in the number of tenants on arable land in West Raynham (Stride 1989, 308–18). The changes began between 1530 and 1570 when some tenants appear to have been enlarging holdings by amalgamation with others. The trend continued at a reduced pace until 1633 at least and possibly 1667. The demesne increased markedly showing that the Townshends were in the forefront of these changes. Further unification of lands in West Raynham by purchase was also taking place in the 1720s (Rosenheim 1989, 144).

A map by Thomas Waterman dated 1617 (NRO BL 33) shows that part of the area of the earthworks was still inhabited then. The hollow way appears to be the road marked '*regia via*'; it left the eastern apex of the triangular Cross Green which had curving sides. The '*regia via*' had buildings on either flank; the earthworks show some signs of these. In 1621 this public road led across a bridge into East Raynham and along the avenue leading to Raynham Hall (Williamson and Taigel 1991, 86). Some of the westerly group of earthworks seem to have been crofts attached to houses on the eastern side of the green while those of the third group were tracks and field boundaries. An area east of St Margaret's church was labelled 'Rectory

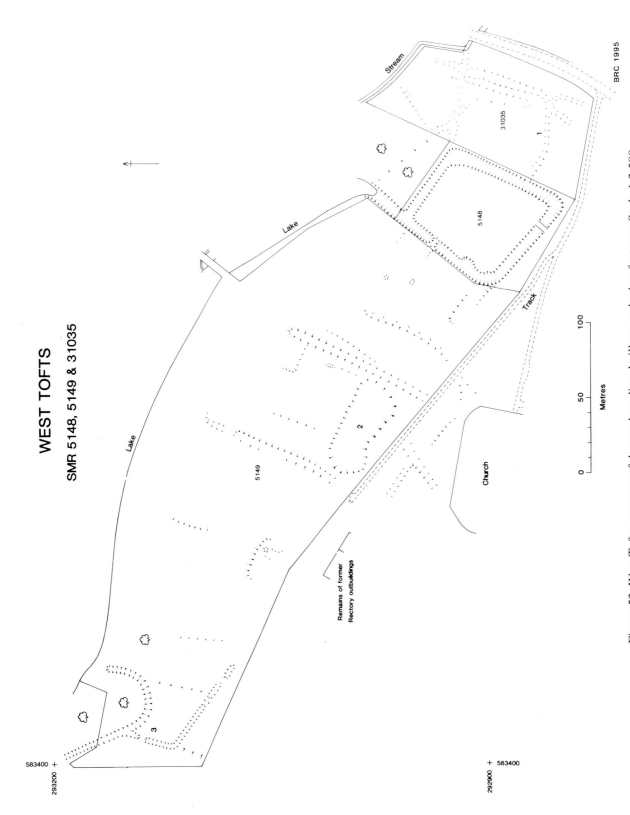

WEST TOFTS
SMR 5148, 5149 & 31035

Figure 53 West Tofts, remnant of deserted medieval village and other features. Scale 1:2,500

82

voc(ato) Old Churchyard'. Faden (1797) shows the eastward road apparently diverted southwards around a western extension of Raynham Park; this must have happened when the lake was dug in 1724 (Williamson and Taigel 1991, 88). St Margaret's church was abandoned about 1735 (Batcock 1991, 123).

The abandonment of this portion of West Raynham was not the result of medieval contraction but a product of post-medieval landscape changes.

West Tofts SMR 5148, 5149, 31035; TL 836 930
(Fig.53)

A medieval moated platform and scanty relics of a deserted medieval village which was later emparked and finally absorbed into the Stanta military area in 1942.

West Tofts lies within Breckland in a small tributary valley draining westwards to the Wissey. It is just over 10km north-north-west of Thetford in the modern civil parish of Lynford.

The earthworks are to the north and east of the church. The most obvious feature is a moated platform (SMR 5148) draining northwards to a lake which once formed part of the landscaped grounds of the former Hall. The entrance to the platform may have been from the west; the present entrance on the south side is modern. Vegetation obscures the surface.

Unobtrusive earthworks east of the moat (SMR 31035) may be related to it. One sinuous depression (1), part of a U-shaped enclosure, may have been a leat, since degraded, feeding the moat. Further subdued features (SMR 5149) north of the church probably represent a part of the medieval village, where linear banks form the remains of property boundaries. A probable extraction pit (2), some 19th-century parkland features in the far west (3) and the foundations of rectory outbuildings are superimposed on these features.

Domesday suggests an average settlement comparable with other Breckland vills. By 1346 (Feudal Aids III, 392) there were three landholders, Belets, Castons and de Toftes. Stability seems to have been maintained from the 14th to the 16th centuries (Hudson 1895, 274; Sheail 1968) and judging by the numbers of communicants in the 17th century, West Tofts was flourishing in comparison with its neighbours, some of which were virtually extinct (Whiteman 1986, 209–210). In 1664 John Jermyn, with nine hearths, headed the eighteen householders who paid the Hearth Tax in 1664 (Frankel and Seaman 1983, 41). A later landholder, Payne Galway, resided within a park then generally south of the church and had a reputation as an agricultural improver (Dymond 1985, 226; Sussams 1995, 109).

Blomefield (1739, I, 547) suggested that the moated site was the seat of the Castons. The earthworks to the west of this had been depopulated by the late 18th century and incorporated into the park. The hall later became the rectory. In 1720 a curious burial was found in wet ground near the moat during the digging of a drainage ditch. This has been suggested as a possible Bronze Age bog burial (Clarke 1960, 71–2; Turner and Scaife 1995, 212).

The remaining parts of the village east of the earthworks were cleared in 1942 to create a military training area, a late and unusual desertion.

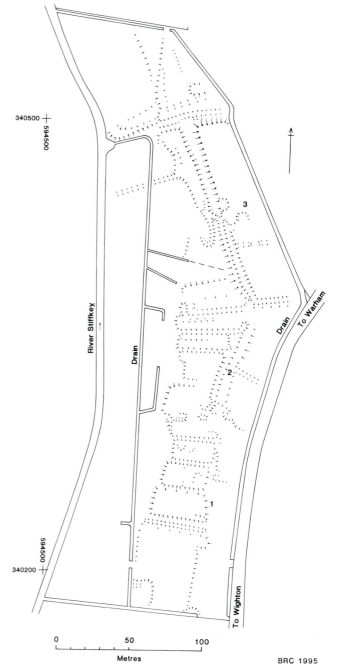

WIGHTON
SMR 1850

Figure 54 Wighton, detached portion of medieval settlement. Scale 1:2,500

Wighton SMR 1850, TF 946 404
(Pl. XIX, Fig.54)

Clearly a deserted part of the existing village, these quite striking earthworks have only a scanty documentary history.

Wighton is about 10km north-north-east of Fakenham; it lies mainly on the western side of the River Stiffkey. The earthworks are situated on the eastern bank to the north of the bridge and beside the road to Warham.

Plate XIX Wighton, medieval settlement earthworks east of the village seen from the north-east.
TF 9440/ABD/FZH 11

The features are in grassland on a low river terrace and include at least six enclosures which back onto the flood plain and face a rather sinuous linear boundary (1) to the east. The most northerly of these have slight east-to-west internal ridges, while two to the south have slight raised areas within. To the north also the eastern boundary becomes more marked, developing into a ditch, possibly a former road (2).

To the north of these enclosures some features are enigmatic and marred by spoil from dredging. The most obvious is a large probably truncated ditched (3) enclosure with a bank to the west broadening into a wide ridge in its northern section. To the north and west of this are various banks extending onto the flood plain; some may be related to an old river crossing and the location of a mill (SMR 15208). Medieval pottery has been recovered from the edges of the large enclosure described last and from the four most southerly ones (Cushion 1995, 35–6).

In 1334 Wighton, together with Holkham, was, in Lay terms, one of two most prosperous settlements in the hundred, a position retained in 1449 (Hudson 1895, 281–2). This suggests a place of some size. It remained large in 1524/5 though Little Walsingham and Wells were bigger (Sheail 1968).

Some evidence comes from a Court Book of 1577 to 1593 (Holkham MSS, Vol 3, Bundle 3, 49). The few details suggest a village which was, by then, largely associated with the west bank. However, there are references to features on the east bank. In 1582 there was an entry referring to lands and tenements in Wighton east of the river. Another concerned a capital messuage and a large acreage in the vill and east field but here the messuage was probably on the west bank. There were several references to the road from Wighton to Warham; a piece of land next Stowehill abutted on this road to the south. There are references to Stowe, Stowe Way (or Sty) and Stowe Crofte. Peasegrene lay to the south of this road. One named street which is not identifiable is Upgate on which there was a messuage with half an acre: it is tempting to see this as an alternative name for the Warham road but there is no other evidence to support it.

Halsey's map (1736, Holkham 29) shows the whole area. It was divided into thirteen small pastures draining naturally into the winding river; there were no buildings and the boundaries do not appear related to the earthworks. The road broadened into Dobbs Common, a feature still shown by Faden (1797). Bryant (1826) shows a straightened river and, like Faden, a group of buildings to the south of the earthworks, but no Dobbs Common. The Tithe Map of 1840 (NRO 218) has modified ditches differing from the modern pattern, possibly reflecting some northern features, and the dwelling with outbuildings and yards.

It appears that the earthworks are medieval and had largely been abandoned by 1577: some late 18th-century settlement then occurred to the south.

WILBY
SMR 31185 & 31186

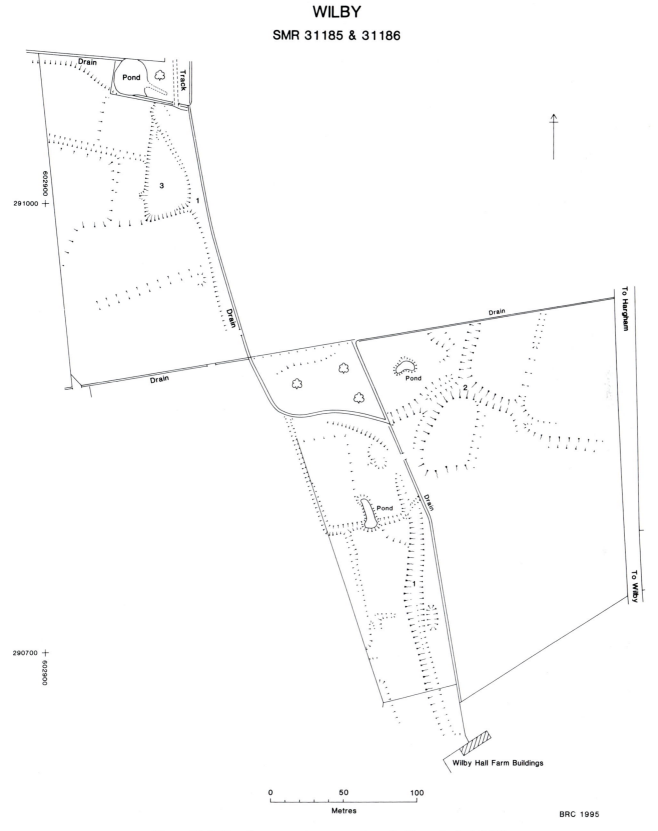

Figure 55 Wilby, former northern extension of village. Scale 1:2,500

BRC 1995

Wilby, Quidenham SMR 31185, 31186; TM 031 908
(Fig.55)

A hollow way and associated enclosures to the north of the surviving village are associated with one of the manors and have evidence of at least Late Saxon origins.

Wilby, a shrunken settlement now within Quidenham parish, lies about 5km south of Attleborough; the earthworks are at the northern end of the village.

A gently sinuous hollow way (1) extends for almost 500m north-westwards from the precinct of Wilby Hall and is only interrupted where it is carried into arable land and a small wood midway along its course. A series of irregular enclosures, probably the sites of tofts, are visible in grassland west of the way and are mostly ditched or scarped, several being truncated by arable land to the west.

To the east of the major roadway is a linked meandering hollow way (2) which diminishes eastwards. This appears to have served some irregular ditched enclosures, one of which may have extended into the wood. The featureless southern portion of the eastern field has been levelled by ploughing in the recent past. The rather vague features in the north-western field which is known as Washpit Meadow appear to represent enclosures but have been marred by an extraction pit (3) and the construction of a sheep dip attached to the pond.

These earthworks are part of the shrunken village of Wilby; the surviving nucleus lies around the church 800m to the south. Wilby Hall is a 17th-century house standing within the remains of a medieval moat. Wilby experienced some decline in the later medieval period and this may have initiated the abandonment of the northward extension.

There were two manors in medieval Wilby: Wilby Hall and Beck Hall. A survey dated 1619 but incorporating an earlier account of about 1566 (CUL Buxton MSS, Box 93, Book 36) and dealing with the southern part of the village mentions a moated manorial site in decay. This appears to relate to a second moated site, now largely ploughed over, which lies between the present Wilby Hall and the village.

The manors were unified in the 17th century when Robert Wilton of Beck Hall purchased the other manor. William Hayward's map of Hargham in 1629 (NRO MC 168/1 P153B) shows the northern part of Wilby as lands of Beck Hall. The earthworks thus seem to have been associated with Beck Hall and it is probable that Wilby Hall stands on the site of medieval Beck Hall. The hollow way probably led to Hargham.

Fieldwalking on the western ploughed-out portions of crofts yielded not only much medieval but also Late Saxon pottery suggesting that the area was occupied by that date. A few sherds of Middle Saxon pottery indicate some earlier activity. Medieval and Late Medieval Transitional pottery found within the copse north of the junction of the hollow ways shows that this conceals part of the occupied area (Davison with Cushion 1999, 257–274).

WOOD NORTON
SMR 33886

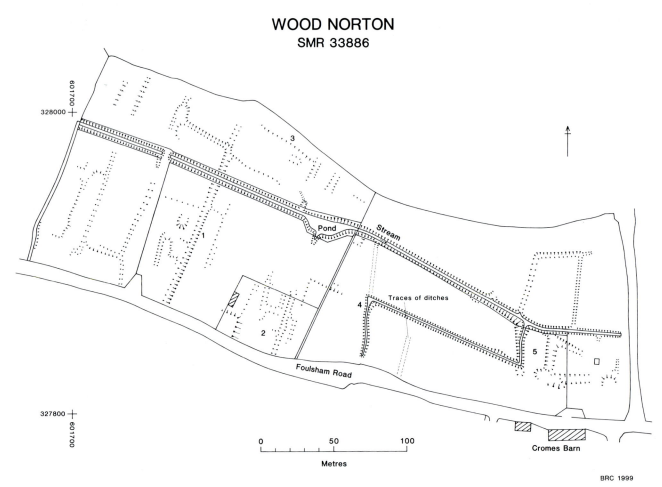

Figure 56 Wood Norton, shrinkage of eastern village extension. Scale 1:2,500

Plate XX Wood Norton, evidence of shrinkage seen from the north-west. TG 0127/K/ASG 30

Wood Norton SMR 33886, TG 019 279
(Pl. XX, Fig.56)

Some rather enigmatic earthworks east of the village with evidence of late-surviving settlement probably represent part of the final contraction of a medieval village.

Wood Norton is a shrunken village about 5km east-south-east of Fakenham. The earthworks lie about 800m east of the church on either side of a small stream on the northern side of the Foulsham Road which formerly also led to Norton Common.

They consist of a series of incomplete enclosures in the western half of the site corresponding, in part, to cottages and closes shown on the Enclosure map of 1811. The best-defined feature is a marked linear depression (1) extending from the road almost to the northern boundary. To the west of it are the remains of four rectilinear enclosures marked by interrupted ditches, scarps or banks.

To the east of the linear depression are only remnants of enclosures; one of these (2) was, until 1842 at least, the site of a cottage near the road. A south-facing scarp (3), almost parallel with the northern boundary, is the southern edge of a track shown in 1811. To the east again features are even less distinct. A curving ditch (4) and a small near-rectangular ditched platform (5) opposite Cromes Barn may be medieval.

Alterations made to improve drainage and some post-war levelling have confused the earlier layout.

Domesday records a church in Wood Norton but by the medieval period there were two, All Saints and St Peter's. The settlement certainly did not suffer excessively in the 14th century as it was allowed only a 7.8% reduction to the Lay Subsidy in 1449, the average for Eynesford Hundred being 19.5% (Hudson 1895, 282–3). Subsequent details indicate a general degree of stability in the 16th and 17th centuries. In 1603 there were ninety communicants and this had risen to 125 in 1676 when there were also forty-two Dissenters (Whiteman 1986, 222), while in 1664 twenty-seven households were charged for sixty-nine hearths, only one house having as many as six (Frankel and Seaman 1983, 19).

Some contraction may be detectable in the abandonment of St Peter's church in the 16th century (Batcock 1991, 52) and the consolidation of the manors with the decline of outlying Lyng Hall, but this was no more than that experienced by many smaller Norfolk settlements after the 14th century.

The evidence gathered from the Enclosure Map (NRO C/Sca 2/152) and the Tithe Map of 1842 (NRO DN/TA 642) suggests that settlement lingered on the Foulsham Road site until relatively recently but by the time of the later map changes were occurring. It appears that the earthworks witness the final stage of contraction of a medieval settlement pattern.

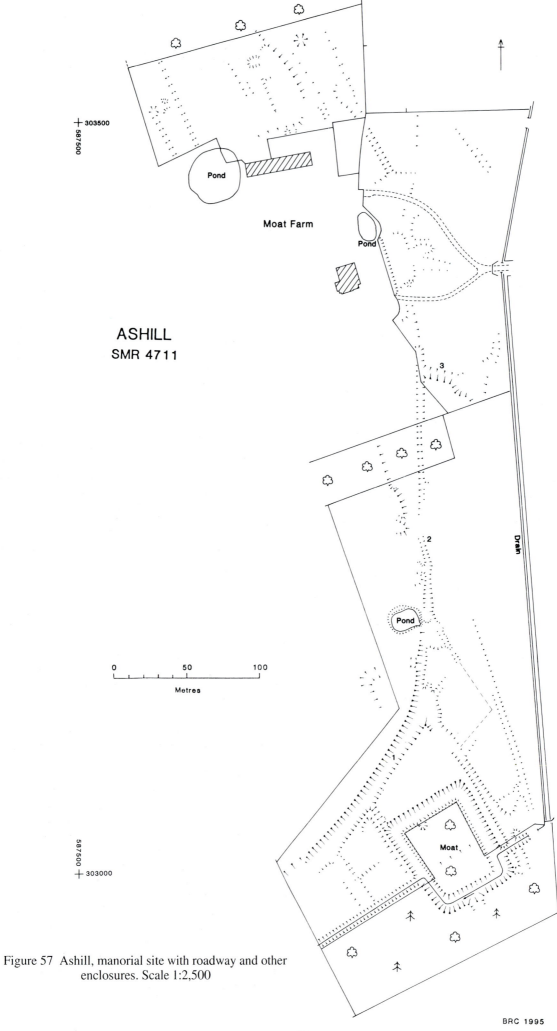

ASHILL

SMR 4711

+ 303500
587500

Pond

Moat Farm

Pond

3

Drain

2

Pond

1

Moat

0   50   100

Metres

587500
+ 303000

Figure 57 Ashill, manorial site with roadway and other
enclosures. Scale 1:2,500

BRC 1995

Manorial Earthworks and other Isolated Sites

Manorial earthworks and other isolated sites are a particularly interesting and varied group. Once again many appear to be located in what has been described as the area of sheep-corn husbandry in the west. It has to be admitted that although some sites such as Shelton, Gayton and Warham Hales are clearly manorial, there remains a number where the distinction has to be subjective or arguable. In the case of Kimberley where there is clearly a manorial site with attendant earthworks, it could also be legitimate to include it, as has been done here, in the section on parkland features.

Manorial sites such as East Harling, Ashill, Middleton Towers, South Creake, Little Dunham and Seething are extremely variable in nature. In certain instances, South Creake and Seething for example, the signs are almost vestigial and are better supported by documentary evidence than by field survival. East Harling is clearly manorial but is a thoroughly confusing site while Ashill, Middleton Towers, Horningtoft, Lyng Hall in Wood Norton and Lyng itself are clear-cut cases. Manorial sites are usually associated with the existence of moats but not many of the moated examples cited here are drawn from the area of boulder clay where they are most numerous (Rogerson 1993, 67). Whereas the boulder clay, being water-retentive, offered many sites where water was easily available or where the drainage afforded by a moat was necessary, of the sites considered here, most are located close to a stream where water was obtainable.

Many of these sites are of interest from the point of view of location though their origin is sometimes obscure through lack of documentation. They include Harling Thorpe which is well-documented and which was in existence at the time of Domesday as a separate manor long since vanished; Thorpe Street itself, an outlying part of West Harling, finally disappeared with the rest of that village in the early 18th century. Seething has what appears to be the earthwork of a circular pound. Others such as Bylaugh, which has no real documentation, Gunthorpe and Crimplesham which are relatively obscure, and Little Appleton, Panworth and Ingworth which pose difficulties in interpretation, are nevertheless intriguing.

Ashill SMR 4711, TF 877 033
(Fig.57)

A moated manorial site, a hollow way and other features are associated with the edge of the former Low Common.

Ashill is a substantial village about 7.5km south-east of Swaffham. The earthworks lie about 1.5km south-west of the present village centre. The most notable is a large trapezoidal moated platform 51m by 41m by 35m, without any obvious building outlines. The moat itself remains substantial and is still used, in part, by a minor watercourse; there is no sign of an entrance to the platform. A ditch to the east appears to be linked northward with a marked hollow way (1), between 11m and 15m in width. After the junction of the two the ditch narrows to become a sinuous depression (2), its uneven floor suggesting infilling. Small enclosures exist to the west and north-east of the moat, the latter having irregularities which are probably the result of ploughing or dumping of spoil.

The narrow extension of the ditch leads north through a wood to form part of the eastern boundary of the gardens of Moat Farm and there is a linked remnant of another depression (3) leading east. It is possible that the gardens once had an eastern extension. The remaining subdued earthworks to the north-east and north of Moat Farm are remnants of subdivisions of possible medieval tofts or closes; some are shown as rectilinear enclosures on 1965 air photographs.

The moat was on the south-western edge of Low Common in 1785 (Reid 1979, 172 citing the Enclosure Award of 1785) with a roadway leading off the common immediately to the north (1) and the edge of the common curving away northwards (2). What remains to be determined is the identity of the moat.

In 1086 Ashill was two distinct places: Ashill and Panworth (Brown (ed) 1984, 21,16;17. 51;5). In medieval times these had become Ashill alias Uphall Manor and Panworth Manor, well to the east.

A survey of 1418 (NRO HMN7/252 772 x 5) of Ashill manor shows that the village was a straggling settlement. References to Goosemere and Gooscroft can be related to Goose Green at the north end of the village and the church, surely in its present position, is mentioned together with a Markaunt Place abutting on Market Gate. The manorial site is unmentioned. The present Uphall Grange on the borders of Houghton-on-the-Hill is suggestive but a map of 1786 (NRO PD 584/87) shows a roughly circular water feature in a Moat Close about 640m south-east of the Grange which may well have been the manorial site. There was a third manor, Collards, Gaynes and Mannocks, originating *c.* 1282 and united with Ashill by 1547 and it seems likely that this was the moated platform. The earthworks to the north suggest common-edge activity which probably disappeared with the amalgamation of the manors, late medieval population decline and the attraction of a probable market to the north-east.

Plate XXI Attleborough: moated platforms, one of which must be the site of the Little Rectory. TM 0294/A/ATW 1

Attleborough SMR 20087, TM 023 947
(Pl. XXI, Fig.58)

Two moated platforms, one of which must be that of the Little Rectory at West Carr.

The earthworks lie to the west of Attleborough town within the parish. The site is divided into two roughly equal portions by one of the headwaters of the River Thet; each contains a rectangular moated enclosure. The southern part has within it the larger of the two moated platforms (1); it measures 37m x 31m and is slightly higher on its southern side, suggesting a more likely position for a building. The southern arm of the moat has two short depressions leading south from it. The eastern one has a small rhomboidal structure (2) on its eastern flank, possibly a building platform. The moat is apparently without a visible entrance but an outlet leat, heavily silted, is at its north-western corner. There are possible inlet leats at its north-eastern corner but they may have been altered by the dumping of spoil. One may have fed a possible fishpond (3).

The second moat (4) is much smaller in scale with an irregular interior (22m x 21m) and has an entrance causeway on its southern side. There are leats linking the eastern and western arms with two roughly parallel ditches, one on either side of the moat. The westerly of these (5) is well-defined and extends south to the stream. The other (6) does not reach the stream but is linked, at its northern end, to a boundary ditch extending east to the road.

The bank alongside the stream on its northern side is spoil from dredging.

These were identified only in 1984 from the air (Wade-Martins (ed) 1987, 38). The name of the farm immediately to the south-west is West Carr Farm and this gives an important clue as to the possible origin of at least one of the moated platforms.

The somewhat confusing Domesday entries for Attleborough, including one entitled 'The Other Attleborough' (Brown (ed) 1984, 50,6,7: 59,1) seems to have been resolved into four major manors in medieval times (Plasset, Baconsthorpe, Chancelers and Mortimers). In addition there were two small rectorial holdings. The larger, the Great Rectory Manor, was two parts of the Rectory; the other, Little Rectory Manor, accounted for the remaining portion. Blomefield reported that the first was on the south side of the church. Of the Little Rectory Manor he stated that 'the Scite is now down, the Close in which it stood, contains 3 acres and is all that remains of ancient demesnes'. He also referred to this as 'commonly called West Ker' (Blomefield 1739, I, 340–367; 354, 355).

It seems likely that these earthworks are the 'Scite now down' though which of the two moated platforms is the Little Rectory remains open to speculation. The larger of the two is the obvious choice which leaves the second unexplained. It may have been an earlier abandoned site or possibly some form of secure place for the Rector's stock or other property. Presumably a bridging point over the stream has been lost.

90

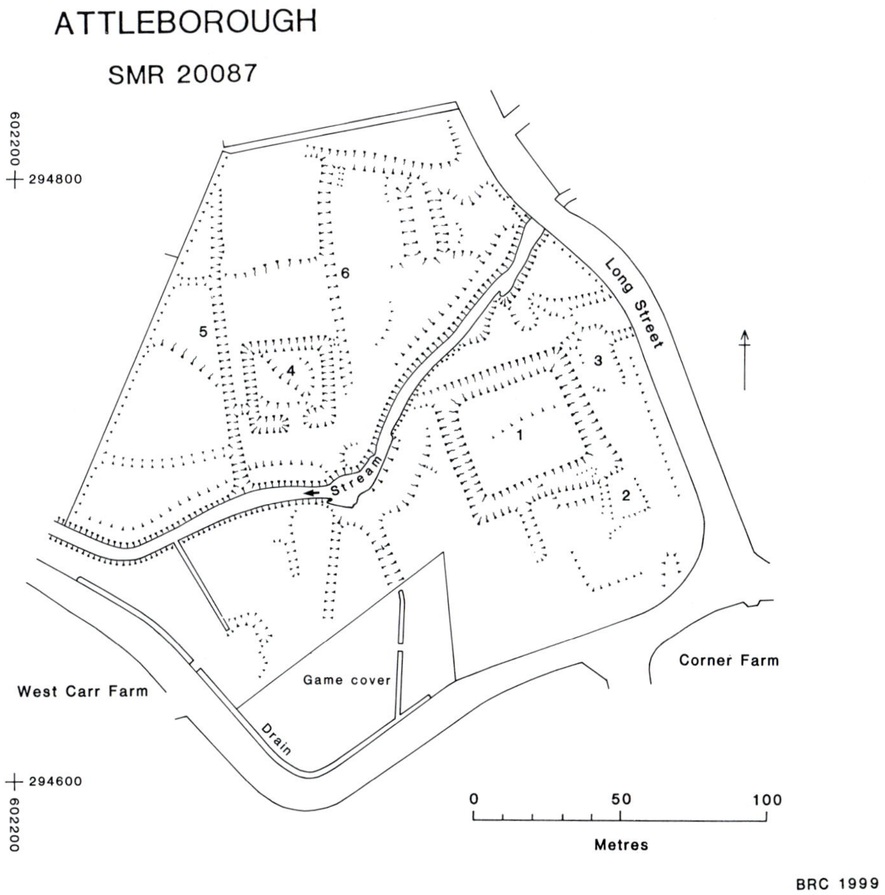

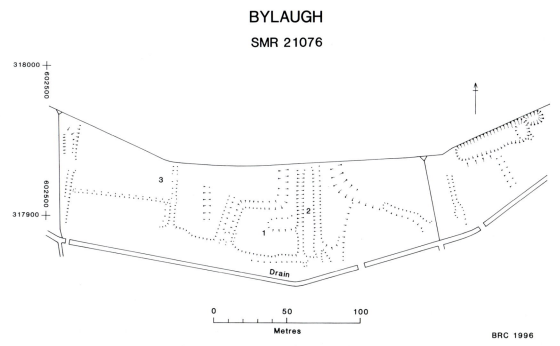

ATTLEBOROUGH

SMR 20087

602200
294800

6

5

4

Long Street

3

1

2

West Carr Farm

Game cover

Corner Farm

Drain

294600

602200

| 0 | 50 | 100 |

Metres

BRC 1999

Figure 58 Attleborough, Little Rectory manor. Scale 1:2,500

BYLAUGH

SMR 21076

318000

602500

602500

3

2

1

317900

Drain

| 0 | 50 | 100 |

Metres

BRC 1996

Figure 59 Bylaugh, detached portion of deserted medieval village. Scale 1:2,500

Bylaugh SMR 21076, TG 026 179
(Fig.59)

Undocumented earthworks, probably medieval, associated with pastures by the Wensum and detached from the deserted medieval village of Bylaugh.

This isolated site lies on a gravel terrace on the northern side of the flood plain of the River Wensum, 600m from the nearest existing settlement within the parish, but only 300m from Castle Farm in Swanton Morley, on the opposite bank of the river.

The earthworks comprise a trapezoidal ditched enclosure (1) abutting the flood plain with a slight internal bank in the south-western corner and a raised building platform against the eastern arm. It is approached by a causeway from the higher land to the north and has a more prominent ditched causeway (2) to its east and other truncated ditched enclosures (3) to the west. A few sherds of pottery occurring on the surface suggest a medieval origin for the site.

It has not been possible to achieve precise identification of the features but they appear to be an outlying remnant of the deserted medieval village of Bylaugh (Allison 1955,145). It seems likely that they represent an early medieval expansion of the village, taking a linear form facing onto riverine pasture. In 1449, after the general economic decline of the preceding century, Bylaugh was allowed a reduction in payment of 28.6% compared with the average for the hundred of 19.6% (Hudson 1895, 282–3).

Thereafter, Bylaugh seems to have gone into gradual decline. A map of 1581 by Ralph Agas (NRO Hayes and Storr, 9/6/87, map 98) shows a landscape, mainly of Sparham, already partly enclosed. The Hearth Tax for 1664 recorded seventeen persons chargeable for fifty-one hearths; sixteen were charged to Henry Bedingfield Esq. (Frankel and Seaman 1983, 21). These figures suggest that Bylaugh had not changed greatly in status since 1500. By the end of the 18th century however, the village had declined considerably. Nathaniel Kent's valuation of Bylaugh (1789) (NRO MS 20757A, 172x) records three farms. Faden (1797) shows only a scattering of buildings close to the present clusters while a sequence of maps, 18th-century or undated (NRO, NRS 4040,4041,4062), shows a landscape largely enclosed. The Tithe Map (1840) shows only Bylaugh Hall (Old Hall Farm), the church, a second farm and four cottages with gardens, and a barn and a yard near the church.

At what point the earthworks were abandoned remains an open question but it is likely to have been before 1500. The original village site remains unknown but it may have been near the church.

Claxton Castle SMR 10304, TG 334 037
(Fig.60)

A very elaborate manorial site which has been much disfigured and has earthworks, probably associated, to the south.

Claxton is a village on the southern side of the Yare valley 11.5km south-east of the centre of Norwich. The castle is at the west end of the village.

Only fragments of masonry (1,2) survive from the castle, not easy to interpret. Around these are remaining portions of a roughly circular moat (3) shown on the Enclosure Map, much disfigured by infilling or by conversion to a drain; precise identification of this feature is difficult. To the north of the manor are very shallow ridges and scarps, one of recent origin; the remainder are not necessarily associated with the castle.

To the south of the road are various earthworks not easy to understand. It is possible that these are the remains of some form of outer enclosure marked by a linear ditch (4), altered for drainage, to the east, a pond-like depression (5) and a more obvious ditch-like feature (6) to the west divided by a modern farm track. Within this is a level area (7) bounded on the north by a shallow ditch. There is insufficient evidence to say that this is an outer enclosure for the moat, as recently proposed (Liddiard 2000, 116), since the easternmost ditch may simply be the boundary of a medieval toft fronting onto the road, and the level ground may be a natural knoll.

To the west again are various features, most notably a sinuous ridge (8) whose shape suggests a headland with a fragment of a further bank to the east and a possible degraded causeway (9) to the north-west. However, the area is too low-lying to be seen as medieval arable land.

Claxton, according to Domesday, was held in 1086 by two men, Roger Bigot and Godric the Steward in several portions (Brown (ed) 1984, 9, 53; 56; 59. 12, 20; 22.). Blomefield states that the manor came into the hands of the Kerdistons (1775, V, 1112). William de Kerdiston was holding the manor together with Ashby in 1316 (Blake 1952, 284) and the other parts of Claxton were acquired by 1326. In 1339 William de Kerdiston obtained licence to crenellate his manor house and, in the following year, received a charter for a weekly market and an annual five-day fair. In 1379–80 his son completed work on the castle (Blomefield 1775, V, 1112).

The Kerdistons sold the manor in 1446 and it eventually passed to the Gawdys. Sir Robert Gawdy was living here in 1624 (Blomefield 1775, V, 1112). At some point in the late 17th century the present house, altered in the 19th century, replaced the castle (Pevsner and Wilson 1999, 264).

The Enclosure Map (NRO PC 6/2 [P 133B]) of 1812 shows that there has been much alteration of the site since. There was almost a complete moat with a narrow entrance to the south and a larger interruption to the north suggesting that the house had been constructed on an infilled part of the moat. This was repeated on the Tithe Map of 1846 (NRO DN/TA 919).To the north lay Mulberry Marsh. Of the ground opposite, Faden (1797) shows the western part as woodland. The farm track has apparently superseded a more sinuous version shown on the 1812 map and this may explain some earthworks while others relate to boundaries shown then.

It is obvious that much has happened to the site since 1906, mainly in the extension of buildings (Rudd 1906, 86–93).

CLAXTON
SMR 10304

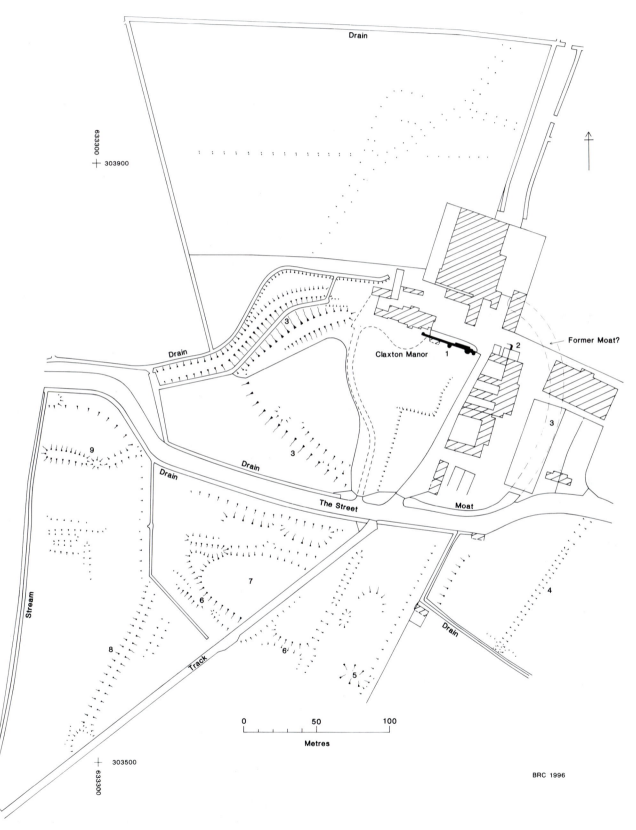

Figure 60 Claxton, major manorial site with other enclosures. Scale 1:2,500

CRIMPLESHAM

SMR 29793

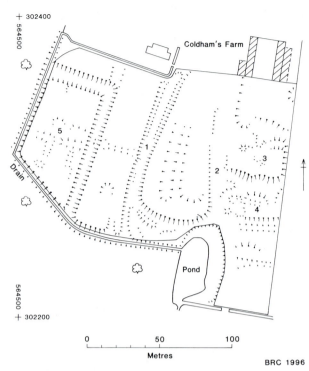

Figure 61 Crimplesham, part of a manorial site.
Scale 1:2,500

Crimplesham SMR 29793, TF 646 023
(Fig.61)

A hollow way and building platforms represent the probable site of Coldhams manor.

Crimplesham is about 4km east of Downham Market. The site lies in an isolated position about 1.5km south of the village in a V-shaped salient of the parish.

The earthworks survive in pasture to the south of Coldham's Farm. The chief feature is a length of hollow way (1) extending south from the farm and turning eastwards before petering out beyond the pond. A scarp which begins as the northern rim of the hollow way turns northwards and forms the western edge of another possible roadway (2). To the east of this are two degraded building platforms (3,4), the former a likely barn. To the west of the hollow way is an inverted L-shaped ditch of some width; the area within this (5) has some irregular ridges of uncertain origin, possibly spoil. This moat-like feature is completed by narrower drains on its western and southern sides.

In 1086 Crimplesham was held by Rainald in three distinct parts with additional amounts held by freemen. This points to a likely initial dispersal of the settlement which was maintained in medieval times (Feudal Aids III, 400, 510). Blomefield (1775, IV, 73–6) gives an account of the manors which, at the Dissolution, came into the hands of the Derham family. He named them as Crimpleshams, Talbots, Coldhams and Wesenhams. Of these there is now very little documentary evidence apart from Coldhams, the sole surviving name on the 1839 Tithe Map (NRO E 6). This shows Coldhams Lane running south from the village to the site.

Faden (1797) is uninformative about the area but Bryant (1826) does show Coldham Farm and the road continuing past it towards neighbouring villages to the south. The One-Inch 1st Edition Ordnance Survey map also shows this road and structures corresponding to the present building and the building platforms on either side. Since the 19th century the site has become even more isolated with the destruction of its southern road link.

The Tithe Map gives additional supporting evidence with the names of fields in the vicinity of the site — 'Coldhams' (three), 'Great Coldhams' and 'Grass Coldhams'. This, together with the occurrence of medieval pottery on this peripheral site, indicate that the earthworks are part of the medieval manor of Coldhams.

Dersingham SMR 1579, TF 692 302
(Pl. XXII, Fig.62)

A surviving moated site within the village may be that of Pakenhams manor, with part of West Hall Yard to the west.

Dersingham is a large village about 13km north-east of King's Lynn with a parish which extends from the Peddars' Way in the east to the coastal marshes in the west. Though a major part of the modern village is located on either side of the Hunstanton road, the Tithe Map (NRO DN/TA 274) shows that this is a modern development on old common land and that the original village was centred to the east. The earthworks lie in this eastern part of the village.

The major feature of the site is an L-shaped moat fed from both north and south and with an entrance on the northern arm. It encloses a level inner platform (1) with no obvious building remains. A substantial bank (2) to the south divides it from enclosures on lower ground where a series of linear ridges and depressions (3) appear to be associated with various types of water management rather than ridge and furrow. To the west of the moat there is an exterior parallel ditch and shallow bank, part of an enclosure linked possibly to a prominent east-to-west bank (4). Remains of a modern sheepwash (5) lie close to Manor Road. The whole site lies to the south-west of the church.

Dersingham in 1086 was a prosperous settlement with a total recorded population of 116 of which 36 were freemen (Brown (ed) 1984, 29,4; 34,2; 66,87). There were two landholders, Peter de Valognes and Eudo. From these, according to Blomefield (1775, IV, 509), the two major manors were derived, Pakenhams and West Hall. Other medieval manors were Gelham Hall, originating out of Pakenhams, Brook Hall out of West Hall, and Snoring Hall.

The earthworks appear to be the only visible survival of a manorial site in the village. Unfortunately surviving records give very few clues as to its identity. A terrier of the 15th century (NRO PD 603/195) gives some information: a pasture called West Hall Yard was next to the manor of Pakenham Hall. It also states that a pasture called Dennyscroft lay in West Hall Yard next to the manor of Brook Hall. This suggests that the two original manor houses lay close to one another and that a third was close by. Another document of 1499/1500 (NRO PD 603/197) mentions a property in Upgate to the east of Pakenham Hall. Upgate may have been a name for Manor Road. On this admittedly slender evidence there is a reasonable probability that the moat was that of Pakenhams Manor. The other earthworks to the west may be associated with it or have been part of West Hall Yard.

94

Plate XXII Dersingham, the probable site of Pakenhams manor south-west of the church. The apparent 'moat' to the south-east, although surveyed, proved unconvincing. TF 6930/C/UU7

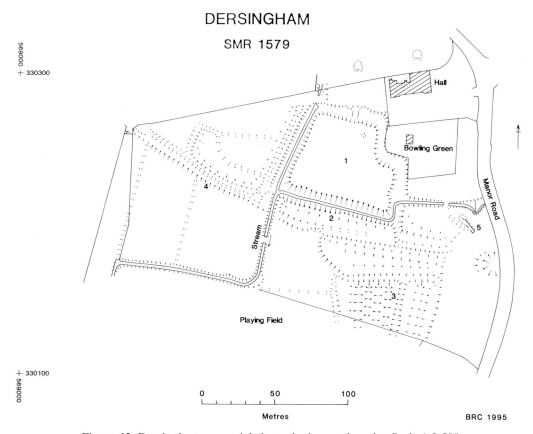

Figure 62 Dersingham, manorial site and other earthworks. Scale 1:2,500

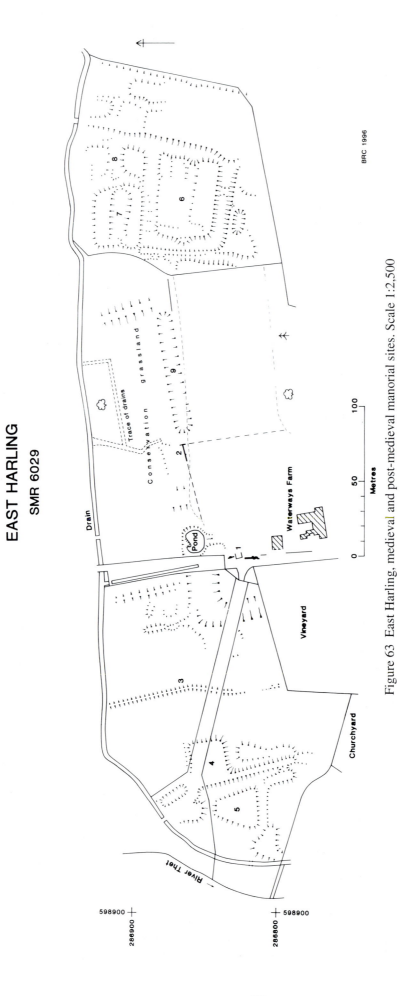

Figure 63 East Harling, medieval and post-medieval manorial sites. Scale 1:2,500

96

East Harling Hall SMR 6029, TL 992 868
(Fig.63)

A very confusing site which includes a moated enclosure, the site of East Harling Hall, built c. 1490, possible fishponds and other features.

East Harling is a large village, formerly a market centre, about 12.5km east-north-east of Thetford. The earthworks lie close to the church and a crossing-place of the Thet, on a terrace above the flood plain.

The somewhat confusing earthworks can be considered in three groupings. The first is close to Waterways Farm and embodies masonry fragments assumed to be associated with East Harling Hall. Two sections of brick walling are visible on a north-to-south alignment; between them is a U-shaped flint outline (1) which is part of a medieval structure. A further excavated length of wall (2) lies to the north-east of this and has been proved to extend south and west almost certainly forming the north-east of an enclosure, probably a kitchen garden. These features probably lay within a moat, marked now by a pond and an L-shaped depression, at its north-western corner.

The second group lies beyond a linear bank (3) to the west, close to the Thet. They consist of a platform (4) at the northern end of a ridge. To the west are two other raised areas, one of them (5) triangular. Considerable quantities of medieval pottery and roof tiles indicate a significant building as part of this complex.

The third group is the most easterly. The most impressive feature is a moated enclosure (6) with raised internal areas. To the north is another enclosure which has degraded internal depressions (7,8), likely to have been fishponds. Other slight platforms and depressions exist to the east of the two enclosures and are bounded by the remains of a ditch.

Between the two moated sites is an area of conservation grassland north of the remains of a linear pond (9); there are only slight traces of earthworks within this area.

Recent resistivity surveys in the eastern areas have shown evidence of enclosures, ditches, walls and buildings (Gurney and Penn 1998, 198, 211) the latter within the kitchen garden.

The early manorial history of East Harling was complicated by divided inheritance which caused a separation of holdings. One at least appears to have been outside the main village at Hill Harling. The manors were eventually united by inheritance, marriage or purchase and became known as 'Harling cum membris' and were eventually purchased by the Lovells (Blomefield 1739, I, 213–218).

According to Blomefield, Sir Thomas Lovell 'built East Harling-hall, on the Tower of which his arms still remain, and a brass bust of his own likeness surrounded with the Garter'. One of the last Lovells, to spite his brother, allowed the house to decay and when he died in 1693 the only course left was to sell it (Blomefield 1739, I, 219).

A particular of 1705 (NRO MS 6689) gives a brief description of the hall at about this time. Harling Hall yards, gardens and orchards and 'Parke ground' were said to encompass 40 acres. The township stood on a 'Pleasant River upon which stands a watermill'. The watermill occupied a position west of the hall where a modern building remains. The hall is shown in 'The Prospect of East Harling Hall' (NRO Rye MS Vol VI; Rye 1889); appearing as a large rambling structure with a substantial gatehouse. There were two eastern wings of differing builds and a much smaller western one. Faden (1797) shows the seat of Revd Mr Wright standing on the site but it is not clear whether this was the original building. Bryant (1826) shows nothing on the site.

The masonry is most likely part of the Lovells' Hall, although the Prospect indicates a much larger building than can be ascertained from the surface details. The other moat may have been one of the other manors or, more credibly, that of an earlier lord. The western earthworks may be in the position of an early watermill, although the size of the raised areas could indicate the hall, in which case the masonry would be more likely to have been an earlier house, re-used in part as a gatehouse. The linear bank is a field boundary of 1804 (NRO C/Sca 2/145). The Tithe Map (NRO DN/TA 869) shows parts of the area as common and makes no mention of the hall. Further geophysical work is expected to assist in interpreting the ground features.

Eccles SMR 10794, TM 024 889
(Fig.64)

A manorial site which was once Episcopal, long since abandoned within a village now markedly scattered but which was still substantial in the 17th century.

Eccles is a small settlement, much shrunken and scattered, lying about 15km north-east of Thetford and 6km south-west of Attleborough. The site is south-east of the church and to the north of Manor Farm.

The earthworks consist of a moated platform (1) with well-defined internal edges except to the east. It has a large depression in the north-western corner, with a small island within it, and a shallow L-shaped central scarp, possibly indicating the position of a building. A curving ditch (2) best seen on aerial photographs, linked to the north-western arm, may be a former edge of the carr to the north, while to the north of the moat is a ridge parallel to it.

To the west and south of the moat are the remains of two abutting ditched enclosures (3,4), rather irregular in shape, which have been degraded by some infilling of the ditches; (3) is bisected by a later drain.

To the west again are fragmentary features. A scarp (5) may be the remains of an enclosure boundary later than 1733 while a mound to the east could be natural but might be a feature linked to the manorial group. To the north-west a ditch leading north from a pond (6) and a north-facing scarp to the south may be the remains of an enclosure of 1733.

Eccles in 1086 (Brown (ed) 1984, 10,21) was held by the Bishop of Thetford as four carucates (480 acres) with a valuation of 60 shillings and a recorded population of thirty-five. It remained an Episcopal manor until the time of Bishop Rugge (1536–50) who was compelled to exchange the Episcopal estates for the Abbey of St Benet at Holme. The property remained with the Crown until 1559 when it was granted to Sir Nicholas Bacon who conveyed it to his son Nathaniel, resident at Stiffkey (Blomefield 1739, I, 275).

It appears that Nathaniel tried to sell the manor of Eccles for the sum of £1700 at various times between 1573

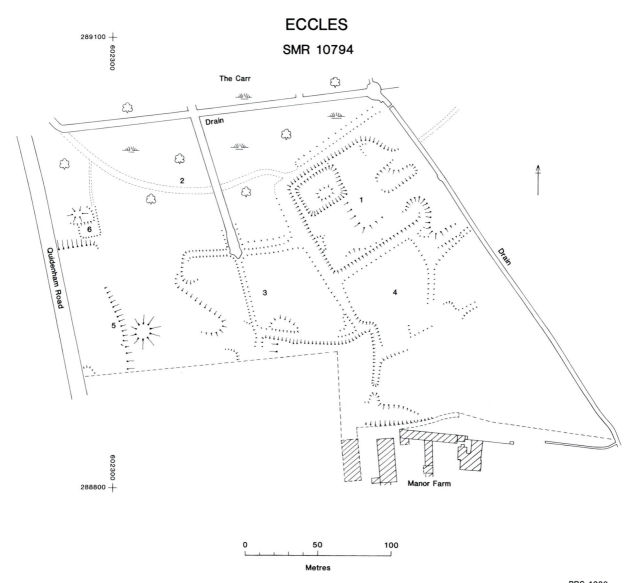

The Carr

Drain

Drain

2

1

6

Quidenham Road

3

4

5

Manor Farm

289100 +

602300

602300

288800 +

0   50   100

Metres

BRC 1999

Figure 64 Eccles, Quidenham, Bishop's manor. Scale 1:2,500

and 1577 (Smith, Baker and Kenny 1979, 98, 99, 197, 231, 260). It seems that Bacon leased the manor in 1586 to George Nunne Gent. (NRO MS 4527A 299 x 5) and that it was still in Bacon's hands some time after 1604 when he received a petition from the 'poore town' of Eccles, signed by twelve people, complaining that his farmers, John and Robert James, were ploughing the heath (NRO MC 571/15 778 x 4).

A map of 1733 (NRO MC 168/4) shows a main village with about forty buildings with the church and other buildings at Overy and on common edges, but no sign of the manor house. The position of the earthwork was named as Court Yard without internal details. Blomefield (1739, I, 274, 276) described the site as being 'now quite ruinated; the motes Foundations *etc.* may be seen in the Low Meadows about a furlong or more SE of the church'. His distance appears inaccurate. He also said that the village was 'much decreased for some time by the Lord's purchasing many of the cottages and small tenements'. This throws some doubt on the dating of the map of 1733. It seems likely that the manorial site gradually became derelict during the late 16th and 17th centuries.

Elsing SMR 3009, TG 040 160
(Fig.65)

A long-standing manorial site with a roadway and a pond which has experienced much later change.

Elsing is a village about 7km north-east of Dereham. Elsing Hall is close to the parish boundary over 1km south-west of the church.

The parkland earthworks lie in the area surrounding the medieval moated site. The hall itself can be dated to the period 1436–1577 but it was heavily restored in 1852 by Thomas Jekyll. Of earlier structures, some foundations of a flint and brick gatehouse (1) and the remains of flint bastions and a western curtain wall (2) still survive. The moat, the southern arm of which has been considerably altered, is fed by a leat from the main stream and the outflow feeds a large rectangular fishpond before rejoining the stream.

The most notable earthwork is to the south-west where a length of hollow way (3) leaves Hall Road in a westerly direction. To the north-east and east of the hall is a rather confusing series of slight linear depressions and banks

98

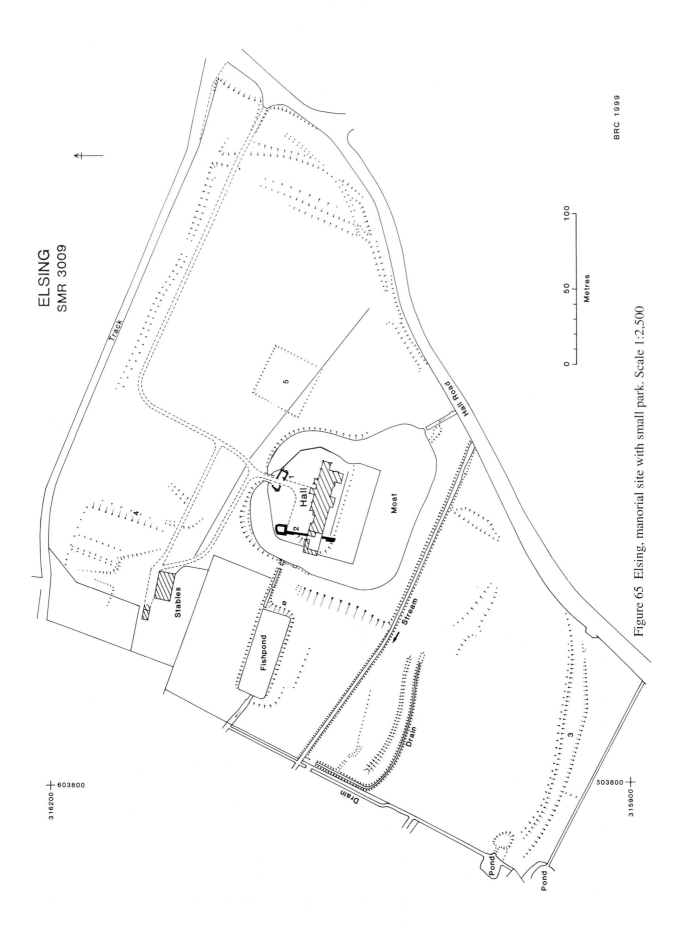

ELSING
SMR 3009

BRC 1999

Track

Hall Road

Hall

Moat

Stream

Stables

Fishpond

Drain

Drain

Pond

Pond

1

2

3

4

5

316200 + 603800

503800 +
315900

0   50   100
Metres

Figure 65 Elsing, manorial site with small park. Scale 1:2,500

99

which are not easily explicable unless they represent previous park boundaries and road alignments.

To the north-west of the Hall are what appears to be a short length of hollow way (4), more pronounced on its western side, and other features to the west including an L-shaped scarp and a low north-to-south bank. Immediately north-east of the moat is a levelled square (5) which may mark a former tennis court (Wade-Martins (ed) 1987, 71).

Elsing has always been held as one manor since before 1066; in 1086 a church was recorded (Brown (ed) 1984, 8,6.). After then it passed through various female heirs until the 14th century, when one of them married Sir Hugh de Hastings who built a new church and who was granted a market and two fairs (Blomefield 1775, IV, 372; Dymond 1993, 77). In the 16th century a Hastings heiress married William Brown whose family retained the lordship until the early 18th century. In 1664 Thomas Brown Esquire was charged for twenty hearths (Frankel and Brown 1983, 21). It is obvious that this site was the home of successive generations and families.

A park appears to have been in existence by 1797 when Faden shows it bounded on the south-west by a track now represented by the hollow way. The Enclosure Map of 1849 (NRO C/Sca 2/106) shows this track as 'footpath stopped up'. This map shows the moat and the fishpond with the house approached by a less direct track which went further north-west before bending back to cross the moat. This appears to explain the traces of the hollow way there. Various buildings called the 'Stackyard' and 'Barn and yards' on the Tithe Map of 1842 (NRO DN/TA 653) lay to the west of this trackway; these probably explain the L-shaped scarp and the north-to-south bank.

Both maps show Hall Road screened by plantations which extend to the stream and the southern margin of the moat, thus obscuring the features mapped there. The Tithe Map refers to the fishpond as the 'Garden Moat'; the meadow to the south of it was called 'Dovehouse Meadow' doubtless recording the site of a vanished manorial perquisite.

Fulmodeston SMR 1068, TF 989 299
(Pl. XXIII, Fig.66)

The site of the medieval manor of Fulmodeston faces south onto a former common and is somewhat distant from the original village.

Fulmodeston is a scattered village 7km east of Fakenham. The parish includes Croxton, a small settlement with a ruined chapel, and, to the south-west, the probable site of Clipston, a Domesday vill. The earthworks lie south of Manor Farm at the extreme southern edge of the parish on the boundary with Stibbard.

They consist of a moated enclosure (1), almost rectangular, with a modern water-course incised within its southern arm, and a slight entrance causeway on its northern one. Its eastern arm has been disturbed by nearby ploughing and has a shallow depression (2) leading into it from the east. A hollow way (3) approaches the moat from the north-east and is joined by a narrow linear depression (4) from the north-west which is part-banked, indicating a probable enclosure boundary. To the south of this and west of the moat are what appear to be enclosures crossed by a ditch which seems later. Immediately to the west of the moat are some vague features of uncertain origin.

It is clear from field evidence, bricks, tiles and medieval pottery, that the moated platform is of medieval origin. Aerial photographs of 1946 show that the remaining features are part of a complex extending eastwards into arable land where cropmarks are now visible.

Fulmodeston was entered in the Domesday Book as one holding. The manor which was held by the Grancourts in early medieval times, was taken by the Crown in the 15th century and remained with it until James I granted it to Edward Coke. It has remained in Coke hands ever since (Blomefield 1769, III, 784–5).

The Enclosure Map of 1810 (NRO C/Sca2/125) shows the area, including the most westerly field named Brick

Plate XXIII Fulmodeston, 1946 RAF vertical of the manorial site. TG 93/TF9930/A 39/TUD/UK50

FULMODESTON

SMR 1068

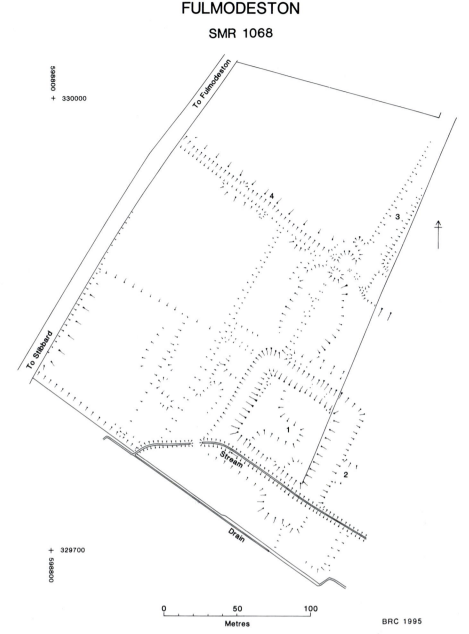

Figure 66 Fulmodeston, manorial site with roadway. Scale 1:2,500

Kiln Close. The land belonged to Thomas William Coke (NRO Hayes and Storr 67). A brick kiln and associated extraction of clay may explain some features west of the moat. Two other maps, the Tithe Map of 1837 (NRO DN/TA 5) and another of 1844 (NRO Hayes and Storr 69) show an L-shaped pool of water in Church Close to the north of the church which is 300m north-north-east of the moat but show nothing of the earthworks. Both reveal the owner of the earthworks area as the (Coke) Earl of Leicester.

Although it is possible that the pool in Church Close may be a remnant of an early moat, the bulk of the map evidence points to this site as being that of the medieval manor of Fulmodeston. Its position as shown by Faden (1797) and the Enclosure Map of Stibbard (NRO C/Sca 2/125) was a little unusual facing south onto the common of Stibbard Green but the Manor House (Bryant 1826), now Manor Farm, supports the identification.

Plate XXIV Gayton, West Manor site with the edge of the former common and remains of ridge and furrow.
TF 7119/C/AFY 9

Gayton SMR 3748, TF 719 195
(Pl. XXIV, Fig.67)

The site of West Manor faces south onto a former common with enclosures and traces of ridge and furrow.

Gayton is a village about 10km east of King's Lynn. The earthworks, a scheduled site, are at the western end of the village in three fields north of the B1145. They consist of a number of ditched enclosures, most prominent in the central field. A possible hollow way (1) leads northwards to a complicated group of earthworks including apparent building platforms (2). The earthworks are bounded to the south by a sinuous ditch (3) denoting the edge of common land enclosed in 1813 (NRO C/Sca 2/129). Slight remnants of ridge and furrow lie to the north (4); this juxtaposition of settlement earthworks and ridge and furrow is rare in Norfolk (Cushion 1996, 40; Wade-Martins (ed) 1999, 60).

Gayton has a confused manorial history in 1086 (Brown (ed) 1984, 8,23–24. 18,1. 19,7. 23,13. 66,23) and this continued into medieval times (Feudal Aids III, 522–23, 450, 581). Blomefield (1775, IV, 538–44) believed that the de Gaytons who held East Hall were descended from one of the Domesday sub-tenants; this

manor may have been near the present hall at the east end of the village.

In the 16th century Thomas Thursby, lord of Gayton manor, was accused of enclosing wastes and commons in Gayton and elsewhere. It is clear from a damaged map of 1726 and a corresponding field book (NRO Bradfer-Lawrence 41/4; BIR/190) that much enclosure had taken place within Gayton, much of it dating back to at least 1671. The map shows the area of the earthworks partly within fields called Bushey Close and West Hall Close; the field book calls the first West Hall Bushey Close and mentions other West Hall Closes of three, four and five acres no longer visible on the damaged map.

A series of Court Books for Gayton West Hall alias Gaytons beginning in 1629 (NRO MF/X/129/8) shows that in the period of the map and field book the manor was held by the Raven family; Blomefield records that in 1730 West Hall was held by Mr Raven, an attorney of Burnham, suggesting the lord was no longer resident. The Court Book shows the Rolfe family acting as bailiffs. The boundary ditch seems to correspond closely with features shown in 1726 and 1797 (Faden). It seems therefore that this is the former manorial site of West Hall facing south onto a common, with open fields to the north.

GAYTON
SMR 3748

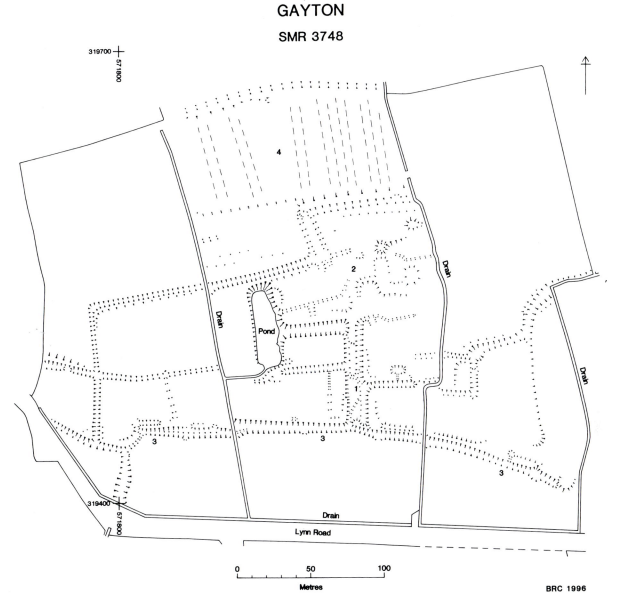

Figure 67 Gayton, common-edge manorial site with ridge and furrow. Scale 1:2,500

Great Cressingham SMR 4687, 4688, 31848; TF 852 020
(Fig.68)

Extensive features within the village include a double-moated manorial site, hollow ways, fishponds and the remains of a further manorial site.

Great Cressingham lies 7km west of Watton. This large complex of earthworks is situated on the south-eastern side of the River Wissey, between the flood plain and the present village street.

There is a moated site, SMR 4687, consisting of two enclosures, the northern rectangle being possibly an earlier site with a hollow way (1) leading to it from the east. The smaller incomplete moat houses the current manor house and is thought not to have had a southern arm. The small linear feature shown on the plan is a more modern ha-ha. A hollow way (2) approaches the southern front of the manor from the south-east and appears to have served not only this but also another probable manorial site, now

partly obliterated by the sewage works, as well as continuing towards a building outline (3) abutting the flood plain. Separate fishponds (4,5) can be seen related to both manors, with a building platform (6) extending into the wood north of the sewage works as the likely other manor house site.

In the east of the surveyed area, the line of a former street is visible as a hollow way (7) just inside the grassland, with enclosures to the west of it. The northern boundary of the site is a double feature (8), including the present field boundary, which was an access trackway to the valley-floor meadows.

Medieval pottery had been found over much of the area to the east and immediately south of the moats, with a limited concentration around the probable second manorial site (6).

To the south of the sewage works are two more possible fishponds (9,10) linked to a ditch on the flood plain edge, a group of low level sub-rectangular enclosures (11) and some fragments of enclosure boundaries (12) which could well be, in part, the rear limits of tofts facing the main street.

GUNTHORPE
SMR 3195

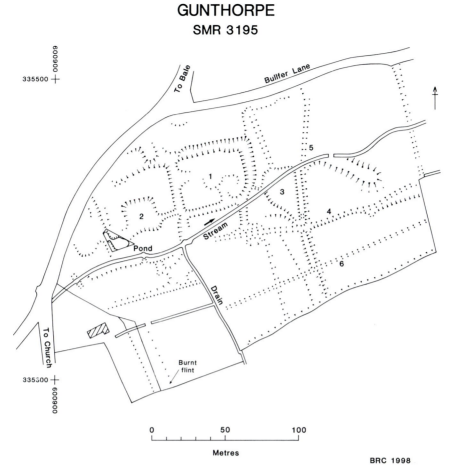

Figure 69 Gunthorpe, probable manorial site with fishponds. Scale 1:2,500

By the 13th century there were five manorial holdings in Great Cressingham. They were the Priory Manor (formerly the Bishop's), Hockham's, Rysleys, Strehall and Glosbridge. Strehall manor lay further south near Water End while Glosbridge lay well to the west (Davison 1994, 73). The identities of the moated sites and associated earthworks are somewhat problematic. 'Hockham's' and 'Rysleys' manors had been united at the end of the 15th century. Hockhams survives on the Tithe Map as a field name to the north-east of the existing moated site. The identity of the latter is likely to lie, therefore, between Rysleys and Priory manors.

A map of 1801 (NRO C/CA 1/14) showed the Dean and Chapter holding north of the road as extending from an old roadway (2) to the south-west boundary of the modern sewage works. In 1801 the moated site was owned by the Chutes of South Pickenham. Some confusion may have begun when the Jenney family leased the Priory manor in 1524. The house on the moat bears the initials of John Jenney and Elizabeth Spring, his wife; from this house they controlled most of Cressingham when John inherited the other four manors from his grandmother. It may thus be the inherited Rysley manor house in which John and his successors lived.

This seems to be confirmed by the statement, in 1647, (NRO PD 131/83) 'The church has the site of the manor called ye Priory with barns built theron lying between ye tenement of Edmund Wolwerd, Christopher Jeny Gent and John Wace.......on the south or southeage the common

called Millmore (but anciently called Deerbought) in pt and an orchd or pitle'. From the same source it is clear that Hall or Priory meadow had the street to the east, the site of Priory manor and Saffron or Barley Close to the west, Deerbought Common in part on the north and a common near the Townbridge to the south. It seems from this that Priory Manor lay to the south of Jenney's house and that its site seems partly obliterated by the sewage farm. It would have been logical for the Jenneys to live on a site they inherited rather than on leased land.

Gunthorpe SMR 3195, TG 010 354
(Fig.69)

A manorial site with fishponds lies in a deserted part of the village which has apparently shifted well to the south.

Gunthorpe is a village about 7.5km south-west of Holt. The present village is linear in form on the southern side of a subsidiary valley of the River Glaven, with the church isolated on an interfluve to the north. The earthworks are in another side valley about 200m north-west of the church.

The major feature of the earthworks is a moated enclosure (1) with an irregular interior. Linked to it are at least two fishponds (2,3) and all are linked in turn to a former watercourse (4) which has been replaced by the present stream which cuts the most easterly pond (3). This pond has a well-defined eastern bank which is prominent

105

enough to appear to be a dam across the lowest part of the valley, continuing upslope to the south. Further fragments of possible ponds are located north, west and south of pond (2). A shallow curving ditch (5) may form part of an outer enclosure for the moat. A straight ditch (6) in the south-eastern portion of the site appears to be a later feature cutting two slight earlier subdivisions.

From 1086 onwards to the late 17th century Gunthorpe seems to have been a comparatively stable community with no undue calamities befalling it (Brown (ed) 1984, 1,28,30; 34,13; Hudson 1895, 280; Whiteman 1986, 226; Frankel and Seaman 1983, 46). In the late 15th century, for example, the manor of Binham Priory had between twenty-one and thirty tenants (NRO MC 619/1 782 x 6).

In medieval times the King's holding became Avenels manor; after the Dissolution the Priory manor passed into the hands of the Church Commissioners.

Court Books (NRO MS 19724 Z 1 J) and Court Rolls (NRO CHC 101423a-c) exist but appear to give no clue as to the identity of the earthworks. From the description it would seem that they are manorial but which manor is uncertain. Their position relatively close to the isolated church is suggestive, particularly as the present village is located very near the parish boundary in a salient, and the moat may have been the site of Avenels.

The Enclosure Map of 1831 (NRO C/Sca 2/137) and the Tithe Map (NRO DN/TA 92) of 1840 give little information. The area was already enclosed by 1831 and was known as Bulfer Meadow with Jarvis Meadow to the south-west and Long Meadow and part of the common to the west. Gunthorpe appears, superficially, to be an example of a village which has moved from an earlier site but there is no firm documentary evidence and, as yet, no archaeological evidence to support this.

Hales Hall, Loddon SMR 1053, TM 369 960
(Fig.70)

An unusual moated manorial site which lies on the edge of Hales Green. The domestic buildings and barn survive with possible gardens to the west, associated enclosures and a hollow way.

Hales Hall, despite its name, is in Loddon parish and about 2.75km south-south-east of the town. It is located at the south-western corner of Hales Green, about one-third of which is in Loddon parish.

The surviving portion of Hales Hall consists of a restored northern courtyard range (1), including a gateway, formerly part of a mansion which had disappeared by the 19th century. On the southern side of the courtyard, and linked to it by a contemporary wall pierced by a gateway, is the magnificent brick barn. The Hall itself lay on the western side of the yard within a moat of which the northern arm, centrally infilled, and much of the eastern remain. The western arm is infilled although a west-facing scarp (2) may be the edge of an outer bank. The position of the southern arm is not readily interpreted, but a slight north-facing scarp (4) may be a remnant of the outer edge. Foundations of walls (3) are visible on the platform together with the remains of two octagonal corner towers.

The moated platform is divided north-to-south by a central scarp (5) suggesting a garden terrace; the lower section is woodland. The wood is surrounded by a narrow

ditch while a broader ditch extends westwards from the north-western corner of the moat. Slight earthworks in the western part of the wood surveyed in 1982 are not convincing although further linear features were noticeable on 1946 aerial photographs to the west and north, before subsequent ploughing.

To the south-east of the barn are other earthworks. An east-to-west hollow way (6) crosses the area and there is one ditched enclosure to the north of it. To the south are vestiges of two more ditched enclosures, one ditch containing a pond; the surfaces of these are irregular and there are signs of possible later disturbance over the whole area. To the north of the entrance to the Hall is another ditched enclosure (7) facing the Green while the remains of an outer moat lie just to the east of the courtyard range. To the north-east of the complex are two ditched enclosures (8) on what was medieval common, one abutting a pond and reportedly the site of a cottage, although this is not confirmed by any early map (Wade-Martins (ed) 1987, 62).

The existing remnant of Hales Hall is that of a late medieval building, by Sir James Hobart, on an earlier medieval site named from the de Hales family. Roger de Hales and his father Walter, acquired much land in the Hundreds of Loddon and Clavering in the late 12th century and, it seems, built a house on the site of the present Hall. Nearby was a deer park, the outline of part of which is still clearly visible on maps. There are also references to a chapel of St Andrew close by the park. Fieldwalking has shown that by the 13th century both sides of Hales Green were quite densely populated.

Much of Loddon passed into the hands of the Mowbray Dukes of Norfolk and when the last Duke of that family died in 1476, the title passed to Sir John Howard. James Hobart, as steward to both, was in a good position to acquire Hales Hall in 1478 and began rebuilding soon after. In the 1640s the Hobarts sold the manor and the house separately; the house was probably demolished in the 18th century.

The site of the Hall appears to include fragments of a formal garden to the west. The area south and south-east of the barn is problematic and may be related to the earlier Hall. There are no obvious signs of buildings and only one sherd of medieval pottery has been recorded there (Davison with Fenner 1990).

Harling Thorpe SMR 6087, TL 946 841
(Fig.71)

An obliterated manorial site with a hollow way and earthworks of former tofts to the east, and possible signs of water management to the west.

West Harling is a deserted medieval village now within the civil parish of Harling. In addition to the core settlement near All Saints' church, West Harling included the important Middle Saxon site of Middle Harling absorbed in the early 16th century (Rogerson 1995), as well as a number of detached street settlements of which Thorpe was one.

The earthworks lie in two meadows on either side of Thorpe Farm; the eastern one is virtually divided in two by Thorpe Cottages and gardens. In this eastern area a hollow way (1) runs roughly from west to east and is interrupted by the cottages. The easternmost section has four probable toft sites facing south onto the way and backing onto the

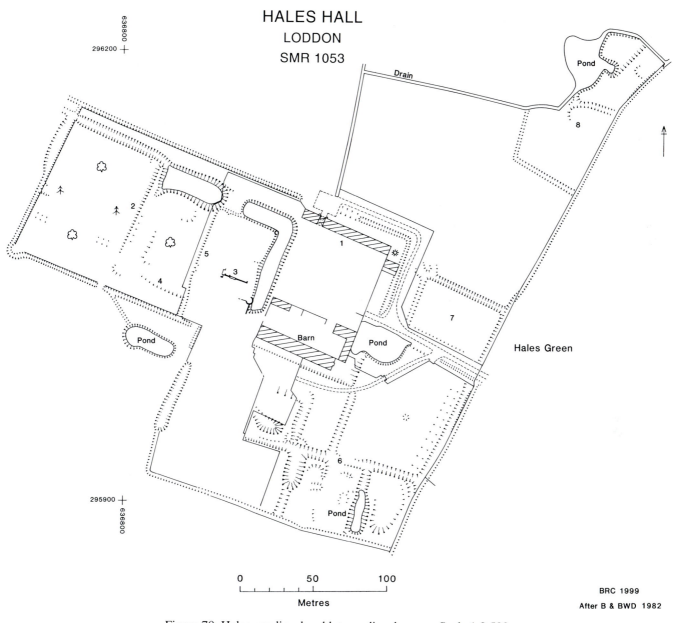

HALES HALL
LODDON
SMR 1053

Drain

Pond

8

296200 +

636800

2

5

3

4

Pond

1

Barn

Pond

7

Hales Green

6

Pond

295900 +

636800

Pond

0   50   100

Metres

BRC 1999

After B & BWD 1982

Figure 70 Hales, medieval and late medieval manor. Scale 1:2,500

flood plain of the Thet. To the west of the cottages the way appears to have been joined by another (2) from the south. A broad depression or drove (3) leads onto the flood plain. West of the farmhouse the major features are a parallel series of ridges and depressions (4) of which the easternmost is linked to the flood plain. As they are straight and on very low ground they are probably the remains of some system of water management. A small length of masonry (m), often stated to be remains of a church, is on a site more appropriate for a watermill, and a millstone has been reported found nearby.

This part of Harling was listed as one of the five 'Herlinga' entries in Domesday with a recorded population of eight, a carucate of arable land and some meadow land. In the 14th century it was held by the Hakefords and later in that century by the Secfords. Subsequently the manor was known as Hackfords or Seckfords and was added by purchase to the others in West Harling in 1564. There are documentary references to a watermill in Harling Thorpe in the 15th century. A description in 1495 of a messuage in

Thorpe shows it as lying between Thorpe Fen to the north and field land to the south and there are references to the 'street called Thorpe' from the late 15th century up to 1709, including some to messuages and hemplands. By that time, according to Blomefield (1739, I, 202), the manor house had been long gone, it probably stood near Thorpe Farm.

By 1737 a new lord, Richard Gipps, whose memorial bust is in the chancel of All Saints', had reduced the number of dwellings in West Harling through systematic purchase and so, by then, the street of Thorpe had virtually disappeared to be replaced by one of the three farms of the West Harling estate.

A quantity of medieval pottery has been found on the site together with some post-medieval pieces. It is clear that this site, certainly in existence in 1066, must be seen as a hamlet or manorial cluster and not as a village. It is of a linear form developed in Breckland valleys as population expanded in early medieval times (Davison 1980, 295–306; 1983, 329–336; Cushion and Davison 1991, 207–211).

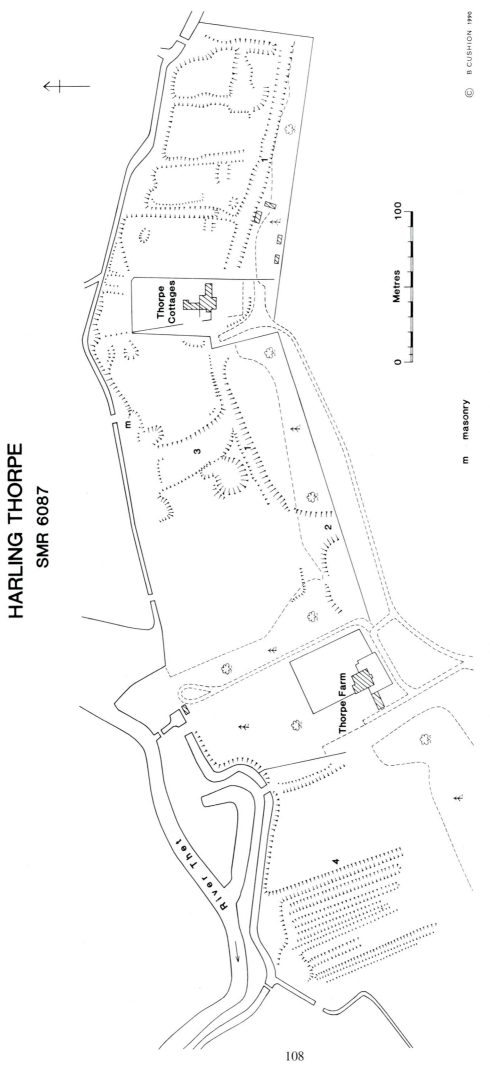

HARLING THORPE

SMR 6087

Thorpe Cottages

Thorpe Farm

River Thet

m   masonry

0   Metres   100

Figure 71 Harling Thorpe, isolated street of deserted medieval village. Scale 1:2,500

© B CUSHION 1990

108

HILGAY
SMR 4454

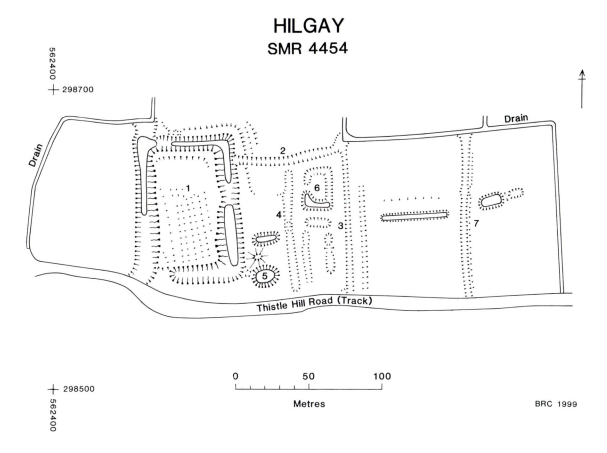

562400

+ 298700

Drain

Drain

2

1

6

4

3

7

5

Thistle Hill Road (Track)

+ 298500

562400

0   50   100

Metres

BRC 1999

Figure 72 Hilgay, complex manorial site. Scale 1:2,500

Hilgay SMR 4454, TL 626 986
(Fig.72)

Earthworks of a probable moated site of the manor of the Abbey of Ramsey lie together with associated enclosures, possible fishponds and a small ditched feature.

On the northern margin of this former Fenland island 5.5km south of Downham Market is this complex group of earthworks. The main feature is a large rectangular moated enclosure (1), with the moat partly water-filled and an outlet leat from the north-western corner. The present entrance at the western end of the southern arm is not a convincing original position, but there is a shallowing of the moat central to the eastern arm which may be the original way in. There is some indication of embanking on the northern side of the platform and externally to the north and north-east. On the southern portion of the platform some slight linear ridges may well represent a period of cultivation. One sherd of medieval pottery and a few brick fragments have been noted from the platform.

Extending eastwards from the north-east corner of the moat is a gently-curving ditch (2) which links with a junction of existing drains and a straight north-to-south ditch (3). These features delineate the westernmost of three contiguous enclosures bounded to the south by the track. This enclosure is at a slightly higher level than those to the east and may once have been divided centrally by a north-to-south depression (4). The western portion contains two ponds, the southernmost (5) linked to the south-east corner of the moat. The eastern portion has a small rectangular moated enclosure (6), with a western entrance. This may have held a building, possibly a dovecote.

To the south are three depressions, the northernmost being the best-defined, which were possibly fishponds. The two enclosures to the east are separated by a gently curving north-to-south ditch (7). To the west, a slight ditch parallel to and east of (3) suggests a flanking ditch of a possible trackway, while a narrow east-to-west pond is central. The easternmost enclosure has two ponds, possibly linked originally, at a different orientation to other features, possibly also fishponds (Wade-Martins (ed) 1999, 57).

Domesday Book shows that a number of landowners held land in Hilgay (Brown (ed) 1984, 1,210. 8,17. 9,230. 14,3. 15,2. 16,1. 66,7.). Of them all only one could be considered really important, Ramsey Abbey which held two carucates (240 acres) of arable. In 1316 the landowners were said to be the Abbot of Ramsey, the Abbot of St Edmundsbury and Earl Warenne (Blake 1952, 266). The St Edmundsbury lands, 58 acres, were assessed in Southery in 1086 suggesting that this holding lay predominantly in the south of the parish near Southery. It seems likely that Ramsey Abbey held the lion's share of the island. Furthermore it held a carucate at Snore in Fordham on the opposite bank of the Wissey to the earthworks (Brown (ed) 1984, 16,2.) now the site of Snore Hall.

It is likely, therefore, that the earthworks may be the site of the Ramsey manor though ultimate proof is lacking. A 15th-century register of the Abbey (NRO Hare 2 232 x) makes scant reference to Hilgay although it is well attested in the Middle Ages (Silvester 1991, 46).

HORNINGTOFT

SMR 7168

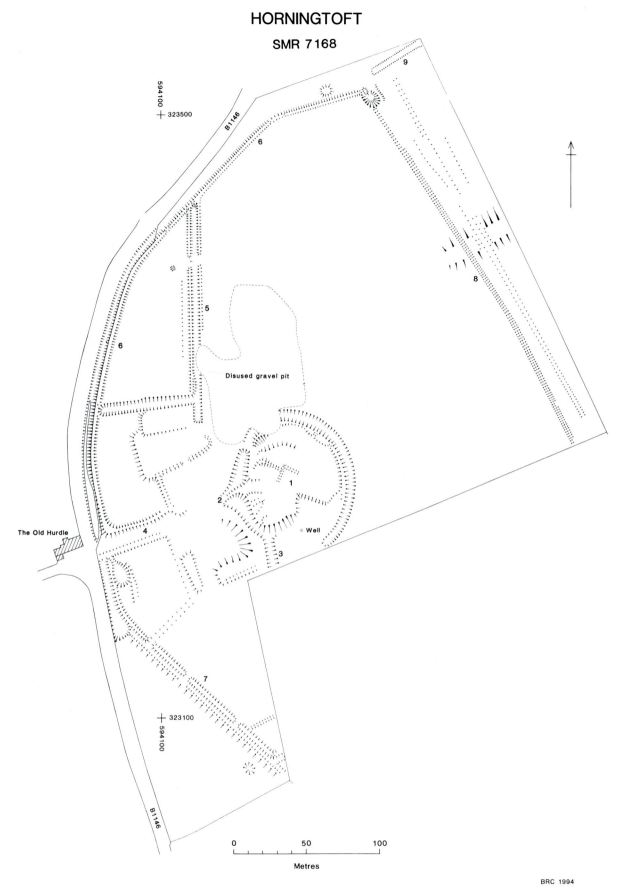

Figure 73 Horningtoft, major manorial site. Scale 1:2,500

Plate XXV Horningtoft, oval moated site with entrance and flanking enclosures within the remnant of an enclosing bank and ditch. 9423/E/AQP 18

Horningtoft SMR 7168, TF 942 233
(Pl. XXV, Fig.73)

An impressive oval moated site has a grand entrance with side enclosures and outer yards, all partially enclosed by remains of a bank and ditch.

Horningtoft is a small village about 7km south-south-west of Fakenham. The earthworks lie to the east of the village and consist of an incomplete oval moated enclosure (1) with its eastern limit defined by a ditch 6m to 8m in width with a partially spread internal bank. The western entrance causeway (2) spans a deeper section of the moat. Gravel extraction has destroyed the moat to the north while the southern part is indeterminate; a channel (3) leading south from the moat may indicate some form of extension. Within the moated enclosure are straight grassy banks, possibly walls, while a lower area contains a well.

An impressive approach to the moated site was along an entrance roadway (4) flanked by yards of varying forms. There are also two pits which may be contemporary with the manorial site, although they have been used as over-flows for surface water from the road.

To the north is a substantial ditch (5) between banks, partly destroyed by gravel working and joined by another from the west. A boundary bank has an external ditch, infilled to the north, but deepened as a roadside ditch. The southern part of this feature (7), aligned north-west to south-east, follows the course of a Roman road from Billingford to Toftrees (Wade-Martins 1977, 1–3) the bank possibly being part of the agger.

The most easterly well-defined earthwork is a narrow ditch (8) which does join the boundary bank at a pit while slight linear features to the east may include a trackway. In the extreme north-east is a length of boundary bank (9) on a different alignment to that further west.

Horningtoft, in 1086, was held by Godric as custodian for the King and was linked with Kipton (Chiptuna), being valued, taxed and measured with it (Brown (ed) 1984, 1,77). As Kipton is generally held to be in Weasenham (Allison 1955, 151) some distance to the west this introduces an early complication. The holding passed to the Earl of Richmond and by 1290 was held by Nicholas de Castello as half a knight's fee from Robert de Tateshale (Blomefield 1775, V, 1021). From then on the de Castello family held Horningtoft throughout the 14th century until at least 1428 (Feudal Aids III, 416, 455, 540, 595). In 1462 a certain Humphrey Castell was lord, presumably an anglicisation of the name, and the family appears to have persisted into the 16th and 17th centuries (Blomefield 1775, V, 1021–22).

It seems most likely that the earthwork was the medieval seat of this long-resident family with the area within the oval moat perhaps modified for later use. The bank (6) suggests that it may be the remains of a medieval woodland boundary, or possibly a deer park (Rackham 1986, 99); the latter might fit the picture of a high grade manorial site. Faden's map (1797) shows the bank as a woodland boundary.

The Enclosure Map of 1816 (NRO C/Sca 2/325) does not show any earthworks, the whole area being part of 'The Great Wood' while the Tithe Map of 1839 (NRO DN/TA 422) shows the woodland reduced in size but covering the site and with a track continuing east from the present road, presumably across the causeway, to join a north-to-south track to the east beyond the earthworks. This last track may be associated with the narrow ditch which follows the same apparent course. The wood probably contributed to the survival of the site after the later Middle Ages.

111

INGWORTH
SMR 7403

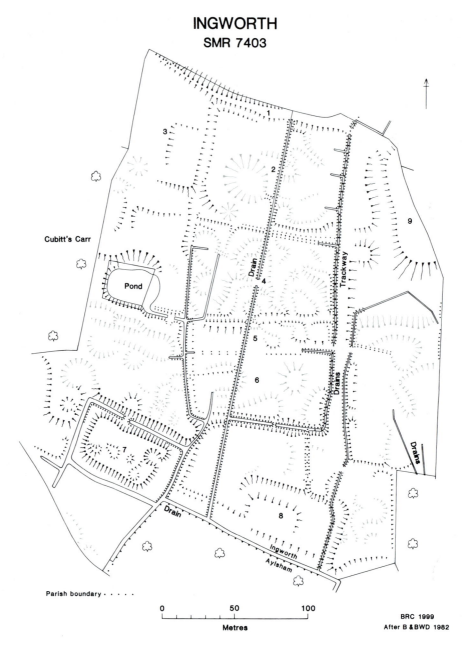

Cubitt's Carr

Pond

Drain

Trackway

Drain

Drains

Drains

Drain

Ingworth
Aylsham

Parish boundary · · · · ·

0   50   100

Metres

BRC 1999
After B & BWD 1982

Figure 74 Ingworth, manorial site. The features in grey appear to be natural or quarry features. Scale 1:2,500

Ingworth SMR 7403, TG 199 290
(Pl. XXVI, Fig.74)

A very complicated site which has suffered from quarrying and which contains at least one partially moated platform and several degraded enclosures.

Ingworth is a small village in the Bure valley about 2.5km north of Aylsham. The earthworks lie in Hall Meadow in the extreme south-eastern corner of the parish and actually extend across the boundary into Aylsham.

The earthworks are very confusing. There are features which are undoubtedly medieval and others which are fairly obviously later, together with still more which appear natural. The plan attempts to distinguish between those of presumed archaeological interest and those with more irregular patterns which appear to be natural or quarry features — these being depicted in grey.

The northernmost feature is a ridge with a distinct north-facing scarp (1), used partly as a field trackway. To the south of it are a number of sub-rectangular enclosures of varying definition. The first of these (2) is separated from (3) by a linear depression which may have been a wide drain or, perhaps, a hollow way leading south towards a part-moated platform (7). The remaining enclosures (4,5,6) are bounded by drains, two of them (4,6) have vague internal features. To the west of them is a large pond.

The platform (7) has two moated boundaries, the northern one and part of the western arm. The southern edge overlooks the flood plain and the eastern one is a broad flat depression. There are no convincing features which might be construed as former buildings on the platform. Another platform (8) is within Ingworth but is less defined though some function asssociated with the manorial site is likely. It is fed by a degraded possible leat from the south-east corner of (6).

112

Plate XXVI Ingworth, a manorial site with other confusing features. CUCAP AQK 21
(Photography by Cambridge University Collection of Air Photographs)

Within Aylsham is a north-to-south trackway and to the east again is part of an enclosure (9) or a natural feature. Over much of the field a system of drains has been imposed on the features and various pits appear to have been dug.

In 1086 Ingworth was in two parts, the most important of which was held by Reynald FitzIvo (Brown (ed) 1984, 21,33). This afterwards came to the Crown and was, in the reign of Edward I, passed to the de Ingworth family. By 1316 it had been split in two halves, one to Henry de Coleby and one to Peter de Brampton (Blake 1952, 274). Subsequently, in 1342, the two portions were reunited. In 1365 the manor was sold to George Felbrigg and so passed to the Windham family (Blomefield 1769, III, 612–13).

There is a description of the manorial site dated 1444 quoted by Mason (1872–3, II, Aylsham parish) '....and the sayd Ryver extend itself further unto the Manner of Sir John of Colby Knight.....and there begyn a certain olde Dyke and extend unto one Mote in the said Manner, and from that Dyke goeth straight forth beyond the said Mote....unto a poste where ye gates of ye said Alice were sett, and there be a certain common way which ledeth unto Erpingham Sygate'.

The Enclosure Map (NRO C/Sca 2/109) of 1812 calls the area Hall Meadow as does the Tithe Map of 1839 (NRO DN/TA 193), both maps show it as property of the Windhams. There is no record in either of common land to the north, though Faden (1797) does suggest it. In 1812 Hall Meadow was approached from the north-west by a private road called 'Clarks Green Lane'. This might account for the northern trackway (1); alternatively this may have been a common boundary.

LITTLE APPLETON
SMR 3501

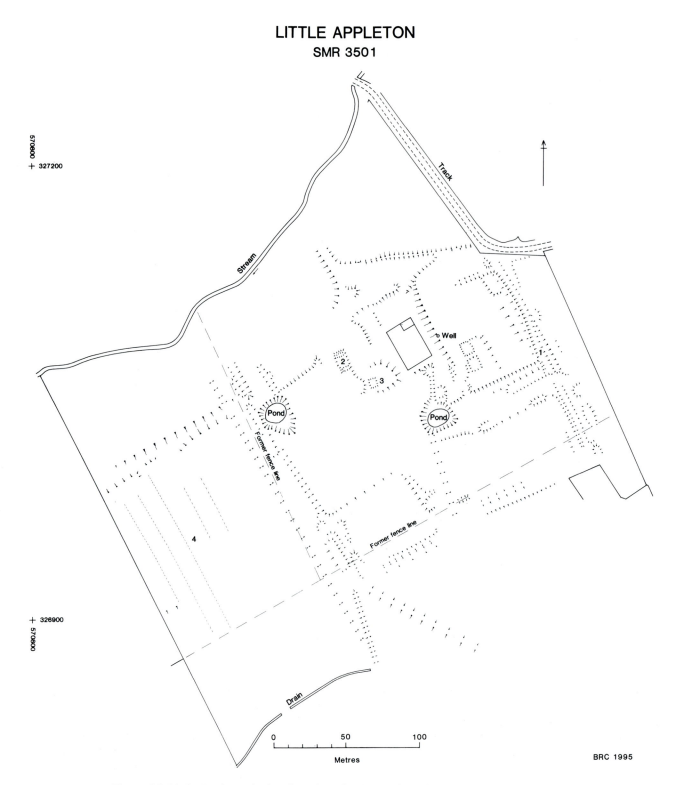

Figure 75 Little Appleton, isolated portion of a deserted medieval settlement. Scale 1:2,500

Little Appleton, Flitcham SMR 3501, TF 710 270 (Fig.75)

An interesting site within Appleton; the earthworks appear to be related to comparatively recent buildings but are almost certainly superimposed on medieval activity.

Little Appleton lies about 500m east-south-east of the ruined Appleton church; Appleton is a deserted medieval village now united with Flitcham about 13km north-east of King's Lynn. Little Appleton is on a low spur with a stream to the north and consists of a hollow way (1) with truncated banks and ditches representing former enclosures. At least two raised platforms (2,3) are probably sites of buildings. A series of faint and incomplete linear depressions and ridges in the south-western part of the site may be remnants of ridge and furrow (4). Limited surface finds suggest medieval activity on this site although most earthworks west of (1) appear post-medieval.

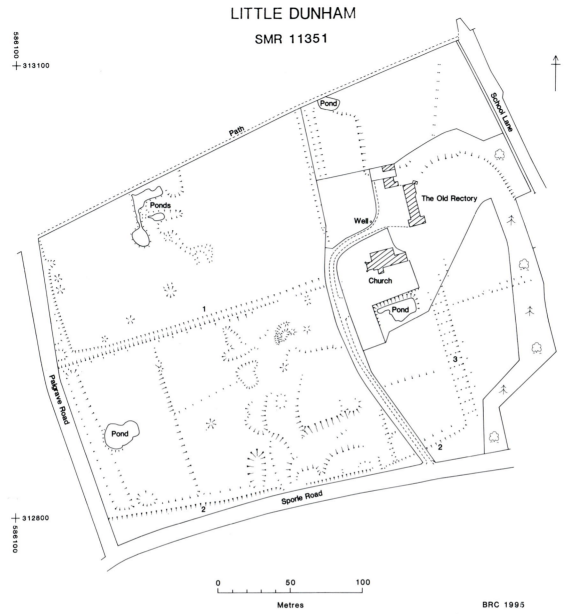

Figure 76 Little Dunham, remnants of a manorial site with enclosures. Scale 1:2,500

The identities of some of the building platforms are suggested by Faden (1797) and the Ordnance Survey 1st Edition map (*c*.1824 with later additions) which show buildings. The 1st Edition names the cluster 'Little Appleton'. An undated book of farm plans (NRO Hayes and Storr 9/6/1987 135) shows Little Appleton Farm. Some of the features shown seem to accord with the earthworks on the plan. Land to the west of the farm is shown as belonging to Edward Paston and this suggests an 18th- or early 19th-century date for the book. A map of 1617 but based on a survey of 1595 (NRO BRA 2524/6) shows a house with three other buildings arranged around a courtyard in this position.

In 1086 two distinct holdings were recorded in Appleton, one, the larger, was held by Roger Bigot, the other by Peter de Valognes. According to Blomefield (1775, IV, 464–7) the larger eventually came to the Pastons who built a hall *c*. 1596. The other was divided, part going to Flitcham Priory. By the 17th century Appleton had declined to a mere handful of people (Whiteman 1986, 228)

and the church had 'greatly decayed' (Allison 1957, 142). Blomefield recorded four or five houses and a ruined church. It seems likely that the two farms recorded by White in 1845 (White 1845, 585) probably broadly represent the two Domesday holdings and that Little Appleton, being one of them and closer to Flitcham, may have occupied part of the Valognes holding.

Little Dunham SMR 11351, TF 863 129
(Fig.76)

The earthworks were encircled by common land in the 18th century and were later partially emparked. A manor house probably stood to the west of the church.

Little Dunham is a small village about 5.75km north-east of Swaffham. The earthworks lie in a pasture immediately west and south-west of the church with other features in pasture surrounding the church and the Old Rectory.

LYNG

SMR 12303

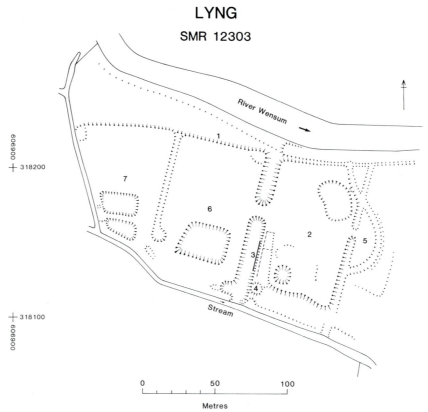

Figure 77 Lyng, manorial site with fishponds. Scale 1:2,500   BRC 2000

The area west and south-west of the church is subdivided by a well-defined linear depression (1) flanked by a bank to the south which leads towards the west front of the church suggesting a possible pathway. At its western end the northern bank suggests a former roadside boundary. To the south a wide shallow depression lies parallel to the present roadside bank and ditch; the partially embanked pond cuts into this showing them to be of different periods.

The southern boundary of the field has a well-defined scarp (2) roughly parallel to the Sporle Road; this may be a pre-enclosure roadside boundary. In the southern half of this field the most prominent features are irregular depressions and scarps in the eastern portion. There is no obvious pattern and there appears to have been some recent infilling from the evidence of a 1946 aerial photograph. Some pits may have been dug for clay.

South of the church the southern boundary bank crosses the present drive to link with a ditched causeway (3) leading towards the Old Rectory; there is a small rectangular enclosure to the west of this. To the north of the house are relics of former garden features.

Faden (1797) shows Little Dunham church and its immediate surroundings completely encircled by common land; this must be the Dunham Moore or Common mentioned in 17th-century Court Rolls (NRO CHC 101423). The earthworks were part of the encircled area. Bryant (1826) shows that the common had been enclosed; this took place in 1796 (Carthew 1877–9, 89,98). Bryant shows a small park around the Old Rectory and a much larger one further to the east at Dunham Lodge. According to Carthew (1877–9, 89) the Lodge was built in 1784–5 by a Mr Parry 'on a highly elevated plot'. The Tithe Map of

1838 (NRO DN/TA 64) names the area to the west and south-west of the church as 'part of Manor Close' but does not show the causeway leading to the Old Rectory.

A plan (NRO Road Order Nox 18, No 1) dated 1849 shows that the railway necessitated a re-routing of a footpath now forming the northern boundary of the area on the earthwork plan.

Medieval records show that the manor in those days was held by the families of de Ryvers and de Dunham (Feudal Aids III, 416, 454, 539, 595); it can be assumed that a manor house then stood near the church and that Manor Close may have been its site. Medieval pottery from the edges of two of the pits further enhances this interpretation.

Lyng SMR 12303, TG 071 181
(Fig.77)

One of the best-documented earthworks, this is the site of Lyng manor, with two further enclosures, one with fishponds, to the west.

Lyng is a village in the Wensum valley about 9km north-east of East Dereham. The site lies about 300m north-north-east of the church abutting the flood plain of the river.

The earthworks consist of three enclosures bounded on the north by a scarp (1) and ditch marking the edge of the flood plain. The easternmost enclosure (2) is sub-rectangular with a clearly defined entrance on its substantial western side. To the south of the entrance is some brick revetting (3), probably medieval. East of this are outlines of buildings including one represented by a depression. The

116

Plate XXVII Middleton Towers, moated site with associated earthworks including fishponds. TF 6717/L/AVF 12

southern edge is less clear. There is a marked south-facing scarp providing an edge to the platform but the moat extends further south and there is a mound (4) beyond the scarp which may represent a corner turret. The eastern boundary is also broken by an entrance leading onto a semi-circular ditched projection (5); this ditch continues north to cut across the corner of the enclosure.

The central enclosure (6) has a large sub-rectangular depression within it and is bounded to the west by a ditch with a bulbous southern end. Access was probably at its south-western corner. The western enclosure (7) contains two depressions connected by leats to a minor stream to the west; though irregular they may have been fishponds. Tiles dating from the 13th century were found on this site in the 1940s.

Lyng, in 1086, was one holding of three carucates (360 acres) of land on the demesne, with a further 24 acres held by five sokemen (Brown (ed) 1984, 4,29). According to Blomefield (1775, IV, 406) the earlier medieval lords were of the Cheyney family; various descendants had parts of the manor but by 1316 it was held by Sir Alexander de Clavering (Blake 1952, 276). His widow made over the manor to Sir Walter de Norwyc (NRO Phi/204 577 x 3) in 1320. It appears to be his son, Sir John de Norwyc, who obtained a licence to crenellate here and at Mettingham (Suffolk) in 1342 or 1344 and the last of the family passed the manor of Lyng to the College of Mettingham in 1373 (Blomefield IV, 1775, 407; Martin 1999, 24).

An agreement between the Master of the College of Mettingham and Robert de Mauteby, lord of Sparham, concerning fisheries at Lyng provides an unusually clear identification of the earthworks (NRO MC 1950/1 899 x 3). Mauteby was claiming free fishing in a new stream belonging to the Master which ran from the west head of Kydholm or Turnepool to the Master's watermill at Lyng below the manor of Lyng south and an alder grove north. The Master claimed free fishing in an old stream from the same point in Kydholm to an old ditch below Sparham manor and Sparham common north and east and an alder grove in Lyng south and west. The dispute was resolved by the Master obtaining the fishery in the new stream and Mauteby having that of the old one. This happened at a date before April 1417 when Mauteby died (NRO Phi/54 578 x 2).

The Tithe Map (NRO DN/TA 570) shows no earthworks but names the area to the north of the river as 'Kidhams'; the parish boundary leaves the river following a minor watercourse (the old river) to include this area near to Sparham Hall and rejoins the river near the site of a mill. The earthworks are thus those of Lyng manor.

Middleton Towers SMR 3393, 3395; TF 670 175
(Pl. XXVII, Fig.78)

A complete moat surrounds a large house partly of 15th-century date with an outer enclosure encompassing fishponds, some elaborate enclosures and at least one possible toft.

Middleton Towers lies about 1.75km north-east of Middleton village and about 4.75km south-east of King's Lynn. The major earthwork is the complete moat surrounding the present house partly of the 15th century, both designated SMR 3393. The remaining earthworks are SMR 3395 where there is a probably contemporary outer

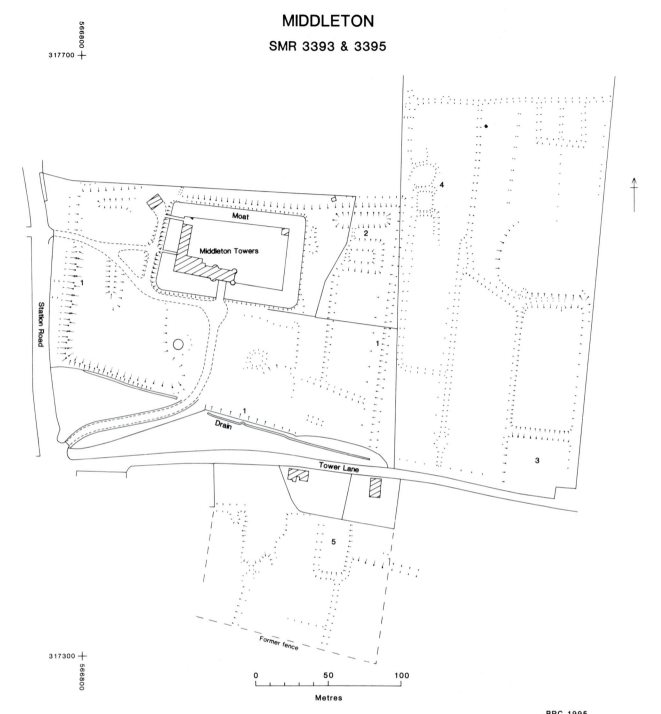

Figure 78 Middleton Towers, major manorial site with adjacent tofts. Scale 1:2,500

enclosure (1), 225m east-to-west and 120m north-to-south, particularly well marked to the west. To the east of the moat are depressions (2), probably fishponds, with a channel leading south. Other features within this enclosure to the south of the moat are remnants of post-medieval gardens.

To the east of the enclosure is a series of rectilinear ditched enclosures, aligned north-to-south. Of these only the small toft-like enclosure (3) in the south-east corner looks convincing as a settlement site. Two raised areas (4) in the north-west are on a spur of land and are possibly related to the house; they may include a dovecote site.

South of Tower Lane some surviving grassland shows banked and ditched enclosures. One (5), now truncated by

cottage gardens, may be a remnant of a toft (Wade-Martins (ed) 1999, 67).

The Scales family held one of the manors of Middleton in the time of King Stephen (1135–54), one of his forbears having inherited by right of his wife. The manor became known as Scales Hall Manor. About 1150 one of the family founded the Priory of Blackborough to the south of the village and it seems likely that a fine moat, now covered in dense vegetation, may have been the initial site of the Scales manor there (Silvester 1988, 129).

The fortunes of the family were enhanced from time to time by distinguished individuals and fortunate marriages, gradually acquiring other manors in Middleton. In 1305 an

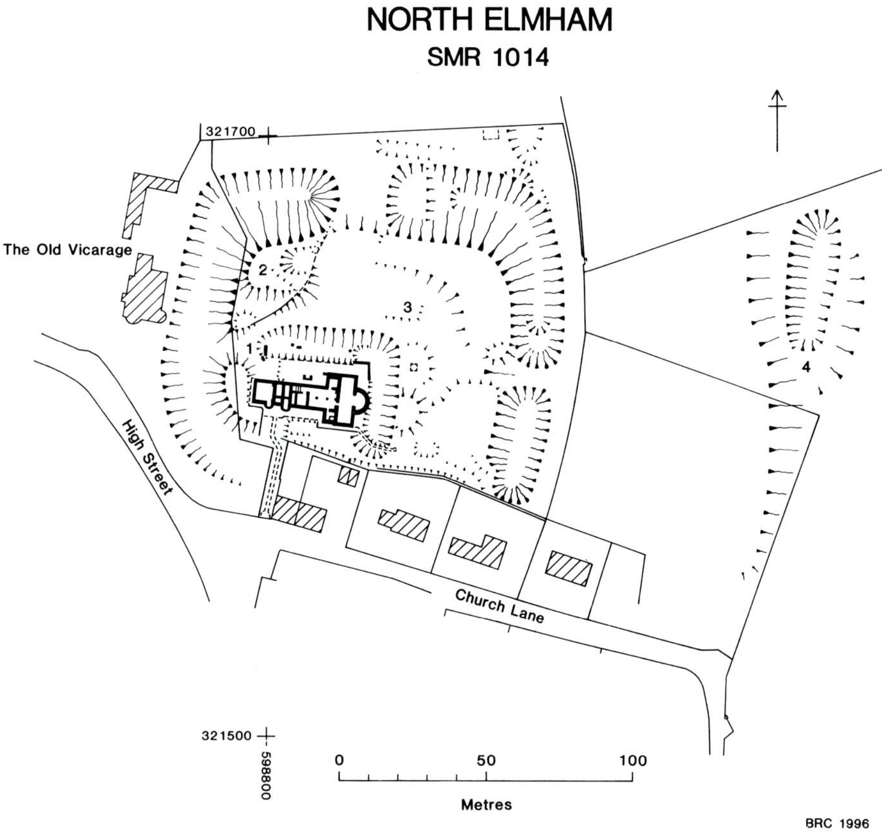

Figure 79 North Elmham, site of Bishop's Palace. Scale 1:2,500

Inquisition Post-Mortem (Cal. Inq. P-M. IV, 220) records that Robert de Scales had held a capital messuage, a windmill, watermill, 260 acres of arable, 69 acres of meadow, 10 acres of pasture with rushes, 5 acres of wood and an acre of turbary in Middleton. Another of 1369 (Cal. Inq. P-M. XII, 401) shows their increasing dominance of the village: Sir Robert Scales died seised of two-thirds of a manor, including a deer park, one-third of another manor, a manor called 'le Castel halle' (Middleton Mount) and 40 acres of arable held from Castle Rising. A later member of the family was Seneschal of Normandy who, after the loss of French territories, met a violent end in the Wars of the Roses. It was he who built the house at Tower End which replaced Middleton Mount and expressed the family's importance.

There is a map (Yates 1981, 75) prepared for hearings in Star Chamber for a dispute *c.* 1550 over the ownership of the Salt Fen. Though crude it shows the road past the Towers, known as Holle Lane or Calseye (causeway), crossing the bridge with a stylised Tower complete with machicolations standing in 'The Tower medowes' which spanned the stream or brook. Three houses were shown standing to the south. An illustration of the Tower before 19th-century building showed it in a ruinous condition and the present structure, dating mainly from *c.* 1860 and *c.* 1900, incorporates the 15th-century brick gatehouse, with a small fragment of contemporary masonry to the north of the house.

North Elmham SMR 1014, TF 989 216
(Fig.79)

A very large moated enclosure, with traces of an outer enclosure to the east, surrounds a smaller one in which the remnant of the chapel stands.

North Elmham is a large village about 8km north of East Dereham. Before 1071 it was the location of the seat of the Bishops of East Anglia. The site is at the north end of the village and contains the remains of a building thought originally to be that of the Cathedral but now considered by many to be a later Episcopal Chapel (Heywood 1982, 1–10).

The earthworks consist of a large moated enclosure with a smaller one in its south-west corner enclosing the remains of the chapel. The southern arm of the major enclosure has been partially destroyed by houses and gardens. The original connecting link (1) between the two enclosures appears to have lain north-west of the chapel. Within the larger one are a somewhat degraded mound (2) at the north-western corner which may be the remains of a prospect mound, an L-shaped scarp (3) which may represent part of a building, and an infilled well to the south.

There are two causeway entrances; that on the northern side is less convincing as an original feature than that on the east which led into an outer enclosure. This feature is now represented by a fragment of an enclosing ditch (4); much of the remaining outline is visible on aerial photographs as a soil mark (Wade-Martins 1980a, pls V–VIII; (ed) 1987, 50).

The site is of early significance as that of the late 11th-century Bishop's seat. Whether the building was of wood (Heywood 1982, 1–10; Fernie 1983, 178) or of stone is arguable (Batcock 1991, fiche 6:E6). A Saxon cemetery nearby, partly excavated, bears witness to its presence (Wade-Martins 1980a, 185–195). The alternative suggestion is that it post-dates the transference of the see to Thetford in 1071 and is merely an Episcopal Chapel built between 1094–1119 by Bishop Herbert de Losinga.

The building appears to have remained in use as a domestic chapel by the bishops until Bishop Despencer, having obtained licence to crenellate, fortified the site c.1387. It is not clear what had happened to the site before that date; it is probable that the manor house of the early medieval bishops stood near; it is possible that the chapel building had already been converted to secular use. Despencer certainly modified the building considerably for use as a house and seems to have been responsible for laying out two moated enclosures as well as the outer bailey. This, apart from the short length and cropmarks which show its eastern limit, is indistinct but it must have linked with the inner enclosure (Wade-Martins 1980a, fig.9, 23) possibly protecting the entrances. The prospect mound would have afforded good views of the surroundings, possibly of the chase.

A survey of 1454 makes no mention of the building or its yards. It was still used as a meeting place for manorial courts in 1535 but the house may have been no longer habitable. By 1561 the building was used as a quarry for repairs to the parish church and by 1568 the site was leased with the proviso that it should revert to pasture. The ditches were referred to in numerous abuttals from 1464 onwards and, in this way, influenced the form of the northern part of the village (Yaxley 1980, 597–600).

The site, owned by the diocese of Norwich, is in the Guardianship of English Heritage.

Panworth, Ashill SMR 4708, TF 897 048
(Fig.80)

The former site of Panworth Hall is identifiable in the north-west corner; the remainder of the earthworks include field boundaries, a hollow way, a headland bank and two possible tofts but because of continued occupation little definite can be said.

Panworth is a small farm settlement in a curious north-eastern panhandle extension of the parish of Ashill, about 7km south-east of Swaffham. It was listed in 1955 as a deserted medieval village in its own right (Allison 1955, 154).

The earthworks in pastures near Panworth Hall Farm are the suggested site of this settlement. The features, however, appear to be of varied origins. The two ponds and a linear depression associated with the fence running south-west (unmapped because it is so obscured by dense scrub) mark the course of the earthwork known as the Panworth Ditch, of probable Early Saxon date (Wade-Martins 1974, 32–34). The northern pond is a remnant of a moat which, in 1581, surrounded Panworth Hall (NRO MS 21123 179 x 4). This was demolished and replaced by existing buildings or their forerunners. Earthworks (1) correspond to the hall site; some of the farm buildings may have survived into the 19th century while other earthworks

nearby include possible fishponds (2) and earthwork banks (3–5) shown as field boundaries in 1581.

In the eastern field in 1581, a dovecote stood near the slight earthworks (6) with common land further east; the complex bank and ditch (7) and its northern continuation seem to represent the common edge, while the hollow way (8) probably marks a track across the common. Its line continues as a soil mark in the arable further east. The low bank (9) with a ditch on its crest may be a headland bank.

Other banks and ditches (10,11) appear as field boundaries on later maps (NRO NRS 21176 (undated 18th century); NRO PD 548/87 (1786) and NRO PD 548/27 (1813)) and thus appear post-medieval. The hollow way (12) was omitted in 1581 but may be medieval as may be features (13,14). The two earthworks which relate to the medieval landscape are enclosures (15) and possibly (16) which may represent tofts on the common edge with crofts extending west (Williamson pers. comm.).

In 1086 Panworth had a recorded population of twenty-two (twenty-five in 1066). It had, with a portion of Ashill, been in the hands of Harold in 1066 but was possessed by Reynold after the Conquest. Ashill, by comparison, had a recorded population of forty-five in 1086 (Brown (ed) 1984, 21,16,17; 51,5). Panworth did not achieve parochial status but remained a manor within Ashill, staying separate from the other manors in the village. It is, therefore, not a deserted medieval village.

The map of 1581 shows it as a very limited settlement, the manor house being surrounded by closes named Asheyarde, The Okeyard, The Oke Close and the Dovehowse, the latter with a building like a house upon it. There was one other building shown named as Clarke's tenement.

Later maps (NRO NRS 21176 and PD 548/87 of 1786) display a different arrangement of farm buildings in similar fashion but the Tithe Map of 1841 (NRO DN/TA 432) shows a considerable alteration. This probably reflects the rebuilding by Holkham Estate between 1813 and 1818. The farm house in the 1870s was described as being brick faced with flint and covered with blue pantiles with two good sitting rooms, kitchens, dairies, five bedrooms and servants rooms (Wade-Martins S. 1980, 146–7).

Seething SMR 10442, 10443; TM 321 979
(Fig.81)

The southern field contains earthworks which are probably part of the hall site with possible fishponds. The northern one has a common-edge boundary and a circular feature, possibly a pound.

Seething is a compact village about 14km south-east of Norwich. The earthworks are in two fields at the north-eastern end of the linear settlement. The northern one, SMR 10442, consists of four ditched enclosures, the two westernmost ones abutting on a ditch, with an entrance causeway, roughly parallel to the present street. Of the four enclosures the north-western one is most clearly preserved and has on its eastern edge a distinct ring ditch (1) 15m in diameter. The eastern boundary is clearly associated with this feature. In the south-western corner of the field is a large bulbous depression which continues into the garden to the south and may be associated with the 'Old Hall'.

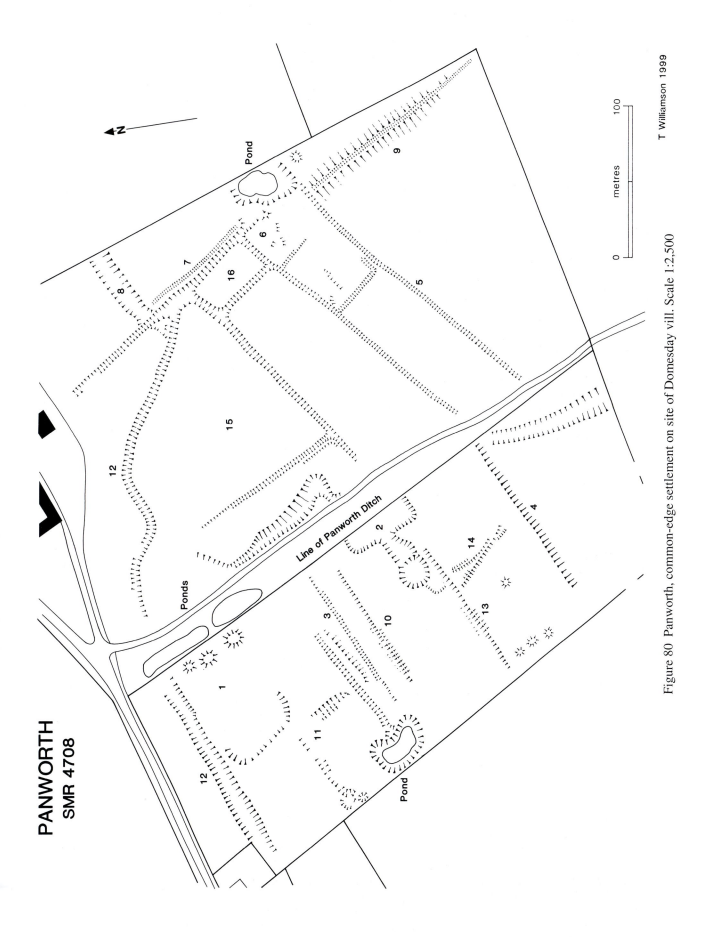

PANWORTH
SMR 4708

Pond

Ponds

Line of Panworth Ditch

Pond

Figure 80 Panworth, common-edge settlement on site of Domesday vill. Scale 1:2,500

T Williamson 1999

metres

0   100

121

SEETHING

SMR 10442 & SMR 10443

Figure 81 Seething, limited manorial remains with a pound. Scale 1:2,500

The southern field, SMR 10443, contains a building platform (2), *c.* 22m by 9m, with an exposed fragment of brickwork, probably medieval, on its eastern side. To the south-east are two shallow degraded depressions (3), possibly remnants of fishponds. The remainder of the field contains various depressions and channels, some forming incomplete enclosures.

Seething in 1086 had a recorded population of about seventy-one of whom there were thirty-five freemen and twelve sokemen and there was more than one church (Brown (ed) 1984, 1,230. 6,5. 9,25;51;62;69;169; 171. 47,5;7). In 1334 it paid the fourth largest sum to the Lay Subsidy in the Hundred of Loddon, but was allowed a reduction of 21.6% in its 1449 payment (Hudson 1895, 269). This agrees with a statement made by Blomefield, quoting a deed of 1361, in which the Abbots of Sibton were freed from responsibility for a chantry chapel in Seething because the deaths of free tenants and villeins had wasted the lands which were meant to support the chantry (Blomefield 1775, V, 1158). The Cistercian house of Sibton had a grange in Seething (Denney (ed) 1960, 115) and some land was also held by the Hospital of St Giles in Norwich (Rawcliffe 1995, 113, 125). Seething seems to have continued without further serious mishap to the present day.

Some indications as to the identity of these earthworks can be obtained from relatively modern maps. The Enclosure Map (NRO C/Sca 2/260) of 1814 shows the church standing on Church Green and this extended southwards along the present street. Its boundary appears as the western ditch, with an entrance causeway, on SMR 10442. The whole field was called Pound Close in 1814 and on the Tithe Map of 1838 (NRO 526), suggesting an origin for the ring ditch which is so well-preserved and is in sympathy with the boundary of the north-western enclosure. If this was a pound, the remains are unique in Norfolk. The bulbous depression was the northern end of a water feature shown in 1838.

Faden's map (1797) has the linear common extending south to Tubgate and beyond and shows not only Seething Hall in a small park north of the church but also 'Old Hall' in roughly the position for SMR 10443. Bryant, in 1826, also has 'Scite of the Hall' here. It seems very likely that the building remains on the platform were part of this hall and that some at least of the other features there were gardens and enclosures associated with it; the name in 1838, Dove House Meadow, supports this.

Shelton SMR 10175, 10182; TM 228 905
(Fig.82)

Earthworks include a fine double-moated site with fishponds together with an irregularly shaped feature, partly water-filled, which may be a second moat.

Shelton is a scattered village 17km south of Norwich. The major earthworks are associated with the present Hall while a second site lies to the south-east.

The most significant feature (SMR 10175) is the double-moated site of the hall. The existing late 18th- or early 19th-century building replaced a house of *c.* 1490 which stood within the square moat. Some fragments of masonry survive in a corner tower (1) and in revetting of the moat. To the south-west is another moat, roughly

rectangular and subdivided by a ditch. A long red-brick barn to the north-east of the moats is also of the late 15th century. Some ponds to the north-west are the remains of former fishponds.

North-west and north-east of the moats is a series of ditched enclosures and linear features, separated by a drain which divides two distinct alignments. One ditch (2) encompasses the fishpond and is aligned as if contemporary with the moat. The north-western group includes a mound (3) near which medieval roof tiles have been found, and a discordantly superimposed post-medieval track. Some of the north-eastern features which are very subdued may be medieval in origin.

To the south-east site 10182 is more enigmatic. The major feature is a long water-filled depression described as a moat on Ordnance Survey maps, and linked to the stream. There are various linking ditches, including two ponds, outlining a strangely-shaped enclosure (4), not entirely convincing. There are also raised areas outside this which may include building platforms, but there is no supporting evidence.

A bank and ditch (5) may link the two sites: it appears similar to one north-west of the hall (6) and they may be parts of a common outer enclosure or park boundary (Cushion 1998, 44).

In 1086 there were two lords of Shelton: Roger Bigot with the largest part and Robert son of Corbucion (Brown (ed) 1984, 9,98; 216. 35,13). According to Blomefield (1769, III, 174) these holdings became the manors of Overhall and Netherhall respectively. In medieval times the dominant lords were the Sheltons who acquired both manors (Feudal Aids III, 411,477,527,585–6). It was the Sheltons who built the hall in *c.* 1490; its appearance was described in later days by Blomefield (3,181):

> 'There was a grand antique manse or manor house here, built by Sir Ralf Shelton, in a square form, with an outside wall embattled, and a turret at each corner, moated in, with a grand gate space at the entrance, and with a turret at each corner of it. In the windows and ceilings were many coats of the matches of the Sheltons *etc.* but the whole is now ruinated. The demeans and the park *etc.* were sold by the Sheltons from the manor, as I am informed, to Sir Rob. Houghton, Knt, Serjeant-at-Law'.

An illustration of the old hall (NRO Rye MS 17, VI,114) has been published (Finch 1996, 91–92). Latterly the Sheltons appear to have lived at Carrow Abbey and, perhaps, at Barningham in Suffolk. The old hall was demolished in the 1720s by a new owner (Finch 1996, 94). There is some evidence from the Tithe Map of 1838 (NRO DN/TA 25). The naming of two enclosures, Great Dove House Meadow and Little Dove House Meadow, may explain the presence of medieval roof tiles around the mound, and the roughly rectangular moat is described as an orchard.

No evidence is available for Site 10182. It is just possible that it may have been the site of an earlier medieval forerunner of Site 10175. Another faint possibility is that it may have been Netherhall, obsolete by the amalgamation of the manors.

Plate XXVIII South Creake, probable site of Beaufours manor, much altered. TF 8536/B/AAN5

South Creake SMR 1017, TF 857 362
(Pl. XXVIII, Fig.83)

An area which has undergone much change and which includes the site of Beaufours manor.

South Creake is about 9km north-west of Fakenham. The earthworks lie to the south-east of the church in a small area completely surrounded by roads. The River Burn flows northwards in a regulated channel at the east side of the area. Two former channels, one original and irregular (1), the other artificial (2), cross the site. To the east of these is a well-defined bank; to the west of them three depressions, two of them bounded westwards by another bank (3).

In the north-western corner is an incomplete building outline (4) with some flint masonry, bounded to the south by a drain linked to the straighter of the abandoned channels. South of this is a possible trackway (5) between the remains of enclosures. A further bank in the south-west corner and the remnant of a platform (6) with some flint masonry in the south survive on the remainder of the site.

A map of *c.*1630 (NRO BL 35) shows this area with the stream in its original irregular channel. To the east of it the area is simply marked 'Scite of Manor of Boffhouse' with a single house facing south onto a triangular widening of the roadway. There were two medieval manors in South Creake, apart from the holding of the Abbey of North Creake; they were Roses and Beaufours. 'Boffhouse' is clearly a corruption. The remainder of the earthwork area was divided unequally by a way called 'Beresty'. To the east of it was Barretts Close with the pond at the north end. To the west of it were two houses, one in the north-west corner and one facing south onto Westgate. Kirkegate bounded the area to the north and Lertamer Way to the west. The two houses appear to account for the two buildings noted in the survey although New Road is a realignment of Lertamer Way and the north-western pond is new.

It is clear that changes had already occurred by 1630 as there was little sign of Beaufours manor. Attempts to reconstruct earlier features from older documents give some features. A survey of 1464 (Holkham MSS Vol 3, Bundle 5, 82) mentions messuages facing south onto Westgate which may refer to this area. The names of roads

SOUTH CREAKE

SMR 1017

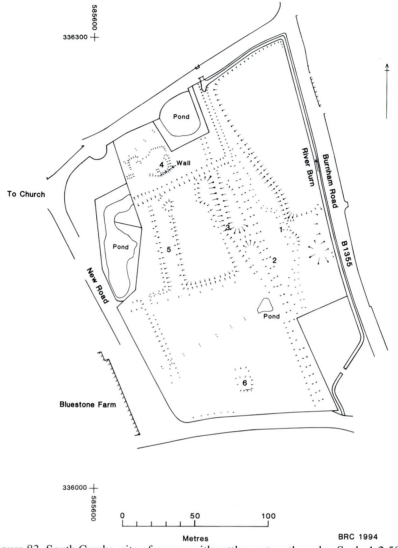

Figure 83 South Creake, site of manor with settlement earthworks. Scale 1:2,500

do not concur easily with those of 1630; various messuages were said to abut west on Beresty and east on Medylgrene and, or, Beresgate. A survey of 1475 (Holkham MSS Vol 3, Bundle 2, 22) states that the furlong beginning at Westgate alias Fletgate and abutting on the Beck and stretching from Beresgate in the east and Beresty to the west is omitted.

Faden (1797), Bryant (1826) and the OS One-Inch First Edition all show buildings in the south-west corner and the latter also has a building in the south-east. It is likely that a site in the centre of a village would receive much alteration, much of it unrecorded, over the years.

Tharston and Tasburgh SMR 9976, 9977; TM 193 959
(Fig.84)

A moated platform with two probable fishponds lies to the east in Tasburgh and is probably Boylands manor. In Tharston little sign survives of Welhams manor or its free chapel.

Tharston and Tasburgh are neighbouring villages about 13km south-south-east of Norwich, separated by a small tributary of the River Tas.

The site in Tharston (9976) known as Chapel Hill is probably a natural feature. There is a record here of discoveries of skeletons and pottery, probably medieval, in 1897. The earthworks recorded now consist of an enclosure (1) marked by an outward-facing scarp except for the south-west boundary which is inward-facing. There is a subdividing ridge running east to west within the

126

THARSTON SMR9976
&
TASBURGH SMR9977

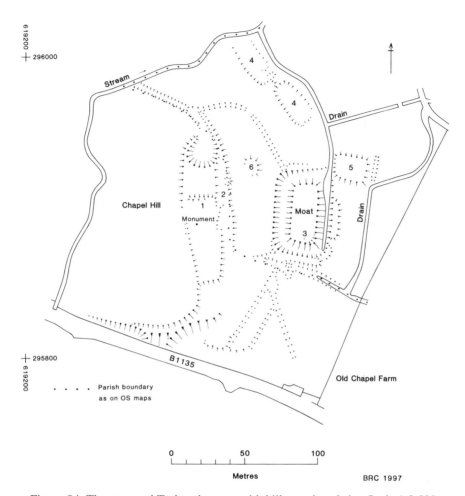

Figure 84 Tharston and Tasburgh, moat with hill-top chapel site. Scale 1:2,500

enclosure. To the east of the enclosure is a lynchet (2) which may have been a trackway. At the north end of the enclosure is a pit linked to a ditch.

The ditch is the likely inlet leat to the moat (9977) which is the major site on the Tasburgh side of the parish boundary. The platform within the moat measures 37m north to south and 17m east to west, with some masonry (3) visible at the southern end, and the moat itself is about 10m wide. The eastern arm contains some water. To the north of the moat are two depressions (4) which may have been fishponds. To the east of it is a near-rectangular raised enclosure (5) while to the north-west is a much smaller platform (6) which may have supported a building. The parish boundary runs north-west to south-east through the sites, following, in part, the lynchet (2) with Chapel Hill to the west and the moat in Tasburgh to the east (Cushion 1997, 33).

The site in Tharston was first noticed in 1897 when human remains and pottery were discovered (Norfolk Arch. Misc. 1906, 79–81); these were probably medieval but some Romano-British finds came to light then and in subsequent years. Blomefield says that Welholmes or Welhams manor in Stratton had its original site near Holm Hill in Tharston. To this original manorial site belonged a free chapel dedicated to St Giles and called Holme or Welholmes Chapel (Blomefield 1739, I, 204). Holm Hill is an old name for Chapel Hill (Addington 1982, 101, 111). This description of the chapel may account for the presence of a possible medieval graveyard and certainly explains the name 'Chapel Hill' recorded on the Tithe Map (NRO DN/TA 390).

It appears probable that the moated site within Tasburgh is that of Uphall or Boylands manor, said by Blomefield (1739, III, 139) to be the capital manor of Tasburgh. In 1289, according to him, William de Narford was allowed free passage under Sir Richard de Boylands' courtyard and his chapel of St Michael to his alder carr. Blomefield said that this chapel was for the use of the family. As alder carr occurs in river valleys on wet land this fits, to some extent, the position of the moated site. Addington (1982, 107, 111) placed Boylands manor here.

It is likely, therefore, that, as Addington pointed out, there were two chapels, one on either side of the parish boundary, a situation which has led to a certain amount of confusion over siting and dedication.

127

TIBENHAM
SMR 29577

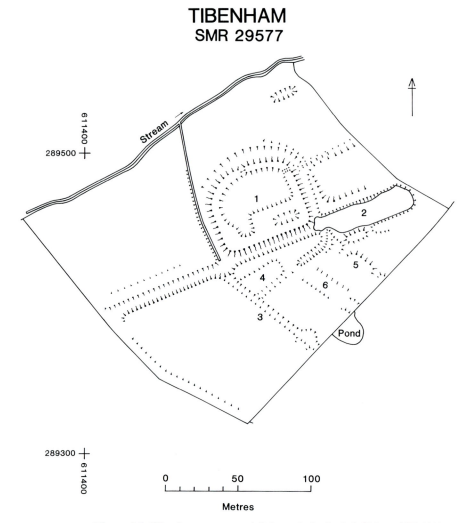

Figure 85 Tibenham, moat and fishpond. Scale 1:2,500   BRC 1993

Tibenham SMR 29577, TM 115 894
(Fig.85)

The site of Tateshalles manor survives with a probable fishpond and an approach way.

Tibenham is a village about 10km south-east of Attleborough on the south bank of the headwaters of the River Tas. The earthworks lie by the side of the stream at the northern end of the parish.

The main feature of the site is a D-shaped moated enclosure (1) with the straight arm of the moat on its southern side. The enclosure is uneven with a platform in the south-eastern corner and an embankment, cut in two places, around the remaining portions. Pottery sherds found within the enclosure confirm the site as medieval. A broad channel, partly embanked on its north side, leads into the southern arm of the moat from the west and continues on its eastern side, ending in a probable fishpond (2). A narrow ditch (3) enters the junction of the channel with the moat coming from the south-east.

To the east of this and south of the moat is an area of further earthworks which appears to include two platforms (4,5) and a possible approach roadway (6). The fishpond is partly embanked on both sides; that on the northern side is

continued around the eastern side of the moat where it is cut by a ditch leading east.

Tibenham has ten entries in Domesday Book (Brown (ed) 1984, 4,56. 9,98;217;223;226. 14,39. 17,65. 29,7;10. 66,107.). The major entry was that of Eudo, said by Blomefield to have been the ancestor of the Tateshalles who held it in the Middle Ages (1769, III, 187).

In 1316 the manor of the Tateshalles was held by John de Orreby (Blake 1952, 282). It later passed, in the time of Richard II, to the Cliftons and so went subsequently with Buckenham Castle. In 1649 Sir Philip Knyvett had it valued; that of the 'scite of the Hall *etc*' was said to be £93 - 15 - 0 per annum. The site of the Hall, known as Tibenham Hall alias Orrebys, Tatersales cum Carleton, was a quarter of a mile north-west of the church (Blomefield 1769, III, 187). Blomefield's distance is rather more than 440 yards in practice but his direction is correct for this earthwork.

The Enclosure Map names a building nearby as Old Hall and the bridge carrying the road to Carleton Rode was, and still is, Old Hall Bridge (NRO C/Sca 2/300) but no sign of the earthworks is evident. According to Blomefield there was said to have been a chapel at Old Hall which was staffed by the Canons of Old Buckenham, 'but I have not met with any certain Account of it' (Blomefield 1769, III, 187).

WARHAM
SMR 1886

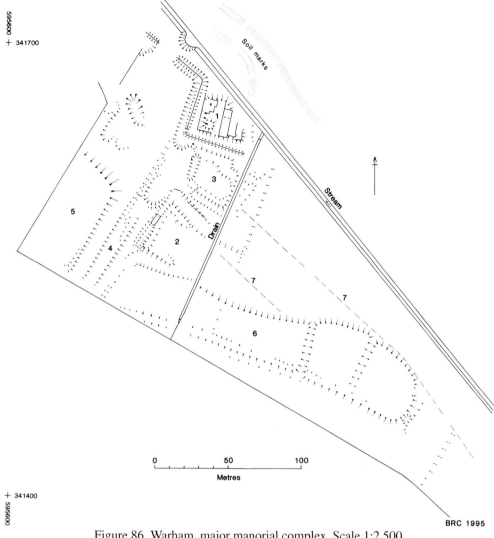

Figure 86 Warham, major manorial complex. Scale 1:2,500

Warham SMR 1886, TF 957 416
(Fig.86)

A well-documented manorial site lies on the boundary of Warham.

Warham is a village about 3.5km south-east of Wells. The earthworks lie in grassland on the margin of the parish of All Saints with some soil markings extending across the stream into Stiffkey.

The partial moat encloses incomplete ground-level building outlines (1) of flint and late medieval brick as well as a mound with much loose flint. Flint and brick revetting is also visible along much of the western and southern arms of the moat and suggest the platform was not rectangular. The western arm of the moat turns north-westwards and soil marks to the north point to an irregular platform destroyed by the cutting of the present stream.

To the south of the platform are two possible enclosures, the more southerly one (2) has signs of structures and may have been open to the south-east. The

northern one (3) has been disfigured by a modern drain and may have been complete. Also visible here are the remains of linear terraces (4) damaged by quarrying, one of which may have been an entrance to the manor. To the south-west is a terraced area (5). To the south-east, beyond a modern drain, are two enclosures with evidence of subdivision; the western one (6) has a southern boundary bank which extends westwards across the drain. Shallow channels (7) denote modern drains.

A field book of 1588 (Holkham MSS, Vol 3, Bundle 1, 2) reveals that this was the site of Hales Manor, one of three medieval manors in Warham. The description given is of the site of the manor called Hales Hall with meadows, yards (or gardens) and an alder carr attached to it and estimated at 12 acres in extent. It lay between the common pasture of Warham in part and abutted to the north on the stream flowing from the watermill at Binham. It abutted to the south on the road from Binham to Wells. To the west was an enclosure called Hall Close divided into four pightles totalling about 15 acres and lying between the road and Cockesfordmedow to the north. This meadow of 3 acres

129

lay to the north of Hall Close and had the stream to the north, a pool in Hales manor to the east and the manorial watermill on the Stiffkey River to the west. There had been a bridge called Hallbrigge to the west.

There had already been changes to the course of the stream by 1588. There is a casual reference to a piece which was described as being part of the old river which was used in common by Warham tenants. It is not clear whether the parish boundary has been redrawn when the stream was finally regulated, but it looks very likely, putting part of the manorial site within Stiffkey.

The Tithe Map for Warham All Saints dated 1838 (NRO 16) shows the area divided into four pieces, two of them called 'Hales' and 'Long Hales'. To the west was a drove and beyond that 'Brick Kiln Close', a name suggesting a possible explanation for quarrying.

Wood Norton SMR 3085, TG 012 289
(Fig.87)

Earthworks of a complicated manorial site almost completely embanked, consisting of a probable house platform, two associated yards or gardens and possible fishponds.

Wood Norton is a village about 9.5km east-south-east of Fakenham. The earthworks lie to the north of the village at the southern end of a lengthy salient extending north from the main body of the parish.

The features are clothed by a thick wood. There is a quadrilateral moated enclosure (1), apparently approached from the south-west. To the south-east of it are two attached moated areas. The smaller of them to the east (2) is separated from (1) by a bank and has an entrance, probably modern, on its south-western corner leading from a more irregular area (3) to the south. This again seems to be linked by a narrow entrance to the approach to the main enclosure (1). To the north and north-east are three depressions; the smallest (4) is linked to the moat, the others are separated from it and each other by embankments. There is a small depression in (5), on one of two slightly drier areas abutting the eastern boundary.

There is a large embankment, widest in the north, which surrounds all the features with the exception of the southern side. It is broken by a continuation of the eastern boundary bank of (5). Central to the southern side of enclosure (3) are two exterior flanking ridges separated by a narrow gap; this may represent an entrance. A slight ditch leaves south-eastwards from this and an irregular depression (6) 70m to the west was probably a clay pit.

Blomefield (1775, V, 452) records that this earthwork was the manor granted to Alice de Luton during the reign of Henry III when it was known as Luton fee. It afterwards passed to the Gerbridge family by 1286–87. John Gerbridge presented to the living of All Saints' church by the right of this manor in 1310 and 1321. 'John Gerberge' was shown as a landowner in Wood Norton in the Nomina Villarum of 1316 (Blake 1952, 276). In 1359 the Bishop acted as guardian of Roger Gerbridge as lord of Ling Hall;

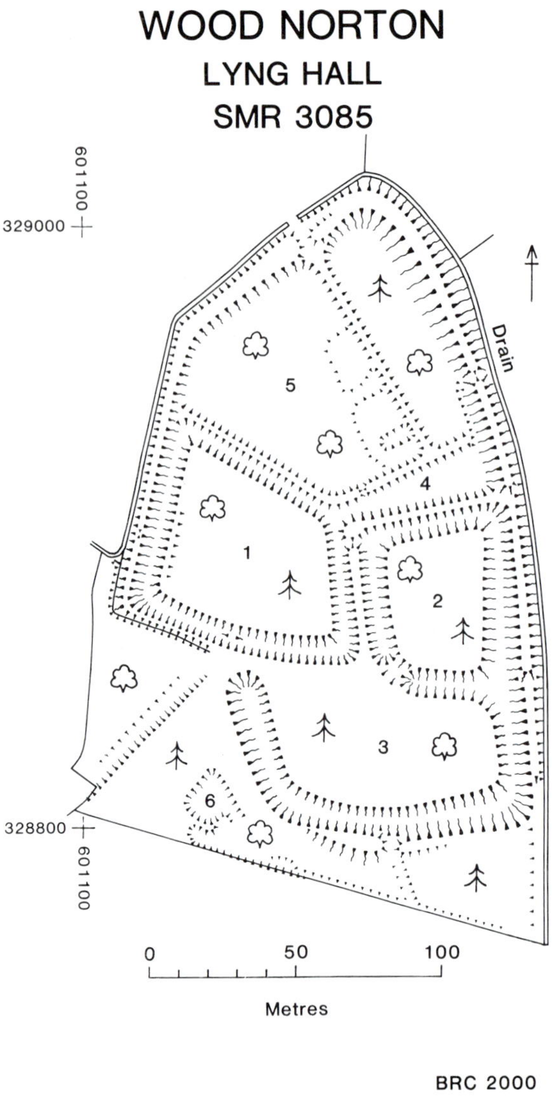

WOOD NORTON
LYNG HALL
SMR 3085

Figure 87 Wood Norton, unusually complete manorial site. Scale 1:2,500

this was the first mention of the name by which it is now known. The Gerbridges appear to have held the manor until at least 1402–03 but thereafter it passed into other hands.

Wood Norton had two medieval churches, All Saints' and St Peter's, the latter in the gift of another manor. St Peter's was abandoned early in the 16th century (Batcock 1991, 52) and it may be that this saw the decline of Lyng Hall with the consolidation of the manors.

The Enclosure Map of 1813 (NRO C/Sca 2/152) and the Tithe Map (NRO DN/TA 642) of 1842 both show the area of the earthworks without internal detail; it was called Lyng Hall Wood on the Tithe Map.

It seems likely that the quadrilateral enclosure was the inhabited site with other yards and gardens nearby. Some at least of the embanked depressions probably were, or held fishponds and there is seasonal water in the ditches. No sign of buildings is evident.

Monastic Sites

Although Norfolk's monasteries have frequently been examined historically and architecturally, less attention has been paid to their earthworks. The following series of plans is an attempt to redress this omission, the only exception being Coxford Priory which has been published recently (Cushion and Davison 1997, 497) and is reproduced here with an abbreviated text for the sake of completeness. The extensive earthworks of West Acre Priory, Langley Abbey and Marham Abbey have been appreciated and fully surveyed for the first time and the earthworks associated with the well-known Castle Acre Priory have been shown to be much more extensive. Carbrooke Commandery and Burnham Norton Friary are two other sites of which relatively clearly-integrated plans now exist.

Some of the remaining sites are less open to interpretation. Wendling Abbey, Wormegay Priory, West Dereham Abbey, Hempton Priory and Flitcham Priory as well as Shouldham Priory have all undergone drastic post-Dissolution modifications. At West Dereham fishponds appear to be medieval but little else is visible above ground. At Shouldham some earthworks survive but their purpose is unclear. Wendling, Hempton and Flitcham have all been adapted, the last being very severely altered.

The sites are a cross-section of the monastic orders. Binham, the remarkable St Benet's and Wymondham were Benedictine while Castle Acre was Cluniac. North Creake, Wormegay, Flitcham, West Acre, Coxford and Hempton were all foundations of the popular Augustinian Order of Black Canons. West Dereham, Langley and Wendling were of Premonstratensian White Canons. Of the others, Shouldham was of the purely English Gilbertine Order, a dual house for men and women; Marham was for Cistercian nuns, a double rarity for Norfolk, as East Anglia was not favoured by the Cistercians who sought wilder places and were reluctant to accept women. Carbrooke Commandery was one of the most important centres of the Knights Hospitallers in England. Burnham Norton was a house of Carmelite Friars and the only Friary with remaining earthworks. This is because of its rural setting. Friars, unlike other orders, were, ideally, mendicants (beggars) who were not allowed to possess lands beyond the sites of their houses and therefore sought to congregate in larger towns where there was an audience for preaching and where there were opportunities to attract offerings. After the Dissolution most urban sites were quickly cleared and used for other purposes; Burnham, on the edge of Burnham Market, has survived to a greater extent.

Binham Priory SMR 2081, TF 982 400
(Fig.88)

An intriguing site which is detached from the existing village with the building still partly in use as a parish church. Speculations about the original site of the village are not supported by any documentary evidence.

Binham is a village in north Norfolk about 7.5km south-east of Wells-next-the-Sea. The Priory lies on the north-western edge of the village centre, on the eastern side of Warham Road (Westgate). The nave of the Benedictine Priory church remains in use as the parish church while the excavated and displayed ruins of the chancel, transepts and conventual buildings owned by the Norfolk Archaeological Trust are in English Heritage Guardianship.

Outside the Guardianship area are the remains of the gatehouse and some 180m of the flint-built precinct wall to the south and outlines of three buildings (1,2,3). Earthworks south-east of the church include a marked scarp (4) which like other scarps and banks nearby, probably represents an enclosure boundary; a parchmark extension (5) of the rere-dorter lies within this group. The large pond is probably post-medieval despite the presence of some medieval masonry and may have been a mill-pond. On the north side of the stream subdued channels and banks appear to be remains of an abandoned water-course (6), and fishponds while the probable site of a watermill (7) is approached by a causeway (8) from the north. Vague features to the north-west (9) are of uncertain origin (Wade-Martins (ed) 1987, 33). The precinct wall is obvious by the Warham Road and the Langham Road probably marks the eastern boundary. The northern precinct limit is less certain as it may have extended north of the old course of the stream.

In 1086 Binham was held by Peter de Valognes; a population of thirty-four was recorded and there were references to a mill and a manor hall but no church was mentioned. It seems unlikely that there was no place of worship. Valognes and his wife founded the Priory, subordinate to St Albans Abbey; it may have been in existence by 1093. A confirmatory charter (NRO MC 619/1) records the grant of the church of St Mary, Binham and all the manor. Henry I granted a Wednesday market and the right to an annual four-day fair in March (Doubleday and Page 1906, II, 343–46). The market was out of use by the 17th century but the market place with its preaching cross remains an open space in the centre of the village (Dymond 1993, 77).

Binham may have moved to this focus from an earlier centre, possibly a linear position along Westgate of which Warham Road may be a survival. If that were so the Priory may have been built over part of the original village with its church replacing a predecessor. There is, however, no archaeological evidence to support this suggestion. The rights of the parishioners to use the nave of the Priory for their own worship were stated clearly in 1432 when they were granted permission to hang a large bell at the gable-end provided that it did not disturb the monks' devotions (NRO MS 9253 8D2 BRA26). When, in 1541, Thomas Paston was granted the houses, buildings, barns, stables, dovehouse, yards, orchards and gardens within the Priory precinct (no mill or fishponds were mentioned) the parish retained that part of the church in which they had rights (NRO MS 2854 3 c 6).

BINHAM PRIORY
SMR 2081

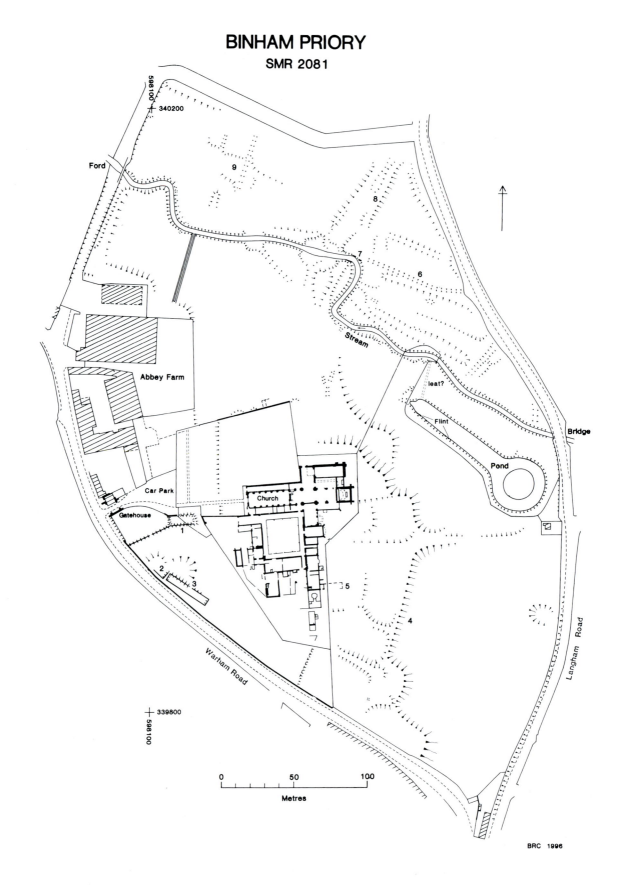

Figure 88 Binham Priory. Scale 1:2,500

132

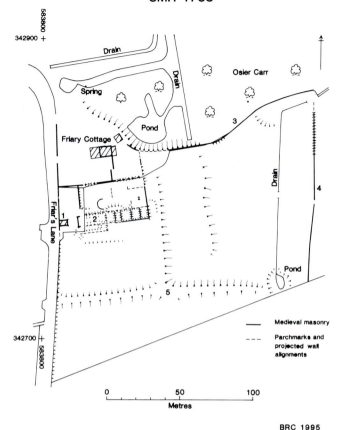

BURNHAM NORTON
SMR 1738

Drain

Osier Carr

Drain

Spring

Pond

3

Friary Cottage

Drain

4

Friar's Lane

1

2

Pond

5

—— Medieval masonry

- - - Parchmarks and projected wall alignments

0   50   100

Metres

BRC 1995

Figure 89 Burnham Norton Carmelite Friary.
Scale 1:2,500

Burnham Norton SMR 1738, TF 839 428
(Fig.89)

The only earthwork site of a Friary which survives in Norfolk, probably because of its rural setting.

Burnham Norton Friary stands about 0.5km north-east of Burnham Market, opposite a school and about 0.3km east of Burnham Norton parish church.

The most obvious upstanding feature is the gatehouse (1), now repaired, which abuts Friar's Lane. There are also remains of a flint precinct wall surviving as a roadside boundary with a gap, possibly a gateway, about 14m to the north. A small courtyard is formed by the wall of Friary Cottage garden and another extending southwards. East of the gatehouse, on a slightly different alignment, are building outlines which incorporate a church (2) and show much further subdivision. Parchmarks suggest a possible south aisle. To the north are incomplete lengths of walling probably bounding a cloister and an incomplete building outline. A large C-shaped flint wall is enigmatic. Friary Cottage appears partly medieval; some north-to-south flint walling extending south from the Cottage is possibly medieval. A sinuous precinct wall (3) overlooks a lowlying overgrown area leading to the River Burn, which may have served as a link to the sea. The eastern precinct boundary (4) remains distinct but the southern one is indeterminate, being either the existing hedge or a low spread bank (5) to the north.

This friary was founded in 1241 by Sir William Calthorp and Sir Ralph Hemenhall. In 1298 they were licensed to enlarge the house by incorporating a rood ($\frac{1}{4}$ acre) of meadow. Thereafter its existence seems uneventful. Presumably the urban activity of neighbouring Burnham Market attracted the Friars but, compared with the Carmelite house at Blakeney which received four grants of enlargement, its success was modest. The gatehouse has important early flushwork panelling and some mouldings which look early 14th century while in the cottage there is an early 14th-century doorway (Pevsner 1962, 105).

In 1538 Thomas Cromwell received a letter from Jane Calthorp asking him to petition the King to allow her to purchase the house as there were only four friars left. They were too poor to maintain the house and were happy to sell it. The King, however, gave it to Sir Richard Gresham; it had not been 'defasde ne rasede' (presumably left intact) (Doubleday and Page 1906, II, 425–6).

The Tithe Map of 1840 (NRO DN/TA 229) shows as standing buildings the gatehouse and the putative church, subdivided in two. Two buildings are shown north of these, one facing onto the road and one on the east side of the claustral enclosure. Friary Cottage and the field to the north of it was 'Friars Common', the field to the south, 'Friars Close'; both were pasture.

Carbrooke SMR 8814, 31424; TF 951 022
(Pl. XXIX, Fig.90)

The extensive earthworks of the Commandery of the Knights Hospitallers which was the most important in England in the 14th century. A large partly moated area with foundations of buildings, fishponds and enclosures can still be seen.

Carbrooke is about 3.5km north-east of Watton. The site is that of the Commandery of St John of Jerusalem or Knights Hospitallers (SMR 8814) and possibly extends into the neighbouring SMR 31424.

The major feature on the site is a three-sided moated enclosure open to the west. Within is a slightly upstanding near-rectangular structure (1) with sides mainly of flint with some signs of an adjoining feature to the south. Remains of a probable building platform lie to the west. Parchmarks indicate other buildings to the north and south, some with subdivisions (2,3,4). Also within the enclosure are two depressions, one much larger (5), probably fishponds; the smaller one is connected to the moat and the two ponds may have been linked. There seems to have been no western limb to the moat. To the east of it is a meandering feature (6), probably an old watercourse possibly feeding the moat. Linked to it are two large depressions (7,8) which may have been fishponds. All these features and the eastern limb of the moat retain water during the winter. To the north-east is a well-defined small moated enclosure (9) with signs of two outlet leats. The remaining features on the site are relatively modern.

Within the school grounds excavation was carried out by the Norfolk Archaeological Unit in 1998 in advance of construction of a new playground. The remains of a kitchen with ovens, hearths, a possible dovecote and probably an infilled fishpond were found. Parts of the outlines of these

133

CARBROOKE

SMR 8814 & 31424

Figure 90 Carbrooke Commandery, Knights Hospitallers' site with adjacent enclosures. Scale 1:2,500

buildings were recorded to the south of the school as parchmarks on the plan prior to the excavation.

The probable northern and eastern boundary of the precinct is a substantial ditch (10). To the north-east of it is

Site 31424. The northern part of this has been modified by the construction of cycle tracks, largely ignored on the plan. The northern area has a small banked enclosure (11) abutting a bank forming the southern boundary of a

Plate XXIX Carbrooke: the site of the Commandery, partly moated with fishponds and enclosures visible.
TF 9502/M/ATU 7

rectilinear enclosure, otherwise still hedged. These faced eastwards onto an old road shown by Faden (1797); the slight ditch (12) extending south possibly marks the line of this.

Two boundary features link to the north-east corner of the supposed Commandery precinct, the east-to-west section (13) bounding a series of more interesting enclosures to the south. One (14) abuts the precinct and is approached from the south by a strip of land crossed by a more recent drain leading from a frequently water-filled depression central to the area. Other smaller enclosures are to the east, with irregular undulations nearer Wood Farm being possibly related to former buildings and small ponds.

The foundation is credited to Maud, Countess of Clare who, in 1182, gave the Knights the advowson of the church and that of Little Carbrooke, now deserted, together with her manor in Carbrooke. It was dedicated to St John the Baptist ('of Jerusalem') and had a chapel. Initially there was a Knight and two brethren who had charge of twelve poor people (Doubleday and Page 1906, II, 423–5; Puddy 1961).

In 1338 a return showed that the annual value was over £192 and that land in Carbrooke, Costessey and Bawburgh was farmed by them. Besides the manor and gardens there were 426 acres (172.4ha) of land, 15 acres (6ha) of meadow, 24 acres (9.7ha) of pasture, two windmills and a dovecote in the manor of Carbrooke. Most significant is the tally of persons which may account for the size of the

establishment. There were a Preceptor and two brethren, the vicar of Carbrooke and his servant, two stipendiary secular chaplains saying masses for the founder's soul, four clerks to collect the offerings of the district, the twelve poor persons, eight servants of the house and occasional guests. Others had connections of varying kinds; there was a steward of the court, a Preceptor's squire, a chamberlain, bailiff, cook, baker, porter, warrener, carpenter, and a gardener, together with two boys of the Preceptor's, a stable boy and kitchen boy and a washerwoman. Some of these must have lived on the premises (Larking 1857, 81–3). At this time the Commandery was the greatest in England (Sire 1994, 183).

By 1535 the house had declined and all that is recorded of the additional people were the vicar and two priests; no reference was made to the twelve poor persons.

Site 31424 is interesting as it survives so close to the known position of the Commandery. Unfortunately there appears to be no firm evidence of the identity of the features there. The more northerly ones appear to be field boundaries of uncertain age. They are obviously pre-19th century as they appear related to a road extant in 1797. The southerly group is more problematic. The confused earthworks near Wood Farm may be remains of former farm buildings or even houses and gardens. Although earlier documents do survive (NRO NRS 20282 43 E3 of the 16th century and NRO MS 3256 4B1 of 1673) they offer little help in the absence of a contemporary map.

Plate XXX Castle Acre under snow, the Priory within its precinct, from the south-west. CUCAP AXA 65
(Photography by Cambridge University Collection of Air Photographs)

Castle Acre Priory SMR 4096, TF 815 148
(Pl. XXX, Fig.91)

The familiar ruins of this Cluniac site are shown surrounded by previously unmapped earthworks within the precinct wall, revealing much more extensive remains.

The extensive ruins of the Cluniac Priory of Castle Acre are among the best-preserved monastic remains in Norfolk. However, some features within the area under English Heritage Guardianship remain as earthworks while, beyond, a much larger range of features lies within the precinct wall to the east and south-east of the upstanding ruins. The precinct wall follows Priory Road in the north and South Acre Road to the east, while fragmentary remains exist beside the River Nar to the south.

Within the Guardianship area the well-defined scarped enclosure of the lay folks cemetery (1) lies north of the nave and to the west of it are traces of a former entrance way (2). To the west of the monastery low banks and platforms (3) with a fragment of masonry indicate further buildings, possibly remains of guest-houses.

In the outer grassland the northern sector has been rendered almost featureless by past ploughing. A small standing building in the north-east corner may have served as a pilgrims' chapel (4). The remaining area is divided by a well-marked channel (5) diverted from the River Nar further east which marks a former leat serving the reredorter and kitchens.

To the north of this channel several enclosures have been truncated by the excavation of the major buildings, one of them being the monks' cemetery (6). An irregular alignment of scarps and banks running north-to-south separates them from other enclosures and small building platforms; surface finds of building materials and medieval pottery have been made on some. South of the channel the main features are a series of north-south depressions (7) which may be remnants of fishponds, one reaching the southern precinct boundary, and a U-shaped ditch (8) enclosing an area of indeterminate depressions, the ditch being probably post-medieval (Wilcox 1980, 231–276; Wade-Martins (ed) 1999, 45).

William de Warenne, before 1088, established the Cluniac order here, giving them the parish church. How far the Warenne holding in Domesday 'Acre' referred to the planned Norman settlement or its predecessor is not known. The position of the church in 1086 is unknown, the present building outside the planned town has nothing before *c.* 1300 and may be on a newer site (Pevsner and Wilson 1999, 242).

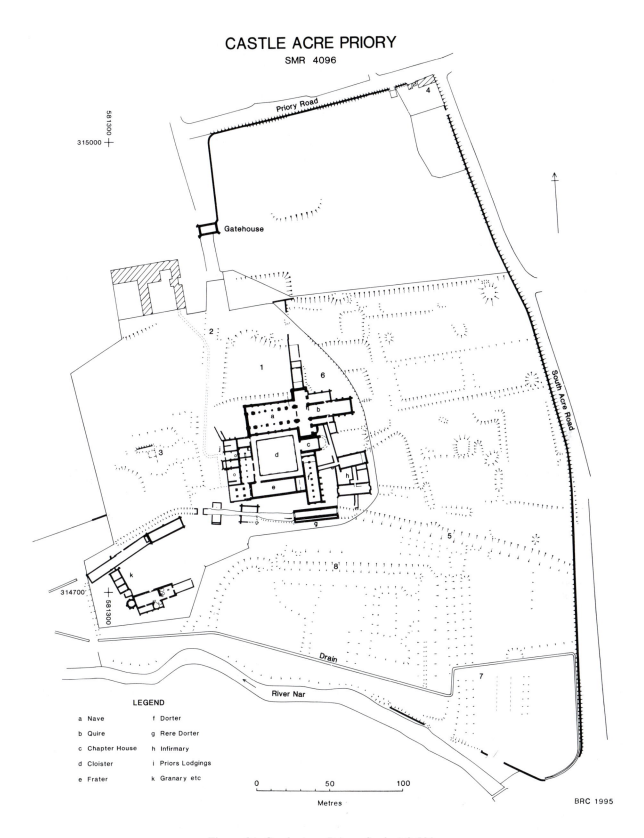

CASTLE ACRE PRIORY
SMR 4096

LEGEND

a Nave   f Dorter

b Quire   g Rere Dorter

c Chapter House   h Infirmary

d Cloister   i Priors Lodgings

e Frater   k Granary etc

0   50   100

Metres

BRC 1995

Figure 91 Castle Acre Priory. Scale 1:2,500

It is not easy to visualise the first Priory within the first-stage castle (Coad and Streeten 1982, 138–301) as it is accepted that the castle only reached its final form in stages beginning *c.* 1140. A later confirmatory charter gave the Priory a new site on two orchards and the cultivated ground between it and the town. (Doubleday and Page 1906, II, 356).

In 1401 the Priory obtained an indulgence for penitents to encourage pilgrims to contribute financially to the church. This may have made possible the building of the gatehouse and a new Prior's lodging *c.* 1500. Dissolution occurred in 1537 when there were ten monks and the Prior. The Prior's lodgings were used in later centuries as a farmhouse so preserving this building relatively intact.

Coxford Priory, East Rudham SMR 3632, TF 847 291
(Fig.92)

An extensive site with scanty upstanding buildings, recently planned for the first time.

The site of Coxford Priory lies on the western side of the River Tat with a broad area of fen to the south. The priory precinct is uncertain apart from about 100m of flint walling by the road south of Abbey Farm.

The major upstanding fragments are the remains of the nave and chancel of the priory church, but outlines of parts of the western and eastern wings of the cloister are visible in an irregular area of earthworks to the south subjected to considerable robbing and disturbance. A virtually complete building outline (1) lies to the south-west within what was a partially moated inner court, while outside to the north are outlines of two significant ranges, one aligned east-to-west (2), the other north-to-south (3). At the north-west corner of the moat are the remains of a bridge (4).

To the west of the moat are one fragment of a small building (5) and a broad east-to-west ridge (6), probably representing a further building range.

The south-west of the complex contains a series of fishponds (7) with a channel (8) leading south-east, probably outside the precinct, and re-appearing south of the present watercourse; this may have formed the southern boundary of the inner court. An enigmatic banked and ditched enclosure (9) lies on lower ground to the south-east, while to the east of the claustral range there are a boundary ditch and a possible east-to-west causeway. Further incomplete boundary channels exist to the north of the main ranges while, in the extreme north, a building outline is probably part of the medieval settlement of Coxford (SMR 29830) (Wade-Martins (ed) 1999, 52).

Coxford Priory was a house of Augustinian Canons founded *c.* 1140. It grew from a community of priests on an earlier site near East Rudham church which moved to Coxford when a new one was given by John de Cheney. His charter (NRO DN/Sun 8) refers to a mill, a fishpond, Caldewellwang, and the land between it and the water of Tattersett, all Ketellesmerewang and Noremerewang and a foldsoke for 300 sheep '*infra Penigsti*'. Another charter concerned a ditch separating the priory from Broomthorpe Common to the south.

'Wang' (ON vangr) is a portion of a field or enclosure (Field 1972, 274) hence Caldewellwang could mean 'the field or enclosure with a cold well', probably referring to the land around Mary Bone's Well (?Marie la Bonne) which is a vigorous chalk spring. The two other fields may refer to the actual site of the priory; Penigsti lay somewhere to the north-west.

The priory received many benefactions including the gift of the churches of East and West Rudham and, when dissolved, had rents in forty-four parishes, five manors and eleven churches; there were then a prior and nine canons remaining. A hospital of St Andrew, founded *c.* 1181 by Harvey Belet, was under the governance of the priory but stood outside the precinct, probably close to the bridging point on the Tat, (Saunders 1910, 284–370; Cushion and Davison 1997, 492–505).

Flitcham Priory SMR 3492, TF 734 265
(Fig.93)

The remains of the Augustinian Priory are probably overlain by the farmhouse and buildings; the remainder of the site is complicated by ditches and depressions, some at least a product of more recent drainage or landscaping.

Flitcham lies about 13km north-east of King's Lynn on the northern side of the Babingley River. The earthworks are to the south-east of the village, around Abbey Farm, and cover *c.* 23ha. They present an involved pattern made more complicated by changes to the part spring-fed drainage system, and include features unlikely to be associated with the Priory.

The most impressive earthworks are nearest the farm, with medieval masonry inside the house suggesting it and the buildings overlie the church and major conventual structures. A major feature is a broad shallow linear depression (1) which once extended south of the present river channel. To the west of it, various banks and ditches may mark old field boundaries, while in the north-west a bank (2) is the rear boundary of tofts abutting a road to the north. To the east of (1) the surface is complicated by ditches and depressions including a rectangular pond (3).

South of the farm, by the river bank, is the flint masonry outline (4) of a rectangular building. A fragment of masonry, associated with a scarp (5) and parchmarks seen in air photographs, lies to the north. To the east of the farm the most obvious feature is a linear depression (6) extending southwards and linking with another depression (7) which links to the main landscaped pond to the west. Further subdivision to the east is mostly incomplete, with a possible precinct wall position indicated by a bank (8), parallel to the present road.

The Augustinian Priory was founded early in the reign of Henry III and became a cell of Walsingham. Sometimes called the Priory of St Mary ad fontes ('at the springs') it was never very large; there were six canons in 1370. In 1514 the barns and other buildings needed repair, farming was neglected and there were debts. It was dissolved in 1538 (Doubleday and Page 1906, II, 380– 81). In 1517 it was found that the Priors of Flitcham and Walsingham had been among landowners converting arable to pasture in Flitcham and that fifteen houses were decayed (Leadam 1892–3, 6; 270, 7; 189). The possible former tofts already noted may be evidence of this.

An early 17th-century map (NRO NRS MS 4290) shows a large house, in part the present farmhouse, facing north onto a courtyard which had entrance by a porch or gatehouse to an outer enclosure. This had a small building with a tower-like structure in the north-west corner; a gate opened onto a road. The area between house and river is blank. The road past the house was Massingham Way which branched southwards from from Houghton Way and by a right-angled turn immediately north of the farm led past the house before curving south-eastwards across the valley near 'Scite of Barnestones' (in 1655 'The Springhead'). Two linked buildings to the west of the house formed an east-to-west range, two more lay in a north-to-south range to the south-west, possibly the present main barn. Two small buildings are shown in an enclosure to the north-west and two dotted rectangular outlines lay within the curve of Massingham Way.

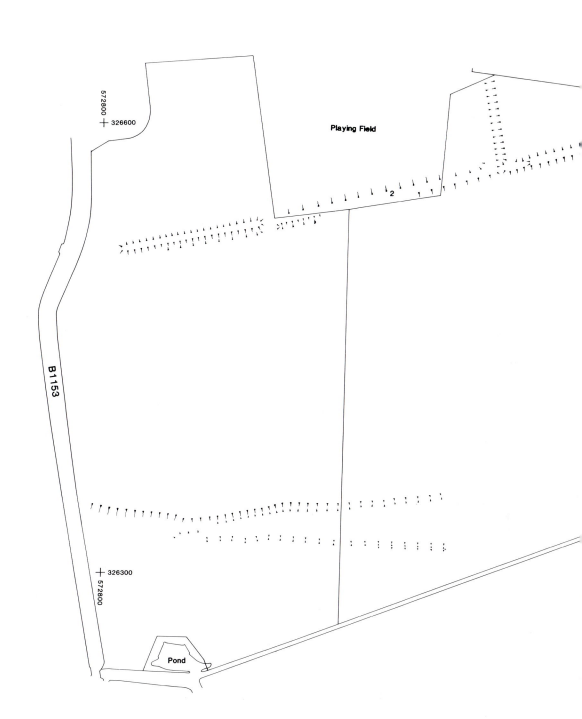

572800

+ 326600

Playing Field

2

B1153

+ 326300
572800

Pond

FLITCHAM PRIORY
SMR 3492

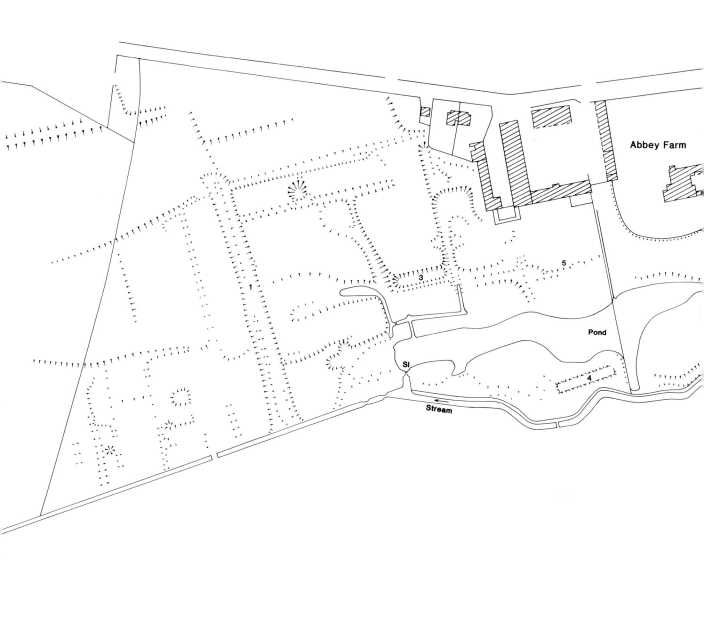

Figure 93 Flitcham Priory, limited monastic remains with evidence of medieval tofts. Scale 1:2,500

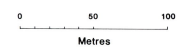

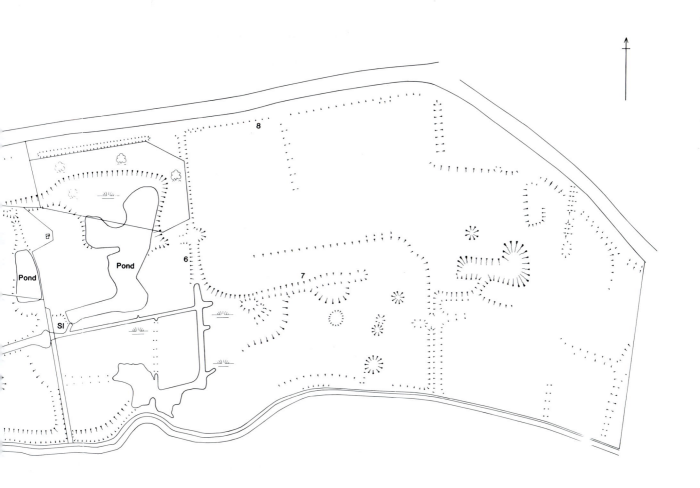

BRC 1994

Figure 93 (continuation)

HEMPTON PRIORY

SMR 7110

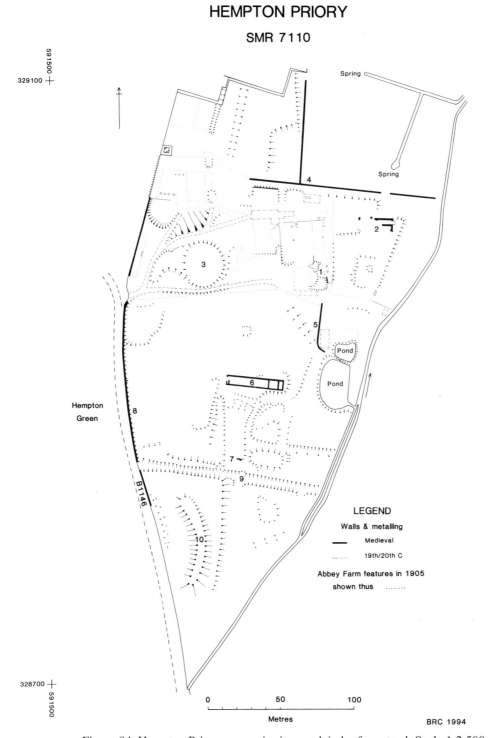

Figure 94 Hempton Priory, monastic site overlain by farmstead. Scale 1:2,500

A map of 1655 (NRO MS 4293) shows the main house with an apparently different distribution of satellite buildings, including one by the river-bank. A 'Provision Lane' seems to match the western linear depression (1) on the plan, with 'Rye Close' to its west. 'Conyvere' was an area north-west of the farm.

A map dated 1728–44 (NRO MS 4295) shows yet another arrangement of buildings. Massingham Way is called 'The Lane' and an apparent curving track is shown leading from the right-angled bend to the river. Provision Lane is not shown. A round pool is shown south-east of the farm; this and a second near the river may have been replaced by the existing ponds.

Faden (1797) still shows Massingham Way; by the 1820s it had been replaced by a direct link to the village. If the maps are reliable they witness periodic remodelling and disturbance of the site, but few details can be matched to the earthworks. This suggests that many features to the south-west of the farm may pre-date the maps and be of monastic origin, but no convincing layout of monastic buildings is indicated here or to the south of the farmhouse.

Hempton Priory SMR 7110, TF 916 289
(Fig.94)

The site of the Augustinian Priory has probably been covered by later farm buildings. Post-medieval features complicate the area.

This triangular site lies in grassland between Hempton Green to the west and a north-flowing tributary of the Wensum to the east. It is at the eastern end of Hempton village. The northern part of the area has seen much change: Faden (1797) shows a Bridewell; the Ordnance Survey 1st Edition, Abbey Farm and Bryant (1826) a windmill as well. The farm, demolished in 1969, has obliterated many older features.

The surface remains of Abbey Farm correspond with details shown on the 25" Ordnance Survey map of 1905 and are indicated on the plan. Some of them can be assumed to cover the major monastic buildings. Some buildings may contain reused flints, while the former farmhouse is indicated by depressions (1). The major medieval remnants are building fragments (2) to the north-east of the farmhouse, including a south-eastern corner buttress. Most notable is a large mound (3) with a ramp, it is likely that this marks Bryant's mill but it may have had an earlier use. Some features, notably a T-shaped wall to the north (4) and a length of wall to the south of the farmhouse may be medieval (5). The latter leads to two possible fishponds, the more northerly of which has undergone partial infilling; they are linked by leats to the stream.

Remnants of a building (6) to the west of the ponds appear to be an isolated building, probably agricultural.

To the south again are ditched enclosures at various levels and a piece of flint wall suggests a building (7). The precinct wall survives by the road to the west (8) showing that the area within was part of the Priory. The most noticeable features are an east-to-west linear depression (9) and a crescentic ridge (10); these may be post-medieval.

Hempton Priory, founded as a hospital before 1135, became an Augustinian Priory c.1200. The original founders were Roger de St Martin and Richard Ward, Ward subsequently becoming an Augustinian canon and prior.

The priory stood at the end of a dam or 'causey' linking Fakenham with Hempton and was sometimes known as Dammesende. The endowment included the Rectory and manor of Hempton and by 1291 it had interests in forty parishes; despite this, its income then was only just over £29. It had two fairs and extensive rights of sheep pasturage, a market and a watermill.

In 1200 it was granted a fair on Whit Tuesday at the causeway to Fakenham. In 1302 the priory was licensed to bring back a watercourse which used to run through the priory to its old channel.

The priory was never strong and on surrender in 1534 there were only three canons and the prior. In 1546 the site, manor and Rectory were all granted to Sir William Fermour and his wife; Fermour was a flockmaster who lived at East Barsham (Doubleday and Page 1906, II, 381–83).

Langley Abbey SMR 10344, TG 362 028
(Pl. XXXI, Fig.95)

The substantial site of the Abbey is isolated beside the flood plain of the Yare. The upstanding portions are within the remains of a moat crossed by a gateway leading to a road approaching the inner court. Building outlines and probable fishponds are also present.

Langley is a scattered settlement about 14km south-east of Norwich; the remains of the Abbey are some 2km north of the church, fringing the flood plain of the Yare.

The survey shows a considerable complex of features within the precinct surrounding the church and other major buildings which were excavated in the early 20th century (Erwood 1923, 175–234).

The precinct boundary is well-defined by a moat (1) to the north-west, south-west, where some infill has occurred and south-east, with subdued earthworks and neighbouring cropmarks showing that it continued onto a gravel terrace further to the north-east, beyond the present boundary. The major entrance (2) lies to the north-west coming from an area shown as common in 1797 (Faden). Interrupting the moat, it leads by a banked roadway (3) towards the inner court gatehouse (4). This roadway is flanked by rectangular enclosures and partial building outlines (5,6,7). One boundary (8) extends via a pond-like depression to form one side of a causeway leading onto marshes further east. Enclosures and probable fishponds (9) lie to the north-east and east of the major buildings, with two substantial building outlines to the south and south-east (10) on the edge of a terrace.

Langley Abbey was founded in 1195 by Sir Robert FitzRoger Helke, the colonising canons coming from Alnwick. The Premonstratensian Order favoured relatively isolated sites and this fulfils this condition on the edge of a gravel spread fringing marshland. Prosperous at first, with a Tuesday market and an annual fair, it began to face difficulties from flooding in the stormy late 13th century and sought help from the Pope in 1343. Despite these difficulties a licence to build and crenellate a belfry was obtained in 1346.

Towards the close of the 15th century Visitations revealed laxity, indiscipline and serious debt. In 1536 there were six canons and twenty-one servants when the abbey was dissolved and the buildings were said to be ruinous and in decay.

143

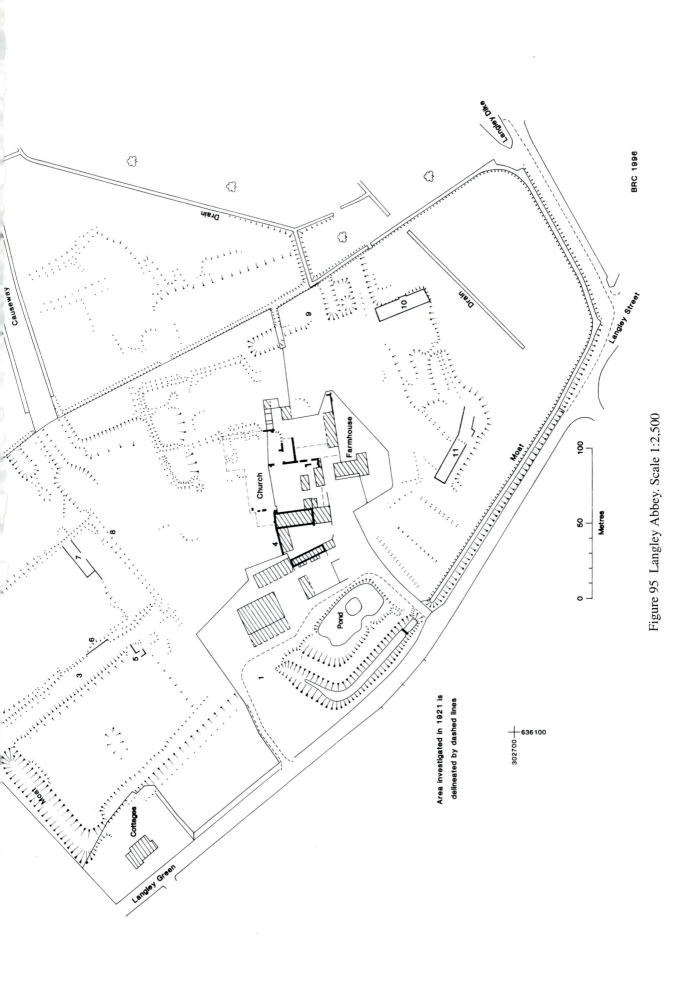

Figure 95 Langley Abbey. Scale 1:2,500

BRC 1996

Area investigated in 1921 is
delineated by dashed lines

302700 —+— 636100

Metres
0   50   100

144

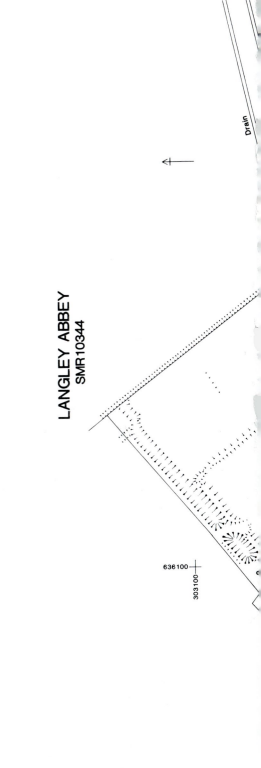

LANGLEY ABBEY
SMR10344

Drain

636100

303100

Plate XXXI Langley Abbey, the northern earthworks viewed from the south-east. TG 3602/Y/ARK 15

A survey in 1575 by John Goodwyn (Erwood 1923, 175–234) described the site as having on its eastern side a 'flete......called Percolis'; to its west the common of Langley Green, a manorial messuage and meadows and another flete next to a common causeway leading to Grenemarshe; on its northern side the river flowing from Norwich to Yarmouth and, on the southern side, common pasture. 'Percolis' may be Langley Dike. The surviving standing buildings have been identified as the Cellarium and part of the Gatehouse and a stable with other fragments of the cloister, chapter house and sacristy. North of the cloister faint outlines of the church remain. Fishponds in this situation could easily have been maintained by ground-water percolation.

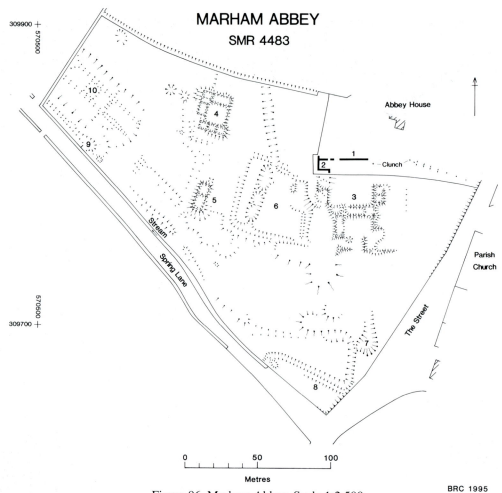

MARHAM ABBEY
SMR 4483

309900 +
570600
Abbey House
10
4
9
1
2 - Clunch
Clunch
5
6
3
Stream
Spring Lane
Parish
Church
The Street
570500
309700 +
7
8

0   50   100
Metres

BRC 1995

Figure 96 Marham Abbey. Scale 1:2,500

Marham Abbey SMR 4483, TF 706 097
(Pl. XXXII, Fig.96)

The only major Cistercian house in Norfolk, also, uniquely, of Nuns; the outlines of the cloisters together with those of other buildings are in grassland next to the scanty upstanding remains of church and parlour.

Marham lies in west Norfolk about 12.75km south-west of King's Lynn. The site of the abbey is to the west of the village street and the survivor of two parish churches, Holy Trinity, St Andrew's having been abandoned in the 16th century (Batcock 1991, 54).

The remains are of particular interest; among the best of the smaller houses in the county, it is the only major Cistercian house (Doubleday and Page 1906, II, 370). They are chiefly in grassland but the south wall of the nave of the Abbey church (1) and three sides of the parlour (2) adjoining to the west are in the grounds of Abbey House. The nave wall has two complete circular windows, one quatrefoil, one sexfoil, and the remains of another.

To the south of these is a group of grass-covered building outlines about 1m in height which represent the claustral range (3), with remains of further buildings adjoining to the south. Two other groups of building outlines can be seen to the west. The larger (4), possibly the infirmary, is U-shaped and open, apart from a wall, to the east. The smaller one (5) appears to be subdivided.

Between these and the remains of church and cloister is an incomplete ditched earthwork enclosure (6) with a shallow channel joining the northern arm. This appears to have been an inlet. The north-east corner of the enclosure appears truncated by the claustral range suggesting it is a possible earlier feature. Within the enclosure is a north-to-south depression, subdivided twice, which may have been a fishpond complex; it is linked to the outer ditch at both ends. Other earthworks include a pit (7), possibly for clunch and probably not contemporary; a possible former roadside boundary ditch and bank (8); a former (modern) sheepwash (9) and a low platform (10) between ditches of unknown age and purpose (Wade-Martins (ed) 1999, 49).

Marham Abbey was founded in 1249 by a widow, Isabella Countess of Arundel, who endowed it with her lands and the manor and services in Marham. The foundation was unique in that it was intended at the outset as a Cistercian Abbey (Thompson, S. 1991, 96) under the initial guidance of the Abbot of Waverley, a male Cistercian house in Surrey. The Nunnery was allowed to have burials and services said by their priest in their own church and to prove wills of those dying within the precinct.

The abbey seems never to have been very wealthy; in 1291 it was excused from contributing to payments because its endowments were small and its value in 1535 was just over £39. At the Dissolution there were an abbess and eight nuns.

146

Plate XXXII Marham Abbey: scanty remains of the church lie within a garden but the remainder of the earthworks are clearly visible. TF 7009/AF/DV 8

North Creake Abbey SMR 1953, TF 856 394
(Fig.97)

Earthworks surrounding the remains of the Augustinian Abbey consist mainly of enclosures and channels.

North Creake is a substantial village about 10km north-west of Fakenham in the valley of the Burn. The remains of the abbey lie to the north of the village on the boundary with Burnham Thorpe.

The earthworks lie in meadows to the north and south of the remains of the Abbey church and the adjoining farmstead which has a walled garden marking the cloister. They consist largely of linear channels corresponding to former watercourses. To the south is an incomplete trapezoidal enclosure bounded by modern drains to the west (1) and north (2) and an old channel to the east (3). The northern drain occupies part of a ditch which extended further west and linked eastwards with the old channel. Within the enclosure are two broad channels linking the western drain with the Burn. Another old channel (4) lies still further to the east. Between the enclosure and the farm is another ditch (5).

North of the abbey are more varied but subdued earthworks including a raised area with brickwork suggesting an old bridge (6). A series of eastward-facing scarps form apparent extensions to a narrow channel and mark the former course of the Burn (7) which can be linked with a fossil meander and cutoff (8) on the opposite bank. A sub-rectangular enclosure (9) lies within a larger one formed by a ditch (10) to the west, an east-to-west linear feature (11) to the north and the present river and roadway east and south. The ultimate western boundary (12) is a degraded bank and scarp while north of the linear feature is a slightly more prominent curving ditch. Dredgings dumped on the western bank of the Burn may have obliterated remains of fishponds.

The first religious building on this site was a chapel dedicated to the Blessed Virgin and founded in 1206 by Alice de Nerford on 40 acres called Lingerescroft. In 1217 Sir Robert, her husband, founded a hospital nearby, with 40 acres more, dedicated to St Bartholomew in thanksgiving for a decisive naval victory over the French (Rodger 1997, 55). In 1227 the master and brethren of the hospital, with Dame Alice's consent, became Augustinian canons. At about this time Henry III granted the new priory the right to hold four annual fairs and in 1231, becoming its patron, made it an abbey. In 1484, having suffered a disastrous fire, the buildings were curtailed. In 1506 the abbot died, the last victim of an epidemic and the monastery was dissolved (Carthew 1879a, 152–68; Bedingfeld (ed) 1966, XV–XVI, XXI; Bedingfeld and Gilyard-Beer 1970).

An 18th-century copy of a map of *c.* 1600 (NRO NRS 3503) shows the abbey remains and farm buildings in an inner precinct. To the south the Burn ran in the old straight channel to the precinct wall and then turned west before following its present course through the farmstead. The ditch partly occupied by a drain and the ditch to the north were field boundaries. In the northern field the Burn followed its former course and to the west the boundary of this field was a trackway while the curving ditch to the north was the limit of the outer precinct. Dovehouse Meadow, to the east of the Burn, had a building standing upon it. In 1812 the Burn north of the abbey was as *c.* 1600,

but to the south it appeared to have been moved further east and then diverted north-westwards to reach the inner precinct wall (NRO MS 18623/36 365 x 3).

St Benet's Abbey, Horning SMR 5199, TG 383 156
(Pl. XXXIII, Fig.98)

Impressive earthworks surround the site of the church and conventual buildings, all enclosed within a perimeter ditch, and include numerous fishponds. They are approached by a causeway from the north-west leading to the remains of a gatehouse.

St Benet's Abbey lies in an eastward extension of the parish of Horning which is about 12km north-east of Norwich. The isolated site is on a low island in riverine marshes on the north bank of the River Bure.

The D-shaped precinct is defined by a water-filled ditch fed from the Bure, possibly a former meander; the entry near the gatehouse from a causeway running across the marshes being obscured by infilling. A bank inside the ditch contains remains of a wall. Licence to crenellate was granted in 1327; besides protection the ditch aided the drainage and supplied water for fishponds.

An inner court is defined by ditches or banks (a) to (c) and (d) and from there to the river or possibly westward by (e). Rectangular foundations on (d) may be those of a gate or tower. Within are the scanty remains of the church; the north wall of the nave remains; the unusually narrow form suggests a rebuilding on earlier foundations. The remainder, apart from the north transept, has largely fallen or is marked by turf banks and mounds. Earthworks to the south mark the positions of conventual buildings, most notably the sunken rectangles of (g) and (h), the first being possibly remnants of the cloister.

An outer court surrounds the inner on the landward side. The rectangular gatehouse has arched gateways on its north-western and south-eastern sides but lost an upper storey in the 18th century when a drainage mill was built. The scoop wheel for this mill is visible on Stark's engraving (Stark 1834). A possible dock lay to the south-west. To the east is a spectacular group of fishponds, still water-filled, while to the south of them are possible further ponds enclosing three rectangular platforms.

The remainder of the periphery consists of a series of enclosures (1 to 10); several of these (1,3,5,6? 7,9 and 10) include water features, probably fishponds of varying forms, others (1,2 and 3) are crossed by leats and there are signs of buildings on (4), possibly a dovecote or viewing point in the north-west corner, and (5) and (9). Some of these enclosures may be gardens, others the sites of farm buildings.

The riverside was also marked by a wall, some remains of which are now beneath the water. The most notable earthwork here is that of the Chequers Inn demolished by 1907. It was approached by a track (j) from the gatehouse passing a depression (m) which was a lined pond or undercroft. Other buildings edged the waterfront; one (t) to the south-east of the Chequers may have been next to a jetty, and there were two more ponds. This area handled the river traffic which supplied the monastery (Wade-Martins (ed) 1987, 36; 1999, 48).

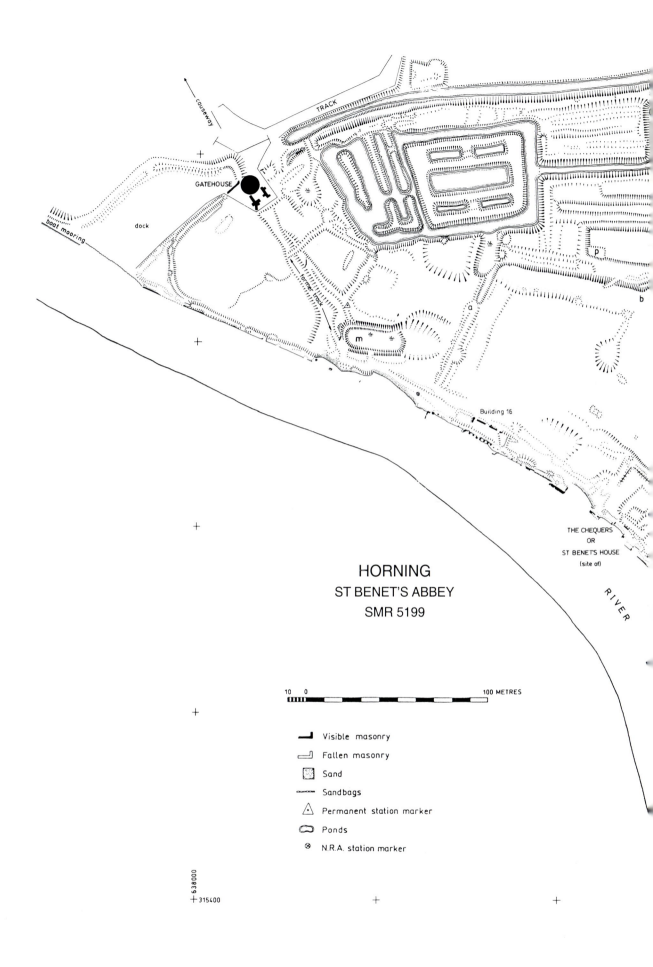

HORNING
ST BENET'S ABBEY
SMR 5199

10   0   100 METRES

⌐ Visible masonry
⌐ Fallen masonry
▧ Sand
∼ Sandbags
△ Permanent station marker
⬭ Ponds
⊗ N.R.A. station marker

638000
315400

Figure 98 St Benet's Abbey, outstanding monastic complex. Scale 1:2,000

GN

DITCH

ENCLOSURE 1

ENCLOSURE 2

q

ENCLOSURE 4

r

ENCLOSURE 3

c

ENCLOSURE 5

f

DITCH

ENCLOSURE 6

ENCLOSURE 7

h

g

ENCLOSURE 8

e

ENCLOSURE 9

d

?wharf

t

638600

315400

ENCLOSURE 10

modern boat
mooring

RCHM
ENGLAND

150

Plate XXXIII St Benet's Abbey, showing the well-preserved fishponds, the gatehouse and remains of the church.
TG 3815/K/AGW 11

This isolated marshland place is typical of one chosen as a pre-Danish monastic site with its accent on solitude rather than acessibility, though this is tradition and not certainty. At some point in the 10th century the site was re-established but it was not until *c.* 1020 that Cnut, attracted by the monastery, refounded it as a Benedictine abbey. By 1046 it had three manors and twenty-eight dependent churches. It figures, with sixty-five entries, as a substantial Domesday landholder.

Although it had numerous holdings in the medieval period, it had only two small dependent houses. One was Rumburgh priory but this became a cell of St Mary's, York early in the 12th century. The other was the neighbouring Hospital of St James, founded in 1153, with a subordinate at Great Hautbois, founded *c.*1235. The number of monks of St Benet's remained quite constant, varying from the low to mid twenties until the end. However, there must have been a substantial number of lay people in attendance.

The abbey had the solitary distinction in England of not being dissolved. In 1530 the King made Bishop Rugge Abbot with all its properties in exchange for those of the Bishopric. The Bishop was required to retain a prior and twelve monks to maintain services but by 1540 the last

monk left and Rugge had stripped the Abbey. The precinct was plundered for building materials and the site was let out to farm. The survey published here was carried out by the Royal Commission on Historical Monuments in October 1994.

Shouldham Priory SMR 4255, TF 679 094
(Fig.99)

Much of this Gilbertine house is concealed by Abbey Farm or is visible as extensive soil markings; these earthworks seem to consist of enclosures and ditches with possible fishponds and are rather problematic.

Shouldham Priory lies to the north of the village of Shouldham which is about 12km south-east of King's Lynn. Much of the priory is concealed beneath the farm buildings or is visible only as soil marks to the north-east and north of the farm (Green 1992, 30,31; Wade-Martins (ed) 1999, 50). It was established as a house of the Gilbertine Order for canons and nuns and was the only one in Norfolk. The few earthworks lie to the south of this complex and have been subjected to some modern disturbance.

SHOULDHAM PRIORY

SMR 4255

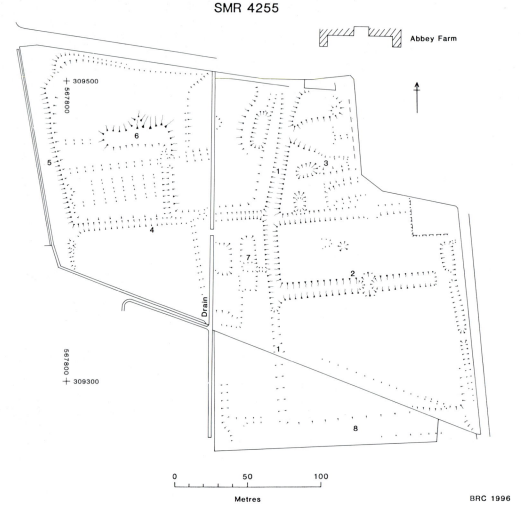

Figure 99 Shouldham Priory, peripheral remains of a Gilbertine site. Scale 1:2,500

The dominant feature is a marked north-to-south channel (1) dividing the area and becoming less remarkable further south. To the east of it are two rectangular enclosures separated by a ditch (2) which has been disturbed by modern activities. A former farm building has intruded on the more northerly one. To the north of these is a remnant of a third enclosure (3) much disturbed and partly obscured by farm buildings.

To the west of the central ditch are two other enclosures cut by a modern drain. They are separated by an east-to-west ditch (4) which extends westwards to a distinct bank which appears to mark an old boundary (5), possibly the edge of a roadway leading northwards and eastwards to approach the priory. The northern one has a mound (6) marking the site of a building. Both include depressions which may represent former ponds, one (7) being linked to the main ditch by a short channel. Both also are marked by shallow internal ditches. The southernmost feature (8), a slight east-to-west linear depression, appears on the line of a Roman road, the cross-section of which was noticed further west in the edge of a ditch (Wade-Martins (ed) 1999, 50).

Shouldham Priory was founded c. 1190 by Geoffrey FitzPiers, Earl of Essex. The foundation charter endowed it with the manor of Shouldham and the two parish churches of All Saints and St Margaret. By 1291 it had an annual income of over £207 and held property in London and in twenty-six Norfolk parishes. However in 1392, it was valued at 200 marks (over £133) having suffered losses to its properties by fire, a gale, and river and sea floods. When surrendered in 1538 there were a prior, sub-prior, eight canons and a prioress, sub-prioress and five nuns (Doubleday and Page 1906, II, 412–14).

It remained with the Crown until 1553 when it was sold to Thomas Mildmay. Surveys made in his day and in those of Sir John Hare, his successor, give very few details of the priory, referred to as 'The Abbey'. The earliest, made at some time after 1553 (NRO Hare 2497) mentions only the 'Abby Grene'; one dated 1633 made by William Hayward lists the 'Site of the Abby', the 'Abby lane', 'Abby field' and 'Abby Greene'. The Abbey Green was common pasture and lay north and west of the site and the Abbey field to the south and east (NRO Hare 2495). It is clear that apart from the western entry already noticed there was another leading to the priory from the two churches to the south-east. The earthworks do not appear to be described and must have been part of the site though their function is unknown. The possible ponds seem unusual in view of the numbers elsewhere on the priory site.

Plate XXXIV Wendling Abbey, vertical photograph showing parchmarks. TF 9312/R/GKH 9

Wendling Abbey SMR 7281, TF 939 127
(Pl. XXXIV, Fig.100)

The Premonstratensian house has some signs of the actual conventual buildings remaining but most of the church is gone. A great deal of disturbance has occurred.

Wendling lies about 5.75km west of East Dereham; the remains of the abbey are about 0.75km east of the church and straddle an eastward-flowing stream. Most of the foundations of the buildings are said to have been removed for road building according to an article and plan (*c.* 1810) printed in 1859 (Bulwer 1859, 38–40).

To the north of the stream building outlines of the claustral range are visible as grass-covered masonry and parchmarks, with some remains of flint and brick on the surface. All that is left of the abbey church is a fragment of flintwork (1) representing the south-western corner of the nave. The 1810 plan gives some indication of how much has been removed. To the east of the cloister (2) was the chapter-house (3), still largely visible, while to the south of the cloister parchmarks and surface masonry (4) vie with mounds and depressions to suggest robbery of the buildings there. A building (5) omitted in 1810 to the east of the cloister may not be medieval but is more likely to be the infirmary.

South of the stream is a fairly complete building outline (6), again absent from the 1810 plan. Also here are two substantial ditches which can be traced in arable land to the east. It seems likely that these are former channels of the stream; the irregular banks of the northern one (7) suggest that this may have been the original course. It appears to link with what may have been a moated enclosure (8), now partially visible in arable land to the east, and of which the more southerly channel formed a part.

Wendling Abbey was founded about 1265 by William de Wendling as a Premonstratensian house. He endowed it with a messuage in Wendling and lands there, in Scarning and the Franshams and buildings in Feltwell.

There are various records of buildings and repairs. In 1411 the Pope granted indulgences to those who, on visiting, gave alms for the repair of the church. In 1478 it had to be rebuilt because it had been destroyed by fire. In 1482 progress in building was noted but speed on work on the church was urged and this was still in hand in 1488 when progress on building church and conventual houses was mentioned. It can be assumed that part of the remains at least are the results of this programme. It seems there was also concern over numbers, the total varying between four and six canons besides the abbot and in 1491 they were ordered to raise the number to eight.

In 1528 the Pope allowed dissolution to Cardinal Wolsey but his fall saved the abbey though confidence may have been lowered. In 1534 the County Commissioners reported that in addition to the canons there were two hinds and ten servants and that there was much decay. It was valued at over £55 in 1535 and was granted to Christ Church, Oxford in 1546 by Henry VIII (Doubleday and Page 1906, II, 421–423; Butler 1961, 226–9).

WENDLING ABBEY
SMR 7281

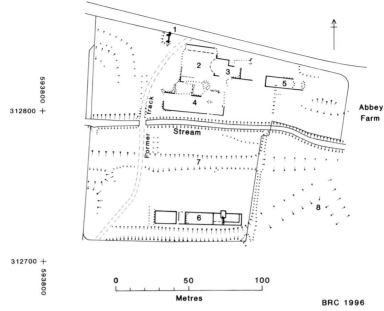

Figure 100 Wendling Abbey. Scale 1:2,500

Plate XXXV West Acre Priory, view from the north-east showing a hollow way and enclosures together with the site of the priory church and associated buildings. TF 7815/R/AUG 10

West Acre Priory SMR 3881, 16580; TF 782 150
(Pl. XXXV, Fig.101)

A large precinct in which the Augustinian house survives as irregular mounds but some upstanding walls and buildings remain. Probable village earthworks, fishponds and a hollow way are notable.

The precinct of the Augustinian Priory, straddling the Nar, contains some 30ha; unlike those of the Cluniac Priory of Castle Acre upstream (pp136–7), only scant remains of the buildings are visible above ground.

The church and immediate surroundings were excavated and interpreted in the 1920s (Fairweather and Bradfer-Lawrence 1929, 359–94) and are represented by the cluster of earthworks north-east of Abbey Farm. Important survivals within the precinct are the barn and, south of the river, the upstanding ruins of a building of unknown purpose. The precinct boundary is most evident in the south-east where flint and ashlar masonry is clearly visible; elsewhere it follows existing roads apart from a length near the 14th-century gatehouse and the parish church.

Earthworks south of the Nar fall into three groups. In the extreme south-east are interrupted lengths of a linear depression (1); it joins a deeper linear feature (2) and extends to the valley floor. To the east of this is a small

sub-rectangular mound with a surrounding bank interpreted as a possible Iron Age square barrow (SMR 16580).

In the south-western corner are ridges, banks and ditches with a short length of masonry (3) on one scarp. On the valley floor opposite the conventual earthworks are depressions of various sizes and forms, one water-filled being one of a pair of fishponds together with a building (4) outlined on a causeway leading to the river.

North of the river and east of the churchyard is a probable hollow way (5) with three small banked enclosures on its northern flank. Near the river are two large depressions (6,7), the latter water-filled, both with leats leading to the river, again probable fishponds. South-west of the barn is a circular mound (8) at the west end of a shallow causeway; this may have been a mill-mound.

The priory was founded by Olivet, priest of Acre, who formed a community following the Augustinian rule around the church of West Acre. In the early 12th century Ralph de Tosny endowed the community and the priory church and buildings were constructed (Vincent 1993, 490). The surviving portions of the priory church show Norman and Early English characteristics (Pevsner 1962, 371).

There is little firm evidence about the nature of features in the precinct. A way which used to pass through the midst of the priory-court was diverted outside in about 1208

(Blomefield 1775, IV, 749–53). This might refer to the modified hollow way (2) in the south-east of the precinct; it appears to have led towards a fording point on the Nar and a footpath just outside the precinct wall reaches the same ford. Another possibility is the short hollow way east of the churchyard, but this looks more like a back way to properties on its northern flank perhaps taken into the precinct. It is also possible that the old way through the midst of the priory-court was diverted to become Sandy Lane.

In 1343 the Priory was licenced to enlarge its 'manse' by enclosing two acres of common in Custhorpe (south of the river) in exchange for two acres of pasture (Cal. Patent Rolls 1343, 5). This might refer to the upstanding building south of the river but Pevsner (1962, 372) dates it c. 1400; it does show that enlargement of the precinct did occur. The enigmatic features in its south-western corner may have formed part of the hamlet of Custhorpe.

The medieval watermills recorded (NRO BIR/1 396 x 2) were apparently outside the precinct. Some of the depressions in the valley floor were undoubtedly fishponds though other works may have been for osiers or alders. However, in 1494 the Bishop's visitation criticised the sub-prior for devoting too much time to rearing swans on the water near the priory, sending them as presents to important persons without profit to the House (Doubleday and Page 1906, II, 402). This implies something more extensive and enclosed than the river channel.

In 1537 only eight canons and the Prior signed the surrender. In 1538 it was granted to the Duchess of Richmond and, after her death it reverted to Sir Thomas Gresham. In 1577 it was reported that his agents were selling freestone from West or Castle Acre at 20d the load (Smith, Baker and Kenny 1979, 251).

West Dereham Abbey SMR 4396, TF 663 003
(Fig.102)

Earthworks lying to the south of the Abbey site (Premonstratensian) have now largely vanished. Possible fishponds lie within a pattern of ditches and linear depressions, some of them probably comparatively modern. The ditch surrounding the site may be 17th-century.

West Dereham is a straggling village about 5km south-east of Downham Market and the abbey site is about 1.5km south-south-east of the parish church. The site is enclosed within a large rectangular ditch. Aerial photographs have revealed the outlines of the abbey buildings although virtually nothing remains above ground. The cropmarks of the monastic church are obscured but a buttressed gatehouse and a probable barn are clearly visible to the north. Other buildings include probable cloisters and a chapter house; an infirmary lies to the east. A detached building outline to the south has been identified as a rere-dorter (Edwards 1978, 89–92; see also Wade-Martins (ed) 1987, 34; Green 1992, 46).

To the south are the earthworks not previously planned. The most northerly is an isolated near-rectangular depression (1) within which is a figure-of-eight system of ditches. To the south of it is a complicated pattern of ditches, some probably modern, linear depressions and what may be former fishponds. The pond within a hollow is linked seasonally with a drain but is at the northern end of a broad linear feature (2) leading south with a westward link. There is a lengthy sinuous channel (3) east of the pond linked by a leat to smaller ponds to the west. A large dry, partly infilled depression (4) lies in the north-eastern corner and is linked to another linear one. These appear to be fishponds. The south-eastern area has a series of sub-parallel linear troughs (5) too widely separated to be ridge and furrow.

The abbey was founded in 1188 for Premonstratensian Canons. They were known as White Canons and were more austere than the Black Augustinian order, having a preference for remote sites. They were granted a weekly market in 1199 and a three-day annual fair. In 1285 they were allowed to enlarge their site on the western side at the end of their close called Fishecroft. In 1535 the annual value was over £228; it appears to have been a well-run house and the Abbot received a substantial pension (Doubleday and Page 1906, II, 414–18).

At the Dissolution it came to Thomas Dereham with possessions including 'the fishery in the waters of West Dereham'; this may refer to the Wissey. Blomefield (1775, IV, 80–93) described the gatehouse as still standing, brick-built, embattled, with an octagonal tower at each corner. Blomefield says that on each side a later Sir Thomas Dereham built a wing with a quadrangle and a cloister to the south. This probably refers to an inner gatehouse since aerial photographs show no sign of a later building near what is clearly a gatehouse to the north (Edwards 1978, plate 19).

The only evidence for the southern earthworks is the 1850 Tithe Map (NRO DN/TA E8). This shows the main features on the survey. The northern depression was a simple pond while several drains, particularly the western, eastern and southern ones, are shown as field boundaries only. This may indicate subsequent dredging. The southern pond was not linked to the present drain. Of other depressions, linear or otherwise, there is no indication on the Tithe Map; each division being simply described as part of the lawn. It might be assumed that some at least were medieval fishponds, but some may well be associated with the later mansion. The ditch surrounding the whole site incorporating both the cropmarks and the earthworks was designated 'The Moat'. It is not possible to say whether this was an original feature or a name applied to later work. There is a strong possibility that this was constructed by Dereham to surround his 17th-century house.

WEST DEREHAM ABBEY

SMR 4396

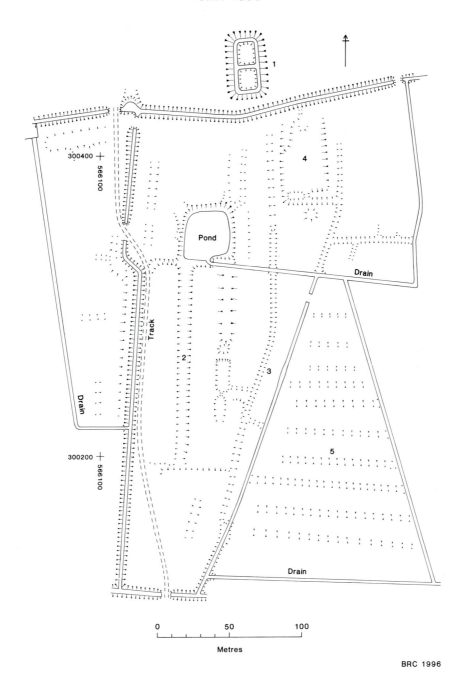

Figure 102 West Dereham Abbey, peripheral features of a monastic site and post-dissolution house. Scale 1:2,500

WORMEGAY PRIORY

SMR 3456

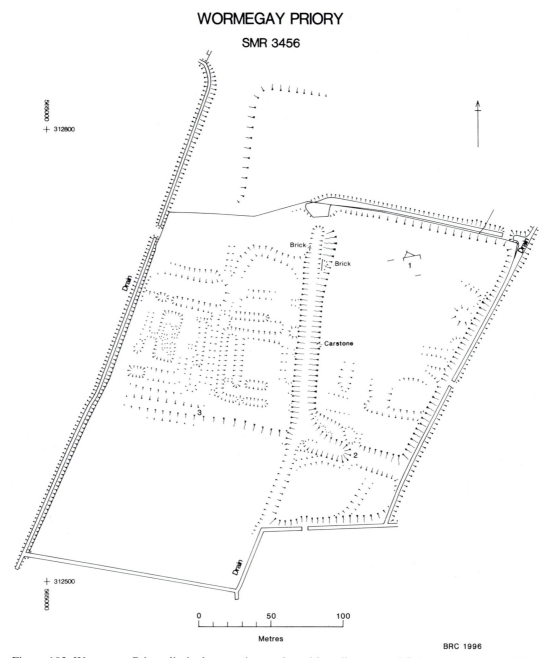

Figure 103 Wormegay Priory, limited monastic remains with well-preserved fishponds. Scale 1:2,500

Wormegay Priory SMR 3456, TF 652 126
(Pl. XXXVI, Fig 103)

Of this somewhat unsuccessful Augustinian house nothing can be seen; the earthworks consist of a moat lying to the east of a system of depressions, channels and ridges comprising the fishponds.

Wormegay Priory is almost 1km north-east of Wormegay Castle and village. No visible upstanding remains exist but there are some 4ha of earthworks. The most prominent feature is a large trapezoidal moat enclosing the highest part of the site. Within this, modern farm buildings existed until the 1960s and some foundations of these can still be seen, (1) possibly incorporating an earlier structure. The moat is well-defined and contains water seasonally; the western arm and part of the southern one are 2m deep and

over 15m wide. The remainder of the southern limb has been degraded by infilling and the original entrance was probably there (2). The eastern and northern arms are narrower and are used by a modern drain. Some masonry is visible at three points on the edge of the western limb.

To the west lie the earthworks of a rectilinear network of depressions, channels and ridges interpreted as a system of fishponds. Infilling and ploughing have obliterated some detail, especially along what appears to have been a southern boundary bank and ditch (3) and also to the north. Several of the channels within the area appear to be linked to the western limb of the moat and it is possible that this intricate pattern may not have been created at once but may be the outcome of additions and modifications over a period of time.

The history of the priory is obscure. Until recently it was believed to have been founded by William de Warenne

158

Plate XXXVI Wormegay Priory, the trapezoidal moat and fishponds. TF 6512/M/AST 15

at some time between 1189 and 1209 (Doubleday and Page 1906, II, 407). However it is now known that it was established at least fifteen years earlier. Henry II's confirmation charter, dated early in July 1175, describes it as the church of Sts Mary and John at nearby Setchey and a fair was licensed to be held for the Canons on Holy Cross Day and the two days following. The obligation to minister to needs of a house already built to support thirteen lepers was also stated; this was a common form of development for an Augustinian house and must refer to the Wormegay site. The founder was Reginald de Warenne and, as this was a confirmatory charter, the original foundation must have been between 1166, when he succeeded to the barony, and 1175 (Vincent 1999, 307–312).

The priory was never wealthy; in 1291 it was valued at over £37 but in 1324 the Exchequer Barons investigated a claim from the priory that it held its lands in free alms and was therefore exempt from payments. Eventually because of extreme poverty, it was annexed in 1468 to the neighbouring Augustinian house at Pentney and was for the remainder of its time valued with that priory. Blomefield recorded (1775, IV, 213) that there were, in his day, no visible remains to be seen.

WYMONDHAM ABBEY
SMR 9437

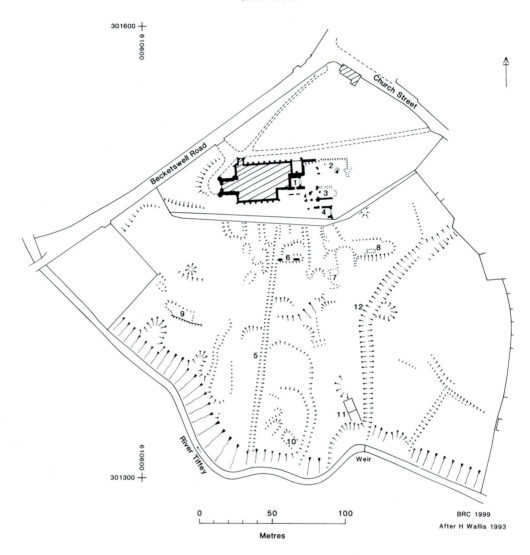

Figure 104 Wymondham Abbey. Scale 1:2,500

Wymondham Abbey SMR 9437, TG 107 014
(Pl. XXXVII, Fig.104)

The earthworks lie to the south of the present churchyard and include some of the conventual buildings and others which are unexplained.

The abbey lies on the south-western margin of Wymondham. The parish church is virtually all that remains of a Benedictine monastery which shared its church with the town. The original Norman church had a central tower separating nave and chancel, transepts, twin western towers, a chancel with apsidal end, two aisles and apsidal chapels east of the transepts. The conventual buildings lay to the south. Later the western towers were demolished and a new one was added from 1448 onwards. A new crossing tower had already been built about 1400 (Pevsner 1962, 393; Margeson, Seiller and Rogerson 1994, 51; Pevsner and Wilson 1999, 792–7).

After the Reformation the nave of the church continued to serve as parish church, much of the remainder being removed except for the central tower (1) which remains as a shell. Fragments of walls immediately to the east represent the locations of a Lady Chapel (2), St Andrew's Chapel (3) and the chapter house (4). The eastern end of the chapter house still stands to nearly its full height. The remainder of the conventual buildings lie to the south in a field extending to the River Tiffey. A straight ditch (5), probably of 19th-century origin, cuts through the cloister.

Two fragments of flint masonry (6) represent part of the south wall of the refectory which formed the range to the south of the cloister. Other building positions capable of identification include the rere-dorter (7) and the infirmary (8).

Parchmarks on aerial photographs give a much clearer impression of these buildings, as well as three other isolated structures further south, but the thick long grass makes ground identification very difficult. Of the three additional structures, the westernmost (9) is a low platform with a southern boundary wall still visible. The central one (10) is a sunken outline with additional depressions to the north-west, positioned to the west of a curving ditch which

160

Plate XXXVII Wymondham Abbey, the surviving church, associated earthworks and parchmarks from the south.
AAF194/17 *Photo by Eileen Horne 27 July 1979, copyright Aerial Archaeology*

broadens into a pond-like feature to the north. The easternmost structure (11) is an almost completely subdivided building outline, abutting the scarp which is part of the natural bluff overlooking the river. It is close to the point where a broad depression (12), extending from the north-eastern boundary of the field, reaches the river. This separates the area of buildings from the more even south-eastern part of the site where some incomplete subdivision is noted. No convincing earthworks of fishponds are seen, although the likeliest location is within the depression north of (10) (Wade-Martins (ed) 1987, 35).

A priory was founded here in the reign of Henry I by William de Albini as a cell of St Albans. As part of his benefaction he granted lands before the church doors to gain privacy, obtaining royal licence to divert a highway for this purpose.

The priory was faced with two major problems. The first was its relationship with St Albans which insisted on imposing priors despite the foundation charter's stipulation to the contrary. The second was with the townspeople whose original church had been replaced by the Priory church. Neither problem was completely resolved until the 15th century; by then the church was formally divided, while the Pope granted the monastery abbey status in 1448.

By 1500 the number of monks had sunk to eleven but Visitations of 1520 and 1526 showed that conditions in the abbey were much improved. The abbot and ten monks subscribed to the King's supremacy (Doubleday and Page 1906, II, 336–343).

A Road Order of 1826 (NRO Road Order Box 11, No 11) shows that the original western road was much closer to the church buildings while the ha-ha separating the abbey and the meadow containing the earthworks was dug only in 1834.

Plate XXXVIII Baconsthorpe Castle, the elaborate house within its moated enclosure is shown together with the later mere, outer gatehouse and formal garden. TG 1238/P/ASJ 26

Castles

Castles are a post-Conquest feature of Norfolk and were not constructed after the 15th century. The most obvious example, Norwich, has not been considered here. The only royal castle in the county, its earthworks are now virtually confined to the motte on which the surviving keep stands, subsequent developments in town life having removed all other features. For that reason it has been excluded from this study pending the results of the Castle Mall and other excavations. The motte within the Roman fort at Burgh Castle, formerly in Suffolk, though an interesting site, has also been omitted as surface remains are so slight. The castles recorded here embrace a range of forms from the earliest to the latest, where earthworks survive.

Thetford Castle, a tall conical motte, is located within the remains of an Iron Age promontory fort, modified to form a bailey, which guarded crossings of the Little Ouse and Thet, one of the major routeways into Norfolk. Others of the same form but of less significance are those at Middleton, which once had a small bailey, Wormegay which survived as the head of an Honour and guarded the entry to its Fen island, Horsford near Norwich, and Denton, discovered in woodland in the 19th century, very small and with no obvious strategic importance. The other early form of castle, the ringwork, is represented by Red Castle, Thetford, which once had a bailey and guarded another ford on the Little Ouse, and by Wymondham and Hunworth, relatively simple structures with no known history. Most of these were of the first generation of castle building, apparently soon abandoned and in one or two cases, largely forgotten.

Mileham, whose history is little known, is an interesting structure with a stone keep on a low motte with a bailey, all surrounded by a circular ringwork. There is also a rectangular earthwork of uncertain date attached.

Old Buckenham, unusually, was destroyed to house an Augustinian Priory and was replaced by New Buckenham which has a circular keep set within a ringwork with an outer bailey. Subsequent heightening and the burial of a gatehouse saw the creation of a bailey to the west with a new gatehouse giving access. Both sites have been re-examined and interesting additional features have come to light at New Buckenham.

Castle Acre and Castle Rising have seen varying amounts of excavation which have shown that assumptions based on visible surface evidence may be completely wrong. Castle Acre revealed continuing improvement of defences from a fairly simple stone building within a palisaded bank and ditch with a gatehouse, to a stone keep within a walled enclosure and with an outer bailey. Castle Rising shows establishment at the expense of an earlier inhabited area and subsequent development up to the mid-14th century. Recent work by Robert Liddiard has suggested that they may have been in a medieval 'landscape of lordship' designed to impress as much as withstand attack.

The last group are not, properly speaking, castles in the true sense of the word so much as fortified manor houses whose owners were granted a licence to crenellate. Weeting is a very early example of the type and stands within a clearly-defined moat. Great Hautbois is much less familiar and has undergone much destruction and alteration so that comparatively little is known of the site. Baconsthorpe Castle is really a late medieval fortified hall subsequently extended and partially converted before final abandonment and is much better known. Licence to crenellate was obtained after the house was built and was largely a status symbol.

Norfolk is not well-endowed with castles; it was distant from any invasion shore and from any major north-to-south route and this, coupled with the flat landscape, meant that their construction was not necessary or particularly easy. Of those considered here, the two Thetford castles were in the most obvious strategic location. Middleton was of less salient value in this respect; it does command an entry from the west but could equally well have been designed to protect the property of its lord. Wormegay had an administrative as well as a limited local strategic value, Horsford and Denton seem to have been of local significance only as were Hunworth and Wymondham. The development of Castle Acre on the Peddars' Way was gradual while Old Buckenham, New Buckenham and Castle Rising mark stages in the rising prominence of the d'Albini family.

Baconsthorpe Castle SMR 6561, TG 121 381
(Pl. XXXVIII, Fig.105)

A nationally important site, a sham defensive structure set within a later 15th-century designed landscape.

Baconsthorpe is a village about 4.5km south-east of Holt; the castle is on lower ground roughly 1km to the north. The remains of the castle (1) lie within a moat, the southern and western arms of which appear largely unaltered. It is probable that the northern arm is later, the moated platform having been enlarged northwards in *c.* 1480–1504 while the mere to the east, dredged out and re-created in 1972, may be an addition to the moat. The D-shaped apron to the east appears to be an addition to the enclosure.

Surviving buildings on the platform include a mid 15th-century gatehouse (2), the south-western portion of the curtain wall of the same period and the late 15th or early 16th century remainder of the walling together with a roofless building (3) in the south-eastern corner. A late 16th-century outer gatehouse (4) stands beyond the moat to the south and was inhabited until 1920.

The earthworks beyond the moated area are extensive and include the retaining dam (5) to the north of the moat and the north-eastern edge of the mere, beyond which is the dry channel of the stream diverted to the recreated mere in 1972. To the south-east of the mere are the remains of dams (6) which may have formed a pool or planned vista visible from the castle.

To the east of the outer gatehouse and south of the mere is a quadrilateral area bounded on the west by a low degraded scarp (7) and on the east and south-east by the stream. Within this is a central pond, rectangular in shape,

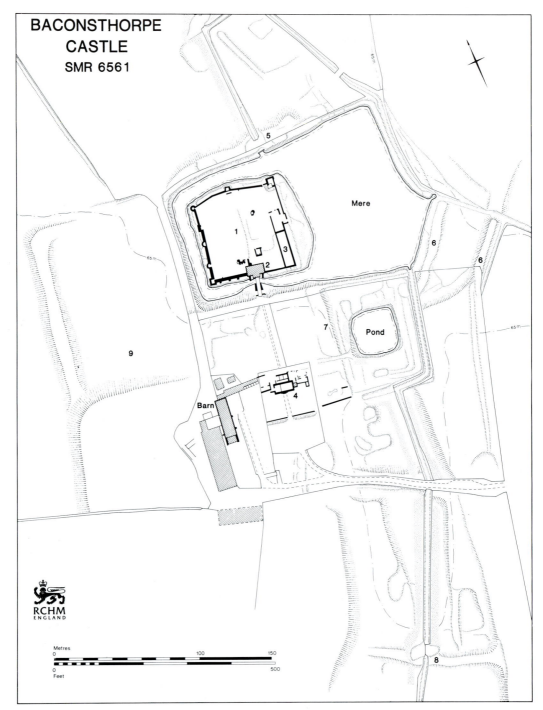

BACONSTHORPE
CASTLE
SMR 6561

Mere

Pond

Barn

RCHM
ENGLAND

Metres
0   100   150
0   500
Feet

Figure 105 Baconsthorpe, an impressive fortified manor house. Scale 1:2,000

a possible viewing platform and raised walks indicating a formal garden. It is possible that the southern scarped edge of the garden may have acted as a dam to form an ornamental pool while a further feature (8) to the south of the present track may have been a causeway.

To the west of the outer gatehouse are a 16th-century barn and the degraded scarps bounding two former enclosures (9), the northernmost one in alignment with the north arm of the moat (Wade-Martins (ed) 1987, 60).

Known simply as Thorpe (Torp) in 1086 (Brown (ed) 1984, 9,177; 33,2) the village later added that of a major landholder to its name. The Bacons sold their estate in Baconsthorpe to William Heydon in c. 1400. The Heydons had been associated with the county since 1221. Leland (Chandler 1993, 315) records that William began to acquire land and that his son John, a noted lawyer, began to build

the facade of a new manor house at Baconsthorpe but died before it was completed. Blomefield (1769, III, 709) recorded that Sir Henry Heydon (son of John; died 1504) built the Hall and described it as 'a spacious sumptuous pile (built) entirely from the ground except the tower (which was built by his father) in the space of six years'. It is possible that it took longer than this. A dragge of 1506 (NRO NRS 23369 Z99) records two manorial sites in Baconsthorpe quite simply as 'Site of Heydon's manor with all the closes and woods adjacent to it' and 'Site of the manor of Heydons called Woodhall with all the closes adjacent' (translation). The first is the 'castle', the other the preceding manor.

A licence to crenellate was obtained in 1561, possibly at the time of the building of the outer gatehouse and court. It was a status symbol and not a serious fortification of the

164

house. At the same time licence to empark 1440 acres around the village was obtained and this may be the time at which the formal gardens were built; little convincing sign of the park remains. The family flourished both locally and nationally, building Heydon Hall in Saxlingham in *c.* 1550 but began to lose ground, especially in the Civil War, and to sell lands in Baconsthorpe. By 1653 Baconsthorpe Castle began to be destroyed, a contract for its demolition being signed by Sir William Heydon in 1654. Blomefield (1769, III, 711) says 'the chief part of the hall was pulled down in 1650, that which is now standing was the tower or Gatehouse'. Since then agriculture, sporting interests, dumping and dredging have all had their influence on the features which remain (Everson and Wilson-North 2002).

The site is in the Guardianship of English Heritage. It is a nationally important site which bridges the gap between landscapes of the early 15th century and those of the early 17th century.

Castle Acre SMR 3449, TF 819 151
(Fig.106)

An elaborate set of earthworks which enclose the final development of the castle, consisting of two wards and with three gatehouses.

Castle Acre is a large village, about 20km east-south-east of King's Lynn and 5.75km north of Swaffham. The village is dominated by the remnants of a large castle, in the Guardianship of English Heritage overlooking the crossing of the River Nar by a Roman road, the Peddars Way.

The remains of the castle include a roughly circular upper ward (1) with a rectangular lower ward (2) to the south-east. To the east of the upper ward is a triangular outwork or barbican (3), with a small semi-circular outer embanked area (4) protecting the entrance. The upper ward is surrounded by a deep ditch, and there is an inner bank surmounted by the remains of a curtain wall. Within it are the excavated remains of a masonry building. The lower ward also has a surrounding ditch and bank with a few remnants of a wall crowning it. Within the lower ward are the outlines, so far unexcavated, of three buildings. There are the remains of three gatehouses; one defending the upper ward. the other two commanding access from the town (5) and the barbican (6).

To the west of the castle are the remaining portions of a large bank, Dyke Hills, and ditch, most complete on its western and southern sides, which enclosed a planned town of *c.* 4.25ha, the gridded street pattern being aligned on Bailey Street. There was a wall on the bank with gates on the northern and southern sides. The northern gate survives with stubs of the wall on either side and there is a small piece of walling (7) blocking the castle ditch at the south-western angle of the lower ward. The southern gate was demolished in the 18th century. Excavation has shown that the northern part of the ditch has been concealed under Stocks Green (Leah 1993, 505) but the north-eastern corner (8) can be seen where it joins the castle ditch. Pales Green may have been the original market place within this planned town (Wade-Martins (ed) 1987, 30; 1999, 43).

It would appear that the de Warennes remodelled their holding in Castle Acre previously held by Toki, a Saxon freeman (Brown (ed) 1984, 8,22), establishing a castle and a priory here. Excavation of the castle carried out between

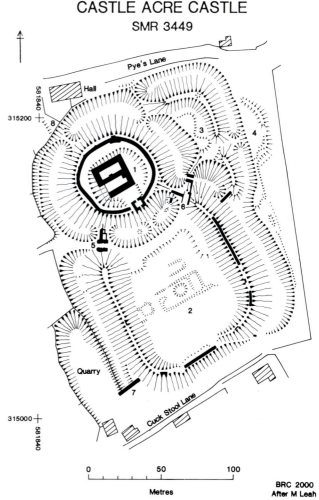

Figure 106 Castle Acre, major earthworks with associated town ditch. Scale 1:2,500

1972 and 1977 has revealed a more complicated structural history than was expected (Coad and Streeten 1982, 138–301). The initial building has been described as a large stone two-storeyed country house, divided internally in two and surrounded by a ringwork entered by a gatehouse, a surprisingly weak fortification. Subsequently the outer walls were thickened and the structure increased in height, the original ground floor was buried and became a basement. This was soon modified by the thickening of the interior wall and the demolition of the southern half of the building leaving a tall narrow keep. This and the raising of the curtain wall was done in the 1140s or 1150s. Later, occupation of this part was largely abandoned in favour of buildings in the lower ward (Kenyon 1990, 49–51). The 'country house' description is disputed by Thompson who prefers the term 'proto-keep' (Thompson, M.W. 1991, 72).

The castle continued to be important into the 13th century with royal visits recorded, but by the end of the 14th century it was neglected and had become derelict. The town, through which Peddars Way had been diverted, seems to have declined at about this time as it was allowed a 40% reduction on its contribution to the 1449 Lay Subsidy (Hudson 1895, 272). However it continued to hold markets into the 17th century (Dymond 1993, 77) and has remained a large village, the centre of which has moved north to Stocks Green and beyond, leaving the planned area outside Bailey Street sparsely built over.

CASTLE RISING
SMR 3307

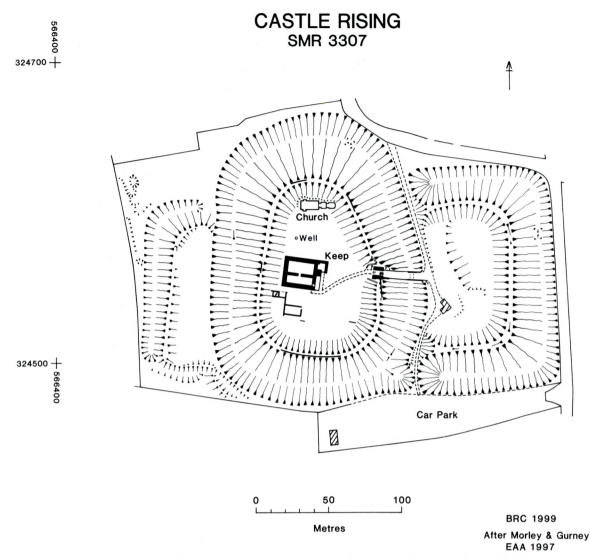

566400

324700 +

324500 +
566400
566400

Church
○ Well
Keep
Car Park

```
0        50       100
|_____|_____|
     Metres
```

BRC 1999
After Morley & Gurney
EAA 1997

Figure 107 Castle Rising, major earthworks surrounding a surviving keep. Scale 1:2,500

Castle Rising SMR 3307, TF 666 245
(Pl. XXXIX, Fig.107)

The earthworks consist of an oval area bounded by a bank and ditch with two outworks, the largest to the east.

Castle Rising is a village about 6.5km north-east of King's Lynn and about the same distance from the modern shoreline to the west. It is also about 1km south of the Babingley River which probably gave access to the sea. Castle Rising achieved borough status in the 13th century (Beresford and Finberg 1973, 139), has elements of planning discernible in its layout, but declined despite sending two members to Parliament until 1832 (Dymond 1985, 163).

The castle stands on a spur overlooking the village to the north and coastal marshland to the west. Surviving buildings within the earthworks include the remains of an 11th-century church, a rectangular keep, and, to the south, the foundations of buildings erected during the residence of Queen Isabella (1331–58). Later buildings in this area were also identified during excavations in 1970–76, and a report of these and later excavations in 1987 has now been published, along with a much fuller analytical description

and an historical background (Morley and Gurney 1997). There is also a 12th-century gatehouse commanding entrance to the inner ward from the east.

The earthworks consist of an ovoid area surrounded by a massive bank and a ditch. To the east, and protecting the entrance, is a rectangular outwork consisting of a high bank with an external ditch. A ramped causeway gave entrance from the north. A smaller outwork, also rectangular, lies to the west where a less impressive bank and ditch enclose a platform raised above present ground level. Excavation has shown that the earthworks of the inner ward were heightened and the ditch deepened, probably *c.* 1200. Material dug was also used to raise the western platform and the eastern enclosure. Slight earthworks, probably dating from an early phase of castle-building, can be seen to the south of the western enclosure (Wade-Martins (ed) 1987, 31).

Earthworks and stone keep have been shown by excavation to be of roughly the same date. Traces of Saxo-Norman settlement beneath the castle (Morley and Gurney 1997, 11), together with the remains of the 11th-century church, suggest that the original Rising, recorded in Domesday as a prosperous outlier of Snettisham (Brown (ed) 1984, 2,4), was removed when the castle was built.

Plate XXXIX Castle Rising, seen from the south-east. TF 1624/ACS/GAQ 2

That the Norman church of St Lawrence in the village was built within the planned layout of the new settlement as a replacement for the earlier building is a familiar assertion.

However, an alternative suggestion is that the church within the castle appears to have been built as a chapel to St Lawrence *c.* 1100, thus making the surviving village earlier than the removed portion which could have been a Late Saxon expansion southwards (Morley and Gurney 1997, 133). The castle was built by William d'Albini after his marriage to Henry I's widow and was a manifestation of his power and standing. The last d'Albini died in 1243 after which the castle passed to another family by marriage.

In 1327 it was conveyed to the Crown and soon after became the home of Isabella of France, Edward II's Queen. She lived there in some state and was a heavy drain on the purses of the burgesses of Lynn (McKisack 1959, 102). The castle had been granted to the Duchy of Cornwall; after her death it was held by the Black Prince who authorised work to be carried out and it was maintained until the early 16th century when, in 1544, it was granted to the Duke of Norfolk. It passed into the guardianship of the State in 1958 (Brown 1989, 81–2) and is now in the care of English Heritage.

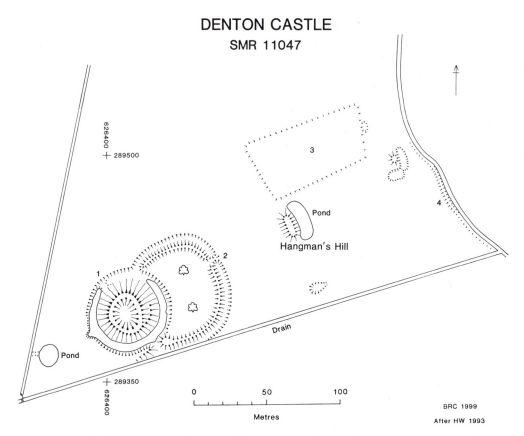

DENTON CASTLE
SMR 11047

626400
+ 289500

3

Pond

Hangman's Hill

4

2

1

Drain

Pond

Pond

+ 289350

626400

0   50   100

Metres

BRC 1999

After HW 1993

Figure 108 Denton, a small motte and bailey with a detached enclosure. Scale 1:2,500

Denton Castle SMR 11047, TM 265 895
(Fig.108)

A very small motte and bailey with the scanty remains of a large detached enclosure to the north-east, levelled since 1884 when it was banked and ditched; little can be said of the history of this site.

Denton is a straggling village about 6km south-west of Bungay. The castle lies in the north-western angle of the parish near Darrow Green almost 2km from the present village. It was discovered in Darrow or Deerhaugh Wood in 1850 and, after the wood was felled in the 1860s, was first examined and planned in 1884 (East Anglian Notes and Queries I, 89; Manning 1884, 335).

The castle is small, the motte measuring only 40m in diameter with a ditch 10m in width. It has a substantial raised rim, up to 2m above the centre which is only 1m above the surrounding field level, and which may be the supporting bank of an oval wooden keep, entered at first floor level. A possible entrance (1) is to the north-west and is directly onto the motte, somewhat strangely, suggesting it is a later feature. The small horseshoe-shaped bailey to the east measures 65m north to south and 35m east to west and has an internal bank 1m in height, except where it joins the motte ditch. Access was by an original entrance (2) to the east.

A scrub-covered regular mound to the east, known as Hangman's Hill, appears to be spoil from the nearby pond, while another mound further east has an L-shaped seasonally water-filled depression to the south and east.

To the north of Hangman's Hill are the slight remains of a trapezoidal enclosure (3) measuring at maximum 80m by 41m. It was shown in 1884 (Manning 1884) as a banked enclosure with an external ditch, and has been levelled since. Part of the eastern field boundary has a length of internal bank (4), possibly a surviving section of a medieval wood bank (Wade-Martins (ed) 1999, 40).

The history of this castle is obscure. It seems likely that it was built on a holding which had belonged to Aelfric in 1066 but had passed to Eudo after the Conquest (Brown (ed) 1984, 1,220. 29,6). It became the manor of Denton with Topcroft which also extended into Alburgh. It is possible that the castle was built by the d'Albinis who rose to prominence in the reign of William II. Their great days were under Henry I and by 1107 they had made their main stronghold at Old Buckenham, so that Denton may have been abandoned soon afterwards.

The site seems oddly-chosen. It is on high ground but in the north-west of the parish well away from the village and surviving roads. However the estate extended into Topcroft and Alburgh; it was close to a linear green linked to others in Denton, Alburgh and beyond. The main crossing-places of the Waveney were at Bungay and Wainford, and Denton is distant from these. The reasons for building Denton castle must remain unknown. The district was prosperous in 1086 (Darby 1952, 113, 117) and in 1334 (Hudson 1895, 276) and it may have been considered advisable to safeguard assets here. It is possible that the reign of Stephen (1135–54) may have seen its construction.

The use of the alternative name 'Deerhaugh' in 1884 can be traced back to 1589 (NRO Frere Ms II/2–20) when a demesne wood called 'Derehaghe' was said to contain 80 acres; no mention of a castle was made. The old name may be derived from OE 'deor' meaning 'animal' or 'beast', usually a deer. The other part could be OE 'haga', a hedge or enclosure or ON 'hagi', grazing enclosure or pasture. Other possibilities include OE 'hagen' or 'haegen' (enclosure) which is found only in Middle English as a park, or ON 'hegn' meaning a grove or hedge (Smith 1956, 25, 130–31, 215, 221). 'Enclosure where deer are found' or a deer park seems appropriate. A deer park may have been associated with the castle or created after the castle had become disused. In 1257 Henry III granted rights of free warren to the lord on his Norfolk estates and this may give a date for the construction of the vanished enclosure and the abandonment of the castle, after which it became woodland. The site is now the property of the National Trust.

Hautbois Castle, Coltishall SMR 7679, TG 261 203
(Fig.109)

The much altered site of a fortified manor house rather than a castle which is not well-documented and of which only foundations remain.

Great Hautbois is a deserted medieval village now lying within Coltishall about 11.5km north-east of Norwich. The site of the castle or fortified house is to the west of a minor road on raised ground on the flood plain of the Bure. The site is a sub-rectangular platform, 60m by 30m, with remains of buildings on the higher northern section (1), and a yard to the south (2).

The castle was approached from the north. A map of 1671 (Dollin 1986, 268–70) shows a roadway continuing from the church and passing to the west of the castle, although access into the castle was from the north-east. The original survey made in 1983, (Dollin 1986, 268–70) showed a causeway with low-lying ground to the west, approaching from the north. Much earth-moving has occurred since and only one side of the causeway (3) now exists, overlooking a smaller low-lying area (4) to the west. A section of masonry previously recorded at the northern end of the causeway has also been destroyed, along with a section a few metres outside the main entrance causeway (5) to the platform. This latter section of masonry has been suggested as part of a probable drawbridge, but the moat must have been considerably wider than now.

The area to the east of the platform has been suggested as an outer bailey, but no convincing evidence for this is apparent, especially as some former drains have been infilled. The causeway entrance is revetted, with substantial terminal flint bastions splayed outwards, while the revetting continues on each internal side of the platform. A small fragment of masonry west of the entrance may be part of a building. The north-western and north-eastern edges of the platform have lengths of flint masonry, the former having buttresses keyed to the wall, the latter with an incomplete building outline (6). The yard at a lower level to the south, separated from the higher level by a very shallow slope, has no identifiable internal features apart from the revetting on its eastern edge. This is the only side of the platform which can justifiably be described as moated, as the others descend to the marshes of the flood plain. A roadway shown continuing to the river

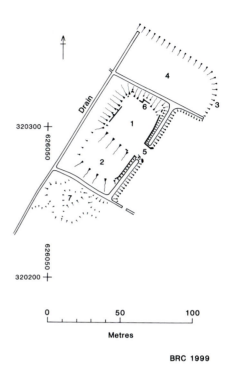

HAUTBOIS CASTLE
COLTISHALL
SMR 7679

Figure 109 Hautbois, limited remains of a fortified manor house. Scale 1:2,500

past the castle in 1671 is unlikely to have been an all-weather access. Some amorphous mounds (7) exist to the south but are not very convincing as contemporary features; they may well represent later dumping.

The manor of Hautbois (Hobwisse — meadow with tussocks; Schram 1961, 149) was in two parts. One was held from St Benet's Abbey by the de Hautbois family. They were responsible for the foundation of a hospice for travellers and poor people, dedicated to St Mary the Virgin, sited north of the ruined church. The church was dedicated to the Assumption of the Blessed Virgin but had relics of St Theobald which attracted pilgrims. The other part was held by the Bainards who, in 1312, built Hautbois Castle. Licence to crenellate was granted in 1313. The manor then consisted of nine messuages, seven cottages, 131 acres of land, 20 acres of meadow, 4 of alder carr, a free fishery and 1.5 acres called Dovehouse Yard. The manor was subsequently linked with Horsford and, by 1671, with Horstead over the river.

A survey of 1613 (NRO Aylsham Collection 54) records 'one piece of ffennye grounde wherein it seemeth hath bin a castle for part of the wales are yett there'. It mentions that the ground was reasonable but could be improved by ditching. A map of the manor dated 1671 shows 'The Manor of Haughtboys Magna' about 600m north of the castle on the edge of a common. This probably represents a replacement for the castle (Dollin 1986, 268–270).

169

HORSFORD CASTLE
SMR 8001

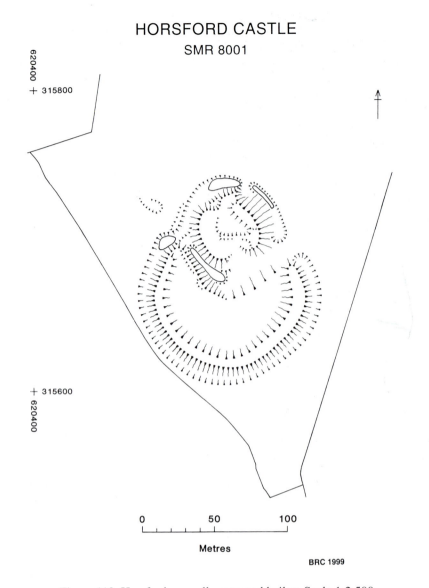

620400
+ 315800

+ 315600
620400

0   50   100

Metres

BRC 1999

Figure 110 Horsford, a small motte and bailey. Scale 1:2,500

Horsford Castle SMR 8001, TG 205 157
(Pl. XL, Fig.110)

A small motte and bailey castle of which the bailey has been partly disfigured by fairly recent ploughing; it had a large medieval park attached.

The castle lies east of Horsford village, about 7km north-west of the centre of Norwich. The castle stands on low ground to the south of a small stream flowing eastwards to the Bure and consists of a circular motte on the northern side of a horseshoe-shaped bailey.

The features, now under pasture, were reduced by ploughing in 1987 when the bailey was ploughed as far as its inner slope, despite the fact that it was scheduled as an Ancient Monument. The motte, *c.* 33m in diameter, is no longer much higher (1.5m to 2m) than the banks of the bailey and is surrounded by a ditch much degraded on its south-eastern flank where it meets the bailey ditch. On top of the motte is an L-shaped ridge and scarp suggesting some form of structure there, perhaps a stone keep.

The bailey measures 82m from east to west and is bounded by an embankment and surrounded by a ditch *c.* 1m deep and generally 10m wide. The only feature seen within the bailey on air photographs obtained before ploughing is a small semi-circular depression possibly representing the approaches to a bridge linking it to the motte where there were also indications of footings of a barbican (Wade-Martins (ed) 1987, 29). No obvious access into the bailey has been identified.

In 1086 Horsford was part of the lands of Robert Malet (Brown (ed) 1984, 7,16) lord of Eye in Suffolk. Horsford was held from him by Walter de Cadomo (Blomefield 1775, V, 1355). Malet had a castle at Eye in 1086 (Rumble (ed) 1986, 18,1) and it seems possible that de Cadomo followed suit at Horsford. According to Blomefield, Camden, in *Brittania* (1610), recorded it as overgrown with bushes and briars and that it had a large park or chase around it, sometimes referred to as 'the forest of Horsford'. This park was recorded in 1310 as being 100 acres, with deer and valued at 10s annually in underwood and herbage (Barrett-Lennard 1904, 267–93).

170

Plate XL Horsford, simple motte and bailey castle seen here from the south-east. TG 2015/ACE/HHQ 15

There is some reference to the park in an arbitration of 1563 (NRO NRS 10381 25 A6) between members of the Graye family in which rights to take forty loads of wood annually, to hunt and to hawk, and to have a free buck and doe are mentioned. An inquiry of 1579 shows that Black Heath and the Old Park were identical and that people of nearby parishes claimed rights there.

Early maps give limited information about the castle and park. A map of 1773 (NOR 48 BCH) shows an area of over 206 acres labelled 'Great Park' with Black Heath on its northern and western sides but no castle. The outline of the park was roughly rectangular with the western side running north to south and marked by a line of trees. The northern one, slightly sinuous, ran from west to east as did the southern boundary which was partly lined by trees at intervals. The eastern side was less regular and possibly encroached upon by two enclosures called 'Great Park Meadows', again outlined by trees at intervals. The Enclosure Map of 1802 (NRO C/Sca 2/170,171) shows a comparable area labelled 'old enclosures' but no castle. A map of 1830 (NRO Aylsham Collection 792) has a crudely-drawn illustration of the castle showing motte and bailey correctly but the Tithe Map (NRO DN/TA 591) shows nothing although it names a field 'Castle Hill Meadow'.

Blomefield (1775, V, 1357–8) described it as enclosed by a circular moat, the keep about 50 feet from the moat and surrounded by another moat. The area on top was, he thought, too small for a large building. In the time of Henry VIII the chase still had deer, but in Blomefield's time, there was only 'a naked heath of 900 acres'.

Hunworth Castle, Stody SMR 1059, TG 072 352
(Fig.111)

A simple ringwork about whose history nothing is known.

Hunworth lies about 3.5km south-south-west of Holt and is a small village now included in the Civil Parish of Stody. The ringwork lies on a wooded spur overlooking the village which is to the south-west, and commanding two crossings of the River Glaven. The slopes to the south, south-east and south-west of the ringwork are steep, declining to the meander below with the ringwork slopes merging with the natural ones, but the northern approach is more gentle.

The ringwork is about 100m in diameter and is on the highest point of the spur. It consists of a circular enclosure of *c.* 50m in diameter surrounded by a bank and ditch, most prominent on its northern side, with a less pronounced and intermittent counterscarp bank. The entrance, probably original, is on the north-western side and consists of a hollowed causeway over the ditch with corresponding gaps in the two banks (Green and Taylor 1966). The central area slopes gently northwards with the inner bank a maximum of 1.5m in height on the eastern side. The eastern side of the outer bank has been altered by a straight field boundary.

Little is known about this fortification. The village has always been small and has not attracted any particular notice from the time of Domesday (1086) onwards. Much of what is known about the castle was discovered during a limited excavation in 1965. The inner face of the bank on the eastern side was examined; some signs of a timber revetment were found together with the remains of a turf bank. On the north side of the enclosure the ditch was originally about 2.9m in depth, had a flat bottom of about 3.3m width and had very steep sides. Rapid infilling had taken place suggesting only a brief period of use. No datable evidence was recovered (Green and Taylor 1966).

The most probable periods of construction were soon after the Conquest and the 12th-century period of anarchy under King Stephen when many unlicensed castles were reported (Garmonsway 1953, 264; Clark 1970, 55). Domesday Book shows that the village was split among three landholders; the King, Count Alan of Richmond, and Walter Giffard, none of whom held much land. However in neighbouring Stody there was a considerable holding by Ranulph, brother of Ilger (Brown (ed) 1984, 1,23; 4,21; 25,22; 36,7), but none of these seems responsible for the ringwork.

There is no certain documentary evidence concerning the ringwork although there is a possible oblique reference to it in Tothill furlong, recorded in a survey made in 1598–99 (NRO NRS 1630 32 C 7) where 'tot' (a look-out place) and 'tot'hill furlong would imply a furlong on or near a look-out hill (Gelling 1978, 146–7; Field 1972, 235–6). Maps reveal little of note. A map of 1726 (NRO NRS 21385) shows only a vaguely drawn hilly area while the Tithe Map of 1838 (NRO DN/TA 370) marks a piece of woodland called Castle Hill with rough hachuring but no convincing shape. Bryant (1826) shows Castle Hill Wood but Faden (1797) and the OS One-Inch 1st Edition appear to ignore the site.

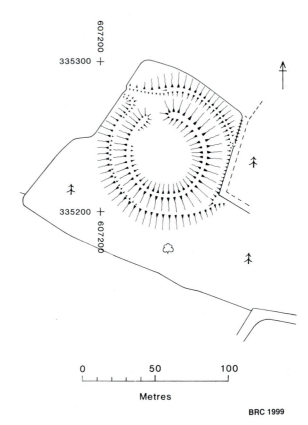

HUNWORTH CASTLE
STODY
SMR 1059

Figure 111 Hunworth, a small ringwork. Scale 1:2,500

Middleton Mount SMR 3394, TF 661 164
(Fig.112)

The surviving motte of a motte and bailey castle; little is known of its history and it was abandoned in medieval times.

Middleton is about 6.5km south-east of King's Lynn. Blomefield recorded this merely as 'an high mount, grown over with bushes, which seems to have been some place of strength and moment in ancient days' (Blomefield 1775, V, 653). It is obvious that its purpose had been forgotten. The almost circular motte stands 10m high, with an additional 3m-deep encircling ditch, 11m wide. The total diameter between outer ditch banks is 59m. A former field boundary bank (1) to the west, a pit (2) to the north, linked by a high-level leat to the motte ditch, and another smaller pit (3) to the south within a slight terraced depression are thought to be of post-medieval origin. Excavation by Andrew Rogerson in 1994 has shown that there had been a small bailey to the east, long since obliterated (Wade-Martins (ed) 1999, 41). The site now stands within a new housing estate and the area of the bailey has been left as a public open space within the development.

The motte stands above the 30m contour with marshy ground to the north, south and west. It probably had a strategic function in guarding the approach from the west but it is likely that its main purpose was to safeguard

MIDDLETON MOUNT

SMR 3394

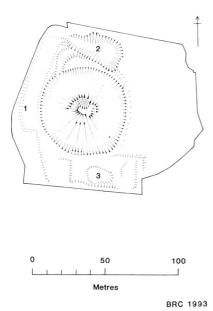

```
0        50        100
|_|_|_|_|_|_____|
          Metres

          BRC 1993
```

Figure 112 Middleton, a motte with archaeological evidence for a bailey. Scale 1:2,500

property. It may well have been constructed just after the Conquest, but there is also the possibility that the anarchy of Stephen's reign may have proved an incentive.

Of four Domesday tenants-in-chief, William de Ecouis seems the most likely to have built this castle; the other lords, de Montfort and Count Alan had sub-tenants and the third, the Abbey of St Edmundsbury, seems to have been of limited significance (Brown (ed) 1984, 4,45. 14,5. 19,4,6. 23,11.). The holding of de Ecouis eventually came, through marriage, to the Honour of Clare and is traceable, through medieval times, as Castle Hall manor (Cal. Inq. Post-mortem VII, 337). The manor of de Montfort came, in the time of Stephen and Henry II, into the hands of the de Scales family and became known as Scales Hall manor; they became prominent in Middleton by a series of advantageous marriages and through distinguished individuals. An Inquisition of 1134 (Cal. Inq. Post-mortem XII, 401) lists the holdings of the Scales family in Middleton and elsewhere; prominent were two-thirds of a manor, including a deer park, which was part of the Honour of Haughley, and a manor of 'le Castelhalle', held of Clare. By this time they had become the major landholders in Middleton and, in the 15th century, one of the family built the large moated house at Tower End. The old castle, or whatever building succeeded it, would soon have been abandoned and largely forgotten.

There are two references in the early 18th century (NRO Church Comm. 164349 and 21843/3 T38A) to Mountshill or Mount Hill, but Faden (1797) does not show it. An Enclosure Map of 1814 (NRO C/Sca 2) shows the mount as a scrub-covered sugar-loaf feature but avoids naming it. White's Directory of 1845 refers to the Tower as the Castle but does not mention the Mount, and the 1st Edition Ordnance Survey map does not show it.

Mileham Castle SMR 7230, TF 916 194
(Pl. XLI, Fig.113)

The considerable earthworks of an impressive castle consist of a motte and bailey surrounded by an outer ringwork; a large rectangular moated manorial site opposite may be part of the original structure.

In 1086 Mileham was a place of unusual significance. The King's holding, previously that of Archbishop Stigand, consisted of 10 carucates (about 1200 acres) of land and had a recorded population of 107. With outlying estates in Litcham and Dunham it was valued at the large sum of £60. Its influence went much further as twenty other places in the county were linked to it either by inclusive valuation or by some degree of soke jurisdiction. Most of these were near Mileham but three were in north-east Norfolk and there was also a small part of Thetford (Brown (ed) 1984, 1,80;212;214;217;232. 4,8. 8,69–70. 9,80. 10,5;53. 13,17. 15,15. 20,7–9. 21,19. 31,39–40. 34,5–6. 66,25;38).

The castle consists of a motte and bailey with, unusually, a surrounding circular ringwork or outer bailey *c*. 200m in diameter. The motte has rather irregular flanks but is essentially circular with the remains of a 15m square flint tower(1), presumably a keep. A fragment of flint wall (2), 30m to the east, abuts the incomplete motte ditch where it shallows and narrows. A ramp running due south from the top of the motte may indicate a bridge to the outer bailey. The inner bailey has a significant internal bank up to 2m high to the west of a ramp where two flint masonry fragments (3) indicate a likely bridge across the ditch which is 15m to 18m wide, and is seasonally water-filled. This access leads from a segment of the outer bailey (4), 150m in length, which has an internal bank broken at the present entrance (5) and also further east, as well as by a triangular depression at its western end. The remainder of the ringwork or outer bailey, except for a portion in the north-east now part of a garden, has an incomplete broad low internal bank. There are two depressions to the south-east, one linked to the inner bailey ditch. To the north-west there is a substantial ditch linking the ditches of the inner and outer baileys. The outer ditch has been much reduced in size, often being little more than a drain alongside a hedge (Carthew 1879b, 10–16).

The village street runs very close to the earthwork and the importance of Mileham may have been the reason for the building of the castle. On the opposite side is a large rectangular moat with a degraded internal bank. Within this, where some subdividing features including drainage ditches are notable, is the site of the medieval Burghwood Manor and the modern Burwood Hall. This feature is apparently misleading as it looks as though it was part of the castle; some unpublished excavations by M.Taylor in 1969 (SMR 7230) revealed medieval pottery of 12th-century date under the bank on the east side. The earthworks of this outer enclosure seem to have extended across the road, thus controlling traffic along what was a major roadway (Wade-Martins (ed) 1999, 42).

Count Alan of Brittany was William I's son-in-law and Mileham was passed to him at some time after the Conquest. It seems very likely that he or his heirs began to build the castle. By 1316 the Earl of Arundel, Edmund Fitzalan, held the Honour of Mileham. An Inquisition Post-Mortem of 1302 (Cal. Inq. P-M IV, 53) mentions a

MILEHAM CASTLE
SMR 7230

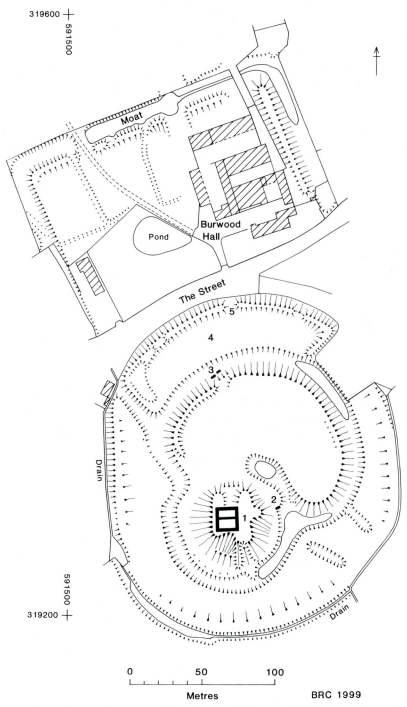

319600 +
591500

319200
591500 +

Moat

Burwood
Hall

Pond

The Street

5

4

3

1

2

Drain

Drain

0   50   100

Metres   BRC 1999

Figure 113 Mileham, a ringwork complex surrounding a keep, with an attached rectangular enclosure. Scale 1:2,500

174

Plate XLI Mileham Castle: the motte and inner bailey are partly hidden by trees but the outer bailey and moated enclosure north of the road are clearly visible. TF 9119/ADF/DPR 4

capital messuage in Mileham, 242 acres of arable, 4 acres of meadow, 4 acres of pasture, together with herbage and underwood in the park, two windmills and a watermill as well as rents. The capital messuage could refer to the manor house rather than the castle. The Fitzalans had holdings elsewhere in England and it may be that Mileham was seen by them as less important and so was allowed to decline. It was mentioned in 1154 when King Stephen acquired it for a short time, with the manor, in exchange for property elsewhere in the county (Brown 1989, 158).

New Buckenham Castle SMR 9200, TM 083 904
(Pl. XLII, Fig.114)

Earthworks consist of a moated ringwork with a large eastern bailey, replaced by a newer gatehouse and smaller bailey to the south-west and accompanied by intriguing additional features.

The castle is situated in Old Buckenham parish immediately to the west of the planned medieval town of New Buckenham. It lies about 6km south-east of Attleborough.

The castle consists of a moated ringwork 175m in diameter, including a water-filled ditch. There is a massive internal bank probably raised when the new bailey (5) was

added, almost burying the original gatehouse which was on the eastern side of the ringwork (Manning 1892, 137–142; Renn 1961, 232–5; Margeson, Seiller and Rogerson 1994, 88). The circular keep (1) is divided by a cross-wall and has outer walls about 3.7m thick. To the east are the remains of a horseshoe-shaped outer bailey (2) with a widely-spread inner bank; the surrounding ditch is not well-preserved having been ploughed and reseeded in 1993. The eastern gatehouse (3) was abandoned in the 13th century and a new one (4) was built on the south-western side. This gave access to a new bailey to the south-west. Air photographs show (Pl. XLII) that this was a small barbican-like enclosure (5) protecting the new entrance, with the surrounding ditch visible as a cropmark apart from the south-western portion, marked by a water-filled ditch. A further area to the south-east near St Mary's chapel may have been a separate enclosure. The chapel is of the 12th century and originally served castle and town before the existing church was built.

Beyond the ditch is a substantial bank (6) which may have been a park boundary, while still further beyond, and partly beside the road, is another bank (7). In the damp area within the banks is an incomplete ditched enclosure (8) with internal depressions, possibly fishponds. There was a 'little park' in 1306 and an alder-holt (Cal. Close Rolls 1302–7, 475). The ditches and banks (6,7) may be park

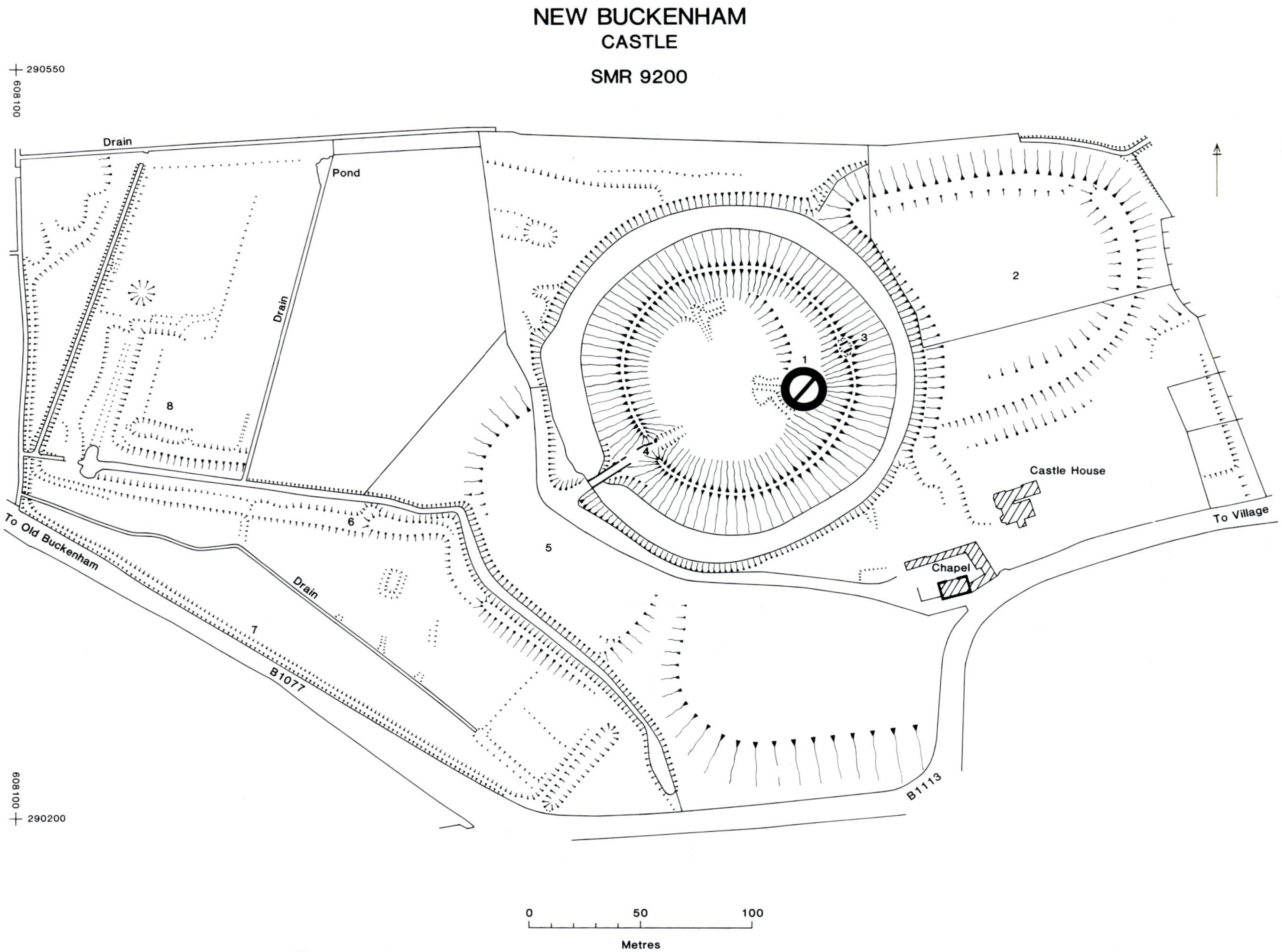

NEW BUCKENHAM
CASTLE

SMR 9200

Castle House

Chapel

2

3

1

4

5

6

7

B1077

8

Pond

Drain

Drain

Drain

To Village

B1113

To Old Buckenham

290550

608100

290200

608100

0   50   100

Metres

BRC 1999

Figure 114 New Buckenham, a developed ringwork with baileys and park. Scale 1:2,500

176

Plate XLII New Buckenham Castle. The moated ringwork is surrounded by trees, the remains of the original outer bailey and the later south-western bailey are visible. TM 0890/C/AEY 10

boundaries; the area was 'Carr Meadow' in 1841 (NRO MC 343/62) and the channels in (8) may have supplied water to the alder-holt rather than to fishponds, unmentioned in 1306 (Wade-Martins (ed) 1987, 32). A map dated 1597 (NRO MC 22/11) shows an area of wood pasture north-west of the castle as 'Parke'. It was bounded to the south-west by 'Procession Lane' and to the north-east by the lane leading north-west from New Buckenham church.

The castle was built as a replacement for an earlier structure in Old Buckenham by William d'Albini and was completed by about 1146 in the reign of King Stephen (Beresford and St Joseph 1979, 226). The site lay beside the road which led from Bury St Edmunds to Norwich and had obvious strategic and commercial significance. The distance from the village of Old Buckenham (about 2km) may well have led to the foundation of the town of New

Buckenham in about 1170 (Beresford and Finberg 1973, 140), formed by the abstraction of about 360 acres of land from neighbouring Banham and Carleton Rode (Beresford and St Joseph 1979, 226). Clearly the town was intended to depend largely on trade and it lay within its own town ditch, scarcely growing beyond it. The chapel of St Mary served the town in earlier days and the later church was founded by Sir Robert de Tateshale.

The castle was acquired by the Knyvett family by marriage with a Clifton heiress. When the last male Clifton died, his nephew John Knyvett succeeded after much legal and factual wrangling and after the eventual Yorkist victory in 1461. Apart from a brief period in the 1480s the Knyvetts remained in possession — not without legal challenge — until an impoverished recusant sold the remains of the castle in 1649 (Schofield (ed) 1949, 130; Virgoe 1992, 1–14, 249–278). Soon afterwards it was demolished.

Plate XLIII Old Buckenham: a corner of the presumed site of the castle is visible, together with part of the outer bailey and parchmarks of the priory. TM 0798/Z/ATA 3

Old Buckenham Castle and Priory SMR 9202, TM 072 925
(Pl. XLIII, Fig.115)

The site of the original castle of Buckenham was abandoned and subsequently altered by the building of an Augustinian priory on or near the site; interpretation is therefore not easy.

This site of castle and priory lies about 3.75km south-east of Attleborough on the north-eastern edge of Old Buckenham village. To the north-east are the signs of a medieval deer park (Yaxley 1993, 54).

The site of the castle is an oblong moated enclosure aligned south-west to north-east, on the north-eastern side of the priory (1). This enclosure measures 110m by 55m has rounded corners and a substantial internal bank, only broken at the entrance, probably original, on the south-western arm. This is considered to be the inner bailey, although no evidence of buildings has been recorded. The substantial outer enclosure to the south-west and south-east is roughly L-shaped and has been bisected this century by the channel with a sluice. The present enclosure to the south-east of (1) has a very broad arm alongside the road, wider than that further to the

south-west. Irregular mounds here may be spoil from this but the only other major point of note is a series of depressions (2) indicating springs in an otherwise gently undulating interior.

To the south-west, the remainder of what may have been an outer bailey consists of a T-shaped enclosure, with the head of the T overlapping the inner bailey. This enclosure is bounded by a moat (3), the south-western arm being partly infilled. The north-western portion has farm buildings and yards post-dating the medieval structures, but north-east of these is a partly-infilled depression (4) with a narrow leat into the outer moat to the north-west. This is part of a pond, possibly for fish, rather than part of an enclosing feature.

The priory remains are within the outer bailey and consist of a lump of flint masonry (5) indicating a north-east crossing pier, with parchmarks of the north transept and part of the choir. Air photographs show marks indicating more of the church outline and a cloister to the north (Pl. XLIII), with surrounding ranges. A small mound to the south of the masonry would seem to be close to the south aisle. A shallow linear depression lies to the south between two curving remnants of banks, possibly originally copse boundaries. The L-shaped farmhouse (6) with some early post-medieval features may represent the prior's quarters.

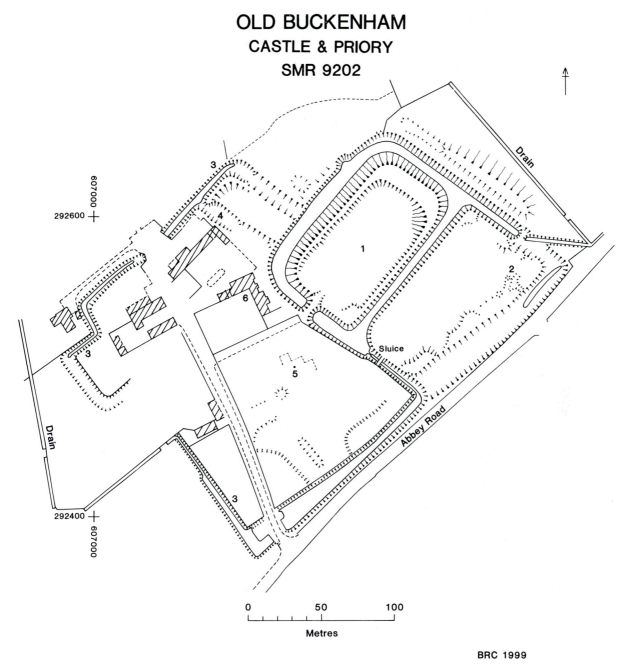

OLD BUCKENHAM
CASTLE & PRIORY
SMR 9202

607000

292600 +

Drain

1

2

4

3

6

3

Sluice

5

Drain

Abbey Road

3

292400 +

607000

0   50   100

Metres

BRC 1999

Figure 115 Old Buckenham, abandoned castle superseded by a monastic house. Scale 1:2,500

The d'Albinis built the castle in the late 11th century. The family was established in East Anglia by William II. It is possible that their early fortress was at Denton but by 1107 they were at Old Buckenham. Marriage of the second William d'Albini to the widow of Henry I saw the building of Castle Rising and the abandonment of this castle for New Buckenham (Brown 1989, 80).

The site of the castle together with its materials were given to the Augustinian canons *c.* 1146 as well as 80 acres of land, woods and meadows and the two parish churches of All Saints' and St Andrews and there were many subsequent benefactions. Its annual value at Dissolution was said to be over £143 (Doubleday and Page 1906, II, 376–8). Sir Edmund Knyvett obtained the lease of the priory and demesne.

Blomefield reported (1739, I, 261) an old sewer arch on the site of the castle and said that the walls of the church were 'quite down, but the foundations may be easily traced'. It had a tower 'in the midst'.

THETFORD
RED CASTLE
SMR 5746

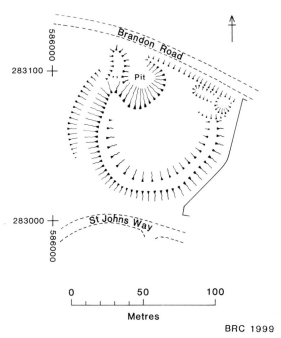

Figure 116 Thetford Red Castle, ringwork with archaeological evidence for a small bailey. Scale 1:2,500

Red Castle, Thetford SMR 5746, TL 860 830
(Fig.116)

An early medieval ringwork which once had a small bailey, built to guard the western entrance to the town as well as a ford on the Little Ouse.

Red Castle lies about 700m from the original centre of Thetford on the southern side of the Brandon Road which leads westwards. It is astride the western end of the line of the Late Saxon bank and ditch which had formed the town's defences.

The surviving earthworks consist of the southern two-thirds of a near-circular raised enclosure, 80m in diameter. An internal bank survives, up to 0.6m high and well spread, as does the western portion of a 2m deep surrounding ditch. Extraction pits have destroyed the northern portion of the ringwork, while road improvements, including work in 1966 (Rogerson and Dallas 1984, 63) have caused further degradation.

Documentary evidence for this castle is lacking. Martin (1779, 9–10) speaks of it as an earthwork on the Suffolk side lying near Ditchingford which was an ancient passage over the river. The 'ditch' may refer to the town ditch which approached the river near this point (Knocker 1967, 121). According to Blomefield (1739, I, 407) the castle belonged to, and was in the fee of, Earl Warenne.

Much of what is known about the site is supplied by archaeological excavation. Knocker's excavation revealed that there was much earlier activity dating from Romano-British, Early, Middle and Late Saxon times. This and similar finds further to the west may indicate an earlier nucleus of Thetford. The castle was not only erected across the Late Saxon town ditch but also around the remains of a Late Saxon church which may have been disused by the time the earthwork was built. Alternatively, it may have continued in use as a church or as part of the defences for some time afterwards. Later excavations in 1964 and 1966 suggested that a further ditch bifurcated from the main one and extended to the west of the earthwork (Rogerson and Dallas 1984, 62–3). Excavations in 1988–9 revealed the existence of a small bailey to the east of the ringwork (Andrews 1995, 68–9).

The likelihood is that the earthwork was constructed about 1146 during the anarchy of King Stephen's reign. It guarded the western entrance to the town as well as the crossing place known as Inselford (Martin's Ditchingford) which probably lay a little further downstream where the river terrace on the north bank approaches the river. A road reached the vicinity of Red Castle from the south, cutting across the Brandon Road, and making its way on the north bank of the river to a place called Potter's Cross (Dallas 1993, 206–07). This emphasises the importance of the location.

The pit dug at some point on the north-western side of the castle may possibly be the result of the sand-digging referred to by Martin (1779, 68) when describing a site on the Brandon Road or, in part, the result of Martin's excavation there, referred to by Blomefield (1739, I, 378).

Thetford Castle SMR 5747, TL 874 828
(Pl. XLIV, Fig.117)

An elaborate Norman adaptation of an Iron Age promontory fort of which a substantial part remains but little is otherwise known.

Thetford Castle lies on the north bank of the Thet in the south-eastern quarter of the town. It commanded the crossing-place of the Icknield Way over the rivers Thet and Little Ouse, now marked by the Nuns' Bridges. It is also close to another crossing of the Thet further upstream near Melford Bridge.

The earthworks are dominated by a circular chalk motte of about 80m in diameter standing some 25m above the bailey which partially surrounded it. The top has a diameter of 20m with a 2m high bank around the rim, with a gap on the western side. A 3m deep ditch surrounds the motte, with two causeways of unknown date crossing it in the north-east and south-east. Remnants of the bailey to the east have chalk extraction pits which have left irregular depressions. To the south and west urban development has encroached upon the former bailey and destroyed part of the outer bank of the ditch.

To the north, the outer bank of the motte ditch forms part of a substantial double bank and ditch earthwork which was the northern boundary of the bailey. A narrow causeway cuts these features which are truncated by further extraction pits and buildings to the west (Davies and Gregory 1992, 1). The inner ditch is 4m deep with a 6m high bank to its south, while the outer ditch, partly infilled to the north-east, is up to 2.5m deep with a 3.5m bank. The north-eastern section also shows signs of disturbance producing an irregular form (Wade-Martins (ed) 1987, 15).

180

THETFORD CASTLE
SMR 5747

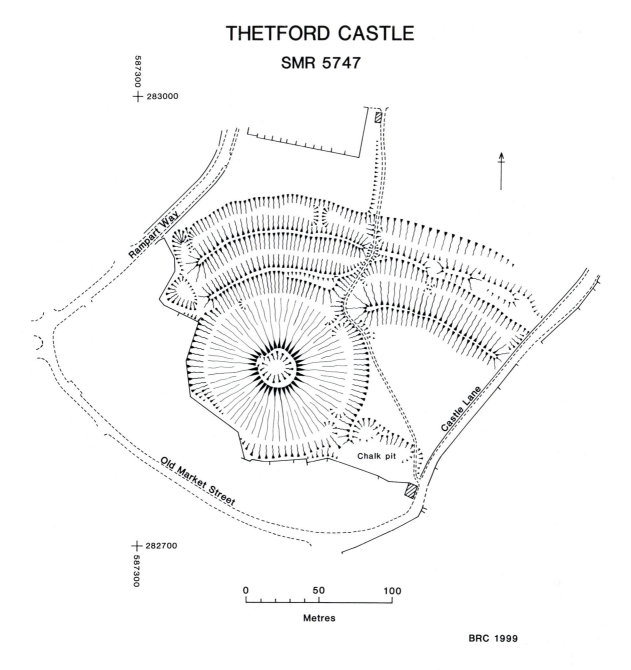

587300
+ 283000

Rampart Way

Old Market Street

Castle Lane

Chalk pit

BRC 1999

+ 282700
587300

```
0          50         100
```
Metres

Figure 117 Thetford, a medieval motte within adapted Iron Age earthworks. Scale 1:2,500

Occasional finds of Iron Age date have been made since the 18th century and have drawn attention to the possibility of an earlier fortification on this site. Excavations carried out in 1962 by Rainbird Clarke showed that the original double banks and ditches were of the Iron Age. The Norman motte and bailey was an adaptation of earlier defences. The excavation demonstrated that there was no sign of a structure on the motte and further investigation in 1985 showed that the original Iron Age fort was open to the south and south-east, relying on a meander loop of the Thet for protection. It was thus a promontory fort, not a complete enclosure. It is probable that an earlier course of the Thet brought it closer to the south-eastern wing of the defences than it is today (Davies and Gregory 1992, 28–30).

The Iron Age fort is one of several such features, most of them in the north-west of Norfolk. Thetford's position

is idiosyncratic in this respect being isolated in the south-west of the county. However, its position guarding the Icknield Way crossing is reinforced by further discoveries of Iron Age activity to the north-west close to the Icknield Way on Gallows Hill. Here a high status large Iron Age large enclosure was excavated in 1980–82 at Fison Way (Gregory 1992). To the south at Barnham in Suffolk there was also a small double-ditched rectangular enclosure (Dymond and Martin 1988, 32).

The Norman castle was not royal but seems to have been erected by Roger Bigot or, possibly, by Ralph Guader before his rebellion in 1075. The purpose is not clear; it may have been built as protection against William I, or to subdue the town, or simply as a recognition of its strategic value (Davies and Gregory 1992, 1). It has, however, also been suggested (Everson and Jecock 2000, 103–4) that it may have been a royal or Warenne creation reflecting

Plate XLIV Thetford Castle, viewed from the north. TL 8782/AV/GCA 11

William I's interest in a very important centre. Its date has been suggested as some time between 1086 and 1088 (Renn 1968, 321). It does not seem to have figured in any way in recorded history and its end is obscure. A castle, probably this one, was demolished in 1172–3 according to Pipe Roll evidence, though this may have referred to the ringwork at Red Castle (p.180). The market extended into the southern portion of the castle and by the early 13th century there were houses and the Chapel of St Mary in the Bailey there. By the late 14th century at least there was a Castle Mill (Dallas 1993, 195–6).

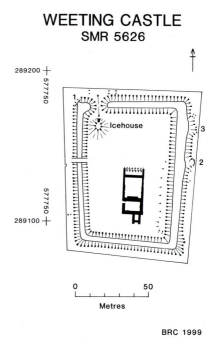

Figure 118 Weeting, a moated fortified manor house.
Scale 1:2,500

182

Plate XLV Weeting, the fortified manor house with the church of St Mary in the background

Weeting Castle SMR 5626, TL 778 891
(Pl. XLV, Fig.118)

This is not a castle but a manor house of considerable standing surrounded by a moated enclosure.

Weeting Castle lies on the eastern edge of the village of Weeting about 2.5km north-north-east of Brandon. The earthwork consists of a moated enclosure, roughly trapezoidal, 80m from north to south, 56m at the northern end and 51m at its southern end. The moat is of variable width and is seasonally water-filled but there is a causeway at the north-western angle which may have been made to afford access to an ice-house. There are brick culverts of modern construction (1,2) which indicate inlet and outlet channels. An embayment (3) may mark the presence of an earlier feature of the same type.

Within the enclosure are the remains of a medieval hall house standing in the midst of the southern half. The building is rectangular and contains a central aisled hall with service rooms to the north and a three-storeyed tower to the south. A narrower range extends southwards from the tower and was probably two storeys high. The northern wall of the service area is marked by an earthern bank over masonry foundations. North of this was a courtyard and north of that again the kitchens, separate from the main

building to reduce fire risk. These are no longer visible on the surface (McGee and Perkins 1985).

Weeting Castle is a high-status manor house rather than a castle. The major part of Weeting was held by de Warenne in 1086 (Brown (ed) 1984, 8,44) and the de Plaiz family held it from them in the early 12th century. They remained there until the late 14th century when, through marriage, it passed to the Howards. It is considered likely that the building was first erected about 1180 and was subsequently altered and added to. The moat is about 80m east-south-east of the surviving church of St Mary and roughly 430m north-north-east of the site of All Saints'. Limited excavation in 1964 suggested that there had been earlier activity — the remains of three ditches dated by Saxo-Norman pottery were found buried beneath the existing structure (McGee and Perkins 1985).

The ice-house is made of brick and covered by an earthern mound and has a northern entrance. It is probably of the 18th century and may have been associated with Weeting Hall, now demolished, in the grounds of which the moated site once stood.

Weeting Castle, referred to as 'Weeting Hall' in 1274 (McGee and Perkins 1885), is a very fine early example of a standard medieval house plan and deserves greater recognition as such (Sussams 1996, 95).

The site is now in the Guardianship of English Heritage.

WORMEGAY CASTLE

SMR 3455

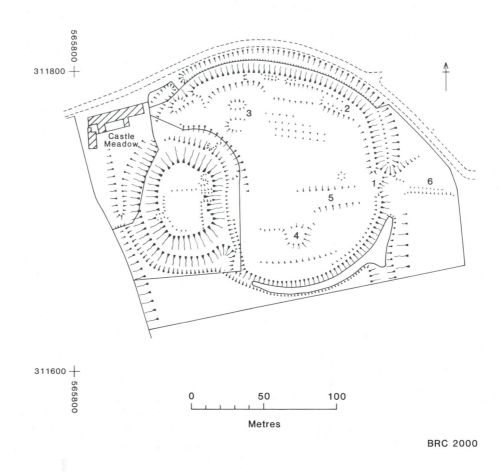

565800
311800 +

311600 +
565800

0   50   100
Metres

BRC 2000

Figure 119 Wormegay, a significant motte and bailey. Scale 1:2,500

Wormegay Castle SMR 3455, TF 659 117
(Pl. XLVI, Fig.119)

A motte and bailey castle of some substance stood on an insular site built over the line of a street which has been diverted round the bailey.

Blomefield wrote (1775, IV, 214) 'Wormegay is environed with water and low grounds, fens and marshes; the chief and most safe entrance is by a causey on the west side, where, on the right hand, stood formerly a castle'. His description is still quite valid as Wormegay stands on a former island about 8.75km south-south-east of King's Lynn with the Nar and its marshy ground to the north and lowlying peat-covered lands elsewhere. The castle, consisting of an earthen motte and bailey, commands what is obviously the entry from the west, and the roadway has been diverted around the bailey (Wade-Martins (ed) 1999, 39). The pre-castle alignment of this way can still be traced west of the castle where it appears as a ridge of soil and gravel about 12m wide on the low ground.

The motte is an oval mound 5m in height surrounded by a narrow berm and motte ditch, considerably degraded along its length adjoining the bailey. The summit of the motte has a raised rim in the south-west and a platform and

ridges in the east suggesting structures flanking an entrance where the motte slope is irregular. The bailey is partly internally banked, with an original entrance (1) in the east, the entrance close to the house being modern. The bailey ditch has been much disturbed to the south of the entrance and also where it meets the northern motte ditch. Features inside the bailey include at least one building platform (2) abutting the northern rim, two more possible platforms (3) further west and one (4) central to the southern half, as well as a central ridge (5) which may represent part of an access way to the motte. A scarp (6) and slight ditch to the east of the entrance may represent the southern flanking ditch of the original roadway before diversion.

The village to the east apparently post-dates the castle. The church stands well clear to the east of the village and this could be the original centre of settlement on the island judging by evidence from surface finds (Silvester 1988, 146–48). To the west of the castle are several channels all of them replacing an earlier natural meandering watercourse.

In 1086 Hermer de Ferrieres held Wormegay (Brown (ed) 1984, 13,4. 66,3.) and he, or one of his probable descendants, the Warennes and Bardolfs, built this castle on the most easily defensible site on the island. They held it as the head of an Honour or Barony clustered mainly in

Plate XLVI Wormegay Castle from the west, showing the diversion of the road. TF 6511/AA/EV8

west Norfolk but with outliers in the rest of the county and also in north Suffolk (Pounds 1990, 132). By the time the Bardolfs ceased to hold it in about 1408, the castle had lost its significance and when the manor came to the Crown in 1537 it had long been disused. In 1544 'le halle yarde', the 'Mylle Pyngell', 'le ley' and the Park were granted to John Dethick but the hall could refer to another site within the Park which lay to the north of the church (NRO MS 3726).

An undated survey, probably of the 18th century, (NRO MS 3770) mentions 'one piece of land called the Castle Yard with a hill in it called Castle Hill'. The stream to the west of the castle was called the 'Myll Load' and was a forerunner of the present channels.

Wymondham Moot Hill SMR 9438, TG 125 018
(Fig.120)

Nothing is known about the purpose or the builder of this ringwork which stands at some distance from the town.

Wymondham Moot Hill lies about 1.5km north-east of the centre of Wymondham very close to the railway line within a wood called Gristle Wood.

The earthwork is an oval ringwork measuring 150m on its longer north-north-west to south-south-east axis and 130m on its east-north-east to west-south-west axis. An outer ditch which is between 15m and 18m in width and about 3m deep is partially wet. There is an entrance causeway in the north-west which is lower than the interior and exterior surfaces. There is an inner bank about 1.7m in height, flat on top, which appears only as a very slight feature in the north. A small break in this bank on the eastern side appears to be recent and may be related to the irregular pond nearby, possibly as a drainage outlet. The outer edge of the surrounding ditch is broken by a leat leading into the ditch alongside the railway; this ditch has disfigured the outer slope of the ringwork ditch on this side.

This earthwork is a mystery. It was probably an early ringwork fortification, soon abandoned and apparently forgotten. It stands well clear of the centre of medieval Wymondham and at no particular vantage point, and the ground is somewhat boggy today. However, in shape and in the position of the entrance it does bear a fairly close resemblence to the similar structure at Hunworth (p.172).

In 1086 Wymondham was recorded (Brown (ed) 1984, 1,215) as having been held by Archbishop Stigand before 1066 but was then in the charge of William de Noyers on behalf of the King. Later medieval Wymondham was divided among a complicated system of manors; of these Grishaugh manor was almost certainly a descendant or remainder of the original great manor (Barringer *et al.* (eds) 1993, 2). The ringwork may date from the early post-Conquest years or more probably, the anarchy of Stephen's reign. Such structures could be speedily and cheaply built (Kenyon 1990, 5–8; Pounds 1990, 52) and soon abandoned.

The name of the wood in which the feature stands, Gristle Wood, is a corruption of Grishaugh Wood, associated with Grishaugh manor (Blomefield 1739, I, 720; Barringer *et al.* (eds) 1993, 12). 'Moot' is almost

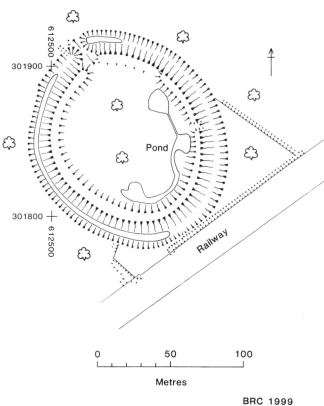

certainly a corruption of 'moat'; the alternative, a meeting-place, is unlikely as the meeting-place for Forehoe was near Carleton Forehoe.

There is no sign of Moot Hill on Faden (1797) or Bryant (1826); the 1st Edition Ordnance Survey One-Inch map shows it as a 'camp' in Gristle Wood. The Enclosure Map of 1806 (NRO C/Sca 2/345) and the Tithe Map of 1841 (NRO DN/TA 448) show the feature but without an entrance.

Figure 120 Wymondham, a small ringwork. Scale 1:2,500

Fishponds, Water Meadows and Oyster Pits

This section is devoted to features depending on the use of water. Fishponds have been a well-known feature of many sites both manorial and monastic. On monastic sites included in this volume those at Coxford, West Acre, Wormegay (Pl. XXXVI), Shouldham and St Benet's (Pl. XXXIII) are clearly recognisable even after the passage of time while others are now less easily distinguishable. On manorial sites survival is less obvious, probably because a fishpond may be adapted and altered for subsequent uses. Some examples of varying certainty may be observed on or near manorial sites at Gunthorpe, Shelton, Middleton Towers (Pl. XXVII), Lyng and Dersingham while existence at East Harling and Seething is problematic. At Kimberley they may have been subsumed by later modification as a water garden or ornamental lake.

The sites shown here are those which now appear to stand alone. Those at Broomsthorpe are clearly recognisable without any other earthworks remaining from a former manorial site, while the marked site at Bodney has only vestiges of the manor which it once served. Bradenham is slightly controversial; it could be a manorial site with fishponds or, as preferred, simply an elaborate system of ponds.

Fishponds are a manifestation of the medieval consumption of freshwater fish, partly for religious purposes, partly to vary the diet. The *Household Book of Dame Alice de Bryene, 1412–13* (Redstone 1931) shows that well-to-do households could acquire substantial quantities of sea fish, salted or dried as well as fresh, crabs and shrimps and supplies of oysters and whelks, the latter brought by a groom with two horses from Colchester. Apart from an occasional mention of eels, presumably freshwater, there is no reference to river or pond fish. Dame Alice lived at Acton, near Sudbury in Suffolk, quite far inland. Nevertheless, it is obvious that much freshwater fish was consumed, and not just in medieval England but in post-medieval times as well (Aston 1982, 266–280). It should be remembered that at least as late as the early 1700s, Roger North, resident at Rougham in Norfolk, not only wrote a treatise on fishponds (North 1713) but was constructing them at Rougham. Their remains, unfortunately, appear to have been partly destroyed by a later brickworks in a wood to the north of the earthworks of the shrunken village (pp62, 64–5).

Water meadows are a fairly recently recognised feature in Norfolk, although the site at Castle Acre is easily distinguishable (Wade-Martins, S. and Williamson 1994, 20–37). Others have been noticed in the past but have been mistakenly identified as ridge and furrow, despite their presence on the flood plain areas of river valleys. Late in archaeological terms, they were a limited success in Norfolk. They seem to have fallen into decay and been forgotten. The remains of water meadows in the Wissey valley and near West Tofts are shown here, with the addition of the first survey of the group at West Lexham which provides an interesting contrast with those downstream at Castle Acre.

The purpose of water meadows was to cover the pastures with water through the winter months. As the water was moving, the chances of freezing were reduced and the ground would remain warm and moist, so giving earlier spring growth. Such systems were expensive to install, the Norfolk climate was more severe than areas further west and south and root crops for winter feed were available, so few experiments were made. The construction of systems seems to have been a feature of the larger estates of the western part of the county which had sufficient resources to cover the cost of installation (Wade-Martins S. and Williamson 1994, 20–37).

For the sake of convenience the curious features at Heacham are also included here. Although there must be some uncertainty about their use, they are water features which were probably for rearing oysters. Again, undocumented, their purpose and existence seem to have been forgotten.

Bodney SMR 5044, TL 829 986
(Fig.121)

Three distinct fishponds survive near a former manor house in a valley subject to many changes of river channels.

Bodney is a deserted medieval village about 9km west-south-west of Watton. The fishponds lie south-west of the church beside what is clearly the former course of a river which has been recently recut to supply landscaped ponds further south. A few metres to the north are two other features; the remains of a moat (1) (marked erroneously as a fishpond on some maps) and, to the south-east of it, the earthworks and foundations of a later building (2) with those of a walled garden (3) to the west.

The fishponds lie in woodland a few metres to the east of a west-facing scarp which marks the eastern edge of the floodplain and an earlier watercourse. They are three in number, the largest to the south and the smallest in the middle of a slightly curving line. The northern one has been slightly infilled and has signs of a leat to the watercourse.

The fishponds appear to have been part of a manorial complex to the north. The Tithe Map of 1842 (NRO 578) shows a three-armed moat; the present feature has been heavily infilled giving only a western arm and a remnant of a northern one. Examination has shown the remains of a southern arm while it is probable that an eastern limb has been infilled. This would seem likely to have been the site of the manor held by the de Montforts and their successors. The building to the south appears to have been constructed at some later time after the manors were united and was described as 'a large convenient old house built of clunch, stone *etc*., with good gardens and walks adjoining to the river side' (Blomefield 1769, III, 372). At some point in the 19th century this old house was taken down and a large farmhouse to the south replaced it. A map (private possession) shows this building extending northwards into what is now the cottage gardens and this may have caused the infilling of the eastern limb of the moat.

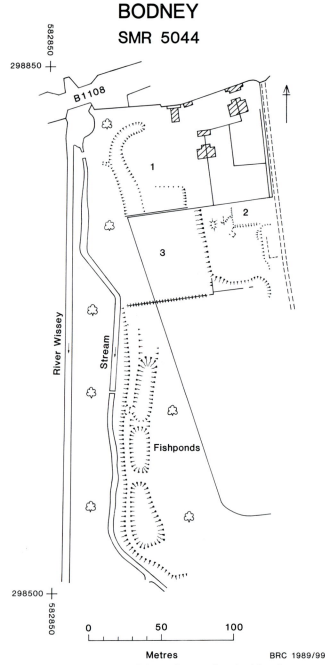

BODNEY
SMR 5044

582850
298850 +

B1108

1

2

3

River Wissey

Stream

Fishponds

298500 +
582850

0   50   100
Metres   BRC 1989/99

Figure 121 Bodney, fishponds associated with a former
manor house. Scale 1:2,500

It is not known when the fishponds were constructed but it seems clear that it was at some medieval date. Thetford Priory obtained the manor of Bodney by 1453 (Blomefield 1769, III, 371). An agreement in 1500 between the Priory and the lord of Langford over intercommoning refers to a boundary 'begynnyng at a close called fyshpondyke on the south part of the common of Bodney' (NRO Phillips 574 578 x 3). Presumably this is an oblique reference to this set of ponds.

There has been much alteration in the courses of the rivers. Armstrong commented 'this water, on the melting of a great fall of snow, or heavy rains, is very dangerous and to be cautiously avoided' (Armstrong 1781, VI, 5–6). The drain next the ponds is a former course of the Watton Brook; the drain followed by the parish boundary further west is an old course of the Wissey. Their old junction was

further south (Faden 1797). The present Watton Brook joins the Wissey much further north. The united stream then leaves its old bed and follows that of the Watton Brook as far as the road bridge to the north of this site before using a new straight channel.

Bradenham SMR 8720, TF 946 085
(Fig.122)

A slightly controversial site: current thinking makes this the site of fishponds although there is a persistent alternative suggestion of a moated manor.

Bradenham, formerly East and West Bradenham, lies about 7km north of Watton; the fishponds are about 1.5km east of the village, close to Manor Farm. They are situated athwart the headwaters of the River Wissey which flows westwards. They form an irregular quadrilateral surrounded by a bank and ditch. The stream enters the south-eastern ditch and flows along the north-easterly side before turning into the north-western one from which it resumes its course. The southern arm is largely dry apart from the south-western corner where some water, probably seasonal, remains. The internal bank, at most 1m high, is unbroken except for a lowering at the south-east corner where temporary access has been made to the interior. Within it, at the north-western end, is a low north-west facing scarp or berm (1), inside which are three depressions, one entire (2).

A steep-sided ditch (3), outside and parallel to the north-western side of the main enclosure, and separated from it by a steep bank, is probably a later development. However, the Ordnance Survey report suggests this may have been a contemporary outer linear pond. Central to the southern arm, a shallow depression (4) approaches from the south. This may have been an original access way. There is no doubt that the earthworks represent a deliberate diversion of the Wissey in medieval times.

There were three medieval manors in East Bradenham (Blomefield 1769, III, 452–57), Huntingfield Hall, Hammonds and East Bradenham. It is the latter which appears to occupy the site of Manor Farm and to which the fishponds belong.

Corbridge's map of 1732 (NRO MS9315 7B9 BRA 26) marks the feature quite accurately with the stream following its present course. It calls it 'The Mote *etc.*' and shows a row of trees growing on its south-western and south-eastern sides. The Enclosure Map of 1800 shows only a vague outline of the area of the feature (NRO C/Sca 2/48). The Tithe Map of 1839 (NRO DN/TA 42) shows it in correct outline, entirely wooded and called 'The Rookery', possibly referring to the then current denizens of the wood. Current Ordnance Survey maps show the features as fishponds, ignoring Corbridge's description. The eastern portion is higher and drier and might have been an earlier house site. However, the internal bank of the entire feature would be unusual for an inhabited site and there is no visible entrance to the platform so that the balance of later opinion favours identification as fishponds.

BRADENHAM

SMR 8720

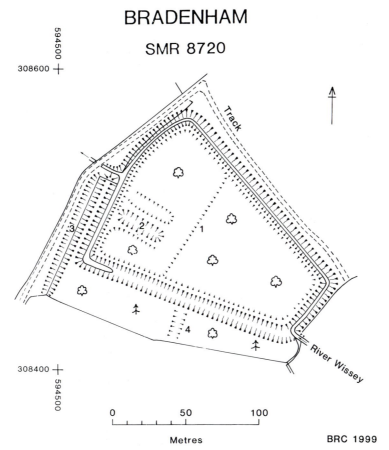

Figure 122 Bradenham, a fishpond complex. Scale 1:2,500

Broomsthorpe SMR 12317, TF 851 284
(Fig.123)

There is documentary evidence referring to fishponds in medieval times near the site of a former manor house.

Broomsthorpe is a deserted medieval village about 7km west of Fakenham; it now forms part of the civil parish of East Rudham.

The fishponds lie in a group of four on the floor of the valley of the River Tat immediately south-east of Broomsthorpe Hall. Three are parallel and of the same dimensions (25m x 9m). The fourth lies at the western ends of the three at right angles to them. It measures 45m by 16m, is less regular in form and is linked to the southernmost of the others by a leat.

Broomsthorpe was always a small place though it once had a church and still had more than ten households in 1428. In 1410–11 William de Pinkeneye had a messuage, land and marsh there with twelve tenants.

There appears to be a reference to the fishponds or some fore-runner in Charter 219 of the Coxford Priory Cartulary. It concerns turbary next to William de Pinkeneye's stagnum (pond) below his house on its southern side. Another charter (217) refers to 13 acres of land next to Pinkeneye's house on its southern side extending down to the head of a causeway and to the river separating Broomsthorpe and Tattersett. This seems to place the sites of the manor house and fishponds with reasonable precision. (Cushion and Davison 1997, 500–501, 504).

BROOMSTHORPE FISHPONDS
SMR 12317

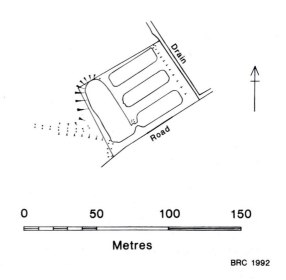

Figure 123 Broomsthorpe, fishponds associated with a former manor. Scale 1:2,500

BUCKENHAM TOFTS

SMR 5090

FLOATED WATER MEADOWS

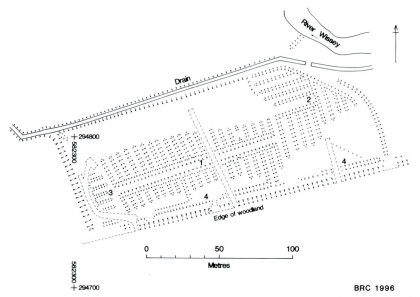

Figure 124 Buckenham Tofts, floated water meadows of varied form. Scale 1:2,500

Buckenham Tofts and Lynford SMR 5090, 31242; TL 824 948, 814 944
(Figs 124,125)

Late 18th or early 19th-century water meadows in the Wissey valley, part of a campaign of landscape improvements carried out by neighbouring landowners.

The features are in two distinct areas of the Wissey valley some 9km north-east of Brandon. The most easterly of the two is within the former parish of Buckenham Tofts, now within Stanford Civil Parish; the other is downstream within the parish of Lynford.

The Buckenham Tofts site is close to a bend in the Wissey and consists of a series of channels, many of them linked to drains on either side of a causeway (1) running east to west. Other channels are grouped in the north-east (2) and to the west (3). Various incomplete feeder channels can be seen with one to the south (4) linking to the main group. The area of the whole site is about 1.75ha and has been subject to some later disruption which has destroyed some linkages. The precise methods of drainage and water distribution are unclear; there is no obvious evidence for culverts or sluices.

The second site is about 1km downstream and is larger being about 7ha in extent although the surviving features are limited to about 3ha. There are three separate areas of ridges and drains differing in form and preservation. The most northerly area (1) consists of fourteen north-to-south ridges separated by channels. To the east of it is a north-to-south drain (2) which turns westward to the western boundary of the field. To the east of this is a second

group of channels (3), the southernmost sections of which are still capable of carrying water. The third group of features (4) lies to the west and is slightly curved; there are about six surviving channels. Subsequent use of the field for pig-rearing may have caused obliteration of some features.

Arthur Young (1804, 396) mentions that Mr Lucas had 'done a meadow of eight acres....at Lyndford'. The reference follows an account of the activities of Payne Galway at West Tofts where Young thought that the flow of water was insufficiently swift to be successful. He also considered that the flow at Lynford might be equally disappointing.

Payne Galway had been working with neighbouring landowners, the Petres at Buckenham Tofts and the Nelthorpes at Lynford, to improve the local landscape with a programme of road alterations and plantations. Floated water meadows appear to have fitted in with this. Mr Lucas had succeeded the Nelthorpes at Lynford in 1804 (Wade-Martins, S. and Williamson 1994, 22).

As with the water meadows at West Tofts, these can be fairly securely dated to the end of the 18th or beginning of the 19th centuries. It seems likely that the same engineer was responsible for all these works. The site at Buckenham Tofts was first recorded in 1971 by Rainbird Clarke who thought they might be the remains of medieval ridge and furrow. Ground inspection and recording by the Norfolk Archaeological Unit has identified them as water meadows. The Lynford meadows were identified from RAF aerial photographs (1069/UK 1634 9 July 1946 5346) in 1995 during the Breckland Archaeological Survey.

LYNFORD

SMR 31242

FLOATED WATER MEADOWS

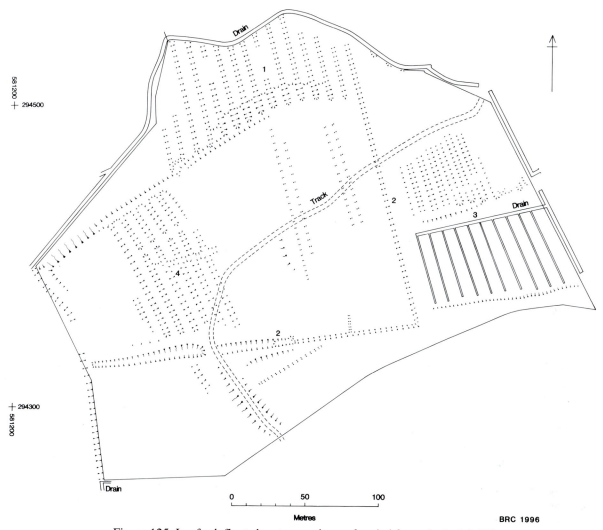

Figure 125 Lynford, floated water meadows of varied form. Scale 1:2,500

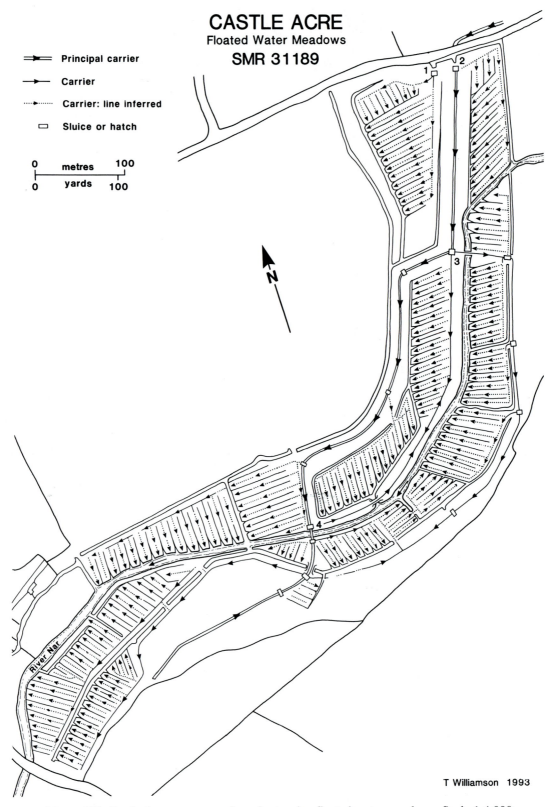

CASTLE ACRE
Floated Water Meadows
SMR 31189

Principal carrier

Carrier

Carrier: line inferred

Sluice or hatch

0 metres 100

0 yards 100

N

River Nar

T Williamson 1993

Figure 126 Castle Acre, reconstruction of extensive floated water meadows, Scale 1:4,000

Plate XLVII Castle Acre water meadows seen from the south-west, with the castle also visible. TF 8215/C/JCW 6

Castle Acre SMR 31189, TF 825 152
(Pl. XLVII, Fig.126)

The best-known example of water meadows in Norfolk; the system seems to have survived until the beginning of the 20th century.

The water-meadows at Castle Acre lie in the Nar valley immediately to the south-east of the village. They cover an area of almost 12ha (30 acres) (Wade-Martins (ed) 1999, 80). The system is divided into blocks of ridges or 'panes', and the sluices are of brick and direct the water along channels and through tunnels. The sluices can still be seen as concentrations of brick rubble. The channels are less easily detected as the ground has been used for grazing cattle in the years since the system went out of use. The accompanying plan shows the complete system as interpreted from the surviving features and fully described by Susanna Wade-Martins and Tom Williamson (Wade-Martins S. and Williamson 1994, 20–37).

Water was taken out of the Nar at Newton and led along the side of the flood plain to two sluices (1,2) which directed water in three directions. Water continuing along the main channel reached another sluice (3) which directed some water across an aqueduct to irrigate seven groups of panes. The main carrier ran west and then south to feed three blocks, then crossed the river on an aqueduct (4) to feed further groups. There is some indication that one section of the main channel at the southern end of its course

runs uphill and must have relied on valley-side springs which no longer flow. In all twenty groups of ridges were watered.

Castle Acre is part of the Holkham Estate and had, in the early 19th century, a tenant called Thomas Purdey who took over the farm here in 1808. He had earlier irrigated land at Houghton St Giles which he had showed Arthur Young in the early 1800s. The details of the contruction at Castle Acre are not available in the estate archives because it was the tenant and not the Estate who was responsible for the work. Some costs are shown as reimbursements in the estate records, including allowances for bricks, some of which must have been for the construction of weirs and sluices. In 1812 Purdey was allowed a sum of money for lime for the water-meadows. In 1810 he was awarded a silver teapot, basin and cream ewer for irrigating 12ha.

It seems that the system remained in use until the early 20th century when the tenant abandoned floating. This was probably the longest surviving system in the county and is the best preserved in the Nar valley. Its success, like those of other eastern examples, was inhibited probably by the gentle topography and the climatic limitations. The water flowing over the surface of the ground was not warm enough to raise the ground temperature and so the improvement in early grass production was insufficient.

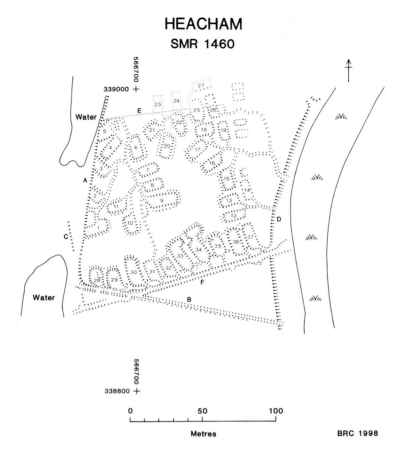

HEACHAM
SMR 1460

Figure 127 Heacham, probable shellfish ponds. Scale 1:2,500

Heacham SMR 1460, TF 667 389
(Pl. XLVIII, Fig.127)

A very singular group of earthworks apparently unique within the county; they are tentatively identified as oyster pits.

The earthworks lie about 1.7km north-west of Heacham church and 400m from the Hunstanton boundary in an area of rough grazing bounded on the east by a silted-up tidal creek.

The earthworks are limited on the west by a boundary scarp (A) of varying height, an interrupted scarp (D) on the east and a ditch (F) to the south. A more recent drain (B) cuts across this last feature. Within these limits the features consist of a series of near-rectangular depressions, some of them embanked, generally of 6 to 8m in width and 10 to 20m in length. They are arranged in groups which are linked by channels which eventually lead either to the former tidal creek to the east (ponds 12–27) or, in the case of the north-westerly group (ponds 1–11), probably originally to the western but later to the southern boundary ditch. Another group (28–37) is aligned on this ditch, each having a leat connecting it to the channel. Two of these have been truncated by the later ditch. A possible land drain (E) appears to have intruded upon the site to the north and there are five possible depressions to the east, one incomplete, which have no links with the system. A slight scarp (C) is the remnant of a drain.

These features were identified from RAF aerial photographs (106G/UK 1571 7 June 1946 3105) and tentatively identified as abandoned salt pans on former salt marsh. However, recent ground investigation failed to find any of the saltern mounds normally seen near sites where salt was produced.

The site proved similar to known oyster fattening pits identified at various places on the coast of Essex (Essex Sites and Monuments Record). Map evidence for their existence at Heacham is slender. An early map of 1592/1623 (NRO L'Estrange OB2/OC2) shows the area as common. An Enclosure map of 1781 (NRO L'Estrange EP4) shows the area with some irregular enclosures on either side of the tidal creek which extends west cutting across a 'New Sea Bank'. By 1820 an Estate map (NRO MF/RO 490/8) shows the southern boundary ditch which suggests that the oyster pits associated with it may be post-1781.

Documentary evidence for an oyster fishery at Heacham is patchy. In 1875 the first specific mention of Heacham was made in a Report on the Fisheries of Norfolk (Buckland 1875). The oyster and mussel fishery at King's Lynn had been prosperous three years previously but had decayed to such an extent that it had been closed for three years. Oysters were recorded as fattening in the Wash at a few sites, one of which was grounds at Heacham Harbour. It seems that mussel fisheries were always more popular although in 1895 oyster pits were noted at Blakeney, Burnham Overy Staithe, Brancaster Staithe and Wells. The arrangement of many pits at Heacham suggests that they depended on tidal inflow and therefore would have been in use before the construction of the sea bank of 1781 (Cushion 1999, 346–350).

Plate XLVIII Heacham, possible oyster-fattening pits. TF 6638/W/UU5

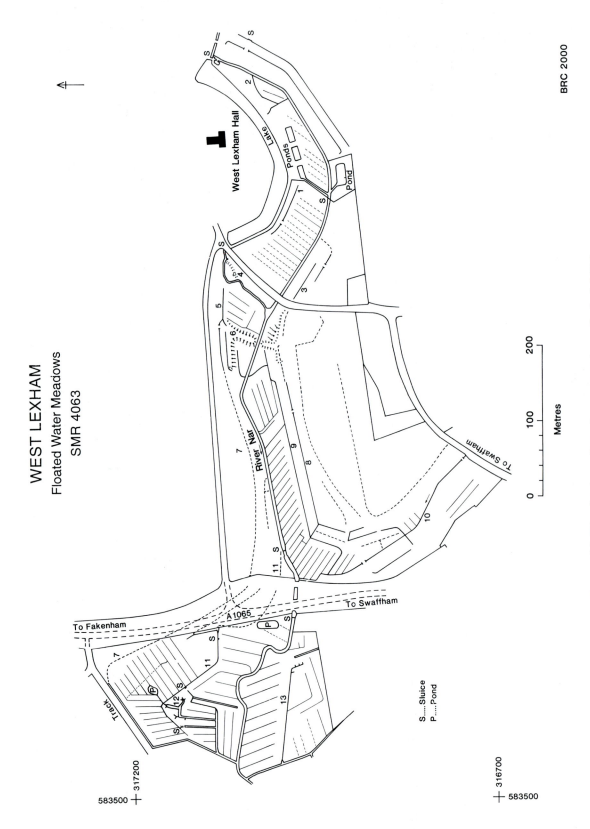

WEST LEXHAM

Floated Water Meadows

SMR 4063

West Lexham Hall

Lake

Ponds

Pond

River Nar

To Swaffham

To Fakenham

A 1065

To Swaffham

Track

2

1

3

4

5

6

7

8

9

10

11

7

11

12

13

S.....Sluice

P.....Pond

BRC 2000

0   100   200

Metres

317200

583500

316700

583500

Figure 128 West Lexham, floated water meadows. Scale 1:5,000

196

Plate XLIX West Lexham water meadows in 1946. TF81/TF8316/A 39/TUD/UK100/Part II 5089

West Lexham SMR 4063, TF 839 170
(Pl. XLIX, Fig.128)

These water meadows are less well-known than those at Castle Acre. They lie upstream in the Nar valley and make an interesting contrast.

West Lexham is a shrunken village in the Nar valley about 8.5km north-north-east of Swaffham. The remains of the water meadows extend 1km downstream from West Lexham Hall. There may have been further features to the east but 1946 photographic evidence is faint and later construction of a lake has destroyed the signs. The surviving portions are in three parts separated by roads.

The eastern section is a series of channels aligned north-east to south-west draining into the river, partly obscured by modern ponds. Some feeder channels (1,2) appear to survive. South of the river is a probable brick sluice with linear channels, one of which (3) seems aligned on a former channel downstream.

The Nar is sluiced at eastern and western ends of the lake to provide a head of water. The western one fed partly into a hydraulic ram (4) (SMR 4066) and partly into a main channel (5) one arm of which formed an aqueduct (6) across the river, the other (7) continuing west. The aqueduct appears to be joined by (3) and feeds into (8) while it may also have supplied (9) which fed the panes draining into the river. After joining, the two are linked to a stream (10).

The third section has been partly destroyed by road widening. A sluice on the Nar provided water for (11) which supplied the southern part of this system while receiving water draining from (7) to the north. Three sluices controlled flow southwards; the broader channels (12) are wider because of stagnation. South of the Nar are more panes fed by (13) the source of which is uncertain.

This is one of a series of schemes laid out in the early 19th century under Holkham Estate patronage (Wade-Martins S. and Williamson 1994, 20–37). It was part of a second phase of interest after 1803 when a prize was offered to whoever could convert the largest area of waste or unimproved meadows into water meadows.

The West Lexham meadows were designed by John 'Strata' Smith on the farm of John Beck and constructed between 1803 and 1806 (Smith 1806). They were paid for by Coke who received a gold medal from the Board of Agriculture in 1806 for the scheme. Further work was undertaken downstream in Castle Acre in 1812 and upstream at East Lexham by F.W.Keppel in 1806.

The work at West Lexham is commemorated in one of the three scenes depicted on the monument to Coke's memory in Holkham Park in 1842 (Bacon *c.* 1850).

Although they are not so easy to interpret or to see as the better-known and more obvious series downstream at Castle Acre, the West Lexham water meadows afford an interesting comparison.

197

WEST TOFTS
Floated Water Meadows
SMR 31157

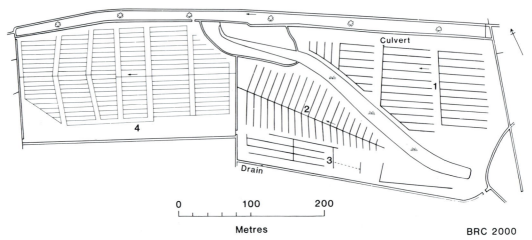

Figure 129 West Tofts, part-surviving floated water meadows. Scale 1:5,000

West Tofts SMR 31157, TL 832 934
(Fig.129)

Constructed about the same time as those in the Wissey valley to the north, these water meadows were mentioned as the work of Payne Galway by Arthur Young in 1804.

These earthworks are close to the deserted village of West Tofts, just over 10km north-north-west of Thetford, at TL 833 934 in a tributary valley of the River Wissey. They consist of a series of banks or panes and ditches laid out in two distinct patterns on either side of a wide canalisation of the natural stream which crosses the area diagonally. This feature, although it may have helped to retain water, may have been a survival of earlier landscaping around the vanished hall some 500m to the south-east.

Water was brought by the construction of a complicated series of leats and sluices which led in from the nearest convenient supply in the River Wissey. The ditches carried the water around the site and drained out through brick culverts, one of which still survives. The eastern area (1) consists of a series of parallel banks and ditches on an east-to-west alignment with outlet ditches at regular intervals. The second area to the south-west (2) has a

herringbone pattern with a central drain or carrier of water; a few small panes (3) are parallel to the southern boundary. A third area (4), now levelled and ploughed and where details have been transposed from aerial photographs, lay further to the west and followed a similar pattern to the first (Sussams 1995).

The water meadows can be approximately dated to the late 18th century. Arthur Young (1804, 396) mentioned that Mr Payne Galway had watered 20 acres at 'Tofts' having employed Mr Brooks, a gentleman 'well skilled in the Gloucestershire method'. Young thought the improvement might be 'exceedingly great' but had doubts about the method used. He thought the panes too flat so making movement of the water too slow.

It is possible that the differing patterns reflect the order of construction; as the exercise was essentially an experiment in irrigation, the differing forms may reflect this. The names of the meadows may support this; in 1845 First Water Meadow was the one south of the central canal, Second Water Meadow was the one to the north, while the third was the Far Water Meadow (NRO DN/TA 866). The central channel was called 'The Lake' which supports the suggestion that it was an earlier park landscape feature.

198

Ridge and Furrow

The distribution of ridge and furrow in Norfolk has invoked much interest in recent years. Compared with the Midland counties where survival is widespread, Norfolk has very little. Either it has been destroyed or it has never been more than very limited in extent.

The most convincing examples are in the western part of the county, the best preserved areas being those at Babingley, Middleton, Tottenhill, Stow Bardolph, Stradsett, Ryston and Hilgay. Their survival here appears to be a matter of local incident rather than any particular influence of soil, although something might be said about situation in the cases of Hilgay and Babingley.

There have been attempts to identify ridge and furrow elsewhere in Norfolk. One certain case was at the deserted village of Caldecote in Oxborough (Wade-Martins P. 1980b, plate VIII) but the site was levelled in 1959. It was particularly interesting in that Caldecote is on the sandy Breckland soils. One argument has been that ridge and furrow could only survive on heavier soils; Caldecote suggests that this was not so. The discovery during archaeological excavation of ridge and furrow under a layer of blown sand at West Stow in the Suffolk Breckland (West 1985, I, 10) and the further example from Brandon Warren quoted by Liddiard (1999, 4) confirm this.

In addition to the sites considered here, areas of ridge and furrow are certainly present at the deserted medieval village of Babingley (Pl. III) and at the manorial site at Gayton (Pl. XXIV) and some faint traces may be present at West Acre High House, Shouldham and, possibly, at Tacolneston. This last possibility is interesting as it is in the eastern part of the county where little other convincing evidence has yet been presented. The interpretation of earthworks at Kirby Cane as ridge and furrow (Silvester 1989, 282; Williamson 1998, 147, 152; Liddiard 1999, 4) has been largely rejected in this volume where it is suggested that they may be ridges produced in connection with the planting of hazel bushes (p.219).

The topic of ridge and furrow in Norfolk was first discussed by Silvester (1989, 280–296) in an article which outlined the difficulties of interpreting from aerial photography and noted the distinct western bias of the examples recognised in the county. In his paper, Silvester differentiated between the wood pasture of south-east Norfolk and the sheep-corn husbandry of the remainder and speculated on the possible effects of the later enclosure in the west on the survival of ridges.

The absence of ridge and furrow from parklands in eastern Norfolk might be explained by events in the lapse of time before the park was created. If, Silvester argued, drainage was the reason for ridge and furrow, why was it present on sandy soils in Breckland and absent from the heavier soil in central Norfolk? He concluded that the west Norfolk examples must be survivals of an extension of Midland practice eastward into the county. Open or common fields of the Midlands seemed to be associated with ridge and furrow; the influence of the variety of common field systems in eastern parts of Norfolk has yet to be determined. He also provided a list of possible sites based on aerial photography; some of these he acknowledged as 'possible'. One of these at Harling Thorpe has since been mapped (Cushion and Davison 1991, 207–211); it is on the flood plain, the ridges are straight and it appears to be some form of water management. Another at Kilverstone Hall seems to consist of property boundaries running down to and across the flood plain (Davison *et al.* 1988, 29).

If, as Silvester argues, the variety of field systems has a bearing, it is possible that study of early post-medieval field books may help. The picture of East Anglian field systems they reveal, admittedly late, is variable in terms of numbers of fields and 'furlongs' of varying size suggesting that these were terms more of convenience than of practical significance. Individual holdings varied in size and there were many closes within the fields. Ridges or 'riggs' are rarely mentioned; perhaps significantly these terms make an appearance in the west at Barton Bendish, Ryston and Stradsett. However, the fact that ridge and furrow certainly existed as late as 1589 in the south-east is shown by a field book entry which refers to a field in Denton which had four 'riggs' at its west end and three at its east end (NRO Frere MSS II/2–20).

The overall picture is of a confusing pattern in a state of fluctuation but which suggests differences from the conventional view of the three-field Midland system and within the county itself. Bruce Campbell has shown that in the Flegg area there was intensive medieval agriculture (Campbell 1981, 18–30) and it is quite likely that this microculture would lead to changes in the farming landscape. The early enclosure of south-eastern parts of Norfolk may have had similar influences.

The form of the ridges shown in the plans is reasonably straight. The characteristic shape of the Midland ridge is a shallow reversed S though those mapped in Leicestershire do not always conform (Hartley 1987). The question of the age of the ridges must come into consideration. The argument that the curve of the S was the result of a team of oxen turning easily on the headland does not appear to hold good for straight ridges. This may be explained by the introduction of the superior traction offered by the horse to plough teams (Rowley (ed) 1981, 17, 122). This may have come earlier in East Anglia. Finds of horse bones from medieval Grenstein show that horses were present in numbers and not apparently as a source of food but of traction (Wade-Martins P. 1980b, 158) although at Thuxton, though they were important, it was argued that their small size was against use in ploughing (Butler and Wade-Martins 1989, 33, 54).

A further consideration is the type of plough formerly in use and the methods of ploughing employed. Ridging would have become pronounced with continued ploughing inwards to the centre (Mitchell 1954, 109–110). Inward ploughing followed by a reversal of direction outwards in a subsequent year would remove the tendency to ridging.

A recent article by Robert Liddiard (1999, 1–6) puts the absence of ridge and furrow in the heavier eastern lands partly down to cross-ploughing or stitching, associated

Plate L Hilgay, ridge and furrow. TL 6197/B/- CUCAP RC8 EB260
(Photography by Cambridge University Collection of Air Photographs)

with enclosed areas which produced a flattened surface. He attaches more importance to the growth in underdrainage on heavier lands which rendered ridging for drainage as superfluous. The 18th-century progress of underdrainage has been considerably underestimated. It did not require the introduction of drainage tiles but relied on networks of parallel trenches filled with brushwood cut across the fields and subsequently covered (Wade-Martins S. and Williamson 1999, 61–67). The examples cited by Liddiard (1999, 4) as exhibiting the former presence of ridge and furrow in south Norfolk are unconvincing despite the validity of much of his argument. The four ridges at Kirby Cane appear to be associated with tree-planting (p.219). The 'ridge and furrow' at Tibenham which he also mentions seems to have been a causeway leading to a common-edge farmstead across a former linear green, a type still shown in numbers by Faden in 1797.

The examples cited in this volume are almost entirely from the west of Norfolk, the sole possible exception being the case of Tacolneston (pp227–8 in Parks and Gardens). It is too early to say that other possibilities will not be found in the east and south; further research may well provide cases there which will broaden the debate.

Hilgay SMR 24136, 24137; TL 618 978, 629 972
(Pl. L, Figs 130, 131)

*The two portions of ridge and furrow comprise the most
extensive areas of the kind surviving in Norfolk.*

Hilgay is the northern portion of a large island in the
Norfolk Fenland about 5.5km south of Downham Market.
There are two areas of ridge and furrow surviving. The
most extensive and best preserved is SMR 24136 which is
a large area to the south-west of the built-up landscape. It
is bordered by Steel's Drove in the north, the A10 and Cross
Drove to the west and south-west and the Ely Road to the
south-east. Much of the eastern boundary consists of a
well-defined headland. Most of the ridges are aligned
roughly from east to west but those in the south-east,
separated by a marked headland bank (1), are on a
north-to-south alignment.

It is in the portion up to the boundary hedge (2) that the
ridges are best preserved and exhibit more curvature, with
their south-western margins marked by a ditch. The
east-to-west ridges vary in height, those in the section
immediately north of (2) being most subdued. The northern
section has suffered encroachment and some disturbance
in the north-east corner, while one area further south
appears to have been levelled by more recent ploughing.
Modern drainage ditches (3) have been cut across several
areas, while earlier east-to-west field boundary ditches
following furrows are marked by thicker dashes in the
central areas.

The second area of ridge and furrow is SMR 34137
south of Wood Hall and consists of three separate portions
which are the best remaining parts of a more extensive area
barely visible in perfect light and surface conditions. The
most southerly group (1) is the most striking, exhibiting
some curvature. That to the north-east (2) has narrower
ridges which appear straight while the remaining area (3)
is rather fragmentary and variable in height and direction.

The soils near Wood Hall are on the better-drained part
of the island and have been described as sandy
glacio-fluvial drift. The larger area of ridge and furrow to
the south-west of the village is on sandy and peaty soils
(Soil Survey 1:100000 map). This area slopes down to the
fen to the west. Silvester (1989, 290) attributes its survival
to the natural slope and the inhibited drainage coupled with
the spring line which renders the edge of the island
unattractive for settlement. The direction of most of the
ridge and furrow here is downslope thus aiding drainage so
it is easier to offer an explanation for the presence and
survival of this group of earthworks.

Hilgay is lacking in accessible documentary evidence
for the medieval period (Silvester 1991, 45–47). However,
all the islands of Fenland to the west have had ridge and
furrow like the Midlands still further to the west and as
Hilgay was formerly a holding of Ramsey Abbey, itself on
a fen island (Darby 1940, 53), it would be logical for similar
methods of cultivation to be carried out on the island of
Hilgay.

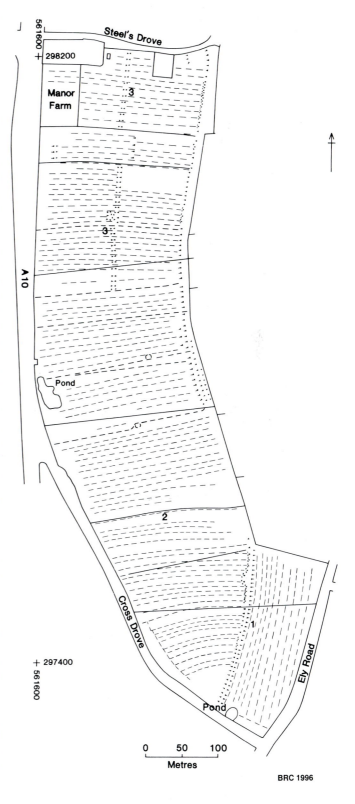

Figure 130 Hilgay, extensive ridge and furrow west of
the village. Scale 1:5,000

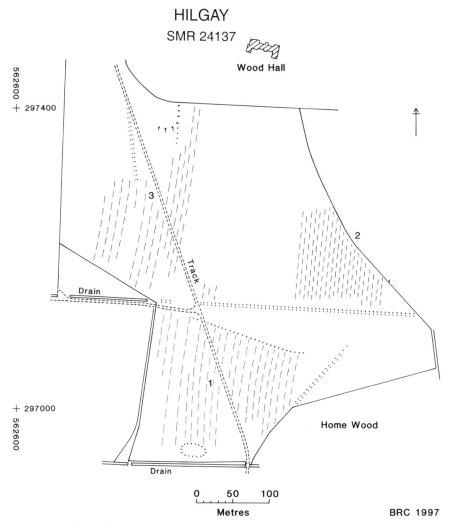

HILGAY

SMR 24137

Wood Hall

562600

+ 297400

3

Track

2

Drain

Drain

1

Home Wood

+ 297000

562600

0   50   100
Metres

BRC 1997

Figure 131 Hilgay, vestiges of ridge and furrow near Wood Hall. Scale 1:5,000

Middleton SMR 31613, 18547; TF 653 162
(Fig.132)

Fragments of ridge and furrow survive south of the A47.

Middleton, near King's Lynn, has earthworks immediately south of the A47(T) close to West Hall Farm near the western boundary of the parish. The area comprises two sites SMR 31613 and 18547. The first is to the south of the existing buildings bounded by a ditch (1) which broadens into a pond at its south-eastern corner. An internal ditch (2) runs north to south while some weak scarps (3) mark the bounds of an old tennis court.

The remainder of the area is SMR 18547 which includes fragments of ridge and furrow with later disruptions. To the south of (1) is a modern straight channel linking it to an irregularly-shaped pond and to the east a north-to-south ditch (4) extending from the road to the southern boundary of the pasture touching the western limit of another pond. Within these ditches are the remains of ridge and furrow (5) with what may be a headland to the north. To the east of the north-to-south ditch are two ditches which are probably modern, but with an earlier boundary (6) to the north. To the east again is a ditched enclosure (7) which extends to the width of the field. Further east again is the best-preserved area of ridge and furrow with the earth-

works of two enclosures (8,9) in the north-east corner, almost certainly superimposed on the ridge and furrow. This may have happened in later medieval or post-medieval times.

Documentation of this portion of the parish is scanty and begins ostensibly with the Church Commissioners' Map of 1751 (NRO Ch. Comm. 21843/3). This shows the land which had belonged to the Priory of Blackborough. This area was part of the West Field 'in which are many inclosed lands' and was labelled as 'West Hall Bushes'. The Enclosure Map of 1816 (NRO C/Sca 2/200) is slightly more informative referring to the area to the south as 'Busy Lands' and showing Calves Pightle to the west of a building on the site of West Hall Farm. Another building is shown to the south of the farm with a second smaller one to the south of it and north-east of a circular pond. This appears to be the southernmost of the three present ponds; the presence of the buildings is not directly apparent on the plan but may account for some of the features shown. The ditch touching the western edge of one of the ponds can be equated with a boundary shown on the map of 1816.

The Tithe Map (NRO PD 640/15) of 1838 shows roughly the area of the earthworks divided into three pasture enclosures, from west to east, House Pightle, Homestall and Bushy Ground, while the farm was 'House and Premises'. On this map no ponds are shown while the Enclosure Map shows only one.

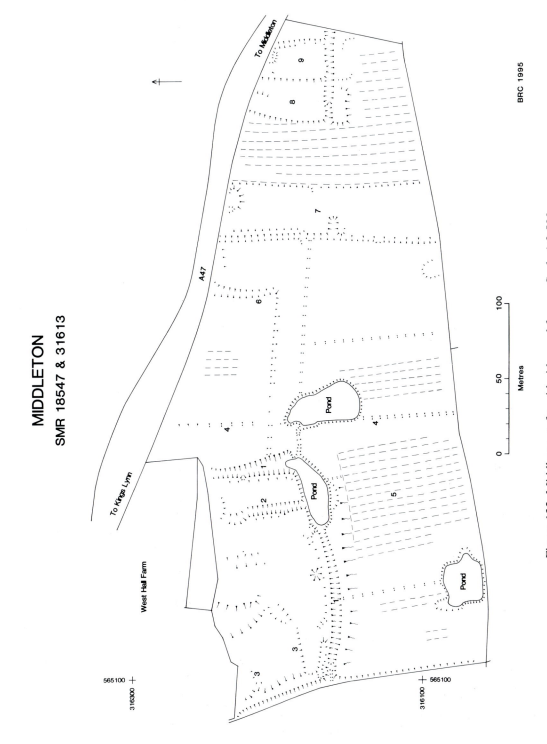

MIDDLETON
SMR 18547 & 31613

Figure 132 Middleton, tofts with ridge and furrow. Scale 1:2,500

203

Plate LI Ryston, ridge and furrow close to the church. CUCAP BRX 103
(Photography by Cambridge University Collection of Air Photographs)

Ryston SMR 2453, TF 622 017
(Pl. LI, Fig.133)

Ridge and furrow survives in grassland near the church of this deserted medieval village.

Ryston is a depopulated village about 1.5km south-south-east of Downham Market. The earthworks are in grassland to the north and south of the church at the north-west angle of Ryston Park. The parish boundary is very close to the western end of the church and some of the features are in Denver.

The field north of the road has as its eastern boundary a linear north-to-south depression (1), clearly a hollow way; this is called 'Lynne Way' on a map of 1635 (Private possession, Ryston Hall). The area west of this has ridge and furrow truncated to the south and bounded by a marked headland (2) to the north. To the north of this is another area which includes, at its west end, short lengths of ridge and furrow. The central enclosure (3), separate in 1635, is bounded by scarps and ditches and is probably a toft with a house site at its southern end. To the west is more incomplete ridge and furrow.

South of the church are more features. The most significant is incomplete ridge and furrow, but also present are the possible former boundary of the churchyard (4) and a causeway (5) across the stream, possibly with

landscaping depressions on either side (Wade-Martins (ed) 1987, 56).

Two field books (NRO PRA 361 379 x 5, 16th century, and PRA 362 379 x 5 of 1586) give an adequate picture of Ryston in early post-medieval times and, with the map of 1635, explain some of the earthworks. These documents show quite clearly that the village had disappeared, most houses being in Roxham with a hall existing in roughly the present position in Ryston.

The land north of the church and west of Lynn Way was part of Church Croft furlong in Ryston Field and was divided into thirteen strips with three 'mere balks' and a row of wood. The most easterly ten lands or riggs, as they were called, had a holt of elm trees at the southern end which may account for the blank area in its south-eastern corner. The area suggested as being a toft is unidentifiable and is probably later. Some of the pieces belonging to the demesne were 'grown with wood' and the more westerly ones abutted on the church wall. The lands to the north of this furlong are remains of Uphouse Furlong in which Lynn Way is said to occupy four ridges. The field books are quite clear in distinguishing pieces of land with acreages and the 'lands' or 'riggs' of which they were composed.

South of the church were Great and Little Church Broke and Church Close. In 1586 Church Close sided west on the other two and north on the churchyard and Church or Market Way. The causeway is a more recent former entry to the hall.

RYSTON
SMR 2453

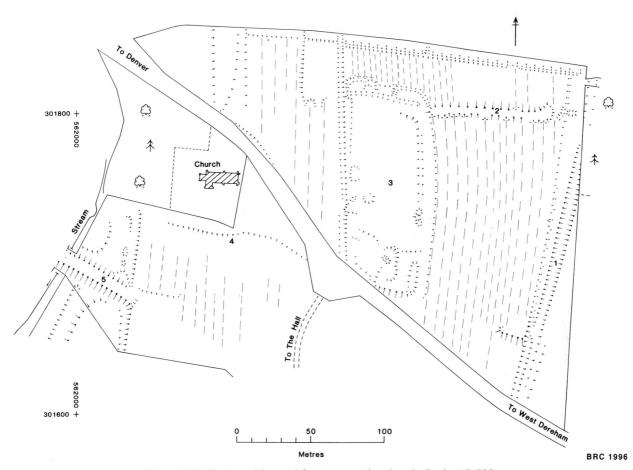

301800 +
562000
562000
301600 +

Church

To Denver
Stream
To The Hall
To West Dereham

0   50   100
Metres

BRC 1996

Figure 133 Ryston, ridge and furrow near the church. Scale 1:2,500

Stow Bardolph SMR 25344, TF 633 053
(Fig.134)

An area of ridge and furrow lies on the old parish boundary with Wimbotsham, which may have been further north in the 17th century.

Stow Bardolph is about 3km north-east of Downham Market; the earthworks lie to the south-east of the village astride the former parish boundary with Wimbotsham.

The westernmost set of ridge and furrow was actually in Wimbotsham; the ridges are aligned roughly north-to-south and are not well-preserved being generally no more than 0.2m in height. A headland bank to the east (1) separates them from a much larger group of ridge and furrow of east-to-west orientation. The parish boundary followed the western side of this before turning eastwards where it is marked by two shallow ditches. No ridges are visible to the south of the first ditch (2). After a small northern bend the parish boundary turned east again along the course of the second ditch (3).

The ridges of the more westerly group run east-to-west and are between 0.2m and 0.3m in height. They are the most consistent in form. Their eastern ends have been cut by a grass track leading north but extensions survive to a degraded headland bank (4) to the east. At this point a bulbous depression seems to have caused disturbance to a

second group on an east-to-west orientation lying to the east. It seems that the depression was formerly a pond now partly infilled.

The last group of strips is well-defined to the north of the parish boundary; two less marked ridges occur to the south of it where a ridge (5), ditched to the east, continues as a causeway into Spring Wood.

A map of Wimbotsham by William Hayward, dated 1626, accompanied by a field book of the same date (NRO Hare Additional 6812/1,2: Hare 4385 213 x 5) and an undated map (NRO Hare 4987 218 x 2) throw some light on these features. Hayward's map suggests that the boundary between the parishes was less certainly marked in earlier days but the north-to-south group of ridge and furrow was part of Short Furlong: the undated map calls it Short Furlongs and states that it was recently enclosed.

Shouldham Way lay to the south of Short Furlong in 1626 and led eastwards before turning north-eastwards appearing to accord with the causeway leading into Spring Wood. Hayward shows that Wood Close lay to the east of Short Furlong; it was the most northerly piece in Harebush Furlong and Stow Wood in Stow Bardolph lay to the north. A headland separated Wood Close from Short Furlong. Hayward's map shows that a portion of the area, Wood Close, had already been enclosed. His map suggests that the boundary between the parishes may then have lain a little further to the north.

205

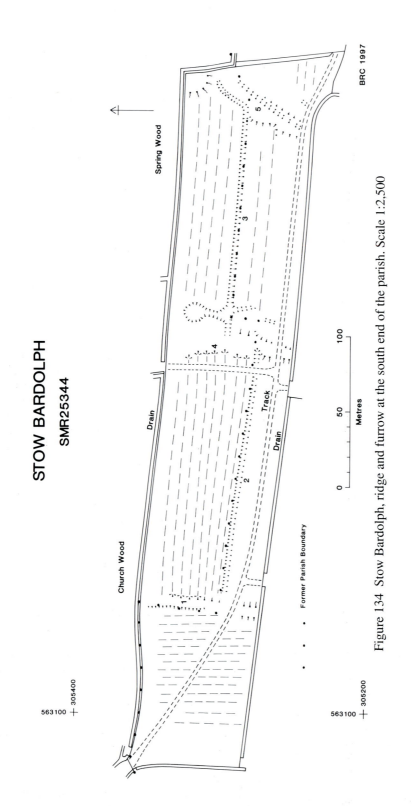

STOW BARDOLPH
SMR25344

Figure 134 Stow Bardolph, ridge and furrow at the south end of the parish. Scale 1:2,500

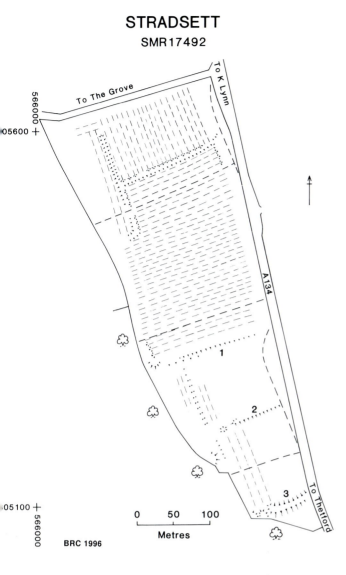

STRADSETT
SMR17492

To The Grove
To K Lynn
A134
To Thetford

566000
05600 +

05100 +
5660000

0   50   100
Metres

BRC 1996

Figure 135 Stradsett, well-preserved ridge and furrow
west of the park. Scale 1:2,500

Stradsett SMR 17492, TF 662 054
(Pl. LII, Fig.135)

*A well-marked area of ridge and furrow, the best remaining
example in a parish where fainter traces survive elsewhere.*

Stradsett is about 5.75km north-east of Downham Market.
The village was emparked in the early 19th century having
already been substantially altered by engrossment and
piecemeal enclosure (Williamson 1998, 281).

The earthworks lie about 0.6km south-west of the
church and consist of the remains of variously-aligned
ridge and furrow. The area is bounded to the east by the
A134 Thetford to King's Lynn road, to the north by a way
leading to The Grove, by a sinuous boundary to the west,
and is roughly triangular in shape.

The northern portion has impressive remains of ridge
and furrow. Headlands form a rough T-shape with the head
of the T facing west. There are north-north-west to south-
south-east ridges to the north of it, a large area of ridges to
the south running west-south-west to north-north-east, and

a few ridges to the west of the head of the T on a slightly
different north-north-west to south-south-east alignment.

The southern portion of the area is much less distinct
with only vestiges of ridge and furrow surviving. A scarp
(1), possibly the remains of a boundary, marks roughly the
southern limit of the best-preserved area. To the immediate
south are scraps of ridges and a ditch. A further scarp (2)
may be a remnant of a headland and between it and a more
pronounced headland (3) to the south are a few more ridges
similarly aligned.

There is a series of maps dating from the mid-17th
century to 1816 at Stradsett Hall which covers many of the
changes to the landscape which have occurred and which
give clues to the nature of this area. However, a map (NRO
BL 14/54) of 1689 illustrates a field book of Stradsett of
the same year (NRO BL Xc/19). In 1689 the landscape was
in a state of transition. The field book records changes in
which enclosures are listed as being formerly parts of
named furlongs. 'Riggs' or ridges are also mentioned in a
way which suggests that at least they were part of recent
memory.

In 1689 the A134 was known as 'Lynn Way', the way
to the Grove did not exist and the sinuous western boundary
was 'Magdalen Lane'. No hint of ridge and furrow is shown
or mentioned; presumably it was of no immediate
significance or it represented the recent past. The sideways
T was a boundary, to the north of which was the newly
enclosed 'Oat Close' formerly parts of Highgate and
Footacre furlongs. To the south and between it and
probably the southern scarp lay 'Tylelath Crofts'. The most
southerly remaining portion is more confusing as a large
rectangular enclosure has been superimposed on what was
there previously; this was 'Mere Pytles' with small
unnamed areas to the north and west. The southern
boundary of this enclosure appears to have been the
pronounced headland with the remainder now occupied by
woodland.

RAF air photographs (106G/UK 1606 27 June 1946
1332) show further ridge and furrow in the park; some
areas survive but are much more subdued.

Tottenhill SMR 14426, TF 636 104
(Fig.136)

*The rather forlorn remnant of a larger area surviving in
1946; in 1776 there were many more in the district.*

Tottenhill lies on the north-eastern edge of Fenland about
9.5km south-south-east of King's Lynn. The earthworks
are of ridge and furrow and cover 1.9ha in a small field at
Thieves Bridge beside the A10.

The ridges lie in two differing alignments within the
field. In the northernmost portion they are arranged in a
north-to-south orientation and are truncated by the hedge
to the north. They are 5.5m to 6m in width and 0.2m high
and are straight.

The second group lies in an east-to-west orientation and
varies in width and in their curved form. The six
northernmost ridges are similar to those in the northern
group and are terminated westwards for the most part by a
narrow ditch. The four central ridges are steeper and fuller
and extend beyond this ditch. The four southernmost ridges
are slightly wider and curve more sharply westwards.

Plate LII Stradsett, part of the ridge and furrow seen from the south-east. TF 6605/G/OGQ7

The western edges of the complete series of ridges are variable in form and difficult to interpret. The north-to-south group is limited to the west by a curving bank but this becomes vaguer and apparently disturbed further south.

Documentary evidence for field systems in Tottenhill is lacking and so it is not possible to attach any specific identification to this relic of open fields. The earliest maps, Faden of 1797 and Bryant of 1826, are uninformative.

The earliest definite reference to this area is an RAF aerial photograph of 1946 (TF 61/TF 6410/A) which shows this and other neighbouring areas of ridge and furrow. These are shown on a map by Silvester (1988a, fig. 104) and are commented upon in a later article (Silvester 1989, 291). The present site is all that remains of these. At Wallington, a little to the south-west, Arthur Young noted, in June 1776, that there were many 'high broad ridges' in this area spreading over a great tract of country; many of the furrows were then 12 inches deep in water so ridge and furrow 200 years ago was more apparent in this area which has more water-retentive heavy soil (Young 1804, 190).

TOTTENHILL

SMR 14426

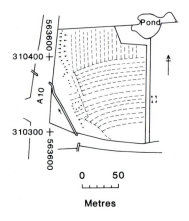

Figure 136 Tottenhill, small surviving area of ridge and furrow. Scale 1:5,000

Parks and Gardens

Parks and gardens have been comparatively lately recognised as earthworks in Norfolk in their own right. Much work on the subject has been carried out by Anthea Taigel and Tom Williamson and reference should be made to their publications (Williamson and Taigel (eds) 1990; 1991; Williamson 1998) for descriptions and details of many sites in Norfolk.

Houghton could be considered the classic case of parkland creation. Its development has been outlined by David Yaxley (1988b) and, more recently, by Tom Williamson (1998, 47–59; 248–251). Because of the survival of the old village earthworks within the park, a plan of the site has been included in an earlier section of this volume (pp50–51) and attention has been confined to that.

The examples selected here are, in some cases, extensions of Williamson's and Taigel's work, others are new examples. West Acre High House is a good instance of an extended survey; not only does it include the site of the original house and probable garden but it adds other features in the surrounding park. These range from an 18th-century brick kiln and signs of 18th-century enclosures to what may be ridge and furrow, possibly medieval in origin. Other examples of extended surveys include Great Melton and especially Hilborough where much additional information has been added.

Tacolneston Park is an example of a new study which includes an assortment of the features that can be preserved within a park which has grown unobtrusively since the last years of the 18th century. They range from roads and enclosures of probable medieval date and ridge and furrow, possibly of similar origin, to post-medieval house sites and various modifications of the later park landscape.

Kimberley could, perhaps, be considered a manorial site, but the extensive and complicated earthworks beyond the confines of the moated platform make it more appropriate in a parkland context.

Gillingham deals with the part of the park which has earthworks which repay mapping; Docking is an interesting study which incorporates medieval features, medieval and post-medieval roadways and enclosures, as well as later features culminating in Second World War relics. Kirby Cane offers some new interpretations of features already recorded while Booton Hall Gardens is a curiously unsatisfactory site; the earthworks obviously precede the documentation and, though not inconsiderable, remain an unexplained vestige of what may have been a more extensive feature. Narborough has been previously overlooked but the survey shows a variety of features of differing dates in somewhat confusing fashion, well worth the investigation.

Booton SMR 7437, TG 116 225
(Fig.137)

Earthworks of a garden of probable 17th-century date are separated from the house by a later ha-ha. A roadway south of the garden is even earlier.

Booton is a scattered village about 1km east of Reepham with a church isolated still further to the east. The hall lies midway between the two. The earthworks lie south of the hall and to the east of the driveway leading to it. The most prominent feature is a ha-ha (1) with a steeper northern edge. It is crossed by a modern causeway in front of the house and has three southern embayments. At the western end a shallow depression continues to the north-west. A tennis court has been constructed to the east altering the southern bank.

To the south is a rectangular feature (2) terraced into the gentle northward slope, partially embanked on the east, and bounded to the north by a terrace or pathway. To the west is a sub-rectangular platform (3) and to the south is a

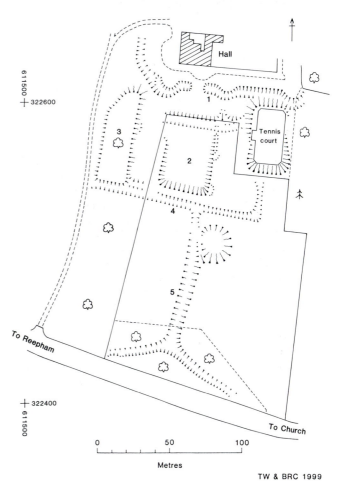

Figure 137 Booton, garden earthworks. Scale 1:2,500

boundary ditch (4) which turns north to be truncated by the tennis court. From this a broad depression (5) leads southwards and forks into two lesser diverging depressions which reach the road. To the east is a large almost circular pit of unknown purpose.

Booton Hall is a 17th-century building modified a century later and lying in a hollow facing gently sloping land. Faden (1797) shows a small park but Bryant (1826) has a much restricted area as park to the south and west of the house; a more westerly area claimed as park by Faden is excluded.

The first detailed map of the site dated 1819 (NRO THS9 386 x 4) and the Tithe Map of 1839 (NRO DN/TA 380) show the whole ha-ha, without embayments, separating the house from the gardens and the park, both maps refer to the area under pasture to the south as 'The Lawn'. By 1839, the area to the west, pasture in 1819, had become arable. The embayments may thus be features datable to a period after 1839.

The area to the south of the ha-ha, which may be of early 19th-century date, appears to contain remnants of an earlier elaborate garden whose southern boundary was the ditch to the platform and terraced square whose purpose, in the absence of documentation, must remain obscure. The northern terrace or possible pathway appears discordant and may be a late feature superimposed.

The north-to-south linear depression is enigmatic also. It is almost wide enough to be a hollow way leading to the hall. If so it must be an entrance earlier than the garden features which must be, at least, of the 18th century. The lesser curving depressions linked to it are also rather puzzling; the map of 1839 and later OS maps show them as bounding a small roadside copse, not shown in 1819.

Originally owned by the Layer family in the late 16th century, the hall was purchased in 1713 by the Elwins who continued to live there until the 1940s. It is probable that 18th-century changes to the garden and park landscape occurred at the same general time as those to the house, but that is only speculation (Williamson 1998, 138–9, 223–4).

Docking SMR 15003, 30502; TF 767 367
(Fig.138)

This park contains many features, including parts of a street with probable tofts, former enclosures and a rectilinear pattern of roads fossilized when the park was created.

Docking is a large village about 10km south-east of Hunstanton. The park and hall lie immediately south of the main east-to-west street; the park has been progressively enlarged since the 18th century.

The major earthworks consist of former roadways which have been absorbed within the park and become disused. One (1), partly hollow and partly terraced, runs southwards from Hall Farm towards London Pond and thereafter divides in two. From London Pond roads extended westwards and eastwards (2), the latter more pronounced with distance from the pond, before reaching a crossroads and continuing eastwards as a terraced roadway (3) to Mill Lane where a surviving road provided a further link to the east. Another roadway (4), embanked on its western side, crosses the east-to-west road and continues south to the edge of the park.

Within this framework are other features. From the western road north of London Pond the remains of another road (5) lead towards the hall, with a short length of terraced trackway leading off to the south. Two complete enclosures (6,7), almost certainly tofts, lie on either side of this road, facing west onto the road leading to London Pond. Some of the other enclosures within the park may well be post-medieval sub-divisions, but some are likely medieval enclosures. One slightly curving broad ridge (8) is a more convincing medieval feature, possibly a headland or an important boundary. (The two sites, SMR 30778 and 30780, relate to military buildings of the Second World War.)

Finds made suggest that there was Late Saxon and medieval activity immediately south of Hall Farm, on both sides of the north-to-south road. Two other areas showed significant activity. One south of the hall produced Late Saxon and medieval finds, the other, to the south of it, was less productive, but included a sherd of Ipswich-type ware.

The finds suggested that parts of the park were once within the settled area of the village since displaced northwards. A survey of probable 17th-century date (NRO NRS 26991 180 x 5) gives no indication of a park, but mentions roads clearly leaving the southern side of the 'mydd strete'. Docking Hall was built in 1612 after the estate was purchased in 1597 (Williamson 1998, 228). A map of 1756 (NRO MF/RO 468/2) shows the hall with an orchard to the west and a garden and orchard to the south; there were enclosed pastures to the south again, some of them identifiable as earthworks.

Faden (1797) shows that a small park had been created bounded on the south by an east-to-west road with a five-way road junction at the south-east corner and an irregular branching of four ways at the south-west margin. The park then was bounded by the three major mapped roadways (1,2,4). North-to-south portions of this road pattern are broadly identifiable in the 17th-century survey. By 1802 plans were afoot to extend the park (Williamson 1998, 228).

A road order (NRO C/Sce 1/11) of 1832 closed the western and southern roads. The Enclosure Map of 1862 (NRO C/Sca 2/96) shows the other roads as stopped and names the two north-to-south roads as London Lane (west) and Wandhams Lane (east). Wandhams Lane continued as Rudham Road, while the easterly projection of the west-to-east road to Mill Lane was Back Lane.

Gillingham SMR 30504, TM 414 921
(Fig.139)

A confusing piece of parkland which probably includes a medieval hollow way, sets of ditches, an old park boundary and other features overlying medieval settlement no longer visible.

The present parish contains the sites of two deserted medieval villages, Winston and Windell, of which little appears to remain. The existing village is about 1.5km north-west of Beccles with the hall and park to the north-east. The surveyed earthworks are to the south of the hall in the southern half of a park in which two medieval churches are situated to the west of the hall, one in ruins. In the northern half of the park, slight earthwork evidence for former roadways is noted but not recorded here.

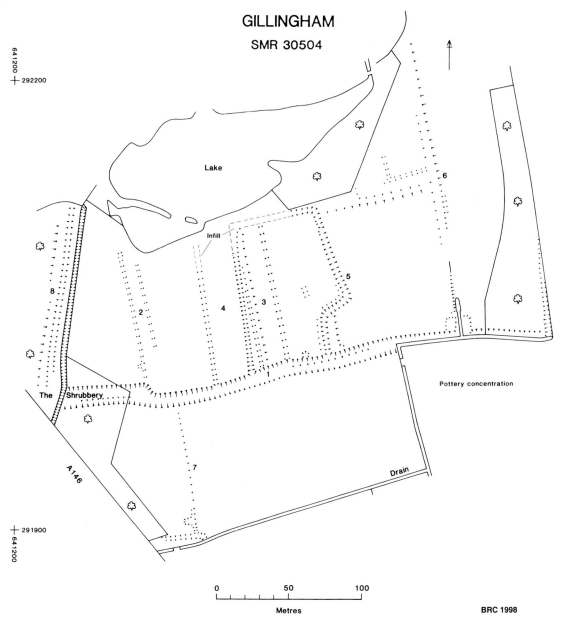

GILLINGHAM
SMR 30504

641200
+ 292200

Lake

Infill

6

8

2   4   3   5

The Shrubbery

Pottery concentration

A146

7   Drain

+ 291900
641200

0   50   100

Metres   BRC 1998

Figure 139 Gillingham, a roadway and enclosures south of the hall. Scale 1:2,500

The main feature of the planned earthworks is a broad hollow way (1), the western end seemingly terminated by a north-to-south ditch, the eastern end with its southern boundary truncated by arable land. To the north of the hollow way are three pairs of parallel ditches, the western and eastern ones (2,3) being similarly aligned. One of the first pair almost links with a kink in the hollow way. The central pair (4) are differently aligned, apparently on the south wing of the 16th or 17th-century hall, and have had their northern ends recently infilled. They are later than (3) since the easternmost one of the pair cuts across the westernmost one of (3) before turning east to form the northern edge of an enclosure with an irregular ditch (5) as its eastern boundary. Further east a north-to-south bank (6) marks a former park boundary, with its southern end bisecting a platform where medieval bricks occur in quantity.

To the south of the hollow way, further west, is a degraded park boundary ditch (7), while the westernmost feature is a terraced path (8), banked to the east, marking the line of a former drive to the hall.

Faden (1797) shows a small park mostly to the south of the hall extending south to features (1), (6) and (7); and also the unrecorded roads and the churches outside the park to the north and west respectively. The park is also shown on landscaping plans of 1812 (NRO MF/RO 336/8), while soon afterwards a Road Order terminated the roads to the north and west of the hall, incorporating them and the churches into the park (Williamson 1998, 236). The Tithe Map of 1839 (NRO DN/TA 829) shows a canal south of the hall; this was enlarged in the 1980s to form the present lake.

The hollow way (1) is too wide to have been a park boundary and was probably a medieval road. Medieval pottery has been found on the mapped earthworks near the southern end of the lake and in arable land to the south-east of the site as well as near the churches, indicating medieval settlement. These facts, together with the position of the churches, suggest that the park conceals a medieval site, abandoned in favour of a more southerly position on the terrace of the Waveney.

Plate LIII Great Melton: the park from the west showing hollow ways. TG 1306/X/HEE 22

Great Melton SMR 21294, TG 137 062
(Pl. LIII, Fig.140)

The surviving portion of a large park of the late 18th century which includes former roadways, tofts and various other features.

Great Melton is a scattered settlement about 6km north-east of Wymondham. The remains of the park (SMR 30505) lie to the west of the two churches, one of them ruined, and the park contains features which are probably substantially medieval.

The most obvious earthwork is a hollow way (1) running north-eastwards from the junction of two roads to the edge of Church Plantation. Linked to this at its southern end are the remains of another hollow way (2) leading towards the site of the early 17th-century Hall (SMR 9277); this has been cut by a clay pit. To the west of it is a small ditched enclosure (3), probably a toft, and to the south of this a short length of ditch and flanking bank. Construction of a bowling green and cricket pitch has removed parts of other features including a ditched causeway (4) and a ridge (5) leading towards an 18th-century dovecote. Also in this portion of the park is an impressive complex feature (6) possibly incorporating a trackway, boundary and headland bank.

A most striking complex linear feature (7), obviously another hollow way, runs from the vicinity of the churches westwards and appears linked to the one coming from the south-west. Near the junction is an L-shaped ditch (8), probably the boundary of a toft. Within Church Plantation are two ditched enclosures. The northern one (9) faces onto the hollow way but its eastern edge is uncertain. The second (10), where much medieval pottery occurs, has been reduced by road construction. Other features within the wood include a linear depression linked to the junction of the hollow ways, possibly an old boundary of sites near the church, and an unlinked narrow depression to the east.

Faden's map (1797) shows a park in existence west of the churches. The northern portion, or 'North Lawn', is now under the plough; the surviving 'South Lawn' contains the earthworks. The park appears to be of the late 18th century, though ornamental grounds east of the hall may have been earlier (Williamson 1998, 263).

Various Road Orders indicate changes leading to the final form of the park. One dated 1776 (NRO C/Sce 2/Box 1, No 9) showed the extinction of the road leading from the present road bifurcation towards the hall in favour of one circling further west. Another dated 1777 (NRO C/Sce 2/Box 1, No 17) showed the suppression of the road running north-east to Church Plantation as well as the east-to-west road which it joined. Other identifiable features are

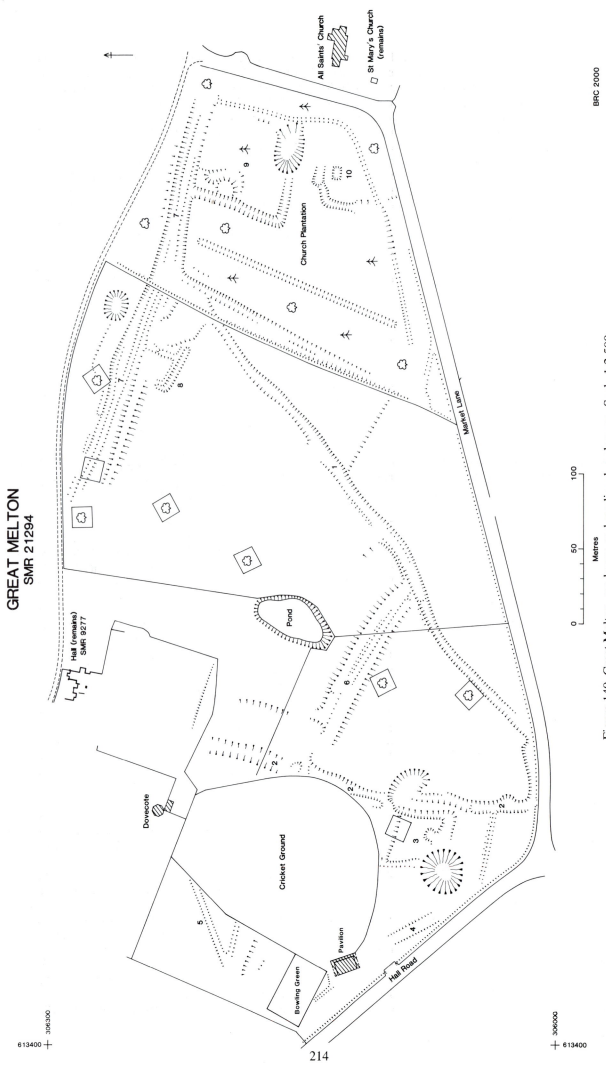

GREAT MELTON
SMR 21294

Hall (remains)
SMR 9277

Dovecote

Cricket Ground

Pond

Bowling Green

Pavilion

Hall Road

Church Plantation

Market Lane

All Saints' Church

St Mary's Church
(remains)

BRC 2000

Metres

0   50   100

Figure 140 Great Melton, roadways and medieval enclosures. Scale 1:2,500

306300

613400

306000

613400

the short length of ditch and bank which was a field boundary in 1818 (NRO C/Sca 2/195) and the ridge leading towards the dovecote which was a path (NRO NRS 4129).

Peverell's manor, with which the advowson of All Saints' church was linked, was described as being east of the church in 1610 (NRO EVL 182/18); it had houses, barns, stables, yards, orchards and gardens attached (NRO EVL 182/19). The second document describes also two 'Playne Closes', one abutting northwards on the way from the church to Barford, and the other abutting east on the way from Bawburgh to Wymondham. The road to Barford was probably the east-to-west hollow way; the second, a road past the church shown by aerial photography continuing south into arable land. It is a possibility that an early site of Peverell's manor was in the wooded area within the park and that, by 1610, it was on a fresh site, but that is mere speculation.

Hilborough SMR 30511, TF 826 002
(Fig.141)

A large park which incorporates hollow ways, probable tofts, ponds and unexplained banks and ditches; probably an extension of a smaller park already in existence in the 17th century.

Hilborough is a village about 15km north-north-east of Brandon. The park lies east of the village and north of the church.

The major feature is a hollow way (1) beginning south-west of the church and curving north-westwards to reach the A1065; it has been partly obliterated by a large pit. A smaller pathway (2) links this roadway with the track leading to the mill. A causeway (3) flanked by a ditch to the south of (1) crosses it and continues north across the stream roughly parallel with the A1065. To the east of the causeway, limited by a bank (4), are the remains of a property, while further west is an enclosure (5) yielding medieval and post-medieval pottery.

To the west of the church, a well-defined hollow way (6) extends northwards but becomes less distinct north of the stream where it is partly obscured by banks and ditches. Two depressions, one containing a pond, are linked to these. East of the pond is a spread bank (7) which becomes less definite as it turns northwards. It is interrupted by two possible access ways, the larger (8) being a broader ridge. The bank is linked by a ridge to the garden boundary and also to a small rectangular enclosure (9), the most definite of a number of vaguer features to the west from which medieval pottery has been collected.

Outside the park is a length of hollow way (10) and an enclosure. To the east of the church within the park are two small oval ditched enclosures, probably modern (11). Beyond the park near the mill is an irregular raised area, part of which may be spoil, on which Middle Saxon and medieval pottery occurs (12).

A field book of 1627 (NRO Hare 4385 213 x 5) refers to a highway west of the church with a tenement and yard further north abutting in turn northwards on the manor house. A marginal note includes the manor house with five other pieces in 'The Parke 40 acres'. As the park is mentioned in the main text elsewhere it is a contemporary feature. Within the park the field book stated that there were two fishponds. It is possible that (6) may have led north to

the manor house with the two hollows, one still a pond, to the east. The existence of this park appears much earlier than the date of *c*.1760 suggested by Williamson (1998, 150, 242). The hollow way may also have served as an earlier way to the later hall.

Other features survived until the 19th century. A Road Order of 1819 (NRO C/Sce 2/Box 8, No 2) shows the ways (1) and (3) still in service while (2) was a loop linking (1) with the way to the mill. The road from Bodney Bridge entered the mill track slightly east of (3). The hollow way (1) continued across the line of the A1065 into a vanished back lane which joined Westgate Street further west. A Road Order dated 1837 (NRO C/Sce 2/Box 16, No 6) shows that (1) and (3) were to be closed and replaced by the present course of the A1065 north of its junction with (1). The Bodney Bridge road was diverted westwards after 1845.

The earthworks north-east of the hall are remains of medieval tofts facing onto the road; one listed in 1626 was 'The Swan', a probable forerunner of the present inn while the hollow way (10) is shown by Faden (1797).

Kimberley SMR 8918, 30466(part); TG 075 041
(Pl. LIV, Fig.142)

A complex set of earthworks within part of a large park containing the moated remains of a hall with outer yards and enclosures and what are almost certainly water gardens together with roadways linking hall and church and a part of a hollow way.

Kimberley is a small village 4.5km north-west of Wymondham: a considerable portion of the parish is within Kimberley Park. The earthworks are in the park and extend eastwards from the church to the easternmost of two woods known as 'The Clumps'.

The outstanding earthwork (SMR 8918) is a substantial moat surrounding the remains of a late medieval Hall. The northern entrance is modern, the original entry was by a bridge in the centre of the southern arm. There were inlet and outlet leats to west and east (1 and 2). Similarly-aligned enclosures to the south (3), somewhat degraded, and a terraced roadway (4) from the west appear related to the hall. To the south-east of the moat is a series of sub-rectangular enclosures (5) separated from those to the west by a later hollow way (6). Two later features, a post-medieval field boundary (7) and a former drive (8) to the present hall to the north-west, are imposed on this group.

The hollow way (6) has been blocked and diverted as a channel into a series of depressions (9) now largely in woodland. These surround a banked oval depression (10), recently partially dredged with the spoil left as a pile in the middle. These features were retained by a now incomplete embankment or dam (11). To the north-east a much smaller rectangular depression (12), almost completely embanked, forms an island within the remnant of a larger depression. These may be interpreted as remains of water gardens linked to the moat (Taylor *et al.* 1990, 155–157), with some features almost certainly fishponds. A ditch (13) to the north-east marks the outer limit of the earthworks and served as a later enclosure boundary (NRO C/Sca 2/65).

To the west are other features in partly ploughed and re-seeded grassland within the park (SMR 30466, part). West of the moat is a depression, partly water-filled, but

Plate LIV Kimberley viewed from the east, showing the moated site with other earthworks including part of a probable water garden in the foreground. TG 0704/N/ATU 12

the major remaining features are fragments of possible roadways leading from the church. The most southerly of these (14), with a bank serving as a possible park boundary, reappears as a causeway further east. The northerly one (15), is partially ploughed out. North of the church is a length of hollow way (16) which was a public road in 1766 (NRO C/Sca 2/65), while a ditch (17) linking with it is probably part of a toft boundary.

There are several surveys of Kimberley which throw some light on these features. A 15th- or 16th-century field book (NRO Kim 1/7/13) gives a description of the area around the hall. A large enclosed park extended east of the churchyard and contained the site of the manor called Kimberley Hall alias Wodehouses with buildings, gardens, a moat, pools of water, pastures, woods and other things pertaining to it. Another field book dated 1622 (NRO Kim 1/7/18) varies the description of the hall. It was situated in a park of 300 acres of pasture enclosed by palings and

consisted of buildings, gardens and yards with pools and fisheries within the park. This does seem to refer to the features thought to be water gardens.

The church stood on the edge of Church or Carrow Green in the 16th century (NRO Kim 1/7/13) and this field book describes messuages around the green and near the church. It also mentions Hall Lane, described as an old road now in the park, and a New Way. It seems likely that one at least of these may correspond with a roadway shown on the plan.

This Kimberley Hall replaced a medieval moat in Fastolfe Wood in the south of the present park, and was in turn abandoned and demolished in 1659 when the Wodehouse family moved to Downham Manor in Wymondham parish. Eventually, in 1712, work was begun on the core of the present Kimberley Hall, 700 metres north of the site shown on the plan (Williamson 1998, 81–83, 148, 152, 256–258).

Pond

4

3

50

Metres

anorial site with

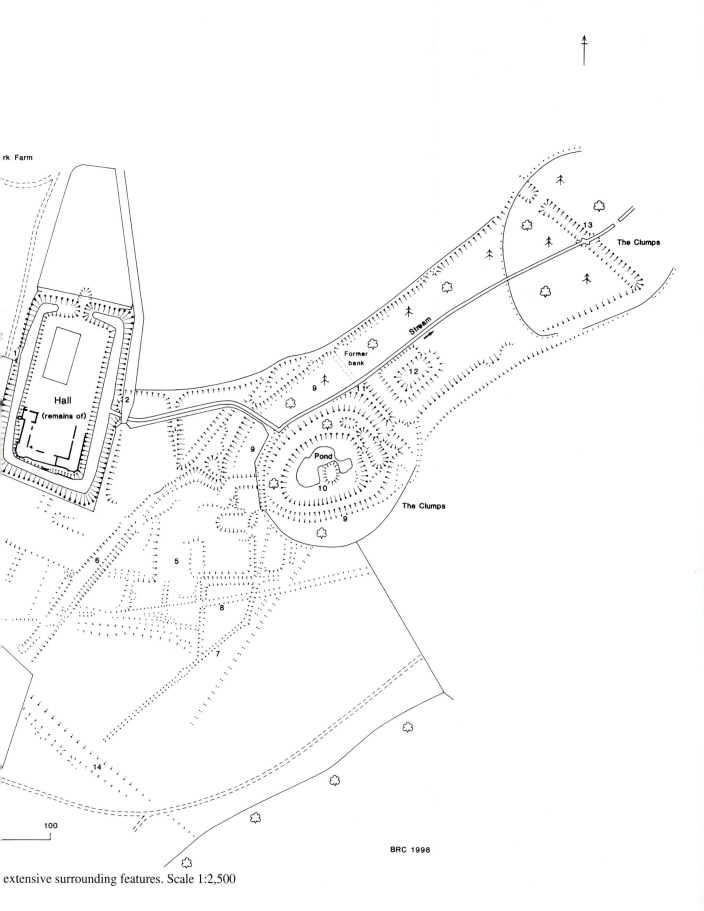

LEY

466(part)

rk Farm

Hall
(remains of)

1
2
9
10
Pond
The Clumps

5
6
8
7
14

9
11
12
13
The Clumps
Former
bank
Stream

100

BRC 1998

extensive surrounding features. Scale 1:2,500

218

Plate LV Kirby Cane: RAF 1945 vertical showing the four rows of trees. TM 39/TM3639/B

Kirby Cane SMR 10690, 29792; TM 371 940
(Pl. LV, Fig.143)

A somewhat enigmatic park which contains old field boundaries, a probable former road line, possible tofts near the church and a very odd group of features in the west, probably ridges introduced for tree planting.

Kirby Cane is a dispersed settlement about 6km north-east of Bungay. Most of the population is now located peripherally leaving the hall in its park in isolation near the church.

The mapped area includes SMR 10690 covering the hall, gardens, ponds and grassland features immediately to the west, thought to be remnants of a moated site. Features here include the remains of an apparent hollow way (1) south of the hall gardens while the area south-west of the hall, 'Moat Yard' on the Tithe Map of 1840 (NRO DN/TA 207), appears enclosed by a double ditch to the west (2) and two linear depressions (3) to the south. Within it is another ditch.

In the remainder of the park is a variety of features. One of these is a curving north-to-south ditch (4) which was the park boundary on Faden (1797) and on the Tithe Map. A major bank (5) extends eastwards from this to cross a large ridge (6) which runs from south-west to north-east. At the crossing a short ridge extends south. At its north-eastern end the long ridge is rather disturbed, but turns east and is terminated by a more recent ha-ha; south of it is a ditched enclosure (7) with an internal bank reinforcing its southern arm.

In the far west is a curious feature: four straight parallel ridges (8) running south-south-west to north-north-east, neatly interrupted at almost the half-way point.

The church was mentioned in 1086 (Brown (ed) 1984, 14,41) but the village may have been dispersed as by 1202 there was certainly a now vanished place called Erwellstun in the north-west (Dodwell 1950, 176; Davison *et al.* 1990, 57). In the 17th century a hall was built with sixteen hearths (Williamson 1998, 258; Frankel and Seaman 1983, 8), the kernel of the present hall.

Many earthworks are related to features shown on the Enclosure Map of 1806 (NRO C/Sca 2/102) and the Tithe Map, but others are interpreted speculatively. Moat Yards was an enclosure in 1840; both maps show buildings in the southern portion. The two ponds have changed; the eastern one now curtailed and the northern one bulbous. Only the name suggests a moat. The long ridge (6) appears a continuation of the western part of Old Bungay Road; the eastern part may well be a diversion. The enclosure near the northern end of this ridge may be a medieval toft but nothing supports this; the area east of the modern drive is featureless on the Enclosure Map.

The four interrupted ridges have been interpreted as ridge and furrow (Silvester 1989, 292; Williamson 1998, 147, 150, 258; Liddiard 1999, 1–6). They lay in an arable field in 1840: medieval features would not have survived. The area only came into the park after 1869. Aerial photographs (TM 39/TH 3693/B of 1946) show rows of trees on the alignment and a post-war eyewitness mentioned hazels growing on the ridge tops. A more viable suggestion is that the straight ridges were 19th-century features raised to contain rows of hazel trees, hence their regularity. Williamson's plan (1998,147) shows them as curved and does not reveal the interruption.

RAVENINGHAM
SMR 30484

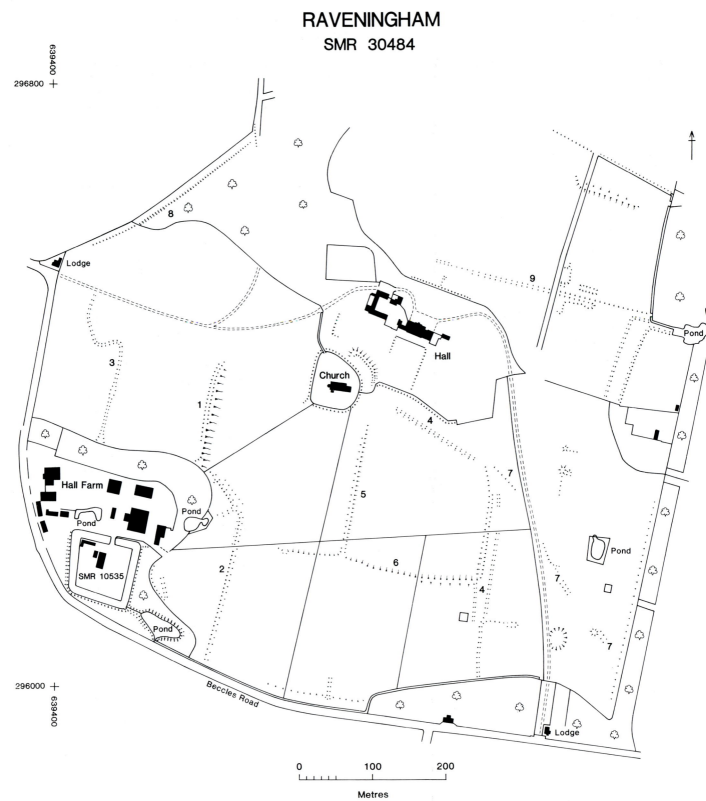

Figure 147 Raveningham, former enclosures and roadways within the park. Scale 1:5,000   BRC 2000

Raveningham SMR 30484, TM 398 963
(Fig.147)

A park which includes old field boundaries dating from the 17th century, a large rectangular medieval moat and former roadways.

Raveningham is a scattered settlement about 6.5km north-west of Beccles and 4km south-east of Loddon. Church and hall lie within a park roughly central to the parish and there is no alternative focus.

The earthworks within the park are largely old boundaries and roadways shown on a map of 1632 in private hands. A tracing of part of this map has been published (Williamson 1998, 145). The only obvious medieval features are the rectangular moat (SMR 10535) and the church. Close to the moat are three ponds, slightly altered since 1632, one of which, to the south-east, may have been a fishpond. Close by also are three field boundaries, one a bank (1) and two which are ditches (2,3), shown clearly on the map of 1632.

The large enclosure to the east of these is still partly detectable with the remains of a roadway (4) along its eastern side leading to the church. This enclosure was divided into four by two internal banks (5,6). To the east again are remains of boundaries of the northern portion of a wedge-shaped field between converging roadways (4,7).

To the north-west of the church is a roadway (8) on the edge of the park; to the north-east are a group of features partially identifiable in 1632. An east-to-west bank (9) is more modern.

Domesday, with twelve entries for Raveningham (Brown (ed) 1984, 1,204,240; 6,7; 9,108; 10,47; 20,36; 31, 10,15; 50,12; 65,17; 66,98), suggests that it may originally have been a scattered settlement which included at least one named satellite, Sudwoda or Southwood (Davison with Fenner 1990, 62).

One family, the Castells, became prominent later and an heiress married Sir Edmund Bacon in 1735. Since then the Bacon family has held the estate (Blomefield 1775, IV, 262–63).

In the last century before the Bacons the area was one of largely enclosed lands. It is not certain that the moated site was still the seat of the family; it is marked 'Situs maner de Raveningham' which may mean abandonment, although two buildings and a cross (or chapel) are shown. Another building lay to the east of the nearest pond. Further buildings lay north of the church; the curved ridge north-east of the church is spoil from the early 20th-century creation of a terrace. Church Close to the south of it was crossed from north to south by Beare Way acting as a subdivision. Its eastern side was marked by a road passing from north of the church to the south. 'An Olde Way' left this to the south-east and in the apex of the junction stood a 'Gulde Hall'.

The Bacons built the present hall in the late 18th century (Pevsner and Wilson 1999, 599) and the road past the church was closed in 1783 (NRO C/Sce 1/Road Order Box 2, No 10).

Tacolneston SMR 32307, TM 139 953
(Fig.148)

A previously unmapped park which includes medieval features in the form of a roadway flanked by tofts and with ridge and furrow surviving to the north — unusual in this part of the county. Also present are features produced during the evolution of the park.

Tacolneston is a village about 7km south-south-east of Wymondham. The hall is north-west of the village and just over 1km west of the church. The surrounding parkland is largely enclosed by plantations.

To the south-east, beyond the stream, are ditched enclosures, either tofts or closes, extending southwards to a scarp (1) marking an earlier line of Hall Road. Another scarp (2), of uneven form, probably representing another roadway, marks the northern boundary of these enclosures. A pond is the eastern boundary of a small ditched enclosure and there is also a banked circular enclosure (3) to the south-east and another, oval in shape, in Hospital Wood.

The area east of the drive has faint ridge and furrow bounded by a subdued remnant of a possible headland to the north and to the east by a drain (4) which is cut by a ring ditch. Other features include a platform (5) apparently aligned with the moat and the drive and, to the south, a rather disturbed enclosure (6) which includes a brickwork base.

West of the drive are various features. In the south-east corner are two scarps, one of them forming the end of a substantial north-to-south linear feature (7) which includes a broad ridge and two ditches, a possible causeway or boundary. In the north are the remains of a curving causeway (8). The western portion of the field is dominated by another causeway (9) more prominent in the north, which crosses an east-to-west ditch. There are four circular platforms of varying size, the largest breaking the line of the causeway.

Blomefield gives no definite information about the hall (1769, III, 107) which is said to date from the time of Queen Anne (Pevsner and Wilson 1999, 691). The partial moat is probably later. There is little firm evidence about the growth of the park which is not mentioned by Blomefield or shown by Faden (1797) who described the hall as the seat of 'Revd Tho. Warren'. Bryant (1826) shows some surrounding plantations. The Ordnance Survey One-Inch 1st Edition (1836–7) shows enclosures to the north and south-west, probably plantations, and, to the east of the present lodge, two buildings separated by a track. The Tithe Map (NRO DN/TA 894 of 1845) shows these buildings which correspond with the small ditched enclosures near the pond and the disturbed area with some brickwork. The eastern boundary of the three enclosures to the south is shown. The ringed embankments here and in Hospital Wood and the ring ditch to the north are woodland clumps on the 1:2500 map of 1906.

West of the drive the northern portion west of the modern drain was pasture in 1845, the southern part arable, thus explaining the degradation of the southern part of the causeway. The four circular platforms shown were woodland clumps in 1906 while the curved causeway to the north was the remnant of a back entrance. The north-to-south causeway by the Lodge was a woodland boundary in 1836.

It seems that the park preserves remnants of tofts, roadways and ridge and furrow of the medieval landscape, borne out by the presence of medieval pottery on adjacent arable land, as well as evidence of the evolution of the park landscape.

West Acre SMR 3887, 3888, 29824, 31636; TF 795 178
(Fig.149)

A very interesting area of parkland incorporating garden remains contemporary with an earlier house, early 18th-century field boundaries, 18th-century brick kilns, possible ridge and furrow, access roads of various dates and other features.

High House, with its associated parkland, lies in the northern part of West Acre which is 7.75km north-west of Swaffham. The grassland surrounding the present mansion exhibits a variety of features representing phases in the development of the landscape.

To the south of the House there are two lengths of boundary ditch (1,2) while a flint-faced ha-ha (3) marks the edge of woodland to the west. On the eastern side, beyond another boundary ditch (4) a sinuous linear depression (5), probably a hollow way, appears to follow the parish boundary. Other features mark the bounds of old enclosures, or tracks leading to them or abandoned driveways to the House sites. To the east of the house are remains of brick kilns close to an irregularly-shaped pit.

To the north of the House features are more complex. Close to the building is a curious three-sided banked enclosure (6) open to the south. A rectangular parchmark has been recorded within it and an abandoned roadway leading towards it is represented by a broad ridge (7). Close by to the north-east, is a series of scarps and depressions aligned north-to-south. Beyond these are what appear to be boundaries of old enclosures.

To the west is a system of ditches, scarps and ridges (8) which extends, in part, beyond the modern road to Home Farm. The grassland to the north of the road contains a number of confusing features including a pit and a linear scarp and ridge (9) leading from the cottages, while the faint remains of what may be ridge and furrow occupy the northern portion. Further possible faint ridge and furrow lies north of Home Farm.

West Acre Priory site and manor passed at the Dissolution to the Duchess of Richmond and later to Sir Thomas Gresham. Eventually, West Acre was purchased by Sir Edward Barkham in 1621. Barkham 'had a large manor-house or hall in this parish called High-House which he built. This being ruinous *etc.*, Edward Spelman Esq., late lord, built a very curious and stately pile near the scite of the Old Hall' (Blomefield 1775, IV, 749–53). A map of 1726 of the manor of High House (NRO BL 14/28) shows the old house slightly to the north of the present site. North of the present site a rectangular feature corresponding to the earthwork (6) described above was shown, possibly a raised terrace walk overlooking a parterre with a central fountain (Williamson and Taigel 1991, 98–100). Buildings shown nearby on the map match the scarps and depressions shown on the plan.

Some of the features in the southern and eastern areas of the park are identifiable as enclosure boundaries of 1726, notably those of Sand-Pitt Close (10). The brick kilns may be those mentioned in a lease to High House Farm in 1763 (NRO BIR/191).

Faden's map (1797) shows the southern boundary of the park following the boundary ditches (1,2), with the western boundary following a causeway to the west of (10). Comparison with the Ordnance Survey 1st Edition One-Inch map (*c.* 1824, with later additions) indicates extensions of the park. It is possible that some features may pre-date the first High House. The 1726 map records Park Brecks and Park Closes and a Lodge Hill Breck beyond the limits of the park; they may refer to an earlier hunting park (Yaxley 1993, 55).

Medieval pottery has not been found on arable land near the ridge and furrow; this absence points to either medieval sheep-grazing or post-medieval agriculture. Large flocks at Stowborough and Wyken recorded in Priory accounts (CUL Dd 8.42) between 1507 and 1510 may have been grazed on open heathland here; Stowburrough Closes in 1726 lay to the west of the park.

TACOLNESTON
SMR 32307

Hall

Moat

Sluice

5

5

4

613600

295500

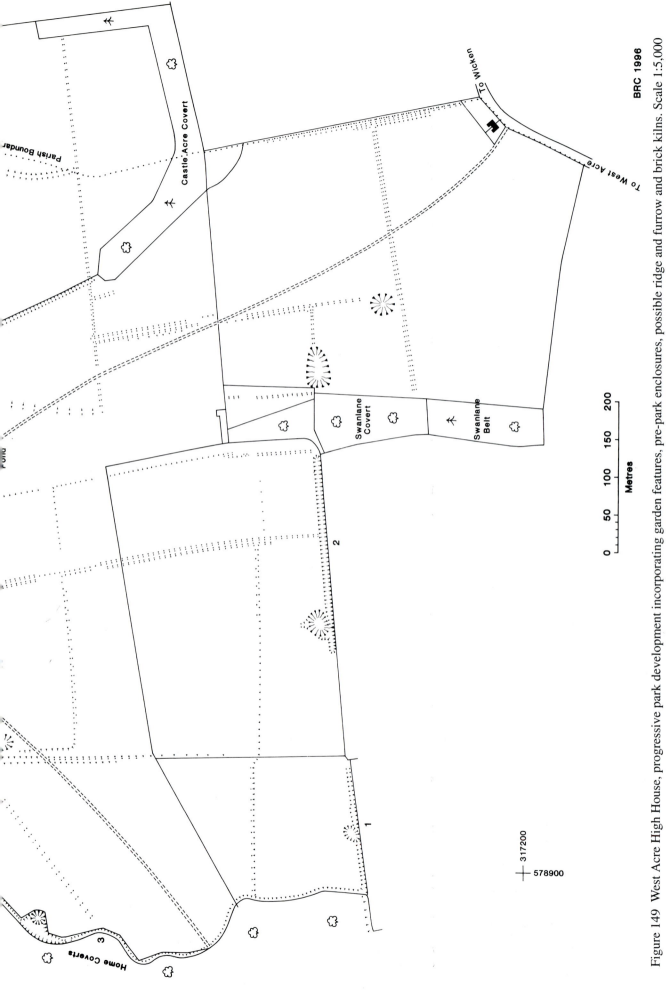

Figure 149 West Acre High House, progressive park development incorporating garden features, pre-park enclosures, possible ridge and furrow and brick kilns. Scale 1:5,000

BRC 1996

Metres

0   50   100   150   200

317200
578900

230

Bibliography

Addington, S., 1982 'Landscape and Settlements in South Norfolk', *Norfolk Archaeol.* 38, 97–139

Allison, K.J. 1955 'The Lost Villages of Norfolk', *Norfolk Archaeol.* 31, 116–162

Allison, K.J. 1957 'The Sheep-Corn Husbandry of Norfolk in the Sixteenth and Seventeenth Centuries', *Agric. Hist. Rev.* 5, 12–30

Allison, K.J. 1958 'Flock Management in the Sixteenth and Seventeenth Centuries', *Econ. Hist. Rev.* 2nd Series, 11, 98–112

Andrews, P. 1995 *Excavations at Redcastle Furze, Thetford 1988–89*, E. Anglian Archaeol. 72

Armstrong, M.J. 1781 *History and Antiquities of the County of Norfolk*, 10 Vols (Norwich)

Aston, M.A. 1982 'Aspects of fishpond construction and maintenance in the 16th and 17th centuries with special reference to Worcestershire' in Slater, T.R. and Jarvis, P.J., *Field and Forest: An Historical Geography of Warwickshire and Worcestershire*, 257–280 (Norwich, Geo Books)

Bacon, R.N., c. 1850 Narrative of the Proceedings regarding the erection of the Leicester Memorial, Norwich Mercury Office

Barrett-Lennard, T. 1904 'Some Account of the Manor or Castle of Horsford', *Norfolk Archaeol.* 15, 267–293

Barringer, J.C., Fowle, R. and Spicer, S. (eds), 1993 *Wymondham in the 17th Century*, (WEA Wymondham Branch)

Batcock, N., 1991 *The Ruined and Disused Churches of Norfolk*, E. Anglian Archaeol. 51

Bedingfeld, A.L., (ed) 1966 A Cartulary of Creake Abbey, Norfolk Rec. Soc., Vol 35

Bedingfeld, A.L. and Gilyard-Beer, R., 1970 *Creake Abbey, Norfolk* (Min. Works Guide)

Beresford, M., 1954 *The Lost Villages of England* (London, Lutterworth)

Beresford, M. and Hurst, J., 1971 *Deserted Medieval Villages* (London, Lutterworth)

Beresford, M.W. and Finberg, H.P.R., 1973 *English Medieval Boroughs: a Handlist* (Newton Abbot, David and Charles)

Beresford, M.W. and St. Joseph, J.K., 1979 *Medieval England, an Aerial Survey*, (2nd edition, Cambridge University Press)

Binns, A., 1989 *Dedications of Monastic Houses in England and Wales 1066–1216* (Woodbridge, Boydell Press)

Blake, W.J., 1951–52 'Norfolk Manorial Lords in 1316', *Norfolk Archaeol.* 30, 232–261, 263–286

Blomefield, F., 1739–75 *An Essay Towards a Topographical History of the County of Norfolk*, contd. by C. Parkin, 1st edition, 5 Vols

Brown, P. (ed), 1984 *Domesday Book: Norfolk*, 2 Vols (Chichester, Phillimore)

Brown, R.A., 1989 *Castles from the Air* (Cambridge University Press)

Bryant, A., 1826 *Map of Norfolk*, reprinted 1998 with an introduction and analysis by J.C. Barringer, (Larks Press)

Buckland, F., 1875 A Report on the Fisheries of Norfolk, ordered by the House of Commons

Bulwer Revd J., 1859 'Plan of Wendling Abbey', *Norfolk Archaeol.* 5, 38–40

Butler, L. and Wade-Martins, P., 1989 *The Deserted Village of Thuxton, Norfolk*, E. Anglian Archaeol. 46

Butler, R.M., 1961 'Wendling Abbey, a note on the site', *Norfolk Archaeol.* 32, 226–229

Calendar of Close Rolls

Calendar of Inquisitions Post Mortem

Calendar of Patent Rolls

Campbell, B., 1981 'The Extent and Layout of Commonfields in Eastern Norfolk', *Norfolk Archaeol.* 38, 15–32

Carthew, G.A., 1877–79 The Hundred of Launditch and deanery of Brisley in the County of Norfolk. Evidences and topographical notes, 3 Vols (Norwich)

Carthew, G.A., 1879a 'North Creake Abbey' *Norfolk Archaeol.* 7, 153–68

Carthew, G.A., 1879 b 'On Earthworks at Mileham' *Norfolk Archaeol.* 8, 10–16

Chandler, J., 1993 *John Leland's Itinerary, Travels in Tudor England* (Stroud, Alan Sutton)

Christie, P. and Rose, P., 1987 'Davidstow Moor, Cornwall: the medieval and later sites. War-time excavations by C.R.Croft Andrew 1941–2', *Cornish Archaeol.* 26, 163–195

Clark, C., 1970 *The Peterborough Chronicle 1070–1154* (Oxford)

Clarke, R.R., 1960 *East Anglia*, (London, Thames and Hudson)

Coad, J.G. and Streeten, A.D.F., 1982 'Excavations at Castle Acre Castle, Norfolk 1972–77; country house and castle of the Norman earls of Surrey', *Archaeol. J.* 139, 138–301

Coke, T.W., 1803 Annals of Agriculture XXXIX

Cornford, B. Edwards, W.F. Leake, G.F. and Reid, A.W., 1984 *The Rising of 1381 in Norfolk*, (Norfolk Research Committee)

Cozens-Hardy, B., 1961 'Some Norfolk Halls', *Norfolk Archaeol.* 32, 163–208

Cushion, B., 1994 'An Earthwork Survey of Anmer, Norfolk', *Medieval Settlement Research Group* 9, 27–29

Cushion, B., 1995 'Wighton, Norfolk', *Medieval Settlement Research Group* 10, 35–36.

Cushion, B., 1996 'Gayton', *Medieval Settlement Research Group* 11, 40

Cushion, B. and Davison, A., 1997 'A Group of Earthworks in the Tat Valley', *Norfolk Archaeol.* 42, 492–505

Cushion, B., 1997 'Tharston/Tasburgh, Ellingham, Deopham', *Medieval Settlement Research Group* 12, 32–33

Cushion, B., 1998 'Shelton', *Medieval Settlement Research Group*, 13, 43–44

Cushion, B., 1999 'Heacham; Earthwork Vestiges of Norfolk's Oyster Industry', *Norfolk Archaeol.* 43, 346–350

Cushion, B. and Davison, A., 1991 'The Earthworks at Harling Thorpe', *Norfolk Archaeol.* 41, 207–211

Cushion, B., Davison, A., Fenner, G., Goldsmith, R., Knight, J., Virgoe, N., Wade, K. and Wade-Martins, P. 1982 *Some Deserted Village Sites in Norfolk*, E. Anglian Archaeol. 14, 40–101

Dallas, C., 1993 *Excavations in Thetford by B.K.Davison between 1964 and 1970*, E. Anglian Archaeol. 62

Darby, H.C., 1940 *The Medieval Fenland* (Cambridge University Press)

Darby, H.C., 1952 *The Domesday Geography of Eastern England* (Cambridge University Press)

Darvill, T. and Fulton, A., 1998 *The Monuments at Risk Survey of England 1995* (English Heritage)

Davies, J.A., Gregory, T., 1992 'Excavations at Thetford Castle, Norfolk, 1962 and 1985–6', in Davies *et al. The Iron Age Forts of Norfolk*, E. Anglian Archaeol. 54, 1–28

Davies, J.A., Gregory, T., Lawson, A., Rickett, R., and Rogerson, A., 1992 *The Iron Age Forts of Norfolk*, E. Anglian Archaeol. 54

Davison, A., 1980 'West Harling; a Village and its Disappearance', *Norfolk Archaeol.* 37, 295–306

Davison, A., 1982 'Petygards and the Medieval Hamlet of Cotes', E. Anglian Archaeol. 14, 102–107

Davison, A., 1983 'The Distribution of Medieval Settlement in West Harling', *Norfolk Archaeol.* 38, 329–336

Davison, A., 1985 'Keburn', *Medieval Village Research Group* 33, 10

Davison, A., 1990 'Norton', *Medieval Settlement Research Group* 5, 27

Davison, A., 1991 'Holverston', *Medieval Settlement Research Group* 6, 30

Davison, A., 1994 'The Field Archaeology of Bodney and the Stanta Extension', *Norfolk Archaeol.* 42, 57–79

Davison, A., 1995 'The Field Archaeology of the Mannington and Wolterton Estates', *Norfolk Archaeol.* 42, 160–184

Davison, A., 1996 *Deserted Villages in Norfolk* (Poppyland)

Davison, A. with Cushion, B., 1999 'The Archaeology of the Hargham Estate', *Norfolk Archaeol.* 43, 257–274

Davison, A. with Fenner, A., 1990 *The Evolution of Settlement in Three Parishes in South-East Norfolk*, E. Anglian Archaeol. 49

Davison, A., Green, B., and Milligan, B., 1993 *Illington: a study of a Breckland parish and its Anglo-Saxon Cemetery*, E. Anglian Archaeol. 63

Davison, A., Cushion, B., Fenner, G., Fenner, A., Reid, A., Wade-Martins, P. and Yaxley, D., 1988 *Six Deserted Villages in Norfolk*, E. Anglian Archaeol. 44

Denney, A.H. (ed), 1960 The Sibton Abbey Estates, Suffolk Records Society 11

Dodwell, B. (ed), 1950 Feet of Fines for the County of Norfolk 1198–1202, Pipe Roll Society 27

Dollin, W., 1986 'Moated Sites in North-East Norfolk', *Norfolk Archaeol.* 39, 262–277

Doubleday H.A. and Page, W. (eds), 1901–06 *Victoria History of the County of Norfolk*, 2 Vols (Norwich)

Dyer, C., 1991 *Hanbury: Settlement and Society in a Woodland Landscape*, Dept. Local Hist. Occ. Pap. (Leicester University Press)

Dymond,D., 1985 *The Norfolk Landscape* (London, Hodder and Stoughton)

Dymond, D., 1993 'Medieval and Later Markets' in Wade-Martins (ed) *An Historical Atlas of Norfolk*, 76–77 (Norfolk Museums Service)

Dymond, D., 1998 'A Misplaced Domesday Vill: Otringhythe and Bromehill', *Norfolk Archaeol.* 43, 161–168

Dymond, D. and Martin, E., 1988 *An Historical Atlas of Suffolk*, (1st edition, Suffolk County Council/Suffolk Inst. Archaeol. Hist.)

East Anglian Notes and Queries I , 1860 (Lowestoft)

Edwards, D., 1978 'The Air Photographs Collection of the Norfolk Archaeological Unit: Third Report', E. Anglian Archaeol. 8, 87–105

Erwood, E.C.E., 1923 'The Premonstratensian Abbey of Langley', *Norfolk Archaeol.* 21, 175–234

Everson, P. and Wilson-North, R., 2002 'The Earthworks', in Dallas, C. and Sherlock, D. *Baconsthorpe Castle, Excavations and Finds 1951–72*, E. Anglian Archaeol. 102, 32–35

Everson, P. and Jecock, M., 2000 'Castle Hill and the early medieval development of Thetford in Norfolk' in Pattison, P., Field, D. and Ainsworth, S., (eds), *Patterns of the Past, Essays in Landscape Archaeology for Christopher Taylor* (Oxford, Oxbow Books)

Faden, W., 1797 *Map of Norfolk*, reprinted 1989 with an introduction by J.C. Barringer, (Larks Press)

Fairweather, F.H. and Bradfer-Lawrence, H.L., 1929 'The Priory of St Mary and All Saints, Westacre, and excavations upon its site', *Norfolk Archaeol.* 23, 359–94

Fernie, E., 1983 *The Architecture of the Anglo-Saxons* (London, Batsford)

Feudal Aids Volume III

Field, J., 1972 *English Field Names* (Newton Abbot, David and Charles)

Finch, J., 1996 'Fragments of ambition: the monument of the Shelton family at Shelton, Norfolk' in Rawcliffe, C., Virgoe, R. and Wilson, R. (eds), *Counties and Communities, Essays on East Anglian History presented to Hassell Smith*, 85–96 (Centre of East Anglian Studies, University of East Anglia)

Frankel, M.S. and Seaman, P.J. (eds), 1983 — *Norfolk Hearth Tax Assessment, Michaelmas 1664*, Norfolk Genealogy 15

Garmonsway, G.N. 1953 — *The Anglo-Saxon Chronicle* (trans; London, Dent))

Gelling, M., 1978 — *Signposts to the Past* (London, Dent)

Gelling, M., 1984 — *Place-Names in the Landscape* (London, Dent)

Glasscock, R.E., 1975 — *The Lay Subsidy of 1334*, Records of Social and Economic History, New Series II (Oxford University Press)

Green, B. and Taylor, M., 1966 — Trial Excavation on an Earthwork at Castle Hill, Hunworth, Norfolk (unpubl. report, Norfolk SMR 1059)

Green, J.P., 1992 — *Medieval Monasteries* (London, Leicester University Press)

Gregory, T., 1982 — 'Romano-British Settlement in West Norfolk and on the Norfolk Fen-Edge', in Mills, D. (ed) *The Romano-British Countryside, Studies in Rural Settlement and Economy* Brit. Archaeol. Rep. British Series 103(ii)

Gregory, T., 1992 — *Excavations in Thetford 1980–82 Fisons Way*, 2 Vols, E. Anglian Archaeol. 53

Gurney, D., 1986 — *Settlement, Religion and Industry on the Roman Fen-Edge, Norfolk*, E. Anglian Archaeol. 31

Gurney, D. (ed), 1990 — 'Excavations and Surveys in Norfolk 1989', *Norfolk Archaeol.* 41, 107–112

Gurney, D. (ed), 1993 — 'Excavations and Surveys in Norfolk 1992', *Norfolk Archaeol.* 41, 522–532

Gurney, D. and Penn, K. (eds), 1998 — 'Excavations and Surveys in Norfolk 1997', *Norfolk Archaeol.* 43, 193–211

Hall, D.N., 1978 — 'Elm: a field survey', *Proc. Cambridge Antiq. Soc.* 68, 21–42

Hart, C.R., 1966 — *The Early Charters of Eastern England* (Leicester University Press)

Hartley, R.F., 1987 — *The Medieval Earthworks of North-East Leicestershire*, (Leicester Museums)

Heywood, S., 1982 — 'The Ruined Church at North Elmham', *J. Brit. Archaeol. Ass.* 135, 1–10

Hudson, W., 1895 — 'The assessment of the townships of the County of Norfolk for the King's tenths and fifteenths, as settled in 1334', *Norfolk Archaeol.* 12, 243–297

Hurst, J.G., 1961 — 'Seventeenth-century Cottages at Babingley, Norfolk', *Norfolk Archaeol.* 32, 332–342

Jurkowski, M., Smith, C.L. and Crook, D., 1998 — *Lay Taxes in England and Wales 1188–1688*, Public Record Office Publications Handbook 31 (Kew)

Kenyon, J.R., 1990 — *Medieval Fortifications* (Leicester University Press)

Knocker, G., 1967 — 'Excavations at Red Castle, Thetford', *Norfolk Archaeol.* 34, 119–186

Larking, Revd L.B., (ed) 1857 — 'Report of Prior Philip de Tham to the Grand Master Elyan de Villanova' in *The Hospitallers in England, 1338*, Camden Series, 81–83

Lawson, A.J., Martin, E.A. and Priddy, D., 1981 — *The Barrows of East Anglia*, E. Anglian Archaeol. 12

Lawson, A.J., 1986 — *Barrow Excavations in Norfolk 1950–82*, E. Anglian Archaeol. 29

Leadam, I.S., 1892/3 — 'The Inquisition of 1517, inclosures and evictions', *Trans. Royal Hist. Soc.* New Series VI 167–314; VII 127–299

Leah, M., 1993 — 'Excavations and Watching Brief at Castle Acre 1985–86', *Norfolk Archaeol.* 41, 494–507

Leah, M., 1994 — *The Late Saxon and Medieval Pottery Industry of Grimston, Norfolk: Excavations 1962–92*, E. Anglian Archaeol. 64

Lewis, C., Mitchell-Fox, P. and Dyer, C., 1997 — *Village, Hamlet and Field* (Manchester University Press)

Liddiard, R., 1999 — 'The distribution of ridge and furrow in East Anglia: ploughing practice and subsequent land use', *Agr. Hist. Rev.* 47, 1–6

Liddiard, R., 2000 — *Landscapes of Lordship; Norman Castles and the Countryside in Medieval Norfolk 1066–1200*, Brit. Archaeol. Rep. 309

Manning, Revd C.R., 1884 — 'Notice of Earthworks at Darrow Wood', *Norfolk Archaeol.* 10, 335

Manning, Revd C.R., 1892 — 'Buckenham Castle', *Norfolk Archaeol.* 11, 137–142

Margeson, S., Seillier, F. and Rogerson, A., 1994 — *The Normans in Norfolk* (Norfolk Museums Service)

Markham, S., 1984 — *John Loveday of Caversham, 1711–1789: the Life and Times of an Eighteenth-Century Onlooker* (Salisbury, Michael Russel)

Martin, E., 1999 — 'Medieval Castles' in Dymond, D. and Martin, E.(eds), *An Historical Atlas of Suffolk*, (revised edition; Suffolk County Council/Suffolk Inst. Archaeol. Hist.)

Martin, T., 1779 — *The History of the Town of Thetford in the Counties of Norfolk and Suffolk from the earliest accounts to the present time* (John Nichols)

Mason, R.H., 1872–3 *History of Norfolk*

McGee, C. and Perkins, J., 1985 — Weeting Castle, (English Heritage Archive Report)

McKisack, M., 1959 — *The Fourteenth Century, 1307–1399*, Oxford History of England (Oxford University Press)

Mills, A. D., 1991 — *A Dictionary of English Place-Names* (Oxford University Press)

Mitchell, J.B., 1954 — *Historical Geography* (London, English University Press)

Moralee, J., 1982/1983 — 'Babingley and the Beginnings of Christianity in East Anglia', *NARG News* 31, 7–11 and *NARG News* 33, 12

Morley, B. and Gurney, D., 1997 — *Castle Rising Castle, Norfolk*, E. Anglian Archaeol. 81

Norfolk Archaeological Miscellany, 1906, 79–81

North, R., 1713 — *A discourse of fish and fish ponds* (London)

Paterson, H. and Wade-Martins, P. 1999 'Monument conservation in Norfolk: the monument management project and other schemes', in Grenville, J. (ed) *Managing the Historic Rural Landscape*, 137–147

Paterson, H. and Wade-Martins, P. forthcoming 'Field monument conservation in Norfolk', in Middleton, B. (ed) *Archaeology and the Rural Environment*

Pevsner, N., 1962 *The Buildings of England; North-west and South Norfolk* (London, Penguin Books)

Pevsner, N. and Wilson, B., 1997 *The Buildings of England Norfolk I: Norwich and North-East*, (2nd edition; London, Penguin Books)

Pevsner, N. and Wilson, B., 1999 *The Buildings of England, Norfolk II: North-West and South*, (2nd edition; London, Penguin Books)

Phillips, C.W. (ed), 1970 *The Fenland in Roman Times*, Roy. Geogr. Soc. Res. Series 5

Pobst, Phyllis E., (ed) 1996, 2000 *The Register of William Bateman 1344–55*, The Canterbury and York Soc. 84 and 90

Pounds, N.J.G., 1990 *The Medieval Castle in England and Wales* (Cambridge University Press)

Puddy, E., 1961 *A Short History of the Order of the Hospital of St John of Jerusalem in Norfolk* (Dereham)

Rackham, O., 1986 *The History of the Countryside* (London, Dent)

Rawcliffe, C., 1995 *The Hospitals of Medieval Norwich*, Studies in East Anglian History 2, (Centre of East Anglian Studies, University of East Anglia)

Redstone, V.B., 1931 *Household Book of Dame Alice de Bryene 1412–13*, (Suffolk Institute of Archaeology and Natural History)

Reid, A.W., 1979 'The Process of Parliamentary Enclosure in Ashill', *Norfolk Archaeol.* 37, 169–177

Renn, D.F., 1961 'The Keep of New Buckenham', *Norfolk Archaeol.* 32, 232–5

Renn, D.F., 1968 *Norman Castles in Britain* (London)

Rodger, N.A.M., 1997 *The Safeguard of the Sea, A Naval History of Britain 660–1649* (London, Harper Collins)

Rogerson, A., 1993 'Moated Sites' in Wade-Martins P. (ed) *An Historical Atlas of Norfolk*, 66–67

Rogerson, A., 1995 *A Late Neolithic, Saxon and Medieval Site at Middle Harling, Norfolk*, E. Anglian Archaeol. 74

Rogerson, A. and Dallas, C., 1984 *Excavations in Thetford 1948–59 and 1973–80*, E. Anglian Archaeol. 22

Rogerson, A., Ashley, S.J., Williams, P., and Harris, A., 1987 *Three Norman Churches in Norfolk*, E. Anglian Archaeol. 32

Rogerson, A., Davison, A., Pritchard, D. and Silvester, R., 1997 *Barton Bendish and Caldecote: fieldwork in south-west Norfolk*, E. Anglian Archaeol. 80

Rosenheim, James M., 1989 *The Townshends of Raynham* (Connecticut, Wesleyan University Press)

Rowley, T. (ed)., 1981 *The Origins of Open-Field Agriculture* (London, Croom Helm)

Rudd, W.R., 1906 'Claxton Castle', *Norfolk Antiq.Miscellany*, 2nd Series 1, 86–96

Rumble, A. (ed), 1986 *Domesday Book: Suffolk*, 2 Vols(Chichester, Phillimore)

Rye, W., 1889 *Catalogue of Fifty of the Norfolk Manuscriptsin the Library of Mr Walter Rye*

Saunders, H.W., 1910 'A History of Coxford Priory', *Norfolk Archaeol.* 17, 284–370

Saunders, H.W., 1930 *An Introduction to the Rolls of Norwich Cathedral Priory* (Norwich, Jarrolds)

Sawyer, P.H., 1968 *Anglo-Saxon Charters, an Annotated List and Bibliography* (London, Royal Historical Soc.)

Schofield, B.(ed), 1949 *The Knyvett Letters 1620–24* (London, Constable)

Schram, O.K., 1961 'Place-Names' in Briers, F. (ed) *Norwich and its Region*, British Association for the Advancement of Science, 1,41–149

Seaman, P. (ed), 1988 *Norfolk and Norwich Hearth Tax Assessment, Lady Day 1666*, Norfolk Genealogy XX

Sheail, J., 1968 'The Regional distribution of wealth in England as indicated in the 1524/5 lay subsidy returns' (unpub. PhD thesis London Univ.)

Silvester, R., 1988a *The Fenland Project Number 3, Norfolk Survey, Marshland and Nar Valley*, E. Anglian Archaeol. 45

Silvester, R., 1988b 'Settlement earthworks at Hilgay and the ring ditches in the silt fens', *Norfolk Archaeol.* 40, 194–198

Silvester, R., 1989 'Ridge and Furrow in Norfolk', *Norfolk Archaeol.* 40, 286–296

Silvester,R., 1991 *The Fenland Project Number 4, Norfolk Survey; The Wissey Embayment and Fen Causeway*, E. Anglian Archaeol. 52

Sire, H.J.A., 1994 *The Knights of Malta* (London, Yale University Press)

Smallwood, J., 1977 'Shouldham Report' *NARG News* 11, 23–26

Smith, A.H., 1956 *English Place Name Elements*, Eng. Place-Name Soc. Vols 25, 26

Smith, A.H., 1974 *County and Court* (Oxford University Press)

Smith, A.H. and Baker, G.M., 1979–90 *The Papers of Nathaniel Bacon of Stiffkey*, Vols I (with R.W.Kenny), II, III, IV (edited by V.Morgan, J.Key and B.Taylor) (Centre of East Anglian Studies, University of East Anglia)

Smith, D., 1969 'A Preliminary Report on the Deserted Village of Shotesham St Mary, Henstead Hundred in the County of Norfolk, England', *Gwynned J.* 170–185 (Pennsylvania, Gwynned Mercy College)

Smith, W., 1806 *Observations on the Utility, Form and Management of Water Meadows* (Norwich)

Stark, J., 1834 *Scenery of the rivers of Norfolk, comprising the Yare, the Waveney, and the Bure...with historical and geological descriptions* (Norwich)

Stride, K.B., 1989 'Engrossing in Sheep-Corn-Chalk Areas: Evidence in Norfolk', *Norfolk Archaeol.* 40, 308–318

Sussams, K., 1995 West Tofts Floated Water Meadows (unpubl. report, Norfolk SMR 31157)

Sussams, K., 1996   *The Breckland Archaeological Survey 1994–6*, (Suffolk County Council)

Taylor, C., 1983   *Village and Farmstead* (London, Philip)

Taylor, C., Everson, P. and Wilson-North, R., 1990   'Bodiam Castle, Sussex', *Medieval Archaeol.* 155–157

Thompson. M.W., 1991   *The Rise of the Castle* (Cambridge University Press)

Thompson, S., 1991   *Women Religious* (Oxford University Press)

Turner, R.C. and Scaife, R.G. (eds), 1995   *Bog Bodies, New Discoveries and New Perspectives* (British Museum Press)

Vincent, N., 1993   'The Foundation of West Acre Priory (1102–1126)', *Norfolk Archaeol.* 41, 490–94

Vincent, N., 1999   'The Foundation of Wormegay Priory', *Norfolk Archaeol.* 43, 307–312

Virgoe, R., 1992   'The Earlier Knyvetts: the Rise of a Norfolk Gentry family', *Norfolk Archaeol.* 41, 1–14, 249–278

Wade-Martins, P., 1974   'The Linear Earthworks of West Norfolk', *Norfolk Archaeol.* 36, 23–38

Wade-Martins, P., 1977   'A Roman Road between Billingford and Toftrees', in E. Anglian Archaeol. 5, 1–3

Wade-Martins, P., 1980a   *Excavations in North Elmham Park 1967–1972*, E. Anglian Archaeol. 9, 2 Vols

Wade-Martins, P., 1980b   *Village Sites in Launditch Hundred*, E. Anglian Archaeol. 10

Wade-Martins, P. (ed.), 1987/1999   *Norfolk From The Air I, II* (Norfolk Museums Service)

Wade-Martins, S., 1980   *A Great Estate at Work* (Cambridge University Press)

Wade-Martins, S. and Williamson, T., 1994   'Floated Water Meadows in Norfolk, a Misplaced Innovation', *Agric. Hist. Rev.* 42, 20–37

Wade-Martins, S. and Williamson, T., 1999   *Roots of Change, Farming and the Landscape in East Anglia, c.1700–1870*, Agric. Hist.Rev. Supplementary Series 2 (British Agricultural History Soc.)

Walters, H.B., 1938–1965   'Inventories of Norfolk Church Goods (1552)' *Norfolk Archaeol.* 26, 248–70; 27, 97–144, 263–89, 385–416; 28, 7–22, 89–106, 138–80, 217–228; 30, 75–87, 160–167, 213–219, 370–378; 31, 200–210, 233–98; 33, 63–85, 216–235, 457–490

West, S., 1985   *West Stow, The Anglo-Saxon Village*, E. Anglian Archaeol. 24

White's Directory of Norfolk 1845, (reprinted 1969; David and Charles)

Whiteman, A., 1986   *The Compton Census of 1676*, British Academy Rec. Soc. Econ. Hist. New Series X (Oxford University Press)

Wilcox, R., 1980   'Castle Acre Priory excavations 1972–76', *Norfolk Archaeol.* 37, 231–276

Williamson, T. and Taigel, A. (eds), 1990   *Gardens in Norfolk*, (Centre of East Anglian Studies, University of East Anglia)

Williamson, T. and Taigel, A., 1991   'Some Early Geometric Gardens in Norfolk', J. *Garden History* 11, 1 and 2

Williamson, T., 1993   *The Origins of Norfolk* (Manchester University Press)

Williamson, T., 1996   'Roger North at Rougham: a lost house and its landscape' in Rawcliffe, C., Virgoe, R. and Wilson, R. (eds), *Counties and Communities, Essays on East Anglian History, presented to Hassell Smith* (Centre of East Anglian Studies, University of East Anglia)

Williamson, T., 1998   *The Archaeology of the Landscape Park, Garden design in Norfolk, England, c.1680–1840*, Brit. Archaeol. Rep. 268

Wilson, D.R., 1978   'Groups of Circles in the Silt Fens', *Proc. Cambridge Antiq. Soc.* 68, 43–46

Yates, E.M., 1981   'The Dispute of the Salt Fen', *Norfolk Archaeol.* 38, 73–78

Yaxley, D., 1980   'Buildings' and 'The Documentary Evidence' in Wade-Martins, P., *Excavations in North Elmham Park 1967–1972*, E. Anglian Archaeol. 9

Yaxley, D., 1988a   *The Priors' Manor-Houses* (Larks Press)

Yaxley, D., 1988b   'Houghton' in Davison, A. *et al. Six Deserted Villages in Norfolk*, E. Anglian Archaeol. 44

Yaxley, D., 1993   'Medieval Deer-Parks' in Wade-Martins, P.(ed), *An Historical Atlas of Norfolk*, 54–55

Yaxley, D., 1994   'The Tower of Houghton St Martin Church', Annual Bulletin, *Norfolk Archaeol.* and Hist. Res. Group 3, 46–50

Young, A., 1804   *General View of the Agriculture of the County of Norfolk*, (reprinted 1969; David and Charles)

Index

238

North Elmham
  moated enclosure *119*, **119-20**
  settlement remains 9, *58*, **58**
North Pickenham 52
  see also Houghton-on-the-Hill
Norton 9
Norwich
  Bishops of 120, 130
    see also Rugge
  Carrow Abbey 123
  Castle 163
  Cathedral Priory, estates 13, 40, 105
  Hospital of St Giles, estates 123
Norwyc family 117
Noyers, William de 186
Nunne, George 98

Oby 10
Old Buckenham
  Castle 163, 168, *178-9*, **178-9**
  Priory 128, *178-9*, **178-9**
  see also New Buckenham
Olivet (priest of Acre) 155
Orreby, John de 128
Otringhithe 9
Oxborough
  Caldecote 19, 199
  Hall *224-5*, **224-5**
Oxford, Christ Church, estates 153
oyster pits 187, 194

Pakenhams manor 94
Palgrave *see* Great Palgrave; Little Palgrave
Panworth 89, **120**, *121*
parks and gardens 9, 10, 209-28
  see also Baconsthorpe Castle; East Raynham; Elsing; Gateley;
    Hales Green; Horsford; Houghton; Shotesham St Mary; West Tofts
Parry, ____ 116
Paston family 115
Paston, Thomas 131
Pentney Priory 159
  estates 221
Petre family 190
Petygards 9
Pickenham *see* North Pickenham; South Pickenham
Pinkeneye, William de 189
Pinkeny family 72
Plaiz family 183
pounds, earthworks indicating 89, 120-3, *122*
Premonstratensian Canons 131
  see also Langley Abbey; Wendling Abbey; West Dereham Abbey
Pudding Norton 9, *59-61*, **59-61**
Purdey, Thomas 193

Quarles 33-5, 74
Quidenham *see* Wilby

Rainald 94
Ramsey Abbey (Cambs), estates 109, 201
Randes, Robert 76
Ranulph, brother of Ilger 172
Raven family 102
Raven, John 46
Raveningham *226*, **227**
Raynham *see* East Raynham; West Raynham
Red Castle *see* Thetford
Reed, John 62
Reynold 69, 120
Richmond, Count of *see* Alan
Richmond, Duchess of 156, 228
Richmond, Earl of 111
ridge and furrow 199-208
  see also Babingley; Gayton; Shouldham; Tacolneston; West Acre
Robert son of Corbucion 123
Rolfe family 102
Romano-British sites 5-6
Roudham 9-10, **62**, *63-4*
Rougham
  fishponds 62, 187
  settlement remains 9, **62-4**, *65*

Roxham 204
Rudham *see* East and West Rudham
Rugge, William, Bishop of Norwich 97, 151
Rumburgh Priory (Suffolk) 151
Ryston 199, *204-5*, **204**
Ryvers family 116

St Albans Abbey (Herts) 131, 161
St Benet's Abbey 131, **148-51**, *150-1*
  estates 169
  fishponds 148, *151*, 187
St Edmundsbury *see* Bury St Edmunds
St Martin, Roger de 143
Saxlingham 165
Scales family 118-19, 173
Scarning 153
Scoulton 47, *66*, **66**
Secford family 107
Seething, manorial site 89, **120-3**, *122*
  fishponds 123, 187
Sefoule family 74
Sengham 72
Setchey 159
settlement remains, medieval and later 9-87, 199
sheep-rearing, as cause of desertion 9
shellfish ponds *see* oyster pits
Shelton family 123
Shelton, manorial site **123**, *124*
  fishponds 123, 187
Shotesham St Mary
  park *67-8*, **67-9**
  settlement remains 9, 10, *67-8*, **67-9**
Shouldham
  Priory 69, 131, **151-2**, *152*
    estate 71
    fishponds 152, 187
  ridge and furrow 69, 199
  settlement remains 9, *69-70*, **69-71**
Shropham 40
Sibton Abbey (Suffolk) 123
Smith, John 'Strata' 197
Snettisham 166
Soane, Sir John 69
South Creake 89, *125-6*, **125-6**
South Erpingham 10
South Pickenham 52, 105
Southburgh 25
Southery 109
Sparham 92, 117
Spelman family 221-4, 228
Sporle 9, 42
  see also Great Palgrave
Spring, Elizabeth 105
Stanford
  Stanford Training Area 10, 83
  see also Buckenham Tofts
Stephen, King 175
Stibbard 100, 101
Stiffkey 129, 130
Stigand, Archbishop 173, 186
Stockton 1
Stody 172
  see also Hunworth Castle
Stow Bardolph 199, **205**, *206*
Stow Bedon *see* Great Breckles
Stradsett 199, *207-8*, **207**
Stratton 127
Swathing family 25
Swathing 25

Tacolneston Park 209, **227-8**, *229*
  ridge and furrow 199, 200, 227-8, *229*
Tasburgh, manorial site **126-7**, *127*
  fishponds 127
Tateshale (Tateshalle) family 111, 128, 177
Tateshalles manor 128
Tattersett 9, *71-2*, **71-2**
taxation records, as documentary source 3
Testerton 59
Tharston **126-7**, *127*

239

East Anglian Archaeology

is a serial publication sponsored by the Scole Archaeological Committee. Norfolk, Suffolk and Essex Archaeology Services, the Norwich Survey and the Fenland Project all contribute volumes to the series. It is the main vehicle for publishing final reports on archaeological excavations and surveys in the region. For information about titles in the series, visit **www.eaareports.org.uk**. Reports can be obtained from:

Phil McMichael, Essex County Council Archaeology Section
Fairfield Court, Fairfield Road, Braintree, Essex CM7 3YQ

or directly from the organisation publishing a particular volume.

Reports available so far:

No.1,   1975   Suffolk: various papers
No.2,   1976   Norfolk: various papers
No.3,   1977   Suffolk: various papers
No.4,   1976   Norfolk: Late Saxon town of Thetford
No.5,   1977   Norfolk: various papers on Roman sites
No.6,   1977   Norfolk: Spong Hill Anglo-Saxon cemetery, Part I
No.7,   1978   Norfolk: Bergh Apton Anglo-Saxon cemetery
No.8,   1978   Norfolk: various papers
No.9,   1980   Norfolk: North Elmham Park
No.10, 1980   Norfolk: village sites in Launditch Hundred
No.11, 1981   Norfolk: Spong Hill, Part II: Catalogue of Cremations
No.12, 1981   The barrows of East Anglia
No.13, 1981   Norwich: Eighteen centuries of pottery from Norwich
No.14, 1982   Norfolk: various papers
No.15, 1982   Norwich: Excavations in Norwich 1971–1978; Part I
No.16, 1982   Norfolk: Beaker domestic sites in the Fen-edge and East Anglia
No.17, 1983   Norfolk: Waterfront excavations and Thetford-type Ware production, Norwich
No.18, 1983   Norfolk: The archaeology of Witton
No.19, 1983   Norfolk: Two post-medieval earthenware pottery groups from Fulmodeston
No.20, 1983   Norfolk: Burgh Castle: excavation by Charles Green, 1958–61
No.21, 1984   Norfolk: Spong Hill, Part III: Catalogue of Inhumations
No.22, 1984   Norfolk: Excavations in Thetford, 1948–59 and 1973–80
No.23, 1985   Norfolk: Excavations at Brancaster 1974 and 1977
No.24, 1985   Suffolk: West Stow, the Anglo-Saxon village
No.25, 1985   Essex: Excavations by Mr H.P.Cooper on the Roman site at Hill Farm, Gestingthorpe, Essex
No.26, 1985   Norwich: Excavations in Norwich 1971–78; Part II
No.27, 1985   Cambridgeshire: The Fenland Project No.1: Archaeology and Environment in the Lower Welland Valley
No.28, 1985   Norfolk: Excavations within the north-east bailey of Norwich Castle, 1978
No.29, 1986   Norfolk: Barrow excavations in Norfolk, 1950–82
No.30, 1986   Norfolk: Excavations at Thornham, Warham, Wighton and Caistor St Edmund, Norfolk
No.31, 1986   Norfolk: Settlement, religion and industry on the Fen-edge; three Romano-British sites in Norfolk
No.32, 1987   Norfolk: Three Norman Churches in Norfolk
No.33, 1987   Essex: Excavation of a Cropmark Enclosure Complex at Woodham Walter, Essex, 1976 and An Assessment of Excavated Enclosures in Essex
No.34, 1987   Norfolk: Spong Hill, Part IV: Catalogue of Cremations
No.35, 1987   Cambridgeshire: The Fenland Project No.2: Fenland Landscapes and Settlement, Peterborough–March
No.36, 1987   Norfolk: The Anglo-Saxon Cemetery at Morningthorpe
No.37, 1987   Norfolk: Excavations at St Martin-at-Palace Plain, Norwich, 1981
No.38, 1987   Suffolk: The Anglo-Saxon Cemetery at Westgarth Gardens, Bury St Edmunds
No.39, 1988   Norfolk: Spong Hill, Part VI: Occupation during the 7th–2nd millennia BC
No.40, 1988   Suffolk: Burgh: The Iron Age and Roman Enclosure
No.41, 1988   Essex: Excavations at Great Dunmow, Essex: a Romano-British small town in the Trinovantian Civitas
No.42, 1988   Essex: Archaeology and Environment in South Essex, Rescue Archaeology along the Gray's By-pass 1979–80
No.43, 1988   Essex: Excavation at the North Ring, Mucking, Essex: A Late Bronze Age Enclosure
No.44, 1988   Norfolk: Six Deserted Villages in Norfolk
No.45, 1988   Norfolk: The Fenland Project No. 3: Marshland and the Nar Valley, Norfolk
No.46, 1989   Norfolk: The Deserted Medieval Village of Thuxton
No.47, 1989   Suffolk: West Stow: Early Anglo-Saxon Animal Husbandry

No.48, 1989   Suffolk: West Stow, Suffolk: The Prehistoric and Romano-British Occupations
No.49, 1990   Norfolk: The Evolution of Settlement in Three Parishes in South-East Norfolk
No.50, 1993   Proceedings of the Flatlands and Wetlands Conference
No.51, 1991   Norfolk: The Ruined and Disused Churches of Norfolk
No.52, 1991   Norfolk: The Fenland Project No. 4, The Wissey Embayment and Fen Causeway
No.53, 1991   Norfolk: Excavations in Thetford, 1980–82, Fison Way
No.54, 1992   Norfolk: The Iron Age Forts of Norfolk
No.55, 1992   Lincolnshire: The Fenland Project No.5: Lincolnshire Survey, The South-West Fens
No.56, 1992   Cambridgeshire: The Fenland Project No.6: The South-Western Cambridgeshire Fens
No.57, 1993   Norfolk and Lincolnshire: Excavations at Redgate Hill Hunstanton; and Tattershall Thorpe
No.58, 1993   Norwich: Households: The Medieval and Post-Medieval Finds from Norwich Survey Excavations 1971–1978
No.59, 1993   Fenland: The South-West Fen Dyke Survey Project 1982–86
No.60, 1993   Norfolk: Caister-on-Sea: Excavations by Charles Green, 1951–55
No.61, 1993   Fenland: The Fenland Project No.7: Excavations in Peterborough and the Lower Welland Valley 1960–1969
No.62, 1993   Norfolk: Excavations in Thetford by B.K. Davison, between 1964 and 1970
No.63, 1993   Norfolk: Illington: A Study of a Breckland Parish and its Anglo-Saxon Cemetery
No.64, 1994   Norfolk: The Late Saxon and Medieval Pottery Industry of Grimston: Excavations 1962–92
No.65, 1993   Suffolk: Settlements on Hill-tops: Seven Prehistoric Sites in Suffolk
No.66, 1993   Lincolnshire: The Fenland Project No.8: Lincolnshire Survey, the Northern Fen-Edge
No.67, 1994   Norfolk: Spong Hill, Part V: Catalogue of Cremations
No.68, 1994   Norfolk: Excavations at Fishergate, Norwich 1985
No.69, 1994   Norfolk: Spong Hill, Part VIII: The Cremations
No.70, 1994   Fenland: The Fenland Project No.9: Flandrian Environmental Change in Fenland
No.71, 1995   Essex: The Archaeology of the Essex Coast Vol.I: The Hullbridge Survey Project
No.72, 1995   Norfolk: Excavations at Redcastle Furze, Thetford, 1988–9
No.73, 1995   Norfolk: Spong Hill, Part VII: Iron Age, Roman and Early Saxon Settlement
No.74, 1995   Norfolk: A Late Neolithic, Saxon and Medieval Site at Middle Harling
No.75, 1995   Essex: North Shoebury: Settlement and Economy in South-east Essex 1500–AD1500
No.76, 1996   Nene Valley: Orton Hall Farm: A Roman and Early Anglo-Saxon Farmstead
No.77, 1996   Norfolk: Barrow Excavations in Norfolk, 1984–88
No.78, 1996   Norfolk:The Fenland Project No.11: The Wissey Embayment: Evidence for pre-Iron Age Occupation
No.79, 1996   Cambridgeshire: The Fenland Project No.10: Cambridgeshire Survey, the Isle of Ely and Wisbech
No.80, 1997   Norfolk: Barton Bendish and Caldecote: fieldwork in south-west Norfolk
No.81, 1997   Norfolk: Castle Rising Castle
No.82, 1998   Essex: Archaeology and the Landscape in the Lower Blackwater Valley
No.83, 1998   Essex: Excavations south of Chignall Roman Villa 1977–81
No.84, 1998   Suffolk: A Corpus of Anglo-Saxon Material
No.85, 1998   Suffolk: Towards a Landscape History of Walsham le Willows
No.86, 1998   Essex: Excavations at the Orsett 'Cock' Enclosure
No.87, 1999   Norfolk: Excavations in Thetford, North of the River, 1989–90
No.88, 1999   Essex: Excavations at Ivy Chimneys, Witham 1978–83
No.89, 1999   Lincolnshire: Salterns: Excavations at Helpringham, Holbeach St Johns and Bicker Haven
No.90, 1999   Essex:The Archaeology of Ardleigh, Excavations 1955–80
No.91, 2000   Norfolk: Excavations on the Norwich Southern Bypass, 1989–91 Part I Bixley, Caistor St Edmund, Trowse
No.92, 2000   Norfolk: Excavations on the Norwich Southern Bypass, 1989–91 Part II Harford Farm Anglo-Saxon Cemetery
No.93, 2001   Norfolk: Excavations on the Snettisham Bypass, 1989
No.94, 2001   Lincolnshire: Excavations at Billingborough, 1975–8
No.95, 2001   Suffolk: Snape Anglo-Saxon Cemetery: Excavations and Surveys